Official History

OF THE

Otago Regiment, N.Z.E.F.

IN THE

Great War

1914 - 1918

By

LIEUT. A. E. BYRNE, M.C.

OTAGO REGIMENT, N.Z.E.F.

WITH MAPS AND ILLUSTRATIONS.

SECOND EDITION.

PREFACE.

THE decision which determined the publication of this Volume found equally its inspiration and its purpose in the desire to place on permanent record the part borne by the Otago Infantry Regiment in the Great War which desolated the World during the years 1914 to 1918, and to give it an honoured and enduring place on the crowded roll of fame among the organised forces that stood for Liberty in those dark days of tragedy and suffering, of heroism and sacrifice hitherto unknown in the armed conflict of nations.

When the compilation of the History was entered upon it became clear that the task of placing on record merely the operations with which the Regiment, in its varying strengths of Battalions, was concerned over a period of four years demanded lengthened, careful and extensive research and inquiry; but to attempt anything approaching a detailed record of the numerous examples of individual valour and sacrifice, of gallant deeds and brilliant service at the cost of suffering and death, would form in itself a monumental epic far exceeding the limits assigned this Volume. In neither instance do official diaries or records, inevitably sparse and sterile in material, always afford the amount of information essential to the requirements of reliable historical accuracy and fulness of incident.

Allowance having been made for shortcomings due to these and other circumstances, it is hoped that the operations of the Otago Regiment, as part of the New Zealand Expeditionary Force, have been invested with some appearance of historical sequence and form, and that a permanent setting has been given to the fame which the sons of Otago and Southland achieved at Anzac and Helles, on the

Gallipoli Peninsula; at Armentieres, the Somme, Messines, Passchendaele, Picardy, Bapaume, and Mormal Forest— the battlefields of France and Flanders. If the History succeeds in keeping fresh the memory of their unconquerable spirit, and if future generations are inspired by the story its chapters unfold, then something will have been accomplished.

It is appropriate at this point that grateful acknowledgment should be made of the generous assistance given by the Senior Officers of the Regiment towards the successful completion of the History, and of the ready response met with on all sides in the search for information bearing on obscure situations, thereby clearing the ground of much that would otherwise have made the work more difficult and less comprehensive.

A. E. B.

DUNEDIN,
NEW ZEALAND.

A TRIBUTE FROM
MAJOR-GENERAL SIR A. H. RUSSELL,
K.C.B., K.C.M.G. (D.), [F.]

———

RICH in its traditions of race and the unpurchasable inherit-
ance of an unconquerable spirit, still vibrant and responsive,
as the historic Call to Arms so splendidly demonstrated, the
sons of Otago stand out conspicuously for the brilliance of
their achievements among the soldiers of New Zealand in
the Great War. Otago could not, however, with its comparatively modest population be expected to provide unaided
the necessary quota for the Regiment which bears its name.
In order, therefore, to supply the deficiency and make up the
requisite strength, men from all parts of the Dominion were
drafted into the Regiment. From this formation it follows
that the Otago Regiment may be correctly described as representative not only of the Province from which it takes its
name, but of the Dominion itself.

At the same time it is fair to assume that its ranks
included a large proportion of the descendants of those early
Colonists who sailed from Greenock in the *John Wickliffe*, or
followed the fortunes of William Cargill, leavened not incon-
siderably by the sons of those adventuring Islanders of our
common stock who in succeeding years made Otago their
home — happy intermingling of Norman, Celt, and Saxon,
to which the English speaking race owes its capacity for
conquest.

It is beyond the power of a Commander in any retro-
spect of the crowded and stormy scenes of war to attempt to
distinguish or differentiate between Battalions in their
relative and contrasting vicissitudes and general treatment
at the hands of Fortune. But it must be said that Fate,
especially in the earlier years, seemed to take a sinister

pleasure in placing the Otago Regiment in the hottest corners of the fight. Pope's Hill, May 2nd, 1915, the raid at Armentieres on July 13th-14th, 1916, and Goose Alley on September 27th of the same year, were hard days ; but each experience only served to put a finer edge on their steel ; and henceforward Fortune smiled on men who had shown themselves independent of her favours and concerned only for the opportunities that appeal to the instinctive fighter.

Esprit de corps was a strongly marked characteristic of all the Battalions ; showing itself equally in the stress and heat of conflict, in the temporary calm of rest billets, and on the march. The record put up by the 1st Battalion of Otago Regiment in its hard and hurried march to Hedauville, in March, 1918, to meet the German attack, when not a man fell out, deserves to take its place among the finest memories of the Regiment as an example of endurance, will-power, and that superb and unyielding spirit which is ever the distinguishing mark of the born soldier.

No word of the Otago Regiment would be complete without mention of the name of Sergeant Travis, first of all scouts and bravest of men, whose epitaph might well be the single word " Undefeated." Asking him one day, half in chaff, if he could produce a prisoner or two for identification, he replied, " Any time you say the word, Sir." He kept his promise.

Under a long list of capable Commanders, Charters, Smith, Hargest and others, the Regiment fought, flourished and brought back to New Zealand a measure of honour of which Otago and Southland may well be proud.

A. H. RUSSELL, Major-General.

A MESSAGE OF GRATEFUL REMEMBRANCE.

As one intimately connected with the New Zealand Expeditionary Force from the day of its birth in August, 1914, up to Christmas, 1917, and more especially associated with the Otago and Canterbury Battalions as Brigadier of the 2nd New Zealand Brigade from March, 1916, to December, 1917, I rejoice to think that the work of the Otago Regiment is to be handed down to posterity, and that the glorious deeds of the Otago men are to be kept evergreen and chronicled in a Regimental History.

No History can adequately describe the fighting qualities and the endurance displayed by these New Zealand men. No task was ever too formidable for them, and to their eternal glory it can be claimed that they never once failed to carry out the duty allotted to them.

Whether the Otago men were scaling the steep and scrubby slopes of Gallipoli, or charging the German wire entanglements under close machine gun fire, as at the Bellevue Spur, Passchendaele, on October 12th, 1917, they always displayed the highest courage, and an initiative surpassed by none and equalled by few other troops.

To have served with the New Zealand Division is an honour in itself, but to have commanded its three Infantry Brigades at various periods is a privilege enjoyed by no other man, and will be my constant pride for the rest of my life.

I hope this History of the Otago Regiment will do full justice to all those gallant souls who came 13,000 miles to uphold their Empire's cause, and especially to those who will never return to their homes in New Zealand.

We must never forget that it is to these, more than to any others, that we owe the Victory.

> " Who shall sing the song of them,
> The wonder and the strength of them,
> The gaiety and tenderness they bore across the sea ?
> In every heart's the song of them,
> The debt that England owes to them,
> The chivalry and fearlessness
> That strove and won her free."

I hope all New Zealand boys will read the histories of their own Regiments.   When they do, the story of the daring deeds of that gallant soul, Sergeant Dick Travis, V.C., D.C.M., M.M., Croix de Guerre, of the 2nd Battalion, Otago Regiment, will surely stir them to the depths.

W. G. BRAITHWAITE,

BRIGADIER-GENERAL,

late Commanding 2nd New Zealand Brigade.

HEADQUARTERS,
    NORTHERN BRIGADE, INDEPENDENT DIVISION,
        BRITISH ARMY OF THE RHINE.

CONTENTS.

PART I.

PART II.

INDEX TO ILLUSTRATIONS.

INDEX TO MAPS.

Part I.
GALLIPOLI.

CHAPTER I.

THE CALL TO ARMS.

LONG after the clamour of historical controversy affecting the reputation of rulers, statesmen and soldiers, whose crimes, genius or virtues have made them outstanding figures in the greatest war of all the ages, has been stilled, and in that more distant time, when the fires of international hatreds shall have burned themselves out, will be read of with racing pulse and swelling pride of race the sudden emergence of this young nation from her sheltered solitude on the farthest edge of the world as an armed and valiant disputant among the war-seamed nations of Europe against barbarism and the lawless doctrine of force.

Instances are rare in history of such spontaneous expressions of loyalty to blood and kindred, of such devotion, at whatever uncounted cost, of sacrifice and suffering, to the ideals and traditions of our race. In the long roll of martyred nations, as of those that have fought and suffered and yet been spared the agony of national annihilation and the destruction of their liberties, there are imperishable examples of sacrifice and achievement ; but nowhere is there to be found inspiration and impulse revealing such splendour of innate and instinctive loyalty, and of chivalry so splendid in its daring than in the instant decision of this Country to stand beside the Motherland in those early days of the gathering storm.

Impressive also and startling in conception was the swiftness with which her rapid decision was translated into action that gave to the Empire and to Freedom an organisation of fighting men unsurpassed in all the higher qualities of courage, endurance and resource that make in combination the most resistless soldier in the field.

3

The assassination of the Austrian Archduke at Serajevo, on June 28th, 1914, was followed a month later by Austria declaring war on Serbia, thus announcing in decisive terms the defeat of British diplomacy, and the triumph of Germany in the first act of the tragedy which was to leave the greater part of Europe in ruins. Events travelled fast under German direction in the development of the great conspiracy which was soon to shake to its centre a world feverishly alive to its imminent peril.

On August 2nd Germany declared war on Russia. At the same moment the German legions were swarming into Russian, French and Belgian territory. On August 3rd a formal declaration of war on France followed this open act of hostilities.

Britain's decision, on which an expectant and excited world, neutral and belligerent alike, waited in breathless suspense, was now taken. On August 4th Britain issued a declaration of war on the leader in the conspiracy against the world's peace.

The heather was now on fire throughout the Empire. New Zealand, in the van among the eager young Dominion States, three days later cabled an offer of an Expeditionary Force to the Imperial Government.

With the acceptance of this spontaneous offer, the necessary machinery was at once put in motion for effecting mobilization of the guaranteed force and its concentration at the four principal centres of the Dominion. In the composition of the Expeditionary Force, so far at least as the infantry side was concerned, one complete brigade was offered. The selection of volunteers was to be made on a purely territorial basis, each geographical area furnishing its quota towards its own territorial regiment. Thus, one infantry battalion from each of the four Provinces, Otago, Canterbury, Wellington and Auckland, each comprising four companies corresponding to and named after the territorial regiments then in existence in the Province or military area, constituted the Infantry Brigade. Under this arrangement the 4th (Otago) Regiment, the 8th (Southland) Regiment, the 10th (North Otago) Regiment, and the 14th (South Otago) Regiment each had its representation in the Otago Battalion, nominally, if not actually, to the extent of

4

one company, which was named after and perpetuated the Territorial Regiment.

The call to arms met with an instant and magnificent response from the young men of the Province, who, animated by the feeling that their Country needed them or by a sense of national honour, or prompted by the spirit of adventure, came forward from far and wide at the first asking. Here was ready material for soldiers of the very finest type—all volunteers and all fortified by the same intrepid courage and armed with the strength and ardour of wonderful youth.

Tahuna Park, Dunedin, was selected as the concentration point for the Province on mobilization being given effect to ; and to this area all recruits were speedily drafted on presenting themselves and being passed as medically and otherwise fit for active service. On August 7th the first draft, comprising seven officers and between 60 and 70 other ranks, arrived at Tahuna Park. Other drafts followed immediately from the districts of which Oamaru, Milton and Invercargill were the centres. Tahuna Park thus quickly became established as the receiving and concentrating point for Otago. Probably three-fifths of the men selected were without previous military training ; but if they were deficient in this respect, there was nothing lacking in their physique, their bearing, and their spirit. The proximity of the projected date of departure of the Expeditionary Force from New Zealand did not permit of the introduction of a comprehensive or exhaustive system of military training ; in the time available instruction in the exercise and discipline of a soldier could be only of the most elementary order.

Orders were issued for everything to be in readiness for embarkation of the New Zealand Force for Europe on August 28th, 1914. This allowed but a limited period of time for equipment and organisation. Subsequently the date of departure was postponed to September 18th, and then later to September 25th. This postponement was a welcome one in many respects, as it afforded commanders an opportunity for more extensive training, and the Quartermaster-General's Department facilities for providing the Force with stores and equipment, as far as the resources of the country permitted.

Ten of the most suitable ships in New Zealand waters at the moment were taken over by the Government and rapidly converted into a state which would provide for the transport of a military force. The two vessels allotted to Otago Province were the *Ruapehu* and the *Hawke's Bay*.

Meantime the Otago Infantry Battalion had been formed at Tahuna Park, and the training and perfecting of the organisation proceeded apace. Lieut.-Colonel T. W. McDonald, N.Z.S.C., had been appointed to command the Battalion, and other officers with territorial experience selected.

THE REGIMENT EMBARKS.

On the morning of September 22nd Otago's first contribution to the New Zealand Expeditionary Force, comprised of troops of the Main Body and the 1st Reinforcements, entrained at Tahuna Park, and proceeding to Port Chalmers, embarked on that date on two transports, and were enthusiastically farewelled by the people of the Province. On the evening of September 24th the Otago and Canterbury transports arrived in Wellington Harbour ; by the morning of September 25th, under escort of H.M.S. *Psyche*, they were ready to join the Auckland and Wellington transports, which had already put to sea.

At this moment, however, orders were issued by the New Zealand Government that, for Imperial reasons, the sailing of the Expeditionary Force was to be temporarily postponed. In accordance with this unexpected development, arrangements were immediately made to disembark all horses and all mounted units. Camps were established in and around Wellington for the mounted units, while the infantry remained on the transports by night, and were taken ashore by day and exercised, for the first time, in tactical operations over the hills around Wellington, one battalion being railed daily to Trentham for musketry practice.

On October 14th H.M.S. *Minotaur* and H.I.J.M.S. *Ibuki* arrived in Wellington Harbour, and on the following day the Auckland transports, escorted by H.M.S. *Philomel*, arrived at Wellington. At 6 a.m. on October 16th the whole convoy, escorted by *Minotaur, Psyche, Philomel* and *Ibuki*, weighed anchor and proceeded out of Wellington Harbour to sea, cheered by large numbers of the people of Wellington and farewelled by His Excellency the Governor, the Military

Headquarters Staff and Ministers of the Cabinet. Once Cook Strait was cleared, the convoy formed up in columns of divisions, in line ahead, with three of the four escorting cruisers steaming at a distance of six miles, one ahead, one on either beam, and the fourth four miles astern, these distances being reduced by less than half during the night.

The strength of the Expeditionary Force, consisting of the Main Body and the 1st Reinforcements, totalled 360 officers and 8,067 other ranks, and included 3,815 horses. Its composition was as follows : Commander, Major-General Sir Alexander Godley, K.C.M.G., C.B., and Headquarters Staff ; one Mounted Rifle Brigade ; one Field Troop ; one Signal Troop ; Mounted Brigade Field Ambulance ; one independent Mounted Rifles Regiment (the Otago Mounted Rifles Regiment) ; one Infantry Brigade (four Battalions) ; Divisional Artillery (one Field Artillery Brigade) ; Divisional Signal Service ; Divisional Transport and Supply Unit ; Divisional Medical Units.

The personnel of Otago Battalion was as follows :—

Officer Commanding, Lieut.-Col. T. W. McDonald, N.Z.S.C. ; Second-in-Command, Major J. B. McClymont ; Adjutant, Captain A. Moore, D.S.O. (Royal Dublin Fusiliers) ; Assistant-Adjutant, Lieut. J. S. Reid ; Regimental Transport Officer, Lieut. H. R. Martineau, V.C. ; Quartermaster, Lieut. V. J. Egglestone. Attached : Medical Officers, Captain C. V. A. Baigent, N.Z.M.C., Lieut. W. G. Scannell, N.Z.M.C. ; Dental Officer, Captain J. H. Don, N.Z.M.C. ; Chaplain, Rev. J. Ross.

Machine Gun Section.—2nd-Lieut. L. G. Wilson.

4th (Otago) Company.—Major R. Price, Captain A. V. Spedding, Lieuts. R. P. Jones, J. S. Reid, J. L. Saunders, 2nd-Lieut. A. C. Boyes.

8th (Southland) Company.—Major J. A. Mackenzie, Captain W. Fleming, Lieuts. W. I. K. Jennings, N.Z.S.C., G. Myers, 2nd-Lieuts. E. M. Gabites, W. F. Tracy.

10th (North Otago) Company.—Major J. H. Moir, Captain F. H. Statham, Lieut. T. H. Nisbet, 2nd-Lieuts. C. St. C. Hamilton, J. G. Cowan, W. M. McKenzie.

14th (South Otago) Company.—Major W. McG. Turnbull, N.Z.S.C., Captain G. S. Smith, Lieuts. J. T. Moroney, R. L. Duthie, H. L. Richards, 2nd-Lieut. D. J. A. Lyttle.

The embarkation states of the Otago Battalion indicated a total strength, inclusive of the Machine Gun Section, of 34 officers and 1,076 other ranks. Of this number 21 officers and 603 other ranks sailed on the *Ruapehu*, officially designated H.M.N.Z.T. No. 5, and Lieut.-Colonel T. W. McDonald was appointed Officer Commanding Troops. On the *Hawke's Bay* (H.M.N.Z.T. No. 9) there were 13 officers and 473 other ranks of Otago Battalion under the command of Major J. B. McClymont ; Lieut.-Colonel Bauchop, C.M.G., being Officer Commanding Troops of the transport.

This eventful voyage to the seat of the European War of New Zealand's first Expeditionary Force may be briefly described. Hobart was reached on October 21st, the convoy sailing again on the following day, and reaching Albany on October 28th, where was found in the sheltered waters of King George's Sound an imposing assemblage of transports carrying the troops of the first Australian Expeditionary Force. At 5 a.m. on Sunday, November 1st, the escort, now consisting of H.M.A.S. *Melbourne*, H.M.A.S. *Sydney* and H.M.S. *Minotaur*, put to sea, followed by the Australian transports. Two hours later the New Zealand transports followed in their wake, and on November 3rd the Japanese cruiser *Ibuki* rejoined the escort. On the night of November 8th-9th the convoy passed 50 miles to the east of the Cocos Islands, and at 6.30 a.m. on the 9th the S.O.S. signal was picked up which resulted in the memorable destruction of the German raider *Emden* by H.M.A.S. *Sydney*, which had hurriedly left the convoy in response to the signals sent out from the cable station on the Cocos Group. The announcement of this fine achievement by H.M.A.S. *Sydney* was received with the greatest enthusiasm on board the troopships. On November 15th the convoy reached Colombo, the victorious *Sydney*, with 138 prisoners from the battered *Emden*, subsequently entering the harbour, when the prisoners were distributed over the New Zealand and Australian troopships. On November 17th the New Zealand transports, escorted by the *Hampshire*, left for Aden, which was reached on November 25th. On the following morning the journey was continued to Suez.

On November 28th information was received by wireless that there was a probability of disembarkation at Suez, which

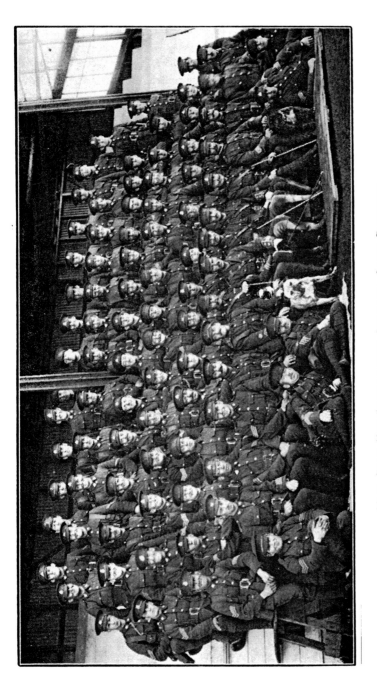

MAIN BODY NON-COMMISSIONED OFFICERS, OTAGO REGIMENT.

Commanding Officer: LIEUT.-COLONEL T. W. McDONALD, N.Z.S.C.

meant that instead of proceeding to England, as was supposed to have been originally intended, the Force was to land in Egypt. This proved to be the case ; but the journey was not yet quite at an end. The great waterway of the Suez Canal, with its defence posts and garrisons of Indian troops, was entered and Port Said reached on December 1st. The *Emden's* prisoners were now transferred to the *Hampshire*, and the convoy left for Alexandria on December 2nd, arriving there on the following morning.

ARRIVAL IN EGYPT.

The New Zealand Expeditionary Force had now reached the end of its long journey by sea. Orders for disembarkation were issued, the transports disgorged their freights of men and horses, and on the evening of December 3rd the first troop train left Alexandria for Zeitoun station, about four miles beyond Cairo. Distant about a mile and a-half from the detraining point, and on the edge of the sun-smitten desert, was the site of the camp selected for the New Zealand troops. More and more trains arrived with men, horses, baggage and stores, and in the course of a few days, with all energies directed to one end, the various lines commenced to assume a well-ordered appearance. There were, of course, the disadvantages inevitably arising from the heat of the day and the eternal sand ; while at the outset, on account of the futility and inadequacies of the local methods of so-called transport, stores were a long time in coming to hand, and certain inconveniences followed.

On December 6th Lieut.-Colonel McDonald was admitted to the Citadel Hospital, Cairo, on account of ill-health ; and a Medical Board deciding that he would not be fit for duty for a considerable period of time, he severed his connection with the Regiment and eventually returned to New Zealand.

It was now proposed to use the New Zealand Expeditionary Force as the nucleus of a Division to consist of Headquarters ; three Brigades, namely, the 4th Australian Light Horse Brigade, the New Zealand Mounted Rifles Brigade and the New Zealand Infantry Brigade (including the Ceylon Contingent) ; New Zealand Field Artillery Brigade ; New Zealand Field Howitzer Battery ; one Field Company New

9

Zealand Engineers ; New Zealand Signal Company ; Otago Mounted Rifles Regiment ; Divisional Train ; three Field Ambulances.

Meanwhile the weather, the great determining factor in all military operations, continued warm by day and cold by night ; the general health of the troops was good ; and training was in full swing over the open spaces which the desert country afforded. The training was of a severe and exacting nature ; and in this connection the long route marches which the infantry daily carried out in full marching order across the sands contributed in a large measure to the high standard of military discipline and the wonderful state of physical fitness ultimately attained. In leisure periods there were afforded opportunities of securing pleasant mental and physical relaxation, either in the city of Cairo, where, it may be said, there was much moral viciousness and much iniquity, or at the great Pyramids of Ghizeh, or the many other places of antiquity which provided unfailing interest and instruction.

On December 18th, owing to the hostile action of Turkey, the suzerainty of that country over Egypt was terminated, and by Proclamation it became henceforward a British Protectorate ; and Abbas Hilmi Pasha, late Khedive of Egypt, because of his adhesion to the King's enemies, was deposed, and the Sultanate of Egypt was offered to and accepted by Prince Hussein Kamel Pasha, eldest living Prince of the family of Mohammed Ali. The new Sultan was proclaimed at Cairo on December 20th, the Regiment being included in the strength which represented the New Zealand Division at the ceremony.

On December 21st Lieut.-General Sir W. R. Birdwood, C.B., C.S.I., C.I.E., D.S.O., Indian Army, who had been appointed to command the Australian and New Zealand Army Corps, arrived in Egypt from Bombay. There was a march of the New Zealand Division and the Australian Light Horse through Cairo on December 23rd, and an inspection by Lieut.-General Sir John Maxwell, K.C.B., C.V.O., C.M.G., D.S.O., Commanding the Forces in Egypt. Sir Thomas Mackenzie, High Commissioner for New Zealand, arrived from London on December 24th for the purpose of extending a welcome to the New Zealand troops ; on December 30th there was a review of New Zealand Forces in honour of the visit of the High Commissioner.

On December 31st Major A. Moore, D.S.O., was appointed to the command of Otago Battalion, *vice* Lieut.-Colonel T. W. McDonald, and was granted the temporary rank of Lieut.-Colonel while holding such appointment. Major J. H. Moir was appointed Second-in-Command of the Battalion, and Lieut. J. S. Reid became Adjutant.

Field training and a further review marked the early days of January. At this stage it was announced that the New Zealand Force was to form the nucleus of a second mixed division, to be known as the New Zealand and Australian Division of the Australian and New Zealand Army Corps, with Major-General Sir A. J. Godley in command. Such is a brief chronological record of the leading events immediately following the Regiment's arrival in Egypt.

TURKISH ADVANCE ON SUEZ CANAL.

On January 25th orders were received for the move of certain troops to the Suez Canal area to support the Indian troops already holding that line against an expected attack by the Turks, who were reported to be advancing on the Canal in three columns. The entrainment of the New Zealand Infantry Brigade commenced on the following morning— Otago and Wellington Battalions were ordered to Kubri, about 12 miles north of Suez ; Brigade Headquarters and Auckland and Canterbury Battalions proceeding to Ismailia. The defences which were entrusted to Otago and Wellington Battalions, in conjunction with Indian troops already established there, comprised a series of posts, Baluchistan, Kubri, Ghurka, and Shalouf, disposed along the eastern bank of the Canal between Suez northwards to the Little Bitter Lake, a distance of about 15 miles. Preparations were at once made for an expected attack in strength by the Turks.

The attack on the Canal and its defences developed on February 3rd. The attempts made to cross the Canal failed signally ; a large number of the enemy were killed and 650 taken prisoners ; and at the close of the fighting on February 4th the enemy was in retreat all along the line. The only point at which the New Zealand Force became seriously

11

involved in these operations was in the locality of Serapeum, where the Turks unsuccessfully attempted to effect a crossing of the Canal by means of pontoons ; and at a later stage in the day's operations the first and only casualties, one death from wounds and one slightly wounded case, were sustained by the New Zealanders. Otago Battalion was in reserve and was not involved in the attack.

On Thursday, January 28th, the 2nd New Zealand Reinforcements, comprising 34 officers and 1,189 other ranks, under Major A. B. Charters, arrived at Suez. Disembarkation was effected and the journey continued by rail to the New Zealand Camp at Zeitoun. The arrival of the 3rd New Zealand Reinforcements, comprising 62 officers and 2,147 other ranks, followed on March 26th.

On March 29th the Division, complete with reinforcements, paraded for inspection by General Sir Ian Hamilton. From this date events immediately commenced to shape themselves in a direction fraught with great and far-reaching consequences.

CHAPTER II.

A GREAT ENTERPRISE.

ORDERS were now issued for the Regiment to be prepared to leave Egypt at short notice as part of the Mediterranean Expeditionary Force which was to be committed to projected operations against Turkey. By the beginning of April General Headquarters had been established at Alexandria, where a great fleet of transports, comprised of captured enemy vessels, was being assembled and made ready for conveying the forces of the Expedition to Mudros, in the Island of Lemnos.

Entraining for Alexandria was to commence on the night of April 6th-7th. An advanced base under Major Charters was being formed at Mustafa, Alexandria, and Zeitoun was to serve as a reinforcing and training camp. Orders were subsequently issued postponing entraining for an interval of 72 hours on account of congestion at Alexandria.

Training was being carried out in long distance route marches, the weight of packs being increased to at least 70 pounds in order to bring the Force up to the state of fitness required for a campaign in the rough and mountainous country of the Gallipoli Peninsula—the scene of the coming struggle. The final preparations of organisation and equipment were now effected, and on Friday, April 9th, entraining for Alexandria commenced.

As Alexandria was reached and detraining completed, embarkation proceeded without loss of time. On April 10th the first of the transports drew out from the harbour where lay sheltered ships of many nationalities. The Regiment was allotted the *Annaberg*, one of the several captured enemy vessels lying at Alexandria, which was like most of the others —filthy beyond description, and abominably louse-ridden.

On departure from Alexandria the Battalion was com-
manded by Lieut.-Colonel Moore, with Major J. H. Moir
Second-in-Command, and Lieut. J. S. Reid Adjutant. The
Company Commanders were as follows : 4th (Otago) Company,
Major R. Price ; 8th (Southland) Company, Major J. A.
Mackenzie ; 10th (North Otago) Company, Major G. Mitchell ;
14th (South Otago) Company, Major W. McG. Turnbull.

A journey of three days brought the transports to Mudros
Harbour, the rendezvous of the Mediterranean Expeditionary
Force. There in the placid waters of the great natural
harbour of the Island of Lemnos, in the Ægean Sea, lay at
anchor ships from the far ends of the world—a fleet of vessels
of war and all the small craft incidental to their projected
operations, transports, and supply ships.

PLAN OF ATTACK.

On arrival at Mudros, the general outline of the plan of
attack to be made against the Turkish defences on the Gallipoli
Peninsula was communicated to Divisional Commanders by
the G.O.C. Army Corps. From the information thus supplied
it was made known that the forces which were to take part
in the operations were as follows : General Sir Ian Hamilton
in Supreme Command. Troops: Australian and New Zealand Army Corps (Commanded by General Sir W. R. Birdwood),
consisting of the Australian Division under General Bridges,
and the New Zealand and Australian Division (two Brigades)
under General Sir A. J. Godley ; 29th British Division under
General Hunter-Weston ; Marine Division under General
Paris ; French Division under General d'Amade.

The decision arrived at by Sir Ian Hamilton and his
Staff was that several simultaneous attacks should be made
on the Peninsula in order as far as possible to mislead the
Turkish Command. Landing places at the extremity of the
Peninsula were selected where an assault upon the Turkish
defences was to be made, principally by units of the 29th
Division. About nine miles along the coast from " Y " Beach
(opposite Krithia) and beyond Gaba Tepe, a point was selected
for a landing to be made by troops of the Australian and New
Zealand Army Corps, who were to work their way up the
heights of Sari Bair, and distract the enemy forces south of

14

Achi Baba by threatening their rear and their communications; the Royal Naval Division was to make a feint attack near the Bulair lines, at the head of the Gulf of Saros; and a landing was to be carried out by the French Division on the Asiatic side, near Kum Kale. The landings were to be carried out under cover of bombardments by the Fleet.

The objective laid down for the Australian and New Zealand Army Corps was the ridge over which the Gallipoli-Maidos-Boghali-Kojadere Roads ran, and especially Mal Tepe. The seizure of this position, it was calculated, would threaten or cut the line of retreat of enemy forces on Kilid Bahr Plateau. On this account and the fact that it would prevent the passage of Turkish reinforcements during the attack of the 29th Division at the extremity of the Peninsula, the capture of the objective allotted to the Australian and New Zealand Army Corps was of vital importance. A covering force, comprised of the 3rd Australian Infantry Brigade, was to accomplish the first landing in the darkness at 3 a.m. The Australian Division was to land immediately after the covering force, followed by the New Zealand and Australian Division. Certainly, whatever the force assembled to meet the effort of the Mediterranean Expeditionary Force, the Turks had had sufficient warning, and ample time to complete the construction of an elaborate and effective system of defence.

A brief review of events, principally of a naval order, which preceded the first serious military undertaking against the Turkish strongholds, will throw some light on the existing state of affairs in relation to the Gallipoli Peninsula at the time when the Mediterranean Expeditionary Force had been assembled at its rendezvous in Mudros Harbour. Turkey entered the lists alongside the Central Empires on October 31st. On November 5th England's declaration of war against Turkey was announced. Curiously enough, on November 3rd, two days previously, an Anglo-French Naval Squadron had opened fire upon the Turkish forts at the entrance of the Straits which divided the European from the Asiatic coast line of the Turkish Empire. This bombardment lasted for a period of ten minutes, and was designed, it was stated, merely to test the range of the guns of the Turkish forts. On February 16th the British War Council decided to despatch the 29th Division, hitherto destined for France, to the Island of Lemnos at the earliest possible date ; to arrange for a Force from Egypt if required ; and to order the Admiralty to prepare transport for the conveyance and landing of 50,000 men. Thus the War Council committed itself to an undertaking which aimed at the occupation of the Gallipoli Peninsula by a military force acting in conjunction with the approaching naval attack. The Navy and the Army were jointly committed to the Dardanelles enterprise ; but the 29th Division did not begin to leave England until March 16th.

By the middle of February, in pursuance of the general intentions, a great fleet of ships of war had been gathered in Mudros Harbour. On February 19th the attack by sea opened on the main Turkish forts at the entrance to the Straits. The bombardment ceased at the close of day and the ships withdrew, to resume their efforts on February 25th with increased weight of ships and guns. On this occasion the outer Turkish forts were compelled to cease fire, and on the following day landing parties of marines went ashore and completed the destruction, though at one point, Kum Kale, they were driven back to their boats with some loss. The absence of serious opposition at this stage emphasised the unfortunate nature of the delays subsequently exhibited in effecting military co-operation with the naval undertaking.

Stormy weather now intervened, and there were no further attacks until March 4th, when a naval squadron, preceded by mine-sweepers, resumed the bombardment of the forts further up the Straits ; but it was difficult or almost impossible to determine when these forts were out of action. The Allied naval operations had not so far accomplished any thing of material value ; the situation in regard to the co-operation of the Army was still vague and unsettled.

On March 18th the first serious attempt to force the Narrows was undertaken. The ships engaged, which included the *Queen Elizabeth, Inflexible, Lord Nelson*, and *Agamemnon*, carried out a heavy bombardment of the several forts, delivering the attack in the form of three successive blows. The conditions were all against the Fleet, and the object was not achieved. The *Irresistible, Ocean* and *Bouvet* were sunk ; the *Inflexible* and *Gaulois* were damaged and beached ; and many of the others sustained serious injury.

It was on the day prior to this costly undertaking that General Sir Ian Hamilton arrived at Tenedos to take command of the land forces. The disastrous results which attended the operations of the Allied Fleet on March 18th presented unanswerable arguments against an attempt to force the passage of the Dardanelles by sea alone ; and almost immediately preparations were commenced for a forced landing and assault upon the Peninsula by the Military Forces acting in co-operation with the Fleet.

The preliminary and subsequent reconnaissances which were made of the north-western shores of the Gallipoli Peninsula from the Isthmus at Bulair to the extremity at Cape Helles, served to convince General Hamilton of the tremendous difficulties which beset the perilous undertaking shortly to be embarked upon, by reason of the generally steep and precipitous country, and the formidable nature of the defences commanding the restricted stretches of beach available for landing troops. From Bulair to Suvla Bay, a distance of approximately 30 miles, the land rose abruptly from the sea, and the general configuration was such that there was no apparent place suitable for a forced landing and subsequent movement of troops. The coast line of the southern half of the Peninsula, stretching from Suvla Bay to Cape Helles, was also, generally speaking, precipitous ; but at certain points there appeared short stretches of coast line the sandy beaches of which at least suggested the possibility of landings being effected. Thus, round the southern extremity of the Peninsula half a dozen such localities presented themselves ; while on either side of Gaba Tepe, about 13 miles northwards of Helles, two apparently good places were located.

Over this southern half of the Peninsula, where prolonged and fiercely contested battles were fought during the progress of the campaign, stood three main geographical landmarks, namely, overlooking Suvla Bay the mountain of Sari Bair, which, from a confusion of spurs and subsidiary features, rose to a height of 970 feet ; further to the south and more to the Asiatic side, the great Kilid Bahr Plateau, rising to a height of 700 feet, and forming a natural protection to the forts of the Narrows against attack from the direction of the Ægean Sea ; and further still to the south, Achi Baba, which rose to a height of approximately 600 feet and dominated the

17

southern extremity of the Peninsula. The Commander-in-Chief was convinced that success could only be expected from a scheme which involved the rapid landing of the whole of the troops under his command, and a clear and practical recognition of the difficulties presented by the restricted nature of the beaches and the strength of the Turkish defences, which could only be successfully dealt with by effecting simultaneous landings at several points, and by threatened landings at others.

Following the arrival at Mudros of the transports conveying the troops of the New Zealand and Australian Division, the available time was fully employed in regrouping troops and practising the hazardous operation of disembarkation from the ship's side. The troops lived on board ship, and at the close of disembarkation practices carried out route marches on shore before returning for the day. Conferences between the commanders of the various units of the Division were constantly in progress. On April 24th, at 9 a.m., a Conference of the G.O.C. and Staff, of Brigadiers, and Officers Commanding Battalions, was held on board the *Lutzow* to discuss points bearing on the projected operations. Secret instructions regarding the landing were now issued.

On April 21st Sir Ian Hamilton issued the following Address to the Troops under his command :—

" Soldiers of France and of the King :

" Before us lies an adventure unprecedented in modern war. Together with our comrades of the Fleet we are about to force a landing upon an open beach in face of positions which have been vaunted by our enemies as impregnable.

" The landing will be made good by the help of God and the Navy ; the positions will be stormed, and the war brought one step nearer to a glorious close.

" ' Remember,' said Lord Kitchener, when bidding adieu to your Commander, ' Remember, once you set foot upon the Gallipoli Peninsula, you must fight the thing through to a finish.'

"The whole world will be watching your progress. Let us prove ourselves worthy of the great feat of arms entrusted to us.   " IAN HAMILTON, *General.*"

The momentous hour for action was fast approaching. At two o'clock on the afternoon of April 24th the *Queen Elizabeth*, with Sir Ian Hamilton and Staff on board, steamed out from the sheltered anchorage of Mudros and headed for the open sea, followed by the other battleships of the Fleet, and then a long line of transports bearing their thousands of the Empire's splendid manhood, many of whom were that day to see the sun go down for the last time. About midnight the New Zealand transports weighed anchor and also moved out to sea, heading for the shores against which there was to be launched an expedition of which there is no parallel in history.

CHAPTER III.

THE LANDING.

THE covering force to the landing to be made north of Gaba Tepe reached its rendezvous shortly after half-past one on the morning of April 25th, and there those who had left Mudros in ships of the Fleet were transferred to their boats ; at the same time the remainder of the covering force was transferred from the transports to six attending destroyers. The whole now proceeded to within some four miles of the coast, steering on a point about a mile north of Gaba Tepe. At 3.30 a.m. the tows were directed to go ahead and land, and forty minutes later the destroyers were ordered to follow.

Through the calm waters of the Ægean Sea, and in the darkness of the yet unbroken dawn the boats carrying those first dauntless elements of the Anzac Force approached the inhospitable shores of the Gallipoli Peninsula. The point originally selected for the landing was actually not adhered to in consequence of the tows failing to maintain the required direction, and as a result the landing came to be made at a point more than a mile further to the north. Along this narrow length of shelving beach, to be immortalized as Anzac Cove, the covering force of Australians leapt ashore from their boats, now under the fire of the enemy on the heights, crossed the intervening stretch of beach, and scaled the face of the ridges which overhung it. So impetuous, so irresistible, was their rush—some of them reaching a point more than a mile inland—that the Turks who had been hurried to the defence of this part of the coast scattered and fled or went down before the onrush ; and so there was established on the broken, scrub-covered ridges of Anzac that precarious footing which, strengthened during the day by the arrival of additional brigades of troops, was to be maintained in the face of repeated assaults hurled against it by an enemy force which at the fall of night was estimated to number several thousand.

With the break of day on April 25th the transports conveying the New Zealand troops were approaching the extremity of the Peninsula, where operations had already been launched ; by 7 a.m. the Headquarters transport, the *Lutzow*, had arrived off shore opposite Gaba Tepe. As the transports arrived at this point the troops clambered down the sides, boarded the attending destroyers, which conveyed them further in shore and transferred them to barges, which were then towed by the steam picket boats to within about 300 yards of the landing point. Now came the desperate task of pulling the heavily laden barges over the intervening stretch of water, an easy target for the fire of the enemy. Jumping from the boats as they grounded, the troops struggled through the shallow water under the weight of their equipment and quickly drew up along the shelter of the ridges which overhung the coast line.

By 9.30 a.m. the personnel of New Zealand Headquarters and the troops contained in the first tow had landed. An hour later verbal instructions were received to the effect that one brigade of the New Zealand and Australian Division was to be utilised to extend the left flank of the 3rd Brigade of the Australian Division, which had formed the covering force for the main operation. Urgent requests were made for reinforcements to be sent to this quarter, and the Auckland Battalion, which was ashore by 12 noon, was at once despatched against Walker's Ridge, to the south-western slopes of which the enemy was now directing accurate shell fire. Half an hour later two companies of the Canterbury Battalion were landed. At 1 p.m. Auckland Battalion was recalled from the position to which it was first directed, and sent more to the right, to Plugge's Plateau, in order more effectively to connect up with the flank of the 3rd Australian Brigade ; while the two companies of Canterbury Battalion were directed to prolong the left flank of Auckland Battalion.

There now followed a complete hiatus in the disembarkation of the troops of the Division ; a fact which in a large measure was to be attributed to the early disembarkations having been more rapidly effected than was anticipated, and the transports further in rear not being hurried on, but adhering to the original times laid down.

Shortly after 2.30 p.m. the first troops of Otago Regiment landed from the tows into which they had clambered from the *Annaberg*. The 8th (Southland) Company, commanded by Major J. A. Mackenzie, landed first, followed by the 4th (Otago) Company, commanded by Major R. Price ; the 10th (North Otago) Company, commanded by Major G. Mitchell ; and the 14th (South Otago) Company, commanded by Major W. McG. Turnbull. By 4 p.m. the Battalion had completed landing. As each Company waded ashore it hurriedly formed up under the shelter of the steep ledges which overhung the beach, just as the previous parties had done, and from there was directed by Colonel W. G. Braithwaite. Otago was at the outset ordered to proceed to the extreme left of the line, but subsequently was recalled and directed to Plugge's Plateau.

Meanwhile the fighting was continuous and was becoming increasingly heavy. The line taken up by the troops who had been landed up to this stage became heavily engaged at every point. The intervals of time between the various landings ; the fact that companies and half companies had on arrival been directed to where they were most urgently required at the moment ; and the broken and precipitous nature of the scrub-covered country, all contributed to confusion and intermingling of units, detachments from all Brigades serving alongside each other. The desperate nature of the situation, and the perilous hold which the covering force had secured and was maintaining over the high ground approximately half a mile east of the beach, demanded that all available reinforcements should be flung into the firing line immediately on arrival. Readjustment and reorganisation of units must follow later. The situation at 5 p.m., when the Headquarters of the New Zealand Infantry Brigade arrived on the beach, was as follows : Otago Battalion on Plugge's Plateau ; Canterbury and Auckland Battalions with Australian units along the front line of horse-shoe shape extending to the left to Walker's Ridge ; and Wellington Battalion on board the troopship.

The troops landed were still without the support of any field guns, while support from those of the Fleet was inade-quate on account of the difficulties of observation and com-munication. The Otago Battalion alone had suffered a considerable number of casualties from the fire of the Turkish guns. About 5.30 p.m. six guns of the 26th Indian Mountain Battery arrived and were posted in support of the New Zealand Infantry Brigade on the Plateau, and by their amazing efforts gave valuable support and encouragement to the sorely tried infantry.

There was no improvement in the general situation towards evening. The troops forming the front line had suffered heavy punishment from the enemy shrapnel and rifle fire ; there were also considerable gaps in the line and serious disorganisation of commands consequent upon casualties and the inevitable intermingling of units. At the outset small detachments in an excess of zeal and gallantry had advanced too far afield, and in the difficult country had been cut off from the main body and there died fighting to the last. A great deal of the ground which had been gained in the first impetuous rush of the covering force had been lost, and the line of resistance, which had resolved itself into a semi-circular position with the right flank about a mile north of Gaba Tepe and the left on the high ground overlooking Fisherman's Hut, the whole commanded by the enemy, was only with the very greatest difficulty maintained by our force, now sadly depleted and greatly outnumbered and assailed by an enemy confident but mistaken in his ability to sweep them into the sea. As this desperate conflict waged far into the night, the wounded painfully dragged themselves or were carried by the tireless bands of stretcher-bearers down to the beach in ever-increasing numbers, and presented a problem which was almost as complex and as difficult as that which the dauntless troops were endeavouring to solve on the heights above.

The New Zealand Infantry Brigade Headquarters now represented to Divisional Headquarters that the landing of guns during the night was imperative if the position won at so much cost was to be maintained. At 11 p.m. the G.O.C., A.N.Z.A.C., arrived from H.M.S. *Queen,* and held a conference at which the G.O.C.'s of the New Zealand and Australian Division and the 1st Australian Division were present. It was decided to reinforce the 3rd Australian Brigade (the covering force) with all available troops, and connect up its left flank with the right of the New Zealand Brigade. So far only one gun, that of the 1st Australian

Division, had been landed. Casualties up to midnight were estimated to have been 1,500, and although the hospital ship had left for Alexandria, the arrangements for clearing casualties were in most respects inadequate. On the whole, it was considered the progress achieved was not as great as was anticipated—a state of affairs which was attributed mainly to the fact that disembarkation having taken place north of the point arranged, subsequent confusion had resulted; that the early stages of the operation having advanced more expeditiously and with more success than was anticipated, the remainder of the disembarkation was not accelerated accordingly ; that the G.O.C. 1st Australian Division, considering the country unsuitable, forbade the landing of the Australian field guns ; and that the Naval arrangements for landing troops towards the close of the day and during the night appeared defective, launches and lighters being scarce and the work in consequence slow.

The whole situation was indeed fraught with great danger. The troops had been subjected to gruelling fire all day, and the power of successful resistance had been reduced by heavy losses and weakened by exhaustion. The seriousness of the situation was represented to the Commander-in-Chief in the course of a communication delivered to him at midnight following the landing. The possibility of re-embarkation was even mentioned. In a characteristic reply Sir Ian Hamilton wrote : " Dig, dig, dig, until you are safe."

Throughout the night an almost incessant and fierce rifle and machine gun fire was maintained. Attacks were delivered by the Turks at several points along the disjointed line ; but all their efforts were successfully resisted, and the break of dawn on April 26th found the line unbroken. By 6 a.m. two guns of the New Zealand Howitzer Battery had been brought ashore. The country in which the landing force found itself was most unsuitable for any artillery, save howitzers ; and even when the guns were landed it was only by man-handling them up seemingly inaccessible heights that they could be got into position.

The enemy's guns opened the day with fire of destructive accuracy along the Plateau and the landing places, and our mountain batteries, the howitzers, and the guns of the Fleet at once took up the challenge. At 9 a.m. orders were issued

Otago Officers on the "Annaberg" waiting their turn to land, April 25th.

Boats on Anzac Beach—April 25th.

*Razorback leading from Plugge's Plateau to Walker's Ridge ;
Sphinx on left.*

Walker's Ridge, Sphinx, and Russell's Top.

Turkish Prisoners at Anzac.

for a reorganisation of units and for effecting, as far as possible, an equitable division of the line held. As part of the various dispositions which this order affected, 10th Company of the Otago Battalion, under Major G. Mitchell, was despatched to reinforce the line held by troops of the 3rd Australian Brigade at a point known as Steel's Post, and remained there for two days. There was continuous and bitter fighting over that period, and the losses were heavy ; among those killed being Lieut. J. G. Cowan. It was for his splendid work during those two days that Sergt.-major A. W. Porteous was awarded the Military Cross, the first to be won by a warrant officer of the Division.

At midday the remaining guns of the Howitzer Battery were landed and brought into action. The general situation still demanded ceaseless exertion in order to maintain the precarious hold gained on the Peninsula. The Turks adopted various ruses in an endeavour to bring about confusion and retirement of units, calling out that the English troops were advancing and not to fire, also blowing familiar bugle calls ; but all these efforts at deception had little or only momentary effect. The strenuous hours of the day were succeeded by a night that was passably quiet along the line of the Plateau ; though on the right the Australians were subjected to a determined attack, which was beaten off.

The efforts made to effect a reorganisation of units had so far been attended with but small success, and the persistent attacks, repeated by the Turks during the 27th, still prevented any advance being made in this direction. Orders were now issued allotting to the New Zealand Infantry Brigade the left section of the line extending from the sea to where the left of Colonel Monash's section ended at the head of Shrapnel Valley. Otago Battalion was to move up the nullah north of the Plateau, thus prolonging the Australian line to the left until a junction was formed with the right of Canterbury Battalion. This was effected during the afternoon and evening of the 27th, the Battalion, with 4th Company acting as a screen, moving up Monash Gully, and taking up its position in defence of Plugge's Plateau.

The enemy's attacks, supported by artillery fire, had been renewed at daybreak on the 27th, and the ridges sloping north-west and south-west to the beach were consistently

25

shelled. By 9 a.m. an attack had developed strongly against the left, at Walker's Ridge, and centre, but was beaten back with loss to the enemy. A desultory fire was maintained throughout the night of the 27th, and frequently the enemy worked up close to our line, but on each occasion was repulsed by rapid rifle fire,—even if the anxieties of the night and the newness of the troops at times led to the expenditure of a great deal more ammunition than was necessary.

Meantime, in rear of the front line and along the stretch of beach, out of chaos was developing a certain orderliness. The establishment of a field dressing station for the reception of wounded, the accummulation of stores and supplies, the construction of communication trenches to counter the danger of ground exposed to fire, the building of dug-outs and shelters along the slopes of the ridges, and the making of roads and tracks, were works that, once commenced, were constantly extended and improved. The fact of the landing having been made at a point more than a mile north of where it was intended, was more a fortunate circumstance than a mistake. Further south there would have been greater space for movement and manœuvre, but more opposition from the Turks by reason of their preparedness, and less shelter from their guns and howitzers, hidden as they were in the high and broken country and secure from our naval guns with their flatter trajectory. But at the point where the landing took place, difficult and broken though the country was inland, the hills, which sloped down almost to the water's edge, afforded a natural shelter for the base of operations, which was an incalculable advantage under the terrific conditions existing.

The following Special Order was issued by Sir Ian Hamilton on April 28th : " I rely on all officers to stand firm and steadfast, and to resist the attempts of the enemy to drive us back from our present position which has been so gallantly won. The enemy is evidently trying to obtain a local success before reinforcements can reach us. . . . It behoves us all, French and British, to stand fast, hold what we have gained, wear down the enemy, and thus prepare for a decisive victory. Our comrades in Flanders have had the same experience of fatigue after hard won fights. We shall, I know, emulate their steadfastness, and achieve a result which will confer added laurels to French and British Arms.''

Throughout the days of the 28th and 29th the advanced line was frequently engaged, elements of the Turks alternately advancing and retreating ; their determination regulated by the fire of the howitzers and the guns of the Fleet. The frequency of these attacks, in which much ammunition was expended, and the fact that they were not pushed through, conveyed the impression that the Turks had now withdrawn a part of the forces, both infantry and artillery, which previously engaged the front, and had sent them to reinforce the troops who were opposing the 29th and French Divisions at the southern extremity of the Peninsula. Nevertheless, a general advance was not feasible because of the limited number of troops available and the non-existence of roads and other vital considerations. To attempt the occupation of a large area of country at this stage of the campaign was out of the question, because of our numerical inability to hold it.

The morning of April 30th was the quietest so far experienced, and the day was spent in relieving detachments from the line and sending them to the beach for a rest and bathing—both urgently needed. The exertions of the past several days, the lack of sleep, the constant digging and fighting, and the ceaseless watchfulness required, added to which was the serious depletion of ranks from casualties, had made inroads on mind and body that must be repaired if the ground won was to be maintained. The strength of the Otago Battalion, as disembarked, was 25 officers and 912 other ranks, and a summary of casualties sustained up to midnight on April 29th indicated the losses, exclusive of missing, as 18 killed and 60 wounded.

CHAPTER IV.

AN ADVANCE ATTEMPTED.

At the close of April plans had been prepared for carrying out an operation having for its object the advance of the general line between Quinn's Post and Walker's Ridge, thereby effecting a much desired improvement in the continuity of our line over this area. The two salient points which it was desired to embrace by means of this operation were, on the right a ridge between Quinn's Post and Pope's Hill—subsequently known as Dead Man's Ridge—not occupied by the enemy, but the possession of which it was important should be denied to him, and which dominated a considerable area of ground extending down Monash Gully; and on the left front a prominence known as Knoll 700, the enemy's occupation of which seriously embarrassed movement between Pope's and Walker's Ridge. The capture of these two points would have the effect of greatly strengthening and consolidating our line. It was originally intended that the assault which the seizure of these positions involved should be launched on the evening of May 1st; but this decision was interfered with by an attack, determinedly made but repulsed, against the left of the 4th Australian Brigade earlier in the evening.

Orders, slightly amended, were now issued for the operation to be carried out on the following day, commencing at 7.15 p.m., and preceded by a bombardment by naval and field guns and howitzers. The troops detailed for the operation consisted of the New Zealand Infantry Brigade and the 4th Australian Infantry Brigade, and one battalion of the Royal Naval Division, one brigade of which had landed as reinforcements on the evening of April 28th. As no move was to be made by the Australian Division, the right of the 4th Australian Brigade was to stand fast in order to maintain connection. The New Zealand Brigade was to advance with its right directed on Knoll 700; while the left battalion of the 4th Australian Brigade was to advance from the northeast and make good a line connecting Knoll 700 with the left flank of Quinn's Post. The battalion of the Royal Naval Division was to form a general reserve. In the further division of tasks Otago Battalion, commanded by Lieut.-Colonel Moore, was detailed to seize the line of the Knoll to a point 400 yards north-north-west ; while Canterbury Battalion, pushing forward from Walker's Ridge, was to prolong the line of Otago Battalion to the left.

At 7 p.m. the bombardment of the Turkish trenches on the Ridge and to the north commenced as arranged, and at 7.15 p.m. lifted on to the enemy's rear slopes and supports. At the appointed time, 7.15 p.m., the 16th Battalion of the 4th Australian Brigade advanced north-east up to the head of the valley, and by 7.45 p.m. had secured a footing on the ridge, although suffering heavy casualties from the enfilade fire of Turkish machine guns. They then commenced to dig in, and were followed by the right of the 13th Battalion of the same Brigade, which gained the high ground to the left and prolonged the line still further to the left towards the Knoll. Unfortunately the Otago Battalion did not arrive at the junction of the valleys at the foot of Pope's until 7.45 p.m., and the first company, which was 4th (Otago), did not clear Pope's, from which point the attack was to be delivered, until 8.20 p.m. The great advantages of simultaneous attack were thus entirely lost.

Otago Battalion, in order to reach its position of assembly, had left Walker's Ridge shortly after 4.30 p.m., proceeding along the beach and up Monash Gully, but was subjected to delays which even the time allowed did not meet. The failure to arrive at the appointed time was attributed to three causes, namely, the activity of enemy sharpshooters in the trenches at the head of Monash Gully commanding certain points of the approach ; congestion due to stretcher parties moving down the valley towards the beach ; and, principally, the half battalion of the Naval Brigade in Monash Gully not having cleared the road sufficiently. Thus the two attacks, which should have been delivered simultaneously in order to benefit to the fullest extent by the preliminary bombardment, took place at an interval of about one and a-half hours.

There were other circumstances which militated against success. It was a night operation; there was the final rush and hurry in the endeavour to recover some of the time lost during the approach march; and the country was exceedingly steep and difficult, there being occasions moving up to assembly positions when the machine guns had to be hauled up steep faces by means of ropes. In face of all these adverse conditions, the Battalion nevertheless advanced to the attack immediately it arrived at its starting point, which was a few yards in advance of the Pope's Hill trenches.

The advance was to be directed towards the enemy position generally known as Baby 700; but with the exception of 4th Company, which was leading in the attack, the direction followed by the assaulting troops ultimately proved to be too far to the right. The advance of 4th Company continued almost unchecked for a distance of from 200 to 300 yards. The first of the enemy trench systems which defended Baby 700 was reached; but the Turks, who previously had withheld their fire, now swept the ranks of the attacking force with deadly effect. Against this sudden burst of machine gun and rifle fire, which, owing to the fact that the Turkish position was sited on a curve, was delivered in enfilade as well as from front, the attack was abruptly smashed. It was at this stage that Major R. Price, commanding 4th Company, Captain A. V. Spedding, and Lieut. R. E. Egglestone were killed. A few of the attackers actually reached the parapet of the foremost Turkish trench. Lieut. J. L. Saunders, the only remaining officer of the Company, took command, but could muster only five men. No support was forthcoming; but this mere handful resolutely maintained their position for some hours, until, all being wounded, they were compelled to withdraw. In this phase of the attack 4th Company suffered exceedingly heavy losses; only 45 out of an initial strength of over 200 responding to the roll call.

Advancing towards Dead Man's Ridge away to the right, 8th (Southland) Company, commanded by Captain W. Fleming, encountered machine gun fire of such a destructive nature that the momentum of its attack was checked almost from the outset. After advancing for a distance of about 200 yards those of the Company who were left reached a point where the nature of the ground afforded temporary shelter from the enemy fire, and after slight reorganisation had been effected the advance was continued. On gaining the high ground again the same destructive fire was encountered, and it was therefore decided to dig in along a line which was only about 30 yards from the enemy's position. The remaining strength of this attacking force now represented about 40 all told. Finally established in two short trenches, they set up an isolated defence which was remarkable for the stubbornness and determination displayed against overwhelming advantage of numbers and position. Swept by fire from the Turkish trenches, assailed by showers of bombs, confronted by the constant threat of being overwhelmed, cut off from all support, and from supplies of food, water and ammunition, and given up as lost, they grimly retained their hold on this advanced position for a period of three days. During the second night the enemy had constructed a new trench at the head of Walker's Ridge, and from this point the garrison was harassed in enfilade. Every effort of the enemy to storm the position was valiantly beaten off. On the morning of the 4th Lieut. L. Richards was killed. The strength of the garrison was being gradually reduced. On the days of the 3rd and 4th runners were sent back to apprise the Commanding Officer of the situation ; but no orders reached the party in return.

It now became evident that it was impracticable to continue to hold the position indefinitely owing to its complete isolation and the impossibility of obtaining support or supplies, and the two senior officers, Major Moir, who as Second-in-Command had led forward the right half of the Battalion in the first stage of the operation, and Captain Fleming, agreed that the only course open to them was to withdraw under cover of darkness. It was subsequent to coming to this decision, on the evening of the 4th, that Captain Fleming was wounded and succeeded in making his way out escorted by two slightly wounded men. The withdrawal was commenced during the night, and at 1 a.m. on the 5th a part of the garrison reached the beach and there rejoined the remainder of the Battalion. By

31

some unfortunate circumstance a section of the garrison which occupied the foremost trench, under Sergt. E. F. Selby, who commanded a platoon of 8th Company from the outset of the operation, did not become aware of the intention to withdraw, and experienced very considerable difficulty in getting back, being compelled to move over towards Walker's Ridge and then down the gully owing to the fact that they were being shot at by our men in the belief that they were the enemy.

Apart from the two remarkable isolated achievements recorded above, the general attack failed to reach its objective, and the losses sustained were exceedingly heavy. In view of this fact support from Canterbury Battalion was despatched, and two officers were instructed to get into touch with Lieut.-Colonel Moore and inform him that reinforcements had been sent to his assistance. With the exception of one company, however, this assistance did not materialise within a reasonable time ; and the Commanding Officer's intention of delivering another assault on the Turkish positions had to be abandoned, the Battalion, with the exception of the advanced elements previously referred to, withdrawing to the beach under orders ; a resumption of the attack being now considered impracticable.

The Divisional estimate of casualties sustained in this action was approximately 800 all ranks. Otago suffered badly, losing practically half its strength in both officers and men. In addition to those already mentioned, the list of officers who fell in this operation included Lieut. J. S. Reid, and 2nd-Lieut. D. J. A. Lyttle. The net results in respect of ground permanently gained were *nil*. The Otago Battalion was now placed in general reserve on the beach.

*View showing Pope's Hill on left, Deadman's Ridge in centre,
and corner of Quinn's Post on extreme right.*

SERGT.-MAJOR A. W. PORTEOUS, M.C., (D.)
(Killed in Action).

CHAPTER V.

THE REGIMENT AT HELLES.

On the evening of May 4th, two days after the launching of the operation which aimed at an extension of the line between Pope's Hill and Walker's Ridge, orders were issued for the withdrawal by the New Zealand and Australian Division and the Australian Division of one brigade each for temporary transfer to Cape Helles, where a fresh advance had been determined upon.

The forced landings on April 25th by the 29th Division at the extremity of the Peninsula, signalised by deeds of splendid heroism and accompanied by fighting of the bloodiest order, were followed by the launching of a general advance on April 27th, in co-operation with the French Corps, now withdrawn from Kum Kale. On the 28th, in the determination to make all possible headway before fresh enemy reinforcements arrived, a further general advance was commenced on Krithia, beyond which was the dominating feature known as Achi Baba.

The utmost limits of the advance fell short of Krithia, and owing to the inadequacies of artillery support, the limitations of supply, and the inability of the exhausted and depleted forces to withstand successive determined counter-attacks, much of the ground gained had actually to be given up. A momentary lull followed, interrupted by heavy fighting, which broke out on the night of May 1st and continued until midday on the 2nd.

The result of all this fighting, begun with such sanguinary desperation on April 25th, and carried on with very little interruption for ten days and nights, was the holding of a line approximately 5,000 yards inland from the extremities of the Peninsula. The Turkish forces were now thrown back to a line previously selected and prepared, and of great tactical strength ; it was to secure possession of an intervening stretch of ground and test the resistance of this new line of entrenchments and redoubts that operations were now planned.

For this offensive, launched on the morning of May 6th, selection was made of one brigade each of the New Zealand and Australian Division and the Australian Division. The New Zealand Brigade was relieved in the line on May 5th by two battalions of the Royal Naval Division, and on completion of relief in the early afternoon concentrated in its position of assembly south of Walker's Ridge in readiness for embarkation and the journey by sea to Helles. At 8.30 p.m. embarkation commenced, the effective strength of the New Zealand Brigade being set down at 88 officers and 2,724 other ranks. The main embarkation was somewhat delayed, but was accomplished during the night, and early on the following morning the destroyers conveying the Brigade arrived off shore immediately east of Cape Helles. There the troops disembarked and marched to their point of bivouac, and by 9 a.m. were concentrated in the Brigade area near Sedd-el-Bahr.

At the point of disembarkation there was evidence of the grim struggle which marked the landing at " V " Beach. Aground was the steamer *River Clyde*, from the specially adapted sides of which the landing troops had poured in face of a hurricane of fire ; on the steep bluff to the right the battered and crumbling fort of Sedd-el-Bahr ; ahead the defensive trenches and wire entanglements. Leaving this evidence of a conflict never to be forgotten because of the heroism and the tragedy associated with it, attention was attracted to the open country, well-watered and clothed with verdure, affording a striking contrast to the steep, scrub-covered terrain and limitations of space at Gaba Tepe.

The Regiment, as part of the New Zealand Brigade, was now included in a Composite Division under Major-General Paris. During the day of May 6th, when the attack was opened, the New Zealand Brigade was held in general reserve. The 29th Division, the left of which rested on the coast about three miles north-east of Cape Tekke, had led off the attack, its right moving in line with the south-eastern side of Krithia ; while the French Corps, with the 2nd Naval

Brigade, attacked as its first point the commanding ridge running north and south above the Kereves Dere. By 1.30 p.m. the line had been advanced for a distance of from 200 to 300 yards. The main enemy position was still out of reach. The attack was renewed on the following morning. On the extreme left it was again found impossible to cross the open ground owing to the cross-fire of machine guns concealed in the scrub on the ridge between the ravine and the sea ; at other points the advance was also checked. A further attack was now ordered for 4.45 p.m., the whole of the 87th Brigade to reinforce the 88th Brigade, and the New Zealand Brigade to be in support. Excepting the left, the line was thrown forward for a distance of from 200 to 300 yards, and the exhausted troops dug in for the night on the ground gained.

Once again, on the morning of May 8th, the advance was to be taken up along the whole line. On this occasion the New Zealand Infantry Brigade was to advance through the line held overnight by the 88th Brigade and press on towards Krithia ; simultaneously the 87th Brigade was to threaten the enemy works on the west of the Ravine. With the commencement of the attack, timed for 10.30 a.m., and preceded by a bombardment from ships and land batteries, the order of Battalions from right to left was, Canterbury, Auckland, and Wellington, with Otago in reserve on account of its numerical weakness after the attack of May 2nd.

On the late afternoon of the 7th the New Zealand Brigade commenced its approach march. Following a course approximating to the western coast-line of the Peninsula, the three Battalions which were to take part in the attack reached their assembly positions under cover of darkness, and were then established along a line about 400 yards in rear of the front line as it then existed. In the meantime Otago Battalion, to be in reserve to the attack, had advanced from its area of bivouac near the Stone Bridge on the Krithia Road, and taking the same course as the remainder of the Brigade, covered a distance of about two miles and there dug in for the night. Just before dawn on the 8th the advance was resumed, the Battalion finally reaching some old trenches in the locality of Pink Farm. The initial stages of the approach had been made in artillery formation ; but later enemy fire compelled the Battalion to move in extended order.

About 10 a.m. the New Zealand Brigade, less Otago Battalion, advanced under heavy machine gun fire to the existing front line. At 10.30 a.m. the attack was launched. The assaulting infantry almost instantly encountered a blast of machine gun fire equal in its destructive power to that which had stemmed the tide of advance on the previous day. By 1.30 p.m. the attack had been definitely checked, and the losses sustained were exceedingly heavy. Canterbury Battalion, on the right, had advanced about 200 yards beyond the foremost trenches gained by the 88th Brigade ; two companies of Auckland Battalion had reached about an equal distance in the centre, but the right company had been compelled to fall back again owing to machine gun fire making a point known as Fir Tree Knoll untenable ; while on the left flank Wellington Battalion had encountered heavy and destructive fire from a Turkish trench from which machine guns dominated the entire area of advance. The Brigade was therefore compelled to dig in on the ground gained. Away to the right of the attack the French found it impossible to advance up the crest of the spur west of the Kereves Dere until the line on the left had been pushed further ahead.

The Commander of the Composite Division now ordered a resumption of the advance by the whole of the New Zealand Brigade ; to commence at 5.30 p.m., and to be covered by an artillery bombardment. This was subsequently cancelled and orders issued for a general advance along the whole line. The 29th Division was to attack in a north-easterly direction, with the Composite Division attacking in a parallel position on the right. The objective assigned to the New Zealand Brigade embraced the village of Krithia and the adjoining trenches ; the Brigade to attack in a north-easterly direction with its left flank resting on the ravine leading to Hill 472 inclusive, and its right flank on a stream flowing south-west from Krithia. The Australian Brigade was to attack in a north-easterly direction to the right of the New Zealand Brigade. The 88th Brigade was to support the attack of the New Zealand Brigade.

At 5.30 p.m. the infantry moved forward to the assault. A full measure of success was again denied the attacking troops. The furthest limits of the advance did not extend beyond a few hundred yards, and some of the ground gained could not be held owing to the exhausted state of the troops and the losses sustained. It was during this second gallant effort that the Auckland Battalion made its memorable charge over a level stretch of ground, 200 yards across, immediately to the left of Fir Tree Knoll. It was across this open space, to be remembered as the " Daisy Patch," that four successive waves of Auckland Infantry advanced, each to be literally swept away by the concentrated fire of Turkish machine guns concealed in the dense scrub to the left. The last gallant effort of the day of the 8th had now expended itself. The material gains were small ; the expenditure in human lives woefully heavy. Many of the wounded lay out over the battlefield during the night owing to the extreme difficulties of evacuation.

It was in support of this last effort of the day that Otago Battalion was called upon. In the early afternoon 4th and 8th Companies had moved forward in support of Auckland Battalion, and an hour later 10th and 14th Companies moved up, but more to the left towards Wellington Battalion, each exposed to enemy fire as it hurriedly crossed the short stretches of level fields, to be remembered as " Daisy Patches " ; but not such bloody patches as that crossed by Auckland Battalion.

There were serious gaps in the line held that night, the result of severe casualties, inevitable disorganisation and loss of direction in the darkness in the effort to effect a readjustment. During the afternoon the New Zealand Brigade was ordered to take over the line right of the Krithia Nullah ; the 88th Brigade to be prepared to give immediate support. Otago Battalion was to connect between the troops of Wellington and Canterbury Regiments ; but when the relief was commenced by night the Essex and Royal Scottish troops did not consider it prudent to withdraw owing to the numerical weakness of Otago Battalion. On the following morning (the 10th) New Zealand Brigade Headquarters reported to the 29th Division that owing to the casualties of the Brigade and the fact that the flanks were much further forward than the centre it would be difficult to take up the whole line without retaining some of the 88th Brigade. A reply was received that

G.H.Q. would arrange the whole matter. On the 11th the New Zealand Brigade was ordered to hand over the section to the Manchester Brigade of the 42nd Division, which had landed on the Peninsula two days previously. The relief commenced shortly after 8 p.m., and command of the section passed between two and three o'clock on the morning of the 12th ; Otago Battalion being relieved by the 8th Manchesters. The Regiment now returned to the area of its former bivouac near the Stone Bridge on the Krithia Road.

The New Zealand Brigade's participation in these operations had resulted in casualties which were set down as totalling 800 ; Otago Battalion's proportion of this number being 102 all ranks. It was in the shallow trenches finally taken over by the Battalion that Lieut. R. Duthie was mortally wounded.

On the morning of the 8th a Reinforcement draft for the New Zealand Brigade, numbering about 900 all ranks, under the command of Captain D. Colquhoun, arrived at Cape Helles, and although joining the Brigade subsequent to the attack, was for the most part held in reserve.

The Regiment now remained at the Stone Bridge for several days, providing working parties, constructing roads, and unloading ammunition and stores. On the afternoon of May 19th advice was received that Anzac was being attacked and that the New Zealand Brigade was to return there with all possible despatch. This was the first occasion, so far at least as the Regiment was concerned, that the term " Anzac " was employed to indicate the front held by the Australian and New Zealand Army Corps, and the officers among whom the movement order was circulated were for a time puzzled to know where " Anzac " really was. Thus hurriedly recalled, the Regiment embarked over the *River Clyde* on board the *Eddystone*, and before midnight had moved out to sea. On the following morning the Regiment was back in its old area of Anzac. Here it was ordered into general reserve along with the New Zealand Brigade and bivouacked in Reserve Gully.

BACK TO ANZAC.

During the absence of the Battalion at Cape Helles several events of interest had occurred at Anzac. The New

Zealand Mounted Rifles Brigade under Brigadier-General Russell, and the 1st Australian Light Horse Brigade had arrived from Egypt. On May 13th Brigadier-General Russell assumed command of the No. 4 section of defences, and the N.Z.M.R. Brigade took over and occupied Walker's Ridge. On May 18th enemy mounted troops and guns were observed moving north and east of Krithia in a westerly direction towards the coast, and a warning was issued that this might mean that a hostile attack was contemplated against the Anzac line. At 4 a.m. on May 19th hostile gun fire broke out, and a report was received that the Turks were massing against the left of the 1st Australian Division. The attack quickly developed, and before long practically the whole line had become seriously involved. A succession of assaults, delivered with great weight and persistence, were beaten off with heavy loss to the enemy. In some instances the attacking waves had been simply mown down by accurate machine gun fire. By the afternoon this apparently great effort on the part of the Turks had expended itself, and the Anzac line had held firm. On the following morning Otago Battalion, along with other units of the New Zealand Brigade, on being hurriedly recalled from Helles, had returned to Anzac.

About 6 o'clock on the evening of the 20th it was reported that Turks in large numbers were moving along the sunken road in the valley east of Johnstone's Jolly. At the same time white flags appeared at many points in the enemy lines. This was at first suspected as a ruse and preparations were made accordingly ; but by means of white flags and the Red Crescent the Turks secured a cessation of fire. Their firing line stood up in the trenches, and in some instances came forward with the flag parties as they advanced. Meantime an interrogator had gone out to meet the enemy, and the answer received was that they wished to bury their dead and remove their wounded. They were peremptorily informed that a flag of truce should be sent on the following morning along the beach from Gaba Tepe.

The enemy party appeared on the following morning as agreed upon, and was met by a patrol and conducted through the lines to Army Corps Headquarters. The outcome of these pourparlers was the arrangement of an armistice or cessation of hostilities between the hours of 7.30 a.m. and

4.30 p.m. on May 24th for the purpose of burying the dead and removing the wounded between the opposing trenches. At the appointed time firing ceased all along the line, and the delimitation parties from either side, having met on the beach at a point two kilometres north of Gaba Tepe, proceeded to move down the centre of No Man's Land and mark out with improvised white flags the line of demarcation. This completed, the burial of dead, the removal of wounded, and the clearing of the area of the wreckage of battle was commenced by the fatigue parties from either side. The task was a heavy one, for the Turkish dead in some places lay almost in heaps—it was estimated that 3,000 Turkish dead were scattered over the area—and it was soon found that it would be impossible to carry out the original intention of each side burying its own dead. Otherwise the terms of the agreement were adhered to ; although there were mutual recriminations as to the amount of curiosity being displayed regarding the opposing trenches both by the Turks and ourselves. By 4 p.m. everyone was under cover again, and the resumption of firing shortly after 4.30 p.m. signalled the close of this remarkable armistice.

On May 21st the 3rd Australian Light Horse Brigade arrived and bivouacked in the gully south of the New Zealand Infantry Brigade, and was followed by one squadron of the Otago Mounted Rifles Regiment, which was despatched to Walker's Ridge.

May 25th, the day following the armistice, was no less memorable because of the sinking of H.M.S. *Triumph* by an enemy submarine, when lying off-shore about a mile from Gaba Tepe. The vessel heeled over shortly after being struck, and sank within a few minutes, a tragic sight for all those who watched her from Anzac.

Quinn's Post, situated on the outer circumference of the semi-circle which represented the Anzac line, and at the furthest point from its diameter, now became the centre of bitter and prolonged fighting. On the retention of Quinn's Post depended not only the stability of the general line, but the security of the communications in rear, in Monash Gully and Shrapnel Valley. Recent developments had suggested that the enemy intended to make a determined effort to gain a strong foothold at the head of Monash Gully.

*Entrance to Trenches,
Courtney's Post.*

At Quinn's Post.

Troops Landing on Improvised Pier, Anzac Beach.

In view of the pronounced salient which the Anzac position formed, the loss of any post was calculated to imperil the retention of the whole line ; and further, the ground in the vicinity of posts was generally so restricted and difficult that direct and effective assistance to any post could rarely be given ; while difficulty was invariably experienced in making full use of all men at the disposal of post commanders owing to the narrowness and intricacy of the communication trenches. Thus handicapped and restricted from the outset, the situation was made more complex by the fact that before very long the retention of a vulnerable point was not to be determined alone by what took place above ground. In other words, fighting was being carried on under ground as well as above it by a process of burrowing and cross-burrowing, and then listening for indications of the enemy's presence and endeavouring to counter his activities in the same work. These operations were always hazardous, and frequently there was necessity for blowing in galleries in order to counter the development of enemy mining. The explosion of an enemy mine at Quinn's Post on the early morning of May 29th was followed by heavy bombing attacks. The left of the post was isolated by the explosion and No. 3 subsection of the defences rushed and seized by the enemy. An hour and a-half later the lost trench was retaken, but the enemy, now reinforced, again attacked in a determined manner, and in answer to the demand for reinforcements, 4th Company of Otago Battalion was despatched to the locality, and remained there for 36 hours ready for emergencies.

It was at this stage that orders were issued which resulted in the New Zealand Brigade taking over the line held by the 4th Australian Brigade in the No. 3 section of defences. This was in accordance with a general scheme of relief which was to be effected gradually, and was commenced on the closing day of May. On completion of the relief Courtney's Post was occupied by Auckland Battalion, with Otago Battalion in reserve ; Quinn's Post being held by Canterbury Battalion. Interchange of battalions was to be effected every eight days. During one of these periods of occupation of Courtney's a new trench in advance of the foremost line was constructed by Otago and Auckland Battalions in conjunction. Three saps were driven forward for a distance of 30 yards and an underground trench constructed ; the remaining few inches of overhead crust being broken through when the task was completed, and the new line then occupied. In the process of digging operations, the body of a dead Turk was met with, and it was decided that those who were brought in contact with such an unpleasant object should receive a fortifying issue of rum. A continuance of this stimulant the parties engaged were successful in securing by producing nightly, as evidence, a piece of the same dead Turk.

On June 9th reinforcements, the 4th, were received to the number of four officers and 239 other ranks. Owing to the reduced strength of the Regiment these were urgently required. There was a daily toll of casualties, even under what might be regarded, in a comparative sense only, as normal conditions. On the morning of June 5th Captain V. J. Egglestone, Battalion Quartermaster, who had rejoined the Regiment when it was at Helles, was killed while drawing rations at the Brigade Dump. Lieut. A. C. Boyes succeeded to the post of Quartermaster.

Relief of the garrisons of the Posts within No. 3 Section was now effected. In the holding of Courtney's two companies of Otago Battalion were disposed along the crest line, with two companies in immediate support in the terraced bivouacs below. The garrison of the forward line was periodically violently harassed by the enemy, and on these occasions numerous casualties were suffered and the defences badly breached. There was, however, some compensation when a gun of the 26th Indian Mountain Battery firing from Courtney's, engaged two enemy guns on Mortar Ridge and silenced them, for a time at least, after an exciting duel.

On June 28th a fire demonstration was carried out along the Corps front with the object of preventing, as far as possible, any move of enemy troops from the Anzac zone to the southern or Cape Helles zone, where the 8th Corps was launching an attack with the object of advancing the outer left flank of the British line. The close of the month of June was remarkable for a heavy attack which the enemy delivered against the positions facing the Nek in No. 4 Section, occupied by troops of the mounted regiments. Commencing at 1.30 a.m. on June 30th fierce fighting broke out and lasted until dawn. According to a prisoner, the attack had been ordered by Enver Pasha himself, with orders to drive the enemy into the sea ; but after the most desperate fighting it was sanguinarily repulsed. Otago Battalion had been relieved in the holding of Courtney's on June 26th ; on July 8th it again took over these defences. On the morning of June 30th no attack was delivered against the front of the New Zealand Infantry Brigade.

Serious attention was now being given to the organisation and formation of hand-grenade parties for use offensively against an entrenched enemy ; and orders were issued for the establishment of regular company grenadiers ; of permanent arrangements for ensuring and regulating the supply of grenades ; and for the training of grenadiers in handling and tactical methods. In the course of the bitter struggles which had waged round the more vital points of the line in the past the effectiveness of the enemy's bombing methods and the profusion of his supplies had been only too apparent, and served to emphasise the serious difficulties under which our garrisons laboured in this all too one-sided phase of close conflict. One result of this development of bomb-fighting was the setting up at Anzac of a bomb factory, from which grenades of various types, the commonest being the jam tin variety, were improvised from material at hand. The necessary organisation had also recently been developed for the prosecution of counter-sniping on a much wider scale than hitherto.

UNPARALLELED SUFFERING.

In no other theatre of war in which our infantry afterwards served did the conditions under which they lived and fought ever approach those which prevailed on the Gallipoli Peninsula. From the moment of landing they had lived in a narrow strip of country with the sea at their backs and surrounded on all other sides by the enemy. At the most it was only a mile in depth ; and whether in " rest " or in the line the men were always within rifle shot of the enemy, and nowhere were they free from the harassing attentions of his guns. The landing had been effected in the face of an enemy superior in numbers and gun power, and securely established in positions which in peace-time manœuvres would have been regarded as impossible for infantry attack. Their superb physique, iron endurance, and perfectly trained condition were the prime factors that enabled them not only to distinguish themselves by their prowess in battle, but to withstand the strain of the incessant and heavy fatigues, the constant exposure to heat by day and cold by night, the unchanging monotony of the diet and the lack of water. At the outset they had landed with light packs, but these had been discarded on the beach in order to enable them more easily to scale the hills and spurs which rose abruptly almost from the water's edge. Many were thus left without change of underwear or without greatcoats; and at that season of the year, although the days were agreeably warm, the nights were very cold.

Over the first few days there had been no organised line, units were inextricably mixed, and it was only in the intervals of fighting and repelling the violent counter-attacks with which the enemy sought to eject them from their precarious tenure on the hill-tops that trenches were dug and units were gradually sorted out and resumed their identity. And all this while parties from the reduced ranks had to be provided for the arduous work of carrying stores, ammunition and water from the beach to the line, and of transporting by some means or other—for there were many casualties and few stretchers—the wounded to the dressing stations on the beach. Until the arrival from Malta of the Pioneers, fatigue parties were drawn almost exclusively from the ranks of the infantry; and so when men were withdrawn from the line it was never in any sense a rest. All the stores had to be carried ashore from the lighters which came in under cover of night, and the water, which was brought overseas, had to be pumped ashore from the great iron barges. The arrival of the Indian Mule Corps made it possible to ease considerably the burden of the carrying parties; but the muleteers could not go everywhere, nor could they cope with it all.

While they remained in the line the infantry were obliged to work incessantly in order to strengthen their positions and increase such protection as they afforded. Interior communications had to be extended and covered ways provided where necessary. Out of the line they were little better off.

They were not permitted to enjoy the doubtful comfort of the bivouacs and shelters they dug for themselves on the sides of the gullies where they rested. By day, and more frequently by night, they were called out to carry, to dig, or to labour at one or other of the heavy fatigues. As the season advanced and the weather became warmer, the place swarmed with myriads of flies, which found a congenial breeding ground in the primitive sanitary arrangements provided, particularly in the crowded bivouac areas near the beaches. Dysentery became rife ; in a mild form it was almost universal, and its effect on men already fighting and toiling may be imagined. But the hardest tasks of all were yet to come.

CHAPTER VI.

A GREAT OFFENSIVE.

THE military situation on the Gallipoli Peninsula had now reached a stage which called for the development of a plan of operations which it was strongly hoped would definitely determine the final success of the campaign. From the date of the landing, April 25th, up to the close of July, the troops had been engaged in fighting as constant as it was desperate. Against the odds of enemy superiority in numbers and position, hampered in movement by the extreme limitations of space, and contending against the apparently irremediable disabilities of supply arising chiefly from the isolation of the seat of campaign, this force had not only maintained its first grip on the Turkish Peninsula, but had strengthened it in face of the determined opposition of the enemy. But it was becoming more and more evident that it was impossible for the existing force to go beyond the point then reached ; and there was the evident danger of the campaign settling down to one of indefinite trench warfare, instead of action and movement leading to decisive and early results. The most recent operations undertaken had only served to show that neither the forces at Anzac nor at Helles were strong enough in themselves to carry out the task to which they were committed in conjunction with the Fleet, namely, the forcing of the Narrows.

In view of this situation, the Commander-in-Chief had requested as far back as May 10th that two fresh divisions should be despatched to enable him to bring the campaign to a conclusion. Again on May 17th Sir Ian Hamilton cabled to the authorities pointing out that if they were to be left to face Turkey on their own resources two Army Corps additional to the existing forces at the Dardanelles would be required. One division had been sent to the Peninsula, but between its despatch and arrival the situation in Russia was such as to set free several Turkish divisions for employment in the Dardanelles. During June the addition of three regular divisions, plus the infantry of two territorial divisions, was promised, the foremost of these troops being due to arrive at Mudros by July 10th, while their concentration was to be completed a month later.

The manner of employment of these fresh forces in order to achieve the greatest measure of success in the speediest and most decisive manner, had now to be determined. Four alternative methods presented themselves to Sir Ian Hamilton, as follows :—

(1). Every man to be thrown on to the southern sector of the Peninsula to force a way forward to the Narrows.

(2). Disembarkation on the Asiatic side of the Straits, followed by a march on Chanak.

(3). A landing at Enos or Ebrije for the purpose of seizing the neck of the isthmus at Bulair.

(4). Reinforcement of the Australian and New Zealand Army Corps, combined with a landing in Suvla Bay. Then with one strong push to capture Hill 305 and, working from that dominating point, to grip the waist of the Peninsula.

In setting out the objections to the first course, the Commander-in-Chief maintained that the capture of Krithia could no longer be counted upon to secure the dominating height of Achi Baba, an entirely new system of works having lately appeared upon its slopes—works so planned that even if the enemy's western flank was turned and driven back from the coast the central and eastern portions of the mountain could still be maintained as a bastion to Kilid Bahr. The practicability of the second scheme was discounted by the fact that the expected reinforcements could not permit of a double operation, which would be necessary if Chanak were to be seriously enough threatened to cause the Turks to relax their grip upon the Peninsula. The third proposal, which would mean an attempt to cut the land communications of the whole of the Turkish Army, presented naval objections which were considered well-nigh insurmountable. The elimination of the first three of the four schemes above outlined left the fourth, namely, an offensive from Anzac, combined with a landing at Suvla Bay, as the most practicable; and it was this scheme which the Commander-in-Chief selected.

" The Australians and the New Zealanders," Sir Ian Hamilton pointed out in the course of his Despatch, " had rooted themselves in very near to the vitals of the enemy. By their tenacity and courage they still held open the door-way from which one strong thrust forward might give us command of the Narrows."

Once committed to this great undertaking, which it was hoped would decisively seal the success of the Gallipoli Campaign, all energies were directed to the one end. The most vital preparations within the Anzac area involved the construction in the gullies of terraced bivouacs to give cover from both view and fire to a great assembly of new troops; the construction and improvement of interior communications to ensure the rapid and easy movement of troops within the area; and the provision of covered positions where artillery could be concealed from the observation of enemy aeroplanes—unusually active at this period. All these preparations had to be carried out by the troops on the spot; and for the most part work had necessarily to be undertaken by night.

Thus was completed the Beach Road, such as it was, from Anzac Cove to No. 3 Post, a road connecting Rest Gully with Reserve Gully, and the widening of what was known as the Big Sap, which provided communication from the northern spit of Anzac Cove to No. 3 Post on the extreme left. In addition to these works there were the thousand and one details of reorganisation and arrangement necessary for the transport and concentration of the new forces destined for the offensive and for the landing and handling of guns and vast supplies of stores, ammunition, water and material; altogether a tremendous undertaking. Throughout the whole of the work there was no complaining, no slackening of effort; all were inspired with the thought that the impending effort would prove to be the crowning reward of their labours and their sacrifices. How near to realisation their hopes came and how far they failed, has yet to be told.

Anzac Cove, before the August Offensive.

Looking up Sazli Beit Dere: Rhododendron Spur on right.

Pope's Reserve Gully.

On the night of August 5th-6th the New Zealand Infantry Brigade concentrated in Happy Valley, immediately to the north of Walker's Ridge, preparatory to the offensive.

The opening day of the great attack to be launched at Anzac was fixed for August 6th. Here, where the real issue was to be fought out by troops of the Australian and New Zealand Army Corps, the ultimate object and essence of the battle was to gain and occupy a line along the summit of the main Sari Bair Ridge, the capture of which must have meant opening the door to Maidos and the Narrows. The Sari Bair system represented one of the main geographical features of the southern part of the Gallipoli Peninsula. Running parallel to the sea, its lofty crest line looked down over practically the whole of the Anzac positions ; but its great strength lay more in the extraordinary diversity of the country which represented its under features than in its own actual height. From the main mass of Sari Bair a series of spurs or ridges extended down to the sea, not in any uniformity or regularity of direction, but irregularly and brokenly, and in places terminating abruptly in steep faces or cliffs ; while separating the whole of these spurs were deep ravines or gullies, even more confusing in the diversity of their direction and the precipitate steepness of their sides. The enemy's hold on the main Sari Bair Ridge, a position of great natural strength in itself, was thus doubly fortified by this difficult and broken country which barred the way to the heights.

For this special reason direct assault was out of the question. Leading up to Chunuk Bair, one of the main features of the Sari Bair system, were two valleys known as Chailak Dere and Sazli Beit Dere ; while leading up to Koja Chemen Tepe, the highest point of all, was a third ravine called Aghyl Dere. It was the passage which these ravines provided that was to be utilised in order to deliver the assaults on the main ridge. But before these important assaults could be delivered the ravines themselves had to be secured. Thus the extraordinary complexity of the terrain called for the planning of a series of subsidiary operations which, if successful, were to culminate in the final combined assault which aimed at securing possession of the dominating heights of Sari Bair and the ultimate holding of a line represented by Quinn's Post, cross roads near Scrubby Knoll, Chunuk Bair, Koja Chemen Tepe.

The plan of operations provided for two covering forces preceding the main attack by two assaulting columns. The right covering force was to seize Table Top, Old No. 3 Post, and Bauchop's Hill, which commanded the foothills between Sazli Beit Dere, Chailak Dere and Aghyl Dere ; on the success of this enterprise would depend the opening up of the ravines mentioned for the advance of the assaulting columns. The left covering force was to move northwards along the beach and seize the ridge known as Damakjelik Bair, about 1,000 yards north of Bauchop's Hill ; this operation would protect the left flank of the left assaulting column during its advance up the Aghyl Dere, and at the same time, it was hoped, assist and protect the right of the 9th Corps in its landing between Suvla Bay and the mouth of the Asmak Dere. The right assaulting column was then directed to move up the Chailak Dere and the Sazli Beit Dere and assault the line of the ridge of Chunuk Bair. The left assaulting column was at the same time to move up the Aghyl Dere and prolong the line of the right assaulting column by storming Koja Chemen Tepe.

In addition to the main operations, there were subsidiary undertakings intended to serve the purpose of diversions and influence the enemy in the disposition of his reserves in a manner favourable to our interests. At Anzac frontal attacks were to be delivered by the 1st Australian Division from the right and centre of the Corps front, namely, against the Lone Pine entrenchments and the works known as German Officers' Trench, both on the right of the front ; followed by assaults from Russell's Top against the enemy positions known as the Nek and Chessboard. In addition, there was to be a big attack at Helles ; a surprise landing by a small force on the northern shores of the Gulf of Xeros ; and demonstrations by French ships along the Syrian coast.

A reconnaissance of the north-western slopes of Sari Bair and of the various lines of approach led to the decision that the main attack must be delivered by night, the actual assault on the summit being timed to take place well before daylight. Just as the reinforcing troops for the offensive were smuggled into Anzac by night, so the main attack on the Sari Bair position was to be launched as a night operation ; and to the tremendous difficulties which the country presented was to be added the confusion inseparable from darkness. But on the other hand the advantages which lay with the enemy in the matter of position were so overwhelming and the nature of the operations such that the great thrust would require to be well advanced before daylight broke.

The forces at the disposal of General Birdwood totalled approximately 37,000 men and 72 guns, with naval support from two cruisers, four monitors, and two destroyers. Actually this force was to constitute two main divisions. The New Zealand and Australian Division, the 13th Division (less five battalions), the 29th Indian Infantry Brigade, and the Indian Mountain Artillery Brigade were entrusted with the task of delivering the assault upon Sari Bair. The 1st Australian Division, to which was added the 1st and 3rd Australian Light Horse Brigades, and two battalions of the 40th Brigade, was committed to the task of holding the existing Anzac position and of delivering frontal assaults from that base. The 29th Brigade (less one battalion) of the 10th Division, and the 38th Brigade were held in reserve.

THE ATTACK LAUNCHED.

The August Offensive, memorable by reason of the desperate and sustained nature of the fighting no less than by the narrowness of the margin by which victory was missed, may be said to have been launched with the assault delivered by the troops of the 1st Australian Infantry Brigade against the Lone Pine entrenchments. The Lone Pine attack was set down to draw the enemy's attention and reserves from the impending main operation ; and it not only accomplished this but served decisively to wrest from the enemy a defensive work of main importance. Against a terrific enfilade fire from north and south the Australians gained the enemy's trenches, only to find them protected by an over-head cover of stout pine beams. Both by tearing up these beams and by working round the communication trenches the attackers broke into the entrenchments, killed or captured the Turkish garrison, and finally held their ground against a succession of counter-attacks which were maintained with unabated fury until the morning of the 9th, and in the course of which the losses sustained on both sides were exceptionally heavy.

The opening of this sanguinary encounter was followed by a second frontal attack delivered a few hours later by the 2nd Australian Brigade against German Officers' Trench to the left of Lone Pine ; and early on the morning of the 7th by assaults delivered by the 3rd Australian Light Horse Brigade against the Nek and Chessboard Trenches, opposite the centre of the line. In these attacks there were tragic losses, sustained by machine gun fire against which the utmost bravery was unavailing.

With the launching of the important diversion against Lone Pine the hour was rapidly approaching when the first move in the real drama was to be made, namely, the opening up of the Deres by capturing the positions which commanded them. Between the fall of darkness and 9.30 p.m. the Navy commenced the shelling of the Nek and Old No. 3 Post, bringing searchlights to bear over the area at intervals, a performance that had been practised nightly for some time and to which the enemy had apparently grown accustomed. At 9 p.m. that portion of the Right Covering Force, the Auckland Mounted Rifles Regiment, detailed to attack Old No. 3 Post, crept forward from under cover of the outposts, and half an hour later the searchlights were switched off. This was the signal for the attackers, who moved swiftly and silently out of the darkness. The enemy was overwhelmed, and in an incredibly short space of time the position was in our hands.

At the same time and in the same manner, the Wellington Mounted Rifles Regiment, moving up the Sazli Beit Dere, effected the capture of Big Table Top, with its steep and rugged sides and its summit honeycombed with trenches. Simultaneously, the Otago and Canterbury Mounted Rifles Regiments, assisted by the Maori Contingent, moved across the Chailak Dere to the assault of Bauchop's Hill—a confusion of ridges and ravines and enemy entrenchments—and shortly after one o'clock on the morning of the 7th this position was also in our hands. Lieut.-Colonel A. Bauchop, C.M.G., Commanding the Otago Mounted Rifles Regiment, fell mortally wounded in this action ; the success gained was largely influenced by his fine leadership and example.

As the attack against the seaward slopes of Bauchop's Hill progressed, the Left Covering Force made its way northwards by way of the Beach Road for the attack on the Damak-jelik Bair. Crossing the Chailak Dere, the march was continued to the mouth of the Aghyl Dere, though exposed to a certain amount of fire from the spurs of Bauchop's Hill not then captured. The Left Covering Force launched its attack against the Damakjelik Bair, and by 1.30 a.m. on the 7th its capture was reported to have been effected. The line represented by Destroyer Hill - Table Top - Bauchop's Hill-Damakjelik Bair was now held and the Deres opened up for the assaulting columns.

At midnight on August 6th, when the right and left covering forces had either effected their tasks or were actively engaged in their completion, the Right Assaulting Column, which included the New Zealand Infantry Brigade, and was commanded by Brigadier-General F. E. Johnston, was moving up the Chailak and Sazli Beit Deres, the two selected lines of advance, and the Left Assaulting Column was approaching the Aghyl Dere. In accordance with the order of battle for the Right Assaulting Column, Canterbury Battalion, on the right of the front and moving by way of the Sazli Beit Dere, was to attack Rhododendron Spur from the west, and thence continue the advance to Chunuk Bair. Otago, Wellington and Auckland Battalions were to move to the attack by way of the Chailak Dere ; next in order to Canterbury from right to left across the Brigade front Otago Battalion was to attack Rhododendron Spur from the north-west, then in conjunction with Wellington Battalion moving on Chunuk Bair. By 10.20 p.m. the left column of the New Zealand Infantry Brigade had arrived at No. 3 Post ; a few minutes later the capture of Bauchop's Hill was reported by the covering force, Otago Battalion having assisted to clear its southern slopes. All the attacks by the covering force had been carried out with the bayonet alone ; magazines being empty.

A short distance beyond the entrance of Chailak Dere Otago Battalion, which was leading, came under fire from a concealed Turkish position on the right of the Dere. Lieuts. T. H. Nisbet and H. R. Ker rushed the position with the leading party and cleared it of the enemy. The Battalion then pushed on towards Big Table Top, some distance ahead ; but there was direct evidence that there were still parties of the Turks to the right who had not been disposed of. After a consultation between Lieut.-Colonel Moore, Captain Colquhoun, commanding 14th Company, which was leading, and Major Statham, commanding 10th Company, it was decided that 14th Company should push ahead, and that 10th Company should attack round to the right. In the course of this operation 10th Company accounted for 100 prisoners. The Battalion then continued the advance on its main objective, Rhododendron Spur, but met with considerable opposition from the enemy entrenched across the Dere, and had to resort to bombing attacks to clear these positions. Heavy machine gun fire from the Chessboard also swept the advance and caused severe casualties. At daylight Otago Battalion had gained its objective and was then joined by Canterbury Battalion, which had been delayed owing to losing direction on the previous night.

Three hours later the Battalion withdrew under orders from the line taken up, and under heavy machine gun and rifle fire from the direction of Walker's Ridge moved across Table Top into the Chailak Dere. Companies were re-formed, and later moved up to the Apex, which represented a continuation of Rhododendron Spur to the left ; they were then in rear of Wellington Battalion.

The confused and broken nature of the country, the difficulty of maintaining direction in the darkness, and the opposition of the enemy had greatly retarded the progress of operations; also the element of surprise, which was to have counted for so much in the attack on Chunuk Bair, was fast disappearing. But the most advanced troops now pressed on beyond Rhododendron Spur, realising that if advantage was to be taken of the measure of success already achieved, then the attack on Chunuk must be driven home without delay. Against increasing enemy opposition the assault was renewed by Auckland Battalion and by the 10th Ghurkas, who were on the left of the New Zealand Brigade and linked up with the left assaulting column. This force came under heavy fire from the outset, and it was not long before it was brought to a standstill.

The advance overnight of the Left Assaulting Column had also been seriously retarded. This force had advanced up the line of the Aghyl Dere until it reached a point approximately 2,000 yards from the sea, and there the 4th Australian Brigade branched off to the left and followed the line of the north fork of the Dere ; the 29th Indian Brigade diverging to the right at the same point and moving up the south fork and the spurs to the north of it. At dawn the Australians were on the line of the Asmak Dere, and the 29th Indian Brigade on a ridge west of the Farm and along the spurs to the north-east. Brigadier-General Cox, commanding the Left Assaulting Column, then ordered Brigadier-General Monash to collect his Brigade, with the addition of the 14th Sikhs, and move to the assault of Koja Chemen Tepe. The growing opposition of the enemy, now strengthened by the hurried arrival of reserves, and the exhausted state of the Column prevented the assault from being delivered.

The situation at 3.30 p.m. on August 7th was as follows : Brigadier-General Johnston's Column on Rhododendron Spur and ridge ; the 29th Indian Infantry Brigade on the Farm ridge below Chunuk Bair and along the spurs to the north-east ; the 4th Australian Infantry Brigade on the line of the Asmak Dere, the next ravine north of the Aghyl Dere. The Right Covering Force was in occupation of Old No. 3 Post, Big Table Top, and Bauchop's Hill. The Left Covering Force was in occupation of the Damakjelik Bair. The forces detailed for operations from the Nos. 3 and 4 Sections were in occupation of their original lines. The troops comprising the two assaulting columns had been actively engaged throughout the morning and the early afternoon, and were still holding firmly to what they had gained, but were exhausted by fighting and lack of sleep. It was therefore decided to halt on these positions until nightfall before making another attempt to gain a footing on the main ridge of Sari Bair. The Turks continued to hold portions of the low ground towards the left of the line of the attack between the ridge and the sea, and showed little disposition to retire from there.

Nor had the co-operation looked for from the north, on which hopes ran high at this crucial moment in our fortunes, materialised, even though the breaking dawn disclosed to many eager watchers the presence of numbers of our ships close in shore to Suvla Bay.

CHUNUK BAIR.

During the afternoon of August 7th reconnaissances were made with a view to the launching of another attack on the Sari Bair position, and following upon this orders were issued for an advance in three columns. The objective of the right Column, which included the New Zealand Infantry Brigade, was defined as Chunuk Bair ; that of the centre and left Columns the prolongation of the ridge north-east to Koja Chemen Tepe, the highest point of the Sari Bair system.

The renewed assault was timed for 4.15 a.m. on August 8th. Preceded by an artillery bombardment of one hour's duration of the Turkish defence system, the advance commenced as arranged. On the right was Brigadier-General Johnston's Column, headed by the Wellington Infantry Battalion, and supported by the 7th Gloucestershire Regiment, the Auckland Mounted Rifles Regiment, the 8th Welsh Pioneers, and the Maori Contingent, the whole led by Lieut.-Colonel Malone ; in the centre the 39th Infantry Brigade and the 29th Indian Infantry Brigade ; on the left the 4th Australian Infantry Brigade. The order of battle placed the Wellington Battalion on the right of the line, the Gloucestershire Regiment on the left, with the Welsh Pioneers forming the second line ; the Auckland Mounted Rifles and Maori Contingent in the third line ; the Otago Battalion to be in reserve at the head of Rhododendron Spur.

With the launching of the attack, the Wellington Battalion, in one determined assault, gained the south-western slopes and crest of the main knoll of Chunuk Bair. The left troops of the Gloucestershire Regiment, shortly after the advance commenced, had come under heavy enfilade fire, which caused the line to edge over to the right and away from its objective. The captured Turkish trench on Chunuk Bair, which represented the most forward line, was eventually found untenable under the weight of enemy assaults ; and save for a few elements who hung on tenaciously to the last, the foremost troops withdrew and entrenched along a line immediately in rear but still on the slopes of Chunuk.

Now ensued an ordeal of supreme self-sacrifice and extreme physical endurance. With the position battered by fire of almost every description, exposed to the enfilade

LIEUT.-COLONEL A. MOORE, D.S.O., (D.)

(*Killed in Action*).

MAJOR F. H. STATHAM, (D.)
(Killed in Action).

The Farm and Road leading down the Aghyl Dere, with Suvla Bay in the distance.

Photograph taken from Chunuk Bair in 1919 by CAPTAIN C. V. BIGG-WITHER, Auckland M.R.)

fire of enemy machine guns, and harassed by persistent bombing attacks, the garrison of this forward line, exhausted and reduced by casualties, refused to yield the ground gained, and at the close of day the Wellington Battalion was still in position on the slopes of Chunuk. It was late in the afternoon before two squadrons of the Auckland Mounted Rifles Regiment succeeded in reinforcing the right of the line, after being temporarily held up by fire ; while the Maori Contingent, which constituted the same line, had swung more to the left, in the direction of the Farm.

While the right Column of the forces committed to the renewed assault on Sari Bair had thus succeeded in gaining a footing on Chunuk Bair, the efforts of the centre and left Columns had not been attended by the same measure of success. The centre Column, advancing from the positions occupied over-night, moved along the gullies which led up to the Sari Bair Ridge ; the right moving south of the Farm against Chunuk Bair, and the left moving up the spurs north-east of the Farm against that part of the ridge which extended north-east of Chunuk. So severe was the enemy's rifle and machine gun fire that little progress could be made ; although a certain amount of ground was gained on the spurs to the north-east of the Farm. Away to the left, the 4th Australian Infantry Brigade had advanced from its position on the Asmak Dere against the lower slopes of the Abdel Rahman Bair with the intention of then wheeling to the right, forcing a passage up the spur and attacking Koja Chemen Tepe. Strong opposition was met with from the outset, and in spite of every effort no material progress could be made. Finally, seriously threatened by the approach of large enemy forces, the 4th Australian Brigade was forced to withdraw to the line which it had previously occupied on the Asmak Dere.

The result of the day's fighting, therefore, was that the right Column held the south-western slopes of Chunuk Bair ; the centre Column was in occupation of the Farm and the spurs to the north-east of it ; and the left Column was contained on the Asmak Dere. This was the situation when it was decided to break off the fight for the day, preparatory to launching a further attack on the main Sari Bair Ridge, using the foothold gained on Chunuk Bair as a pivot.

The Otago Battalion, along with the Wellington Mounted Rifles Regiment (which had come under the orders of the Brigade) was ordered to relieve Wellington Battalion at dusk in the forward trenches on Chunuk Bair. By this time Wellington Battalion had been reduced to a strength which was almost negligible, and but few officers remained. Lieut.-Colonel Malone, a brave and resourceful officer, had been killed. Other units in line had suffered almost correspondingly heavy casualties. In compliance with orders for the relief of Wellington Troops, Otago Battalion proceeded to move forward at dusk, and under the greatest difficulties reached the advanced trenches on the slopes of Chunuk, when the remnants of Wellington Battalion withdrew. It was now decided to extend the original line to the right. Under this arrangement the forces committed to holding the defences of Chunuk were disposed as follows : Two-thirds of the strength of Otago Battalion holding the left front of the line ; Wellington Mounted Rifles next in order to the right ; and one-third of Otago Battalion's strength, represented by 4th Company, occupying a flanking position on the extreme right.

A day remarkable for the fierceness of the struggle was succeeded by a night perhaps even more desperate. No food or water reached the garrison ; there was no possible chance of getting the wounded away ; and the already exhausted defenders, though constantly menaced by the enemy, were forced to exert themselves throughout the night in an endeavour to deepen the shallow trenches— a difficult business owing to the hard formation. Shortly after 4th Company had taken up the position which formed a defensive right flank, movement was observed to the front, but there was some doubt as to its origin. Lieut. J. E. Cuthill accordingly moved out to the front and was able to convince himself that the Turks were massing for attack. This assault was eventually delivered in considerable force ; but our men withheld their fire until the enemy had advanced to within 15 yards of the line, when it was so well and truly delivered that the enemy was most sanguinarily repulsed. When beaten off they retired behind the ridge and reformed for a further effort.

As daylight broke on the 9th considerable numbers of the enemy appeared to the right rear, and at the same time a determined attack, preceded by a storm of bombs, was delivered against our front. The enemy's apparent intention was to drive in the front and then attack the garrison in the flank as it withdrew. The first line of trenches was entered, but the enemy was subsequently driven out, and the occupants of the rear trench, temporarily changing their front, dealt with the enemy threatening the flank. This attack was thus beaten off ; at all other points the enemy was equally unsuccessful.

The casualties during the night had been exceedingly heavy. Lieut.-Colonel Moore, who had commanded the Battalion from its first days on the Peninsula, was wounded, as also was Major Moir, Second-in-Command. Command of the Battalion was then taken over by Major G. Mitchell.

A FINAL STRUGGLE.

During the afternoon of August 8th a further reconnaissance was made of the lines of approach to the enemy's positions, and orders issued for a further assault, the third, against the Turkish strongholds on the Sari Bair Ridge. The line to be attacked was that of Chunuk Bair—Hill " Q," under cover of the footing gained by Brigadier-General Johnston's Column. The assault was again to be carried out by three columns. No. 1 Column, which included the New Zealand Infantry Brigade, was to hold and consolidate the ground gained on August 8th, and in co-operation with the other columns gain the whole of Chunuk Bair ; No. 2 and No. 3 Columns were to assault the position known as Hill " Q,' No. 3 Column being responsible for the main attack.

At 4.30 a.m. on August 9th the Naval and all other available guns commenced a bombardment of the enemy defences on Chunuk Bair and Hill " Q " ; and with increasing intensity this was continued until 5.15 a.m., when it was directed against the flanks and reverse slopes of the positions to be assaulted. Brigadier-General Baldwin, commanding the No. 3 Column, was to form up his battalions immediately in rear of the trenches occupied by the New Zealand Brigade, and from that point launch his attack in successive lines, keeping as much as possible to the high ground. In accordance with this plan arrangements were made to keep the narrow track clear of all obstructions in the way of upward and downward traffic, and guides were provided for the Column. But in spite of all these precautions, the troops were seriously delayed and hampered in their approach march by the difficult, scrub-covered country which had to be traversed in darkness, and losing direction inclined too far to the left. At the hour of attack the 6th Ghurkas of the 29th Indian Brigade (No. 2 Column) had pressed up the slopes towards Sari Bair, and were successful in crowning the heights of the nek adjoining Hill " Q." The co-operation of the troops of the No. 3 Column at this, one of the great moments of the August offensive, would have been invaluable. But as if the advantages which the high ground gave them were not sufficient, the Turks were again to have all the chances on their side. Before our grasp had tightened on this success the enemy, apparently perceiving the consequences of this new hold, counter-attacked heavily, and the Ghurkas bent before it. Almost at the same moment as the Turks had launched this counter-stroke, the Commander of the No. 3 Column, finding that he was too late to share in the operations as arranged, had deployed for attack where he stood, which was to the left of the New Zealand Brigade's support trenches at the head of Rhododendron Spur. But his attack had barely been launched when it came under a terrific fire directed by the enemy from the slopes in front and Hill " Q." So violent, so destructive, and so sustained was this blast that the assault reached but a short distance beyond the Farm—there its momentum ended.

The New Zealand Troops—Otago Battalion and Wellington Mounted Rifles Regiment—who were still grimly holding on to the slopes of Chunuk, had anxiously awaited the relief which this attack, had it been successful, would have brought them. When the completely exhausted state of the defenders of these advanced trenches, and the seriousness of their losses had been represented, encouragement was given by the announcement that Brigadier-General Baldwin's force— the No. 3 Column—was to advance and seize the Turkish positions to the left. The defenders had now witnessed the launching of this action and its failure ; and had to some extent suffered in the counter-blast delivered by the enemy.

During the day an effort was made to send up reinforcements ; two platoons of North Lancashire troops made an effort to reach the position and failed.

The fact that the troops in occupation of Chunuk Bair had now been fighting almost continuously for three days and nights rendered their relief imperatively necessary. It was pointed out that two battalions would be required to hold the position ; and it was urged that the relief should be effected that night. The outcome was that orders for relief were issued at 8 p.m. on the 9th. The line held by General Godley's force at that stage extended up the Rhododendron Spur to the forward trenches on Chunuk Bair, thence in a north-westerly direction through the Farm, and from there northwards to the Asmak Dere. As to the Chunuk Bair position, the trenches extended a distance of about 200 yards across the height, and were shallow in depth. The troops detailed to relieve Otago Battalion and the Wellington Mounted Rifles Regiment were the 6th Loyal North Lancashire Regiment and the 5th Wiltshire Regiment, of the 13th Division ; the 10th Hampshire Regiment to connect with the troops about the Farm. Towards midnight on the 9th the North Lancashire Regiment had arrived ; but it was 2 a.m. on the 10th before the whole of the New Zealand troops on Chunuk Bair were relieved. The Regiment, a mere fraction of its original strength, withdrew to the advanced trenches on Rhododendron Spur, and passed into reserve. Delayed by the intricate nature of the country and the shelling encountered during their progress up the Chailak Dere, the remainder of the relieving troops, the 5th Wiltshire Regiment, had not yet succeeded in reaching the positions to be taken over.

With the break of day on August 10th the great struggle for Sari Bair was abruptly and dramatically cut short in its development. By one overwhelming, fatal blow the hold on Chunuk Bair was to be irredeemably lost, and the hopes which this footing, gained at so much sacrifice, inspired of ultimate and complete possession of the Sari Bair Ridge — and Victory — were relentlessly shattered. The enemy had now made the fateful decision of throwing the whole of his available reserves into the conflict. Preceded by a bombardment of considerable intensity they swept over

the crest in an alarming preponderancy of numbers, down
the slopes of Chunuk Bair and Hill " Q," across the foremost
trenches—now vacated—on the first-named ridge ; and even
by the sheer weight of their numbers threatened to turn and
overwhelm the whole line. But as each successive wave of
the enemy, now advancing almost shoulder to shoulder,
swept down the slopes it was caught in the concentrated fire
of the whole of the machine guns and rifles of the New Zealand
Brigade, now manning the reserve trenches on Rhododendron
Spur. The fire of the warships, of the New Zealand and
Australian Artillery, and of all other available guns swept
through their ranks, causing heavy loss of life. Eventually
shattered and broken by this weight of lead, the enemy onrush
at this point was hopelessly crushed. But around the Farm
and against the spurs to the north-east the onslaught was
such as to cause the line to break and give ground, only to
be restored after fierce fighting by fresh bodies of troops.
Into the area of this desperate conflict the last two battalions
of the general reserve were thrown ; and by 10 a.m. this
extraordinary effort of the Turks, which at certain points
had threatened complete annihilation of the British line,
had expended itself, and those of the enemy who had penetrated far down the ridge began to stream back, although
few of them ever reached their lines again.

The capture, and in no less degree the retention, of the
Chunuk Bair position by the New Zealand troops concerned
had stood as the consummation of an effort remarkable for
sustained gallantry and determination of spirit ; and that
it should have fallen back into the hands of the enemy
occasioned a sense of acute loss and sacrifice in vain. At the
close of the Turkish counter-attack on the morning of the
10th, the New Zealand Brigade's hold on the top of
Rhododendron Spur represented, and remained, the furthest
permanent penetration of the enemy's territory ; and by
virtue of this fact, the position, which formed a pronounced
salient, came to be known as the Apex. From that part of
it which represented the left curve, known as the Upper
Cheshire Ridge, observation was afforded over the area of
the Farm ; Canterbury Slope forming the right curve of
the salient. But in many respects the position was unsatisfactory, mainly because of its exposed nature, the proximity

of the enemy's works, and the high ground to its immediate front ; and strenuous efforts had to be made immediately towards consolidating and making this most easterly point secure against encroachment, which would have forced a readjustment on lower ground. Across the whole front the Turks at the same time appeared to be displaying feverish haste in the construction of entrenchments and the erection of wire entanglements ; whilst on our side it was impossible to carry out a great deal of work on the more important portions of the line during the day owing to the manner in which the enemy dominated the position from the Sari Bair Ridge.

The four days' battle may now be said to have been at an end. The state of exhaustion reached, the disorganisation of units, and the heavy losses incurred prevented any further effort being made in the meantime. Of General Birdwood's forces, it was estimated that the casualties numbered 12,000 ; a total which embraced a high percentage of officers. The general line, it was true, had been appreciably advanced, but the real goal had not been attained ; and the reverse, which had lost to us the foothold on Chunuk Bair, had placed it far out of reach.

SUVLA BAY.

But there were other circumstances which had determined or influenced the course of the action, and over which those who had conducted the offensive against Sari Bair from the area of Anzac had no control. As already explained, simultaneously with the attack from Anzac and as part of the Commander-in-Chief's strategical design for the capture of Sari Bair Ridge, a surprise landing was to be effected at Suvla Bay, north of Anzac. The operation was to be entrusted to the 9th Corps, and according to the prepared plans the first task was to seize the Chocolate and " W " Hills, together with the high ground on the north and east of Suvla Bay. Possession of all the important heights within artillery range of the Bay having been gained, it was intended to direct the remainder of the force through the Anafartas to the east of Sari Bair, and by engaging the enemy from this quarter materially influence the success of operations from the Anzac front.

The landing was accomplished, though not entirely as designed. Initial confusion was succeeded by hesitation, and finally by fatal inaction, chiefly the result of failure to meet the problem of water supply and distribution and the consequent sufferings from thirst of the new and untried army. With the apparent total inability of those in authority to stir their commands into action the situation became so serious that the Commander-in-Chief himself was impelled to hurry to the spot. The days of the 7th and 8th had passed with practically nothing accomplished ; and a belated attempt to advance on the 9th ended in failure. With the arrival of a fresh division of Territorial troops it was decided to make a further attempt to seize the Anafarta Ridge on the 10th ; but the attack failed to get on ; and orders were issued to the Corps Commander to entrench on a line across the whole front from near the Asmak Dere through the Knoll east of the Chocolate Hills to the ground held about Kiretch Tepe Sirt, to the north. Additional troops arrived on August 11th, and a further attack was planned against the heights Kavak Tepe-Teke Tepe. The operation was commenced but not persisted in owing to the Corps Commander's representations that even if the heights were gained it would be impracticable to keep the troops supplied with food and water. Under these conditions the only alternative left was to settle down and strengthen the line held. On the evening of August 15th General Stopford handed over his command of the 9th Corps.

The containing attack delivered at Helles coincident with the launching of the offensive at Anzac was followed by desperate fighting over several days. The success achieved, set down in ground gained, was in no sense pronounced, but the Helles attack had apparently served the purpose for which it was launched, namely, holding down the Turkish forces already in the southern zone and preventing enemy reinforcements being despatched north to Anzac where the main battle was in full blast.

THE SITUATION REVIEWED.

A review of the four days' operations at Anzac would convey but an inadequate idea of the real nature of the struggle were reference not made to the stupendous difficulties presented by the problem of water supply; and by the wounded who poured down to the dressing stations. Long before the offensive commenced efforts were directed towards establishing at Anzac great accumulations of water; and by the utilisation of all possible methods of storage a very great deal was accomplished. But another more difficult phase of the problem presented itself when, the offensive having been launched, this water had to be taken up to the troops for whom it was intended. The extraordinary physical exertions demanded by an advance over such steep and rugged country, combined with the intense heat of a midsummer's day, created a thirst which quickly drained the supply carried by each man. The general advancement of the line, the semi-isolated position of bodies of troops, and the initial absence of direct communication to points which were inaccessible by night and exposed to fire by day, together with the inevitable measure of disorganisation attending the first stages of an attack, made it at times impossible to get water up to those most urgently in need of it. Thus to physical exhaustion were added the acute sensations of a thirst which could not be satisfied.

While all this grim business of fighting and sweating and toiling was in progress on the heights above, another phase of the conflict was presented in the gullies and on the beach below. As the four days' battle progressed, the medical arrangements, despite the greatest efforts of the personnel, could not keep pace with the increasingly heavy toll of casualties. A certain part of these arrangements, owing to the necessity for observing secrecy, had to be effected within the few hours available after the offensive had been launched, while dressing stations had to be established as the advance proceeded. But it was the inability to cope with such a sudden and tremendous rush of casualties that so seriously complicated matters and led to so much delay and suffering. There were hundreds of walking cases, and even badly wounded, who succeeded in struggling down to the dressing stations; but among the gullies and lying exposed on the hills above there were others who, because of their wounds, were unable to move, and had to lie there indefinitely, suffering and hoping against hope that relief of some sort would come their way. But the toiling bearers were already overwhelmed with work; their labours increased by the difficulties of transporting wounded down the narrow gullies which formed the sole means of communication, and through which there passed the constant traffic of mule trains, of relieving troops, of walking wounded, and of the up and down stream of supply. At the beach, barges from the hospital ships and others loaded with mules were filled with stretcher or walking cases as they drew alongside or were emptied, and a way cleared, at least temporarily, for the wounded who continued to pour down from above.

The casualties sustained by the Regiment during the course of these operations and over the succeeding few days totalled 17 officers and over 300 other ranks. Included among those who fell in action during these days of desperate fighting were Major F. H. Statham, Captain R. Wilkinson, Lieut. T. H. Nisbet, Lieut. C. R. Sargood, Lieut. G. E. Waite, and 2nd-Lieut. W. M. McKenzie. Major Statham, a fine powerful fellow, was killed alongside his younger brother and Sergt.-major Porteous, M.C. At the close of the operations there were only four officers of the Battalion left unwounded, this number including Lieut. W. G. Bishop, who was awarded the M.C. Many very worthy non-commissioned officers and men also fell in action. There were several whose bravery earned recognition, the Distinguished Conduct Medal being awarded to Sergt. F. Mitchell for his gallant conduct on the right flank of the Chunuk Bair position ; to Sergt.-major P. C. Boate ; Sergt. A. G. Henderson for his fine work as Battalion Machine Gun N.C.O. ; and to Lance-corp. H. D. Skinner. These days of heavy losses and heroic and exhausting effort saw the arrival at Anzac of the 5th Reinforcements under Captain W. Domigan ; the Regiment thereby receiving an added strength of approximately 300 all ranks. Without any preliminaries this new force was thrown into the violent struggle then raging.

With the breaking off of the offensive on August 10th the forces contained at Rhododendron Spur settled down to a defensive role. All efforts were concentrated on defining and consolidating the new line, in reorganising and regrouping scattered units and, as far as possible, in burying the dead. On August 15th the Apex, except for the southern ridge, was taken over by the Welsh Fusiliers, the Regiment, now under the temporary command of Captain H. Stewart, of Canterbury Regiment, moving below the New Zealand Brigade Headquarters, for a period of three days rest. On the following day a move was made to a new gully which formerly had been occupied by the Turks, and which was named Otago Gully. The recorded total strength of the Battalion on August 16th was 360 all ranks ; this number including the additional strength derived from the 5th Reinforcements. On the 20th of the month the Battalion returned to the Apex, relieving Canterbury Battalion in the holding of the southern ridge.

The losses sustained during the August operations had heavily drained the available forces ; and with the close of the offensive another phase of wastage presented itself. Weariness of mind and body, the persistently bad and cramped conditions of existence, the lack of nourishing food, and the sapping of vitality until it had reached breaking point commenced to levy an alarming toll of sick and diseased men. The evacuations became increasingly heavy. The August offensive had represented the last gallant expenditure of effort ; and wasted bodies simply could not carry on the struggle.

In the course of a Special Order issued subsequent to the Battle of Sari Bair, General Sir Ian Hamilton expressed himself as follows : " The troops under the command of Major-General Sir A. J. Godley, and particularly the New Zealand and Australian Division, were called upon to carry out one of the most difficult operations that has ever been attempted—a night march and assault by several columns in intricate mountainous country, strongly entrenched and held by a numerous enemy. Their brilliant conduct during this operation and the success they achieved have won for them a reputation as soldiers of whom any country must be proud."

On August 21st the 9th Corps undertook operations from Suvla which aimed at gaining ground to the east and capturing the " W " Hills and the Anafarta Spur, in which the left flank of General Birdwood's force was to co-operate. This proved to be actually the last offensive action launched against the Turks on the Gallipoli Peninsula. The main success was achieved by the force operating from the left of the Anzac line. The advance was directed against the line Kaiajik Dere, Hill 60, and Susuk Kuyu, the force carrying out the attack against Hill 60 and the lower portion of the Kaiajik Dere including the Otago and Canterbury Mounted Rifles and about 500 men of the 4th Australian Infantry Brigade. In face of heavy fire the Mounted Rifles reached the south-western slopes of Hill 60 ; while the Australian Infantry gained a footing on the northern side of the Kaiajik Dere. On August 27th a further assault was directed against Hill 60, detachments of the New Zealand Mounted Rifles being again employed. They established themselves on the slopes of the height, and there defied all efforts of the Turks to dislodge them. This signalised the close of the hard fought attacks against Hill 60, and the positions thus gained and held afforded observation over the enemy's lateral communications and a considerable area of the low country towards the " W " Hills and in the direction of Biyuk Anafarta.

On the last day of the month of August Lieut.-Colonel Herbert arrived and took over command of Otago Battalion from Captain H. Stewart (Canterbury Regiment). The Maori Contingent had now been merged into the New Zealand Infantry Brigade ; one platoon being drafted to each Battalion. The reduced strength of Otago Regiment forced a temporary amalgamation of 4th and 8th Companies, designated A Company, and of 10th and 14th Companies, designated B Company.

On September 2nd about 80 men of Otago Battalion were moved up in close support of the Apex. In accordance with the plan of defence issued by Division the New Zealand Brigade became responsible for garrisoning that part of the line which embraced the Apex, Rhododendron Spur and Canterbury Slope. Under the same orders defined outer and inner lines of defence were to be constructed ; and in this connection the Brigade was made responsible for the outer line of trench work round the Apex, the strengthening of the Rhododendron Spur position by several lines of trench work, the construction of communication trenches to the valleys east and south-east of Big Table Top, and trench work extending from the Apex to Cheshire Ridge on the left. On the afternoon of the 10th the Apex positions were subjected to an hour's rapid bombardment from several enemy guns ; seeming to indicate that an attack was developing, but no infantry action followed.

A REST AT MUDROS.

Now came the welcome news that the troops of the New Zealand Infantry Brigade, the New Zealand Mounted Rifles Brigade and the Otago Mounted Rifles Regiment were to move to Lemnos for a period of rest which it was hoped would extend over a month. This was made possible by the arrival on the Peninsula of the 7th Australian Infantry Brigade. The relief of units holding the Apex commenced on September 12th, but on the following day a communication was received from Division to the effect that the move to Lemnos was postponed on account of the cold and showery weather and the fact that there would be no tents available for the troops when they arrived there. The reply to this was that the men would be as comfortable there as in the trenches, even if they were without tents, and a request was made that the matter be reconsidered. To the intense satisfaction of everyone concerned, this was later in the day acceded to. The relief was then proceeded with and completed on September 14th. During the early evening the Regiment moved to Anzac Cove, and embarked on the *Osmanieh* for Lemnos on the following morning. On reaching Lemnos the troops went ashore by ferry steamer, but very little preparation had been made for their arrival. The Battalion marched out to Sarpi Rest Camp (Mudros West), but on reaching there after dark found but a limited number of tents for its accommodation. This was a bad beginning, but the conditions improved in the course of a few days, when more tents were secured, the weather brightened, and the luxuries of hot baths and fresh food, with hours of pleasant idleness amidst peaceful surroundings, were enjoyed. It was a rest and complete change such as was needed to restore mental and physical vitality, so seriously impaired by successive months of hard fighting, lack of nourishing food, the trying heat of the summer, dysentery, and the constant strain and weariness which existence at Anzac imposed. The wastage of man power arising from these conditions was reflected in the numerical weakness of the Regiment when it moved away from the Peninsula—a comparative handful of 130 men.

While at Lemnos the strength of the Battalion was substantially increased by the arrival of the 6th Reinforcements. Light training was now being carried out, and generally the health of the men was showing a marked improvement under the totally changed conditions of living. Lieut.-Colonel Herbert had some time previously proceeded to Egypt for a brief rest; Captain D. White temporarily commanding the Battalion until the return of Captain D. Colquhoun. During this period the Regiment paraded for inspection by General Sir C. C. Monro.

On November 9th this pleasant period of relaxation came to a close, when the Battalion left Lemnos and returned to Anzac, proceeding on arrival into area of bivouac. The New Zealand Brigade again took over the Apex. On the 11th 14th Company of Otago Battalion was sent up from bivouac area to No. 1 Post of the Apex; on the 12th 4th Company was despatched to the same locality. During the 16th there was a good deal of shelling of the Apex, Cheshire Ridge and Chailak Dere, and on the following evening the enemy opened heavy machine gun and rifle fire against the Apex positions. At this period a heavy storm broke over the Anzac area, causing considerable damage to bivouacs and dug-outs, and along the beach. This was but an indication of what might be expected during the dreaded winter months.

CHAPTER VII.

THE BEGINNING OF THE END.

THE close of the August Offensive witnessed the gradual development of a series of events which were to have a pronounced bearing on the prosecution of the Gallipoli Campaign. While the defences and rear and lateral communications of the new front were being improved and extended and a comprehensive scheme of mining developed, the trend of events elsewhere was such as to give rise to a feeling of uneasy apprehension as to the general situation. The entrance of Bulgaria into the war on the side of the Central Powers, the desperate straits to which Serbia was reduced, and the vacillation of Greece, all threatened far-reaching consequences. It was, for example, perfectly clear that more artillery and more ammunition would be made available for Turkish operations on Gallipoli ; and the anticipated employment by the enemy of heavy artillery on a grand scale called for the strengthening of defensive works and communication trenches and the deepening and expanding of the existing system of dug-outs to an extent beyond anything previously adopted or thought of. Again, while the weather up to the middle of October had remained fairly settled, there were unmistakeable indications of the approach of winter, with its violent snow storms and fierce blasts sweeping in from the Ægean Sea. Wasted frames were unable to withstand the wholesale sickness which now gripped the garrison ; and there was apparently no source of supply that could be drawn upon to appreciably replace the losses caused by the evacuations which followed. The most urgent requests made by the Commander-in-Chief for reinforcements could not be complied with ; and it became apparent that the demands of the Gallipoli Campaign were to be subordinated to those of the Western Front. This, it would seem, was the first phase of the developments which pointed to the beginning of the end.

On October 11th Sir Ian Hamilton was cabled to from England and requested to give an estimate of the losses which would be involved in an evacuation of the Peninsula. On the following day he replied in terms which showed that he regarded such a step as unthinkable. Four days later he received a cable recalling him to London for the reason, as he was subsequently informed, that His Majesty's Government desired an independent opinion from a responsible commander upon the question of an early evacuation. In accordance with this decision General Sir Ian Hamilton relinquished his post as Commander-in-Chief of the Mediterranean Expeditionary Force, and, bidding farewell to the "ever-victorious Australians and New Zealanders," departed for England.

General Sir C. C. Monro, the new Commander of the Mediterranean Expeditionary Force, arrived at Imbros towards the end of October, and from there proceeded to the Gallipoli Peninsula to investigate the situation, and to express an opinion as to whether on purely military grounds the positions should be evacuated, or another attempt made ; and if so the number of troops that would be required. The impressions which he gathered are summarised in the following statement : " The positions occupied by our troops presented a military problem unique in history. The mere fringe of the coast line had been secured. The beaches and piers upon which they depended for all requirements in personnel and material were exposed to registered and observed artillery fire. Our entrenchments were dominated almost throughout by the Turks. The possible artillery positions were insufficient and defective. The force, in fact, held a line possessing every possible defect. The position was without depth ; the communications were insecure and dependent on the weather. No means existed for the concealment and deployment of fresh troops destined for the offensive ; whilst the Turks enjoyed full powers of observation and abundant artillery positions ; and they had been given time to supplement the natural advantages which the position presented by all the devices at the disposal of the field engineer." In face of these and other arguments, " irrefutable in their conclusions," General Monro was convinced that complete evacuation was the only wise course to pursue. A visit from Lord Kitchener followed, and the decision to evacuate the Peninsula was apparently then confirmed.

On November 24th orders were received that a period of 48 hours' silence was to be observed, and that no firing was to take place except in case of actual attack by the enemy. This inactivity was faithfully observed; and on the evening of the 26th it was ordered that the policy of silence should be continued until midnight on November 27th. The reasons advanced for the observance of this period of silence were that it was reported that the Turks believed that the Anzac position was about to be evacuated, and that the ruse adopted would induce him to attack; but whatever the real object aimed at, it must have influenced the success of the critical events now pending.

During the closing days of November a blizzard of exceptional severity swept over the Peninsula. The country was covered with a mantle of snow, the outlook generally becoming more repellant and less hopeful as the days dragged their slow length along; while the heavy seas racing before the gale that beat the coast made wreckage of the piers and of the barges moored there. Hard frosts and days and nights of intense cold followed. With the commencement of the blizzard, two companies of the Battalion were at the Apex, one at No. 1 Post and one at No. 2 Post, and two companies in reserve in the Chailak Dere, and with the scanty clothing available and the lack of adequate shelter, they suffered severely. The period of frost was succeeded by a general thaw, and the occupants of the lower areas in particular fared badly; while the recognised tracks and routes became practically impassable. Exceedingly bad as the position was, the high ground of Anzac, with its more effective drainage, had saved the garrison from the disaster which overtook the troops of the 9th Corps on the low levels of Suvla. There in many places water rose to the height of the parapet; and despite the greatest efforts to meet effectively the terrible conditions existing, there were recorded 200 deaths from exposure, while over 10,000 sick were evacuated during the opening days of December. Hard contact with the biting blasts of winter, together with the mountainous seas which raged along the desolate coast and threatened the landing and consequent maintenance of supplies, created misgiving among the garrison at Anzac, and gave rise to depressing thoughts envisioning an ugly outlook if the present was to be taken as the forerunner of even worse conditions both on land and sea.

CHAPTER VIII.

THE EVACUATION.

On December 8th Lieut-.General Sir W. Birdwood, Commanding the Dardanelles Army, was ordered to proceed immediately with the evacuation of Suvla and Anzac. It had been previously determined that the evacuation must be conducted by stages, which would contribute to the secrecy so vital to success. Under this arrangement, the withdrawal of a certain proportion of guns and troops, surplus to the requirements of an ostensibly passive winter campaign, was gradually effected. In view of the extraordinary situation of the Army at Anzac it was imperative that nothing should be done which would arouse the suspicions of the enemy. Bearing in mind also how entirely dependent the success of the operation was on fine weather conditions, and in view of the gales and storms which might be expected at any moment in the Ægean Sea, its rapid accomplishment was of main importance. Thus, with profound secrecy and rapidity as the essential elements of the undertaking, there was presented a military problem which at first sight appeared so complex and so improbable of success that, were it not attended by extraordinary good fortune, to embark upon it was merely to invite disaster. But in so thorough and comprehensive a manner was the scheme for evacuation drawn up, and so expeditiously was it given effect to, that even before the date set down for the final and complete withdrawal a very considerable proportion of men, guns and animals had left the Peninsula, with the enemy apparently quite unconscious of the fact. Though a gradual reduction of the garrison was being effected, there was no departure from the normal life previously pursued both on land and sea. On December 12th 19 guns of various calibres belonging to or attached to the New Zealand and Australian Division were withdrawn.

A memorandum was issued on December 13th authorising the formation of a rest camp at Mudros, where, it was intimated, approximately half the forces of Anzac would rest during the winter months. It was on this day the Regiment moved from its area of bivouac to North Beach preparatory to embarking for Mudros. Owing to the shortage of water transport, however, the Battalion was required to march back to Waterfall Gully. At 5.30 p.m. on the following day, December 14th, the Battalion again moved to North Beach *via* the Main Sap, and under cover of darkness stepped into the waiting barges and silently moved out to the vessel which was to convey them to Mudros and away from the Peninsula for the last time. The official explanation was that the Regiment, in company with other units, was proceeding to the Rest Camp at Lemnos ; but there was more than a suspicion that the move was one of deep significance.

The evacuation was to be concluded to the last man on the night of December 19th-20th. The withdrawal of men, guns and animals, begun after dusk and continued throughout the night, was now in full swing. Everything was proceeding under conditions which promised success. As far as the enemy was concerned nothing had apparently occurred to arouse his suspicions. The remaining artillery was very much in action ; the normal rate of rifle and machine gun fire was being maintained ; the movement of troops along the deres and recognised routes showed no diminution in numbers ; and fires were kept going in deserted bivouacs. The whole area of Anzac bore the appearance of normal occupation. But under cover of darkness, and concealed from the Turks, the machinery of evacuation was silently and effectively working.

On the last night but one the troops of the New Zealand and Australian Division detailed for withdrawal moved down to the rendezvous at No. 2 Post as soon as darkness set in, and were there formed into groups of approximately 400, which was the capacity of the motor lighters employed to convey them to the troopships. Embarkation proceeded with the utmost smoothness, and by 4.45 a.m. the night's quota of 3,490 men had embarked, leaving 3,000 men to guard the lines of the Division. The day of the 19th passed without incident, except that the enemy shelled the Apex with heavy howitzers during the morning and repeated the bombardment during the afternoon. The last 3,000 men of the Division were now divided into three parties, termed A, B, and C. At dusk those of A party marched down to their rendezvous, boarded the lighters, and moved out into the darkness. The B parties followed in their turn, and had completed embarkation shortly after 11 p.m. The C parties were now in sole occupation.

Weak in numbers but strong in resolution, it had fallen to the lot of these men to hold for a few brief hours and then to silently leave and hand over to the enemy what thousands of their comrades had toiled and sweated and died for during a period of eight months of unexampled hardship and suffering. With the last moments inevitably given over to reflection, what wonder if there passed before them the fleeting vision of long lines of gallant souls who, at the price of a shattered body or in the certainty of immediate death, stormed the rugged slopes of Anzac ; of those who by heroism and enduring fortitude immortalized the names of Courtney's, Quinn's, Lone Pine, Chunuk Bair, the Apex, and Hill 60, and above all else, of those thousands who were to be left behind in their last lonely resting places scattered over the hills and through the gullies of Gallipoli. With these thoughts running through their minds, what wonder if the going was harder than the coming.

By 1.30 a.m. the last of the garrison had commenced to withdraw. Men moved rapidly and quietly up and down the trenches and fired shots from the various points from which fire was usually delivered. To give an appearance of occupation even after the last man had left, rifles were adjusted in such a manner as to be subsequently discharged. Barricades had been erected in the main deres and communication trenches, and a final covering position established and manned to protect the points of embarkation should the Turks be suddenly apprised of the situation. Everything that could be of use to the enemy had been either removed, buried or destroyed ; and at the last moment huge piles of stores and clothing, soaked in oil, were ready for destruction by fire. The New Zealand and Australian Division had accomplished the withdrawal of 53 guns, of which 12 had been removed during the two final nights. Only two attached guns were destroyed.

At 2.25 a.m. on December 20th, the barricade erected in the Chailak Dere was closed, and the last of the garrison filed down to the beach. Without interruption or hindrance they stepped into the lighters and moved silently out to the covering ships ready to receive them ; the piles of stores burst into flames—and Anzac was of the past.

RETURN TO EGYPT.

With the Gallipoli Campaign so unexpectedly closed, the Regiment, after resting and recuperating at Mudros, embarked on the old German *Derfflinger* on December 24th and sailed for Alexandria. On arrival the journey was continued by rail to Moascar Camp, Ismailia.

On January 25th, 250 rifles and two machine guns of the Regiment, under Major D. Colquhoun, were ordered to proceed to Bench Mark and Ridge Posts, on the east bank of the Suez Canal, where the duties were of the lightest order and every facility was afforded for healthful bathing in the waters of the Canal. Two days later the 7th Reinforcements arrived from New Zealand, and the Regiment received an additional strength of six officers and 230 other ranks. Reorganisation of companies followed this absorption of strength, and on January 10th a programme of training was commenced. On the 16th the New Zealand and Australian Division was inspected by General Sir A. J. Murray, Commander-in-Chief of the Forces in Egypt. On the 26th the Otago detachment in occupation of the two posts on the east bank of the Canal was relieved and returned to Moascar.

FORMATION OF THE 2ND BATTALION.

With the arrival of reinforcement drafts and the return of men who had been evacuated through wounds or sickness, the strength of forces was steadily growing, and on February 11th orders were received which led to the formation of new and distinct units. This embraced the establishment of an additional infantry brigade. As evidence of the further expansion of Colonial forces, connection with the Australian formation was severed, and on March 1st the New Zealand Division, which now included the 1st and 2nd Infantry Brigades, and the 3rd (Rifle) Brigade, with a corresponding increase in artillery, officially came into being as a distinct and separate unit in the Field. On February 26th the 4th Australian Infantry Brigade had commenced to move out to Tel-el-Kebir at the rate of one battalion daily, thus severing its long association with the New Zealanders. The 1st New Zealand Infantry Brigade was now comprised of the 1st Battalions of Otago, Canterbury, Wellington and Auckland Regiments, and was commanded by Brigadier-General F. E. Johnston, C.B. The 2nd New Zealand Infantry Brigade embraced the newly formed battalions of the same Regiments, Brigadier-General W. G. Braithwaite, D.S.O., being appointed to the Brigade Command. It had been notified that 50 per cent. of officers and from 15 to 25 per cent. of non-commissioned officers from available forces were to be drawn upon for the new Brigade ; but there was considerable readjustment of personnel before appointments to the different battalions were finally made. The postings which were now made in respect of Otago Regiment, and which included a number of officers from the Otago Mounted Rifles, were as follows :—

To 1st Battalion. — Lieut.-Colonel A. B. Charters ; Captain (temporary Major) D. Colquhoun, Captain D. White, Captain S. Rice, Captain W. D. Jolly ; Lieuts. D. H. S. Buddle, W. G. A. Bishop, R. H. Nicholson, P. Mackenzie, W. Ward, W. J. Bevis, G. L. McClure ; 2nd.-Lieuts. W. F. Tracy, T. Gillman, J. E. Cuthill, J. P. Hewat, M. J. White, J. G. Johnston, N. Hall, W. H. S. Widdowson, C. H. Clark, A. P. McCormack, A. G. Brockett, R. R. Gow, A. R. Sutherland, W. D. Stewart.

To 2nd Battalion.—Major D. B. McKenzie, Major J. A. Mackenzie, Captain W. Domigan, Captain W. G. Wray, Captain D. Thomson, Captain W. T. Joll ; Lieuts. G. H. Ferguson, C. St. C. Hamilton, E. B. Alley, A. H. Wright, L. S. Jennings, H. Salmon, H. R. Ker, L. G. Wilson, L. M. Scott, J. H. Barr, P. W. G. Spiers, J. B. Struthers, F. T. Christian ; 2nd-Lieuts. W. K. Dougall, T. Fitzpatrick, M. McP. Watt, J. R. Patterson, J. F. M. Fleming, J. Robertson, A. R. T. McDougall, H. G. Brodie, P. Pile, P. A. Spurdle, A. Craig, C. Barry.

Still further changes were made in commands and appointments in respect of both Battalions ; in some instances due to the posting of additional senior officers to the Regiment.

However, Lieut.-Colonel Charters, who had taken over the 1st Battalion on February 24th (on the occasion of Lieut.-Colonel Moore's departure on account of ill-health) continued in command without interruption; while the posting of Major C. E. Andrews, Auckland Regiment, to the Otago Regiment, determined the appointment of Second-in-Command of the 1st Battalion. With the arrival of Major G. F. Hutton, of the Canterbury Mounted Rifles Regiment, and his appointment to the command of the 2nd Battalion, with the rank of Lieut.-Colonel, Major J. A. Mackenzie relinquished his temporary appointment as Officer Commanding, and filled the position of Second-in-Command. The establishment of Infantry Training Battalions, one for each Brigade of the Division, towards the close of March was responsible for the transfer, though in some instances merely of a temporary nature, of several officers and n.c.o.'s of the Regiment. Lieut.-Colonel Moore, now returned, commanded all New Zealand Training Units and Depots, but later, interchanging with Major Hutton, assumed command of the 2nd Battalion of the Regiment. On April 6th Major G. Mitchell and Major G. S. Smith, both of whom had been evacuated wounded from the Peninsula, returned to the Regiment; among later postings there was on April 12th recorded the transfer of 2nd-Lieut. J. Hargest from the Otago Mounted Rifles Regiment to the Otago Regiment.

All troops of the Training Units were finally transferred to England under the command of Major G. Mitchell.

On March 5th orders were received that the New Zealand Division was to move to Ferry Post Camp, on the east bank of the Suez Canal; replacing the 2nd Australian Division, which was ordered to Moascar. This move commenced forthwith, and on completion the dispositions were as follows : 1st Infantry Brigade, Ferry Post; 2nd Infantry Brigade, half-mile west of Allbury Hill. The New Zealand Mounted Rifles Brigade occupied the front line of defences. The 1st Battalion of the Regiment had remained at Moascar until March 8th, when it marched out and relieved the 28th Australian Battalion at Ferry Post East and Bench Mark Post. On March 20th the Division commenced its return to Moascar, where by the close of the month the whole of its strength was concentrated.

Cemetery on Plugge's Plateau.

Anzac Cove to-day.

ORDERED TO FRANCE.

At the beginning of March it had been made known that the New Zealand Division would at an early date be transferred to France. This, it was realised, meant that the Regiment would sooner or later be thrown into the vortex of the main struggle on the Western Front. Viewed in the light of the immediate prospects which it offered of change of conditions and environment, the announcement was received with general, if subdued, enthusiasm. An exchange of eternal sand for green fields was alluring enough in itself, quite apart from other considerations, real or imagined. Mobilisation parades became the order of the closing days of March ; the thousand and one details of equipment, of fitness, of personnel, of stores, and finally of movement and embarkation now received attention.

Appointments to the principal commands in the Regiment were made as follows :—

1st Battalion.—Officer Commanding, Lieut.-Colonel Charters ; Second-in-Command, Major C. E. Andrews ; Adjutant, Lieut. W. F. Tracy ; 4th (Otago) Company, Captain D. White ; 8th (Southland) Company, Captain S. Rice ; 10th (North Otago) Company, Captain D. H. S. Buddle ; 14th (South Otago) Company, Major D. Colquhoun ; Battalion Quartermaster, Lieut. A. P. McCormack.

2nd Battalion.—Officer Commanding, Lieut.-Colonel A. Moore, D.S.O. ; Second-in-Command, Major J. A. Mackenzie ; Adjutant, Captain D. E. Bremner ; 4th (Otago) Company, Major G. S. Smith, D.S.O. ; 8th (Southland) Company, Captain W. G. Wray ; 10th (North Otago) Company, Major D. B. McKenzie ; 14th (South Otago) Company, Captain L. S. Jennings ; Battalion Quartermaster, Captain H. R. Ker.

On the night of April 5th the Regiment took the first step in the direction of severing its connection with the land of the Pharaohs. This was the entraining of the 1st Battalion at Ismailia for Port Said, where, on the following day, the greater part of its strength stepped aboard the *Franconia,* a small proportion being allotted to the *Ingomia.* The 2nd Battalion of the Regiment entrained at Moascar on April 8th, arriving at Alexandria on the following morning and embarking on the *Llandovery Castle*. The 1st Battalion arrived at Marseilles on April 13th ; three days later the 2nd Battalion had also reached its destination in France.

Part II.

FRANCE
AND FLANDERS.

CHAPTER I.

THE WESTERN FRONT.

THE Regiment had now set its foot on the shores of a land into the interior of which war had long since been carried by a ruthless enemy, whose progress in every direction was marked by ruin and desolation and the sufferings of a helpless non-combatant population. The days of Gallipoli, with their imperishable glories, their suffering and endurance, their heavy burden of unfulfilled anticipation, of hope deferred, and splendour of achievement,—all belonged now to the past. A new campaign was being entered on, and no one doubted but that the Regiment, fighting side by side with the men of England and France—men of the immortal first Armies— would uphold the gallant name it had made for itself on Gallipoli.

It was approaching summer, and the fertile valley of the Rhone, through which the Regiment travelled from Marseilles to the interior, was clothed in verdure of the deepest green. Smiling homesteads, nestled in gardens rich in golden promise of fruit and flowers, provided a refreshing feast for the senses, a tonic for mind and body, after the long drab-coloured days of desert and Peninsula. As an amelioration of the attendant weariness of a long journey by rail, there was everywhere the joyous greeting of an enthusiastic people. And through all there was a leaven of interesting and humorous incident, with impromptu feasting, sudden train stoppages and more sudden resumptions.

The 1st New Zealand Infantry Brigade, which embraced the 1st Battalion of the Regiment, was ordered to concentrate in the Morbecque area, near Hazebrouck, and the 2nd New Zealand Infantry Brigade, embracing the 2nd Battalion of the Regiment, in the Rouquetoire area. The 1st Battalion reached its area on April 16th, detraining at Steenbecque, near the village of Morbecque, at midnight, and marching out to a small camp situated on the Morbecque-Hazebrouck Road. The camp comprised a number of huts, shelters and tents, and was afterwards to become the XXII. Corps School of Instruction. On the following day Battalion Headquarters moved into the village, where the billeting officer found accommodation for personnel and animals in the surrounding farmhouses, and the camp site originally selected was vacated. Three days later the Battalion transport arrived from Abbeville.

The 2nd Battalion of the Regiment reached Hazebrouck on the evening of April 18th, detrained at a small station just beyond, and marched a distance of several miles to Rincq. Rain fell during the night, and in the darkness the guide lost his way, and the march being in consequence unduly prolonged, Rincq was not reached until five o'clock on the following morning. Comparatively good billets, however, offered some compensation for this unpleasant experience. On the 21st the Battalion transport arrived from Abbeville.

This was the Regiment's first experience of being quartered in billets, which demanded an observance of regulations to which the troops had not been previously accustomed. But the conditions generally and the pleasant intercourse with the people of the country provided an agreeable change to men many of whom had only recently gone through the hardships of the Gallipoli Campaign.

The several succeeding days spent in these areas were devoted to route marches, company drill, night alarms, and, of considerable importance, demonstrations by the Army chemical advisers in the adoption of protective measures against the enemy's use of poison gas. At the same time the first quota of selected officers and men was despatched for a course of instruction to the various Army and Corps Schools.

On the last day of April the 2nd Battalion of the Regiment moved out from Rincq to Boeseghen, and on the following day, in company with the whole of the 2nd Infantry Brigade, continued the journey to Doulieu. This involved a march of approximately 20 miles, and carrying heavy packs and 150 rounds of ammunition it proved a stiff test of endurance to which everyone stood up remarkably well. There now followed a further period of rest and mild training, which included throwing live bombs, musketry, and exercise in the several arts of warfare calculated to be useful in view of approaching events.

It was at this stage that the Commanding Officer and the Company Commanders paid a visit to the Armentieres Sector and had their first sight of the German front line. In company with the officers of the 7th East Yorks Battalion, they spent the night of the 6th-7th May there, acquiring a first-hand knowledge of the front, support and reserve positions of the sector, its general defensive dispositions, and the many important details common to relief. On the return of these officers to Doulieu, a conference for all officers was held with Brigadier-General F. E. Johnston, C.B., Commanding the 1st New Zealand Infantry Brigade.

ARMENTIERES.

On arrival in France, the New Zealand Division was incorporated in the 1st Australian and New Zealand Army Corps, which in turn formed part of the Second Army, then commanded by General Sir Herbert Plumer. On May 9th it was announced that the New Zealand Division would at an early date relieve the 17th Division in the line east of Armentieres, relief to be completed by May 20th. The distribution of Divisional troops decided upon in accordance with this relief was as follows : Right sector, 1st Infantry Brigade ; Left sector, 2nd Infantry Brigade ; Divisional reserve, 3rd (Rifle) Brigade. As part of the other details of relief, the 17th Division's Trench Warfare and Grenade Schools of Instruction were to be taken over and maintained for the use of the New Zealand Division. Prior to this date the Regiment had received its first issue of steel helmets.

Orders were now issued for the 2nd Battalion of the Regiment to relieve the 12th Manchester Regiment in the left Brigade subsector of the line immediately east of Armentieres on the night of May 14th, and for the 1st Battalion to take over billets in the town as one of the reserve units to the 1st Infantry Brigade. In pursuance of this order the 1st Battalion moved from Morbecque to Estaires on May 9th, and after remaining there for three days continued its journey to Armentieres, where comparatively good billets were secured. The 4th and 8th Companies were located at Houplines, east of the town.

By this date Captain D. White, formerly in command of 4th (Otago) Company of the 1st Battalion, had been detached for duty as Town Major at Armentieres, an appointment which he retained until the German envelopment of the town in 1918.

The 2nd Battalion of the Regiment reached Armentieres from Doulieu on May 13th. At nightfall on the 14th, after a day of rest and quiet preparation, the Battalion moved up and took over its front line area. Two Companies, 4th and 8th, were disposed along the front line, 10th Company occupied the subsidiary line, and 14th Company was in reserve at Houplines. The relief was effected without special incident or greeting from the enemy, and once the first rush of curiosity as to what was on the other side had been satisfied, the garrison, with that *sang-froid* and adaptability characteristic of the Colonial, soon found itself firmly established in its first sector in France.

The line at Armentieres was at this stage typical of other sectors in France where the merely normal conditions of trench-to-trench warfare prevailed ; its selection for the New Zealand Division being doubtless prompted by the belief that it was a suitable area in which to dispose troops as yet unaccustomed to conditions on the Western Front. But the policy of observing what might be termed a passive resistance was of brief duration ; and while the sector could hardly compare with the furious and unceasing conflict on some of the areas subsequently held, its pacific reputation quickly disappeared with the introduction of colonial aggressiveness.

Armentieres, once a prosperous and populous town, bore impressive evidence of the violence to which its proximity to the front line had exposed it. Most of its terrified inhabitants had fled, and those who remained doubtless did so dreading the menacing uncertainties that life offered elsewhere ; and perhaps in some degree also because of the lure of trade with the troops quartered there. Incidentally, there was a decided shortage of ready money in the Regiment for some

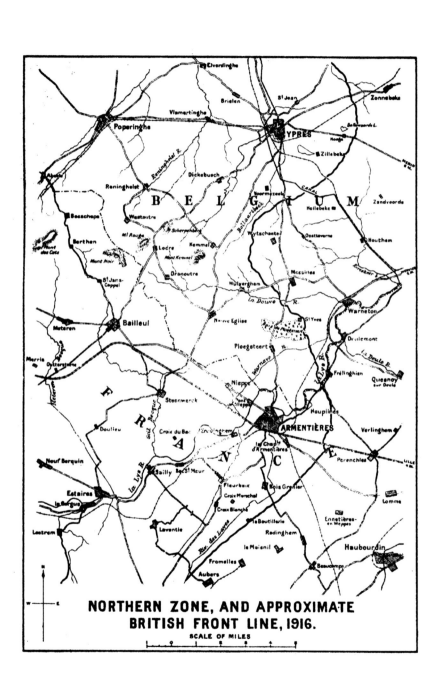

NORTHERN ZONE, AND APPROXIMATE
BRITISH FRONT LINE, 1916.

SCALE OF MILES

time following the first arrival in France. Most of the available resources had been drawn upon during the journey from Marseilles, and the non-arrival of the Field-Cashier accentuated the existing financial embarrassment. Access to Regimental funds was not possible for the same reason, and the difficulty was not overcome, so far at least as the 1st Battalion was concerned, until Lieut. W. Downie Stewart offered and obtained permission to proceed to Dunkirk, where, by means of letters of credit, he raised sufficient money to purchase supplies of vegetables, and straw for bedding. It was perhaps a peculiar circumstance that during this period of temporarily straitened finance the first announcement should have been made of the fact that leave to the United Kingdom was opened to New Zealand troops.

Through " Half-past Eleven " Square and along the devious ways which led through and beyond the town, the forward route extended to the shelter of a solidly constructed communication trench, as tortuous in its winding track as its length was seemingly interminable. From this covered way, incoming traffic debouched on to the support and front lines which, by reason of the low-lying country, were more in the nature of great breast-works than deeply dug trenches. At intervals of a dozen yards or so the front line breast-work was punctuated by traverses or semi-blocks, which restricted the danger arising from the lateral burst of enemy shells ; while in rear of it a second wall or parados protected the garrison from backward bursts. Between traverses were the fire-bays, where from the wooden steps provided sentries stood up throughout the night listening and peering into the darkness which shrouded No Man's Land. This drab breast-work of mud, most of it contained in sandbags, extended into the dreary distance north and south, while out to the front, belts of barbed wire, broken and irregular from shell fire, ran parallel to it. Across the waste of No Man's Land there was a corresponding system of defences, with the vital difference that it belonged to the enemy. And secretly and vigilantly, day and night without cessation, each side moved and watched from the shelter of these sinuous ditches and mud walls and the almost interminable communications which led to them from the outer world. At night men moved out to erect more wire, or to wander round No Man's Land either for the purpose of stalking the enemy who had ventured abroad or for prying unobserved on his movements. The enemy was heard rather than seen ; and thus in time the sense of hearing became more acute than that of seeing. By night hordes of rats, fat and loathsome looking, wandered defiantly over the parapet or duck-walk, devoured all uncovered food, and with their foul bodies pestered those of the garrison who endeavoured to find rest in sleep.

It would be incorrect to suppose that every yard along this irregular front line was garrisoned. In a settled trench system the forward line comprised localities and gaps, the former occupied by the garrison, the latter merely patrolled at intervals or guarded by an isolated post. The existence of these gaps, of considerable length in places, did not necessarily imply a danger, for in the first place their actual location was unknown, or believed to be unknown, to the enemy, and in the event of penetration they were covered from the flanks or rear by supporting strong-points. Normally, a front line system comprised the front line itself, the support line approximately 100 yards in rear, and the subsidiary line from 600 to 700 yards still further back, with the whole linked up by communication and traffic trenches, and strengthened by machine guns disposed so as to deliver cross or flanking fire. Thus a disposition of forces in depth was assured.

Further to the rear, in a complete system of defence, there were established additional strong-points or defensive positions calculated to stem the enemy tide in the event of the front line system being penetrated. Under the arrangement existing at Armentieres on the occasion of the New Zealand Division taking over the line, the front was divided into two sectors, each held by one infantry brigade disposed as follows : Front line breast-works, support line, and strong-points, two battalions ; subsidiary line, one battalion ; in billets, one battalion. The Divisional Reserve consisted of one brigade of infantry, the Pioneer Battalion, and the New Zealand Engineers (three Field Companies).

The routine observed by the garrison of the front-line, where the normal policy was not to make any advance towards the enemy, was as settled and methodical as any organised business. Day and night watches were rigorously maintained without break, patrols were sent out by night to determine or counter enemy movement in No Man's Land, and listening posts established in shell-hole or ditch some yards out from the parapet in order to obtain timely warning of enemy approach. The stability and maintenance of the defences constituted a first essential; trenches were kept clean and free from accumulations of fever-breeding rubbish; the cleanliness of arms and ammunition was insisted upon; and, of paramount importance, rations were brought up nightly from the forward dumps, generally in the locality of the subsidiary line, to which point they were conveyed by the battalion limbers under the direction of the company quartermaster-sergeants.

In the cooking of the daily meals, the closer the cook-house to the garrison the hotter and the better the food when it reached those for whom it was intended. Thus the cook-house, run under company arrangements, was frequently established in the front or support line, and if it were not convenient or desirable to have it there, it was often possible to bring the company cooker, or travelling kitchen, up to the next best place.

The maintenance of ammunition supplies and the for-warding and handling of unlimited supplies of engineering material required for the improvement and extension of the front line system called for the expenditure of further energy during both day and night. Thus the routine of trench life proceeded from day to day, interrupted at times by destructive bombardments, raids and counter-raids, patrol fights, and the various incident of trench-to-trench warfare.

The trench system at Armentieres, when taken over by the Regiment in May, showed every evidence of neglect. It was also deficient of many of the approved principles of defence required to meet effectively attempted enemy penetration. This involved the immediate drawing up of a scheme which had for its object the introduction of considerable improve-ments and extensions, and in this direction the front line system received first attention. The whole of the work to be undertaken was based on a Divisional defence scheme, worked out on the principle of meeting superior forces on the ground allotted to the troops of the Division. Successive defensive positions were to be prepared, and it was laid down that no body of troops detailed to occupy any particular locality was to give it up. If it did happen that ground was lost as the result of enemy action it was to be retaken by counter-attack carried out by troops specially detailed for the purpose ; and in that connection every battalion was to have a plan for counter-attack in the event of its front being penetrated. As to the deficiencies of the foremost system, the wire in front was almost a negligible quantity, the trenches were not capable of affording shelter from heavy bombardments, and there was an absence of suitable positions tor Lewis guns and of means of countering the enemy's sniping and other forms of activity. To give effect to the principle of distribution of available troops in depth and the holding of the front line with a minimum of men, it was essential that these and other improvements should be carried out without delay.

The outcome of all this was that over and above the effective garrisoning of the sector the Division had committed itself to a very extensive works programme. Such, indeed, remained the accepted policy throughout the whole of the campaign on the Western Front. The result was that a sector was invariably left immeasurably stronger in matters of construction and details of defence than it was when taken over. By working on sound and well considered lines, a high standard of efficiency was attained ; although the drawback, expressed from the men's point of view, was that it involved at times an inordinate amount of hard work and constant fatigue parties in the worst possible weather ; and probably extensive works of improvement had only been completed when the sector had to be handed over to a relieving division, which reaped all the benefit. From a broad point of view the policy was, of course, entirely sound, and it had in it the additional and valuable merit of impressive and convincing example. Above every consideration stood out the salient and reassuring fact that stout trenches meant safe shelter under the storm of an enemy bombardment, and in that alone compensated a thousand times for the labour expended and the many weary treks at night between Armentieres and the line during the intervals of so-called rest which alternated with the periods of actually garrisoning the line.

During this first period over which the 2nd Battalion of the Regiment occupied the line east of Armentieres the attitude of the enemy was for the most part passive, though 13 men were wounded, mainly the result of shell fire, and one officer, Lieut. A. C. Boyes, was killed by an enemy sniper.

This first casualty through the agency of a sniper may be said to have had its lesson. On first taking over the line at Armentieres, the German sniper was an ever-present element of danger, full of daring and ingenuity. A liberal equipment of telescopic-sighted rifles and good field-glasses gave the enemy a sweeping advantage. The distribution of field-glasses was not confined to snipers alone. From our point of view, there was a permanent shortage of field-glasses, and they were always professedly difficult to obtain. For example, they were never on issue to infantry non-commissioned officers and Lewis gunners, to whom they would have been invaluable. As a further advantage the German rifle was superior to the British S.M.L.E. weapon for purposes of sniping, but in that respect alone. However, the time arrived when the organisation of the Regiment's snipers and observers was extended and perfected, and by pursuing a combined aggressiveness, the enemy's ingenuity was effectively countered and his ascendency definitely overcome.

Relief of the 2nd Battalion in the line at the close of eight days was effected by the 3rd Battalion of the Rifle Brigade. A return was made to Armentieres for a corresponding period of rest, which really involved nightly visits to the line to repair damage occasioned to trench and parapet by enemy bombardments, or to carry out works of extension and improvement.

In keeping with the series of reliefs then carried out, the 1st Battalion of the Regiment on May 21st took over from the 1st Battalion of the Auckland Regiment in the front line, as the left Battalion of the right Brigade sector in front of La Chapelle d'Armentieres. This represented the 1st Battalion's initial appearance in the line in France, and the process of relief was accomplished shortly after midnight without incident. On the afternoon of the following day the enemy's artillery assumed a decided aggressiveness, and this form of harassment was continued at intervals with varying degrees of intensity during the remainder of the tour.

About this time a message attached to a German rifle-grenade was fired over the New Zealand lines, worded as follows : " Send over the time please, Anzac." It was perhaps more than a coincidence that the Daylight Saving Bill had just come into operation in the United Kingdom, and it was also significant that the enemy was well aware of the identity of the troops occupying the trenches opposite to him. This was the forerunner of other messages which were delivered or posted up from time to time from either side, some of them grim and some of them humorous.

On the third day of its return to the line the 2nd Battalion was subjected to a sustained trench mortar bombardment. Casualties were few, but considerable material damage was occasioned to the trenches. Following this display of ill-feeling, comparative quietness prevailed until relief arrived on the night of 7th-8th June. Under a rearrangement of dispositions given effect to at this period, the 2nd Battalion entered into occupation of the subsidiary line, extending from Buterne Farm (exclusive) to the River Lys (exclusive).

It was at Armentieres that the Regiment was afforded the first evidence of the accuracy of expert gunnery, being the occasion when the enemy registered on the Church of Notre Dame and at the fifth round struck the tower, practically completing its destruction before firing ceased. A few days later the enemy directed similarly destructive fire on the church at Houplines. The systematic shelling of billets and gun-pits was almost unknown at this period, most, if not all, of the retaliatory artillery fire being directed against the garrison of the front line, the battered appearance of which was in striking contrast to the support and reserve lines, where comparative immunity and comfort were enjoyed.

The question of raids was now beginning to receive serious attention by Division. The object of a raid, it might be explained, was in almost all instances primarily to gain information as to the enemy's identity and possible intentions, and secondly to embarrass and harass him. To fight and deal with an enemy successfully, even in trench-to-trench warfare, it was essential to know something about him, who he was, his strength and his temper, his dispositions, and his probable intentions and attitude towards the troops who confronted him. Much of this task of measuring was effected through the agency of patrols and organised observation, but not all of it. Thus a raid, if successful, brought back prisoners who were identified as to their Regiment, a useful guide to the fighting worth of the enemy Division and a contribution to determining the general disposition of his forces. To gain the desired information prisoners were interrogated, and by the adoption of various means persuaded to converse ; while documents and other material seized by the raiding party frequently afforded valuable information. The force committed to an enterprise of this kind approached the enemy's lines in silence, or more often under the protective cover of an artillery barrage which forced the opposing garrison to rush for cover, entered his trenches, seized what prisoners were alive after the bombardment, collected maps and documents from dug-outs, and then made speedily back to its own lines and safety.

Accompanying these raids was a great deal of artillery and trench mortar preliminary and subsequent bombardment, and then retaliatory fire from those who were being raided. Thus as the practice of raiding developed, so did the artillery bombardments increase in frequency and intensity, and if the object aimed at was to arouse the enemy and harass and annoy him, then a great deal of success was achieved. For example, on the night of June 16th, when troops of the 2nd Infantry Brigade carried out a raid on the Breakwater and trenches adjoining, our artillery expended some 5,000 rounds in support of the operation and in conducting a diversion on the Railway Salient near by. Artillery retaliation was a natural sequence, and from this and the other frequent blasts and counter-blasts of artillery fire which a raiding party had directly or indirectly provoked, it followed that the front line trench system and the bewildered and unfortunate infantrymen who garrisoned it were subjected to periods of heavy and destructive battering. The bombardment, per-chance, finally expended itself in intermittent shooting throughout the night, or stopped, as if by mutual consent, as suddenly as it had started. The net results of these provoked or unprovoked assaults were, as they affected the infantry, much mental anguish, some killed or wounded, and a badly battered trench system which must be immediately repaired.

When the 1st Battalion of the Regiment on June 7th, in relief of the 2nd Battalion of Auckland, entered into possession of L'Epinette Salient, which was our closest point to the enemy's line, it involved an increase of the front formerly held by the 1st Infantry Brigade of approximately 1,000 yards. Otago continued to hold the line there until June 21st, which represented an inordinately long spell in the trenches without relief. Raids on the right and left of the sector resulted in the Salient receiving the back-wash of the enemy's artillery retaliation, and casualties were inevitable. The town of Armentieres was also not free from enemy shelling at this period, and at times heavy artillery fire was directed on it. This either preceded our artillery's bombardment of Premesques and Perenchies, to the east of Armentieres, and of other vulnerable spots in the enemy's back areas, or followed as a retaliatory measure. Meantime the cutting of the enemy's wire entanglements by guns of lighter calibre and by trench mortars and the breaching of parapets by howitzers, proceeded apace in view of projected raiding ventures and as part of a general scheme to bewilder and puzzle the enemy. At the same time patrols were constantly out during the night, and brushes and encounters with the enemy, some rather vague as to results, were becoming frequent. In keeping with the avowed policy of aggressiveness it was determined that a mastery of No Man's Land should be obtained. The enemy was apparently imbued with the same offensive spirit, and there was always the possibility of something of interest developing when a patrol from our side crept across No Man's Land under cover of darkness.

On the night of June 13th a party from 14th Company, under Corporal W. White, had just established itself in front as cover to a wiring party when it was assailed at close range by a shower of bombs. Wiring operations had been in progress for some nights previously, and the enemy, apparently aware of this fact, had decided on a scheme of interruption. A brief skirmish in the dark followed this surprise attack, and the outcome was that some of our men were wounded, and one of the enemy, a Saxon, belonging to the 133rd Regiment, was captured and brought into our lines by Corporal White. A single prisoner would in later

TYPICAL FRENCH BILLET.

First Billet occupied by 14th Company, 1st Battalion, near Sercus, on arrival in France, 1916.

days have been regarded as a modest haul, but more curiosity and more interest were exhibited in this bewildered Saxon than the fellow regarded himself entitled to. But he was the first German prisoner captured in France by the New Zealand Division, and as such was evidently entitled to be treated with care and affection.

There were further conflicts with the enemy on subsequent nights, and when a patrol from the 1st Battalion went out with the object of determining if possible how strongly the enemy line was held, it penetrated two rows of wire before being discovered. It was then decided to move to the right, and subsequently, when lying down in the wire, a party was heard moving along the enemy trench. From close range a dozen bombs were hurled, but, as frequently happened, results were unknown.

On the night of June 16th a special party of five officers and 83 other ranks drawn from the different Battalions of the 2nd Infantry Brigade carried out a raid against that portion of the enemy's line known as the Breakwater. The assaulting parties were under the command of Captain E. B. Alley, of the 2nd Battalion of Otago. The particular point selected for the raid was part of the new enemy work opposite Edmead's Farm, and east of Houplines, extending over an approximate distance of 250 yards, with the addition of a portion of the main trench on either side. The raiding troops were divided into wire-cutting and left and right bombing parties, and telephone party. The particular duties of each party had been carefully rehearsed ; a special course of training had been undergone in the arts of close fighting, and a careful study made of the ground. The weapons carried included rifles and bayonets, revolvers, grenades, and knobkerries, and electric torches and wire-cutters were included in the equipment. Whether with the intention of increasing the terror of the enemy or of assisting to lessen the chances of discovery, all ranks had their hands and faces blackened, while the wearing of a white armlet served to distinguish friend from foe once the enemy's trenches were gained.

The assaulting parties, according to programme, moved out from the sally-port into No Man's Land, and lay down 120 yards in advance of our parapet waiting for the artillery bombardment to commence. The bombardment, with medium and light trench mortars co-operating, proved most effective, smashing the enemy's wire and silencing machine guns which opened up from either flank. At the same time a bombardment of the Mushroom was carried out by way of diversion. As the bombardment lifted, the raiders breached the wire ahead without difficulty, and quickly entered the enemy's trenches. Two Germans were bayoneted by the left party, and others were found dead, but a stout barrier of sandbags and wire prevented any lengthy incursion to the right. The party now withdrew as arranged, and returned to the safety of our lines.

Our total casualties were two killed and eight wounded, and included Captain E. B. Alley, who, to the regret of all ranks, succumbed to his wounds. No prisoners were secured as a result of the raid, but it was evident that the enemy was not holding the Breakwater in any strength, perhaps for the very good reason that this new work had not reached a stage of completion. Those who took part in the raid were congratulated by Brigadier-General W. G. Braithwaite, Commanding the 2nd Infantry Brigade, for the fine offensive spirit displayed. Referring to the death of Captain Alley, he stated that it was to this officer's leadership and example that the enterprise owed its success, and had he been spared he was convinced the raid would have been even more successful than it was. It was when approaching the enemy's lines that Captain Alley was mortally wounded, and it was at the same stage that practically all our casualties were incurred.

Comparative quietness was experienced by the 2nd Battalion of the Regiment during the five days succeeding its relief of the 2nd Battalion of Wellington on the night of June 21st. Still there were the usual exchanges of compliments between our own and the enemy's artillery, but the solid breastwork trenches and the shelter which they afforded appreciably minimised our casualties. Patrolling continued as actively as hitherto, and the building up and repairing of trenches damaged by artillery and trench mortar fire, and the strengthening and extending of the system of wire entanglements in front of our line all called for strenuous exertions. Works of improvement were, in fact, being pushed forward with increased vigour.

Clear weather implied good observation, and in the movement by day of large bodies of troops, or transport, or of any considerable firing by artillery, the presence of enemy observation balloons had always to be taken into consideration. It was on their account that extensive movements of troops along roads under direct observation had invariably to be carried out by night, that screens were fixed along certain highways which would otherwise be exposed to view, and that in summer time unavoidable day-time traffic was required to travel slowly and not raise tale-telling clouds of dust. To say the least it was embarrassing to have these enemy "eyes" peering down and probing into affairs that were not strictly their own ; and on the evening of June 26th there was considerable jubilation when our aeroplanes suddenly swooped down on four balloons which were well up behind the enemy's lines, sent three of them crashing in flames, and compelled the fourth to make a hurried descent to escape a similar fate.

In the course of the Regiment's successive tours in the line, special activity was at all times observed in the direction of obtaining early warning of intended or actual launching of enemy cloud gas attacks. The success of such an attack was a matter depending very largely, almost solely one might say, on the direction of the wind and on the weather, and whenever the wind was " dangerous " from our point of view these precautions were naturally doubled. The discovery of an approaching gas cloud or of indications which led the observer to believe that a gas attack was about to be delivered, was to be heralded by the blowing of sirens which warned everyone to adjust his protective helmet, and notified the garrison to assume a defensive rôle in view of possible enemy assault following upon the discharge of gas. False alarms were fairly frequent, and a warning raised by some far-off garrison was repeated for a considerable distance on either side. On June 27th elaborate preparations were commenced for the discharge of gas over the enemy's lines. During the hours of darkness over 140 cylinders were placed in position in anticipation of a favourable wind. This was an undertaking involving a considerable amount of labour, apart from the attendant risks and the necessity for absolute secrecy. Delay in discharging gas already installed was dangerous in view of possible enemy bombardments, and in this instance there was cause for further anxiety. A deserter from a battalion of the 1st Infantry Brigade had gone over to the enemy from the Mushroom on the early morning of June 29th, and a subsequent bombardment of the area over which the cylinders were installed, to say nothing of even more destructive occurrences, seemed to confirm prevailing suspicions. At 10 p.m. on June 30th gas was delivered north of Hobb's Farm. Everything worked without a hitch, and the severity of the bombardment which the enemy directed to our front line and Houplines by way of retaliation conveyed the suggestion that the operation had been attended by success.

AN INCIDENT WITH CONSEQUENCES.

In the ordinary course of events the 1st Battalion of Otago would have relieved the 1st Battalion of Auckland Regiment on the night of the 3rd-4th July, but fearing that the enemy might have received information from the deserter previously referred to, the relief was at the eleventh hour postponed for a period of 24 hours. By that precaution Otago certainly escaped the disaster which overtook Auckland. At dusk, which was the usual time of effecting reliefs, a whirl-wind bombardment suddenly burst over the front and support trench systems of Localities 74, 75, and 76, garrisoned by troops of the 1st Battalion of Auckland. The bombardment was continued with great intensity, so much so that it was considered that an enemy attack was about to be launched against the garrison of L'Epinette. Two platoons of 8th (Southland) Company, under Lieut. R. R. Gow, were accordingly despatched to the front line, and proceeded overland in order to relieve the assumed pressure on Auckland. On nearing the support line they were forced to pass through heavy shelling, and several casualties were sustained, but on arrival at the front line it was found that their services were not required. The party thereupon returned to the reserve line.

The following morning at daylight three working parties were despatched from the Battalion to the front line to assist in clearing the wreckage. An extraordinary scene of destruction presented itself. The unfortunate Auckland garrison had sustained 150 casualties, many of them buried alive in the fire-bays, and these the working parties had to assist in digging out. Had the intended relief not been cancelled, Otago must have shared a corresponding fate. When the Battalion took over the line from Auckland Regiment on the night of the 4th-5th, the parapet was found to be practically flattened out ; there was no evidence of wire in front, no bivouacs remained undamaged, and a travel trench extending from right to left of the sector had to be dug during the hours of darkness. The communication trenches, Plank Avenue and Second House Avenue, the former hitherto presumably unknown to the enemy, were damaged beyond description, and on every side was evidence of the fury and extraordinary destructiveness of the enemy's bombardment.

Thus, by a postponement of the date of relief, the 1st Battalion of the Regiment had escaped the disaster which befell Auckland, but strangely enough, the tour now commenced was destined to be marked by an event even more calamitous in its consequences.

RAIDING AND LOSSES.

In accordance with the promulgated policy of aggressiveness and general scheme of raiding, it was decided that 4th (Otago) Company would on the night of July 13th carry out a raid against the enemy's trenches. The objects of the raid were to obtain information, to harass and mystify the enemy, and to inflict as much harm upon him as possible. The personnel of the raiding party, all told, comprised six officers and 175 other ranks, this number including the assaulting parties, parapet and flanking parties, and the other details of raiding organisation, the whole under the command of Captain W. D. Jolly. Under the prearranged plan scouts and parapet party were to move out from the sally-port 45 minutes before zero hour and the flanking parties fifteen minutes before that time, and take up their positions in shell-holes with the object of protecting the flanks in the event of a counter-raid. The scouts were then to return and lead out the remainder of the raiding party to a concealed position in front of and distant 150 yards from the line to be

101

assaulted. Our artillery was to open with a slow rate of fire 10 minutes before zero, at which moment artillery and trench mortars were to open with full intensity over the enemy's trenches and wire entanglements. Twenty minutes later the trench mortars were to direct their fire against the flanking trenches, while that of the artillery was to be lifted, thereby forming a semi-circular barrage round the area to be assaulted. Scouts and parapet party were then to rush forward, the scouts' duty being to ascertain the condition of the wire, return and lead the raiders through the gaps. The parapet party was to cross the enemy's trench and bomb suspected shelters in rear, while the assaulting parties were to work along the trench itself in four different sections. Meantime, the two flanking parties, facing half-right and half-left respectively, were to guard the flanks from our side of the enemy's wire, while special detachments were to watch the flanks from inside the wire. The 8th (Southland) Company was to provide a patrol to cover the right flank of the raiding party, the 10th (North Otago) Company acting similarly in respect of the left flank. All these duties were made perfectly clear and familiar by practice and training, and nothing was left to chance so far as preparation was concerned in order to ensure the success of the operation. But, alas, through some tragic cause, the whole affair was to prove a ghastly and expensive failure.

During the afternoon the enemy had carried out a certain amount of artillery fire which had all the appearances of a ranging shoot. The misgivings and suspicions aroused in not a few minds by this action were later only too fully confirmed. Every man was in his position in No Man's Land at the appointed time, and the artillery support was forthcoming as arranged. But no sooner had our barrage lifted and the raiding troops proceeded to move forward than a concentrated and murderous shrapnel and machine gun fire fell like a thunder-clap over No Man's Land between our front line and the objective. Under this withering and devastating blast the raiders vainly endeavoured to press forward. The casualties became increasingly heavy ; all the officers were either killed or wounded, and when finally the order came to withdraw, merely a handful of men remained to stagger back to our lines. The whole affair was a tragedy ; and though no definite information could, of course, be obtained on the point, the natural conclusion come to was that the enemy had secured warning of the raid, and the 4th Company walked into a trap only too well prepared.

The casualties sustained were :

Killed   ...   4 officers and 31 other ranks.
Wounded   ...   4 officers and 118 other ranks.
Reported missing   6 other ranks.

This represented a total loss of 163 of all ranks. The casualty list included the following officers : Killed—Captain W. D. Jolly, Lieut. L. Millard, Lieut. T. Gillman, and 2nd-Lieut. G. Black ; Wounded—Lieut. M. J. White, Lieut. J. G. Johnston, Lieut. E. Salmon, 2nd-Lieut. C. H. Clark.

The Battalion Commander was immediately confronted with the formidable task of getting in the many dead and wounded lying in No Man's Land. Every available man was requisitioned for stretcher-bearing purposes, and although everyone worked desperately hard throughout the night, and certainly no one harder and more regardless of danger than Pte. J. D. Stark, the task had barely been completed when daylight broke and put an end to operations. Further bearer parties were out on the following night over the track of the ill-fated raid, and one wounded man and 17 bodies were recovered. It was on the occasion of this renewal of the search that 2nd.-Lieut. A. G. Brockett was killed.

By all these losses of officers, non-commissioned officers and men the Regiment sustained a heavy misfortune ; certainly the worst that had befallen any of its companies in so short a space of time during its fighting days in France, and reinforcements, both in officers and men, had to be asked for at once. The Battalion formation was now temporarily reduced to one of three companies instead of four ; and in consequence of this fact and the extended line being held owing to the transfer of certain divisions to the area of the Somme, the three Companies, 8th, 10th, and 14th, were called upon to hold the line for a period of 32 continuous days without being afforded the opportunity of going back to the subsidiary line.

Major C. E. Andrews had now left for the United Kingdom on duty, and Major D. Colquhoun succeeded to the post of Second-in-Command of the 1st Battalion.

A raid on the enemy's lines had also been undertaken by the 2nd Battalion of the Regiment, then in reserve at Armentieres. The preliminary training was carried out at the Brigade Trench Warfare School of Instruction, and everything augured well for the success of the operation, which was timed for 1.30 a.m. on July 12th. At the appointed time assaulting, flanking, bombing and blocking parties took up their positions in No Man's Land, but the party sent across in advance returned and reported that they had failed to find any gaps in the enemy wire after patrolling and examining it over a distance of 100 yards. Captain D. E. Bremner, who was in command of the enterprise, reached within 20 yards of the enemy wire with his assaulting party. From there it was ascertained that the wire was intact, and deciding that it was impossible to breach it in the short time at his disposal, he made up his mind to withdraw. On the return journey some casualties were incurred as a result of an alarmed enemy's artillery and trench mortar fire.

Our artillery's assistance on the night of this operation was all that could be desired, fire being brought to bear on the enemy's front, rear and communication trenches. A diversion was also created over the Railway Salient. The enemy retaliated with a heavy barrage over our front and support trenches, opening and ceasing almost in unison with our own guns. Briefly, the raid was a failure because, primarily, the wire had not previously been cut by our guns and trench mortars as required, although those who were in command of the trench mortars claimed that the wire had been dealt with, and that the raiders went to the wrong place. The fact remained that the wire which confronted the raiding party was so thick that it could not have been cut sufficiently to afford a passage through in the time available under the rapid programme. Casualties numbered four killed and nine wounded.

On July 16th the 2nd Battalion of the Regiment took over the line from the 2nd Battalion of Wellington. Three days later a raid was carried out by troops of the 1st Infantry Brigade on enemy trenches immediately north of the Railway Salient, and on the right of Otago's sector, in order to give support to an attack by the XI. Corps in conjunction with the 5th Australian Division against the enemy system extending from Faquissart to La Cordonnerie. By way of participating in the minor operation, Otago Battalion had a considerable strength posted in No Man's Land in anticipation of and in order to check a possible counter-attack by the enemy. No action, however, developed as far as Otago troops were concerned.

RENEWED VIGILANCE.

At this period a particularly active patrolling of No Man's Land was being maintained, and the number of patrols operating was unlimited. The enemy was evidently more or less alive to this activity, and as ours were fighting patrols, as distinct from reconnoitring parties, there were frequent clashes. In some instances large numbers of the enemy were observed or encountered and engaged by our patrols with varying degrees of success. It was not always possible to establish the results of these bombing encounters, but it was at least clear that the enemy did not escape damage. But there was also the danger of our own patrols clashing, and in the darkness mistaking each other for the enemy, and there was pretty conclusive evidence that this did occur on more than one occasion.

On July 21st Major J. A. Mackenzie left the 2nd Battalion and proceeded to England to take over command of the New Zealand Details Camp established at Codford, whereupon Major G. S. Smith, D.S.O., succeeded to the position of Second-in-Command of the Battalion.

The appearance in the line of parties of the Royal West Kents (122nd Brigade of the 41st Division), led to conjectures of possible relief and a move to a new locality. These anticipations, however, were not realised, and all that the visit of troops of another unit, ever a prolific source of conjecture and rumour, meant on this occasion was the possibility of the 122nd Brigade taking over the left sector, then held by the 1st Infantry Brigade. But before the time arrived for this order to become operative it was cancelled.

On July 9th the order by which all troops forming the garrison of the front line were to remain awake throughout the hours of darkness was cancelled, and to each group of two or more bays there were to be eight men on duty, two furnishing double sentry, two awake and sitting on the fire-step within immediate call, and the remainder asleep in the trench but fully equipped and ready to man the fire trench on an alarm being given. It was also laid down that an officer was to be constantly on trench duty, in the same manner as an officer was on watch on board ship. It was further ordered that the garrison of the front line system, except those furnishing the day sentry groups, carried out at least four hours manual labour in improving the defences.

The hours of darkness were still very brief indeed ; but on July 28th the times of standing-to were readjusted so as to extend from 9.30 p.m. to 10.30 p.m., and from 3.30 a.m. to 4.30 a.m. By this alteration the intervening night hours of extreme vigilance were lengthened ; but the disappearance of the long summer days was still some distance ahead. The routine of stand-to and stand-down was that at the time appointed in the evening the whole of the garrison took up a definite position in the fire-bays, fully armed and equipped, and remained at their posts for a period of approximately one hour, when the order to stand-down was sent along. The regular watches were then set and maintained throughout the night, and all members of the garrison whose presence was not immediately required in this direction or who were detailed for other duties of routine, retired from the fire-bays. At the appointed time in the morning the order to stand-to was again sent along the line, and once more all arms turned out fully equipped and took up their stations, remaining there until the order to stand-down was received. The reduced day watches were then set and carried on. The general idea of this scheme originated in the almost uniform experience that approaching dusk and approaching dawn were the two most likely moments of enemy attack, and that at these times the garrison should accordingly be fully prepared for any such emergency. And so the system was maintained until the termination of trench warfare in the closing days of 1918. At times the observance of this custom could only have been regarded as more or less formal, yet it continued to provide the opportunity for ensuring that every man knew his correct battle station and that he was possessed of his full fighting equipment, while it also served to accustom everyone to turning out rapidly and effectively. If, of course, the morning and the outlook were foggy, stand-down was not given as usual, and very often it was on this account unavoidably prolonged.

There was no order more welcome to men in the line, and none more cheerfully passed along, than the morning " stand-down," for it implied that the majority of the night sentries could retire to their shelters for that long-deferred sleep ; while in winter time it was immediately followed by the platoon commander or sergeant on his rounds with the ever-welcome rum. The rum issue was unquestionably a great institution, for it assured an exhilaration and warmth of body which lasted until sleep caught the chilled and weary soldier. Where, it might be asked, is the war-worn veteran of a winter campaign who has not confessed that the morning's tot of rum has " saved his life " after a night's vigil in the merciless cold and pelting rain, perchance after standing knee-deep in mud, or after crawling about in the filth and uncertainties of No Man's Land, or lying exposed in the slime of a listening or advanced post out beyond the comparative friendliness of the parapet ?

A Divisional Order issued at this period served to reveal something of only one of the many methods employed to determine pending enemy activities. For some time, it was stated, a listening apparatus had been installed within the New Zealand area and close to the front line trenches. Taking into consideration the position both of the instrument and the signal offices from which messages were intercepted, and the proximity of the German trenches, it was quite certain that the enemy, if in possession of a similar apparatus in the vicinity, was overhearing our messages. Events had happened on the Divisional front which must lead to the conclusion that in many cases the enemy had intercepted our telephone and buzzer messages, and thereby obtained important military information. There was good reason to believe that in this manner the enemy had obtained previous warning concerning two raids carried out by the Division, the result being that he was prepared to meet them, and we in consequence suffered heavy casualties and were unsuccessful. It was therefore laid down that the use of telephones and buzzers was forbidden in advance of the subsidiary line except in cases of extreme urgency, and in all other cases was to be confined to the signal service and artillery forward observing officers. The greatest care was also to be exercised in the transmission of all messages, and no map locations were to be mentioned over the telephone or buzzer.

It was a long cry from Armentieres to the Somme, but during the month of July it was decided that special vigilance was to be observed along the whole of the Second Army Front in order to prevent the enemy withdrawing troops from opposite our front to the region of the Somme, where the great British offensive was then in full swing. In keeping with this important order and to give effect to its purpose, the Division was to be prepared to face greater risks and greater casualties. In other words, the enemy was to be engaged so actively that he would regard it as unwise or unsafe to move any troops away to the south. No Man's Land was to be our land ; our artillery was to be more active ; the enemy's wire was to be cut ; his parapets demolished ; billets bombarded ; frequent raids were to be carried out and others threatened, and counter-battery work actively engaged in. The supply of ammunition for 18-pounder guns in particular was to be unlimited, and no restrictions were to be placed on the amount of shooting to be done by light guns and trench mortars because of retaliation. To what extent the Regiment was intended to participate in this programme of organised fury was never fully realised, for very soon it was to be much more vitally concerned in this same Somme offensive.

It was not until August 6th that the 1st Battalion of the Regiment moved out of the line at L'Epinette after completing a memorable tour, the commencement of which dated back to July 5th. Four days later a warning order was issued to the effect that the New Zealand Division was to be relieved in the Armentieres sector by the 51st Division. On August 15th, the day after the relief of the Division commenced, officers of the 6th Battalion of the Black Watch visited the sector in view of their taking over from the 2nd Battalion of Otago, which was then in line. Relief was accomplished on the 17th, and Otago marched back to billets.

THE REGIMENT RELIEVED.

The Regiment was now clear of the line for a definite period, after three months' occupation of the sector lying east of Armentieres. It was the Regiment's first sector on the Western Front, and its tenure had provided a drastic introduction to methods of trench-to-trench warfare where both sides were very much in earnest. The period spent at Armentieres was remarkable for the strenuous conditions it imposed on the garrison. Enemy artillery bombardments were of great frequency, and at times of considerable intensity ; and over and above the formidable list of casualties which this involved, it also meant that there was an insistent demand for fatigue parties at all hours of the day or night for repairing damaged trenches. From the point of view of the infantry the Armentieres period was a very hard and exacting one.

On coming out of the line, particularly after a tour that had been unduly prolonged, the most gratifying aspect of the change-over was the opportunity afforded of obtaining a hot tub at the Divisional Baths established at Pont de Nieppe. There, with the aid of liberal supplies of hot water and soap, it was possible to get rid of the filth and vermin of the trenches, followed by an issue of clean underclothing, all of which produced a feeling of such delightful invigoration and freshness as to make the miseries and hardships of the preceding few weeks seem almost worth while.

The Regiment was now committed to a period of rest and training which was to prepare it for its approaching participation in the operations of the great offensive of the Somme. Immediately on coming out of the line it departed for the South, and after a journey by road and rail extending over several days, reached the localities of Citernes and Airaines, south-east of Abbeville. On arrival no time was lost in settling down to business. The Regiment was definitely committed to an early participation in the Somme Battle, and bearing in mind this fact, special attention was directed to practice in attack operations and in trench consolidation ; while for the officers there were in addition frequent conferences and discussions in relation to the most recently evolved offensive tactics.

On August 25th Lieut.-Colonel A. Moore, D.S.O., relinquished command of the 2nd Battalion of Otago in order to rejoin his Regiment, the Dublin Fusiliers, and two days later Major G. S. Smith, D.S.O., was appointed to the command of the Battalion.

The programme of training mapped out for the Regiment aimed at producing an all-round high state of fighting efficiency, and of fitness of mind as well as of body ; and when on September 2nd the Division broke camp and headed for the area of the Somme, it was calculated that everyone was in perfect fighting trim.

It was decided that the journey to the new sphere of operations should be relieved by frequent and regular halts, during which training was continued. The route of march brought the Regiment into and along the valley of the Somme River, and though the weather on occasions was showery, being late summer, the journey on the whole was pleasant because of the changing scene, and from a military point of view highly beneficial. There were some stiff marches *en route*, but the high standard of mental and physical fitness attained during the course of training operations was reflected in the comparatively airy manner in which these tasks were approached and carried out.

CHAPTER II.

BATTLE OF THE SOMME.

THE formidable assault which was launched by German arms in the middle of February, 1916, against the great Fortress of Verdun, and which had been maintained at an enormous cost in lives and material, had by the month of June reached what was considered to be its highest point of intensity. Up to that stage the valiant French Armies had withstood the most desperate German efforts to reach their objective ; but it was nevertheless seriously felt that the time had arrived when some great counter-stroke should be launched in order to relieve the French of this continuous and most exhausting pressure. It was, indeed, not long before this feeling was to find formidable expression ; for preparations were at once begun for the opening of a great British Offensive on the Somme front. The projected offensive had really a two-fold purpose, as in addition to the fact that it was calculated primarily to divert German reserves from Verdun to the north, it would also represent a great endeavour to break through the vaunted German lines of defence which had been built up there during two years or more of incessant labour and engineering skill.

On the morning of July 1st, 1916, the first burst of the British attack swept like a hurricane over the enemy lines, extending from the terrible salient of Gommecourt in the north to Frise in the south. How the terrific succession of British assaults on that memorable opening day broke with such murderous results against the formidable walls of the defences of Gommecourt in the north, and how at the close of the day the enemy line had been smashed between Fricourt and Frise in the south, and of the ebb and flow of victory during succeeding days and weeks, must remain among the most memorable and most sanguinary events in the history of the War.

It was into the vortex of this Somme Offensive, or rather series of distinct Somme Battles, that the Regiment, as part of the New Zealand Division, was thrown during the month of September. Though it had not up to that date been identified with any major operations on the Western Front, the Regiment had conclusively proved its worth during several months of active trench-to-trench warfare. But its participation in the Somme Battle was to earn for it a newer and wider fame and reveal its higher qualities as a fighting force, with initiative and extraordinary determination and intensity of purpose as its outstanding characteristics. Thus, along with the several units of the New Zealand Division the Otago Regiment entered the Somme with that dominant fighting spirit ever the fruitful parent of valorous deeds, and also with a lively anticipation of desperate adventure on hand. And in the whole series of operations in which it was engaged, its best fighting reputation was more than maintained. The sacrifices demanded were exceedingly heavy, but when in the early part of October the Regiment, woefully thinned and weakened, marched out of the Somme, it had made for itself a new and a greater name and worthily merited its share of the splendid tributes bestowed on the New Zealand Division by the Higher Commands.

It would be well to preface the account of the Regiment's participation in the Somme Battle by a description of the country over which the general operations extended. The enemy's main position was sited on high undulating ground which, rising to more than 500 feet above sea-level, formed the watershed between the Somme on the one side and the rivers of south-western Belgium on the other. On the southern face of this watershed, which ran generally from east-south-east to west-north-west, the ground fell in a series of long irregular spurs and deep depressions to the valley of the Somme. Along the forward slopes of this face the enemy's first system of defence, starting from the Somme near Curlu, extended first northwards for 3,000 yards and then westwards for 7,000 yards to near Fricourt, where it turned nearly due north, forming a great salient angle in the enemy's lines. Approximately 10,000 yards north of Fricourt the trenches crossed the River Ancre, a tributary of the Somme, and continuing northwards passed over the summit of the water-

MAJOR-GENERAL SIR A. H. RUSSELL, K.C.B., K.C.M.G., (D.), [F.]

General Officer Commanding New Zealand Division.

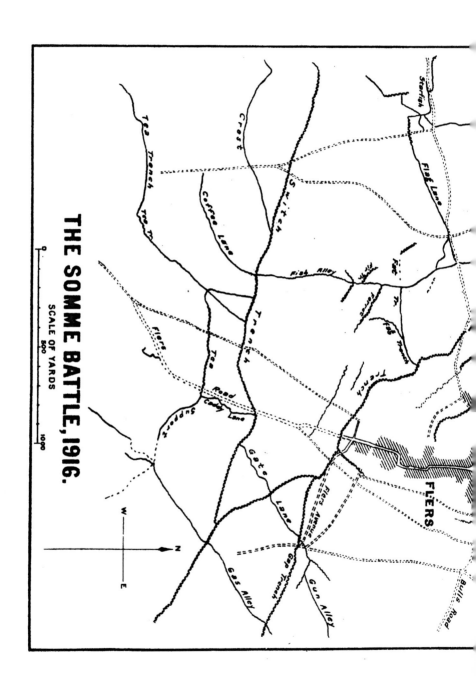

THE SOMME BATTLE, 1916.

SCALE OF YARDS

0   500   1000

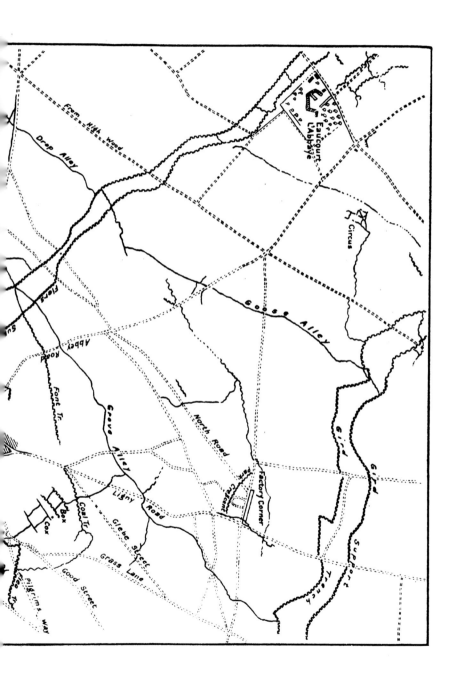

shed, about Hebuterne and Gommecourt, and down its northern spurs to Arras. Between the Somme and the Ancre, on a frontage of about 20,000 yards, the enemy had a second strong system of defences, established generally on the southern crest of the highest part of the watershed, at an average distance of from 3,000 to 5,000 yards behind the first system of trenches.

The whole of these defences, as a result of about two years' preparations, had been rendered very formidable indeed. The first and second systems comprised several lines of deep trenches, protected by great belts of wire entanglements. The woods and villages between these systems had been converted into fortresses, and the existing cellars and chalk-pits supplemented by elaborately constructed dug-outs. The enemy salients were particularly well defended, and every provision made for bringing enfilade machine gun fire across the front. Spacious dug-outs afforded shelter to the garrisoning troops during periods of heavy bombardment, and concrete machine gun emplacements were so arranged as to enable the trenches to be swept in the event of their capture. The whole system was one of extraordinary strength and depth. The enemy had other prepared lines of defence behind his second system of trenches. Between the Somme and the Ancre our trenches ran parallel and close to those of the enemy, but below them ; and while good direct observation was afforded over the German front system and also over the defences on the slopes between the first and second systems, the latter in many places could not be observed from the ground held by us. North of the Ancre the opposing trenches ran transversely across the main ridge, and there the enemy defences were equally formidable. At that point the enemy enjoyed no material advantage in the matter of command of ground ; though mainly owing to the nature of the country our direct observation over the enemy country was not as good as it was further south.

The 11th September found the Regiment within close call of battle. The two Battalions were resting, the 1st at Fricourt, and the 2nd outside Mametz Wood, and at both places the final preparations and finishing touches were being effected prior to going into action. During the succeeding few days officers of both Battalions availed themselves of every opportunity of becoming acquainted as far as possible with the ground over which the impending attack was to take place; lengthy conferences were held, maps were closely studied, and everything possible done by exhaustive preliminary preparation to ensure the success of operations.

In leaving the Armentieres area and moving to the area of the Somme, the New Zealand Division had passed from the Second Army, under General Plumer, to the Fourth Army, under General Rawlinson, and was now incorporated in the XV. Corps.

On September 12th it was announced that the Fourth Army and the Reserve Army, together with the French, who were on our right, were to attack the enemy simultaneously on September 15th. The Fourth Army was confronted with an ambitious programme. It was to attack the enemy's defences with a view to the capture of Morval-le-Boeufs, Gueudecourt and Flers, and at the same time break through the strong enemy defences in the areas of those villages. The attack was to be pushed home with the utmost vigour until the most distant objectives had been reached. For the preceding two and a half months, it was pointed out, we had been unceasingly wearing down the enemy until his *morale* was badly shaken; and it was therefore confidently hoped that a combined and determined effort, such as that about to be made, would result in decisive victory. It is true that British strength and British valour had been employed against the iron walls of the great German defensive system for two and a half months; that artillery beyond anything previously used or thought of had been brought to bear against him; but fortified as he was behind those terrible barriers of wire and other ramifications of almost impenetrable defence, it is doubtful if his *morale* was as severely shaken as might reasonably have been supposed. The desperate and sustained nature of his resistance certainly did not justify this conclusion.

The participation of the XV. Corps in the attack included the New Zealand, the 14th, and the 41st Divisions; and in line of battle the New Zealand Division was placed on the Corps left, while the 47th Division, of the III. Corps, was in turn on our left.

The objective assigned to the New Zealand Division was to be attacked by the 2nd Infantry Brigade and the 3rd (Rifle) Brigade, with the 1st Infantry Brigade in Divisional reserve. The 2nd Infantry Brigade was selected to attack and capture the first objective, with a limit of two battalions for that purpose, and with the remaining two battalions intact and not to be used without reference to the G.O.C. Division.

The various lines of the Corps objective will serve more clearly to illustrate the scope and nature of the task in which the New Zealanders were to be employed. Enumerated in order, they were briefly as follows:—1st — The line of Switch Trench. 2nd—The line of Flers and Fat Trenches, extending along the front of Flers village and running practically parallel to Switch Trench. On the left there was a divergence from Flers Trench in the direction of and along the high ground of Fat Trench and thence back to the point of the cross-roads junctioned by Flag Lane in order to straighten out the general line. 3rd—The village of Flers, and a line extending from Flers support on the left up to Abbey Road, and thence across the rear of the village and along Bulls Road to the right. 4th—The final objective, which was to embrace the village of Gueudecourt and its northern outskirts, and the intervening country and trench systems. The 2nd Brigade attacking troops were to assemble forward of Worcester and Tea Trenches (two battalions), and in Savoy and Carlton Trenches (two battalions) ; and the 3rd Brigade troops just forward of the two 2nd Brigade rear battalions and to the left of Longueval ; while two battalions of the 1st Infantry Brigade were to assemble in Mametz Wood, and two battalions (including the 1st Battalion of Otago) in Fricourt Wood, ready to move at 15 minutes' notice in the event of being required.

The 1st and 2nd New Zealand Field Artillery Brigades, and the artillery of the 14th Division, were immediately supporting the New Zealand Division's share in the general attack. A heavy and devastating bombardment of the hostile defences over the area we are concerned with had commenced on the 12th September, and the sullen roar and rumble of hundreds of guns of many calibres pounding at and endeavouring to destroy the extensive German defence system already augured well for the 15th.

In not a few respects the impending attack had new and strange features for the Regiment. The weight of concentrated artillery employed was infinitely greater than anything hitherto experienced ; the attack was to be carried out behind what might be described as the protective screen of advancing walls of steel—technically known as the creeping barrage ; there were to be in the air contact aeroplanes which would keep in constant touch with the infantry and register for the information of those concerned the line or points which had been reached, determined by spotting the ground flares lit by the infantry when on their objective, or by personal observation ; and, of more moment and interest than all else, the occasion was the first on which tanks, those monstrous and fantastic creations of the mechanical mind, were to make their appearance. How much the tanks actually fulfilled of all that had been predicted of them, on this occasion at least, is a matter that invites some argument. The number employed with the New Zealand Division was four, and in view of the fact that at least three of them were quickly out of action owing either to mechanical troubles or inability to cope with the great craters and shell-holes and upheavals which they encountered, it might perhaps have been wiser to have delayed their appearance until such time as they could have been assembled in greater numbers. One of the four tanks allotted to the Division did actually perform extraordinarily effective work, reaching and passing beyond the village of Flers, breathing death and destruction as it lumbered along its track and instilling fear of a kind hitherto unknown into those of the enemy who encountered it ; for, gazing at it for a second, in terror they fled precipitately.

In keeping with the policy of attack laid down for September 15th, no pause was to be made on the line of Coffee-Crest Trenches, which were to be dealt with by " mopping-up " parties specially detailed. On reaching the first objective no further advance was to be made until one hour after zero—which, clearly expressed, is the time the attack opens —after which the artillery barrage was to begin creeping forward towards the line of the second objective. Two hours after zero the infantry were to advance for the capture of the third objective ; and four and a half hours after zero they were to move forward to the assault and capture of the final objective and the formation of a defensive flank facing west. It will be agreed that an attack must be laid down on specific and express lines of procedure ; in other words, on the basis of a time-table, in order to produce unanimity and co-ordination of action at all points and to work out a definite and accurately timed programme of artillery co-operation. This is what is aimed at, and normally what would be achieved; but there are incidents and various checks and fluctuations in the tide of battle which at times rather seriously interfere with the execution of this pre-arranged programme, and it is then that initiative and quick decision translated into rapid action on the part of those in command of the situation are of priceless value.

To resume the narrative of the Regiment's operations, on September 12th the 2nd Battalion, at fighting strength, marched up to the right front of High Wood and took up a position, handed over by the 3rd (Rifle) Brigade, in Wood Lane, Worcester Trench, and Seaforth Trench, Battalion Headquarters establishing itself in an old German dug-out. During the night patrols went out towards Crest Trench, which was then part of the German front line, while digging parties connected Farm Trench with Wood Lane. The following day the Battalion commenced an important work in the construction of a new line, to be named Otago Trench, which extended to the west and connected Tea Trench with the Apex near High Wood. This work was taken over next day by one company of Wellington Battalion and one company of Canterbury Battalion and completed. At this stage the 1st Battalion of Otago had reached Fricourt Wood, arriving there about 11 o'clock at night and bivouacking. This brings us to the evening preceding the attack. The 2nd Battalion was in position and ready for the serious events of the morning. To make assurance doubly sure Lieut.-Colonel Smith had a long conference with his Company Commanders on the task that lay before them, and with a feeling that everything was in order, there was no reason to doubt that on the following morning the Battalion would acquit itself gallantly and well in this new phase of fighting. Much useful information had been gained by Sergt. R. Travis as a result of an exhaustive night reconnaissance of the area of Switch Trenches.

THE REGIMENT IN ACTION.

The weather broke fine on the morning of September 15th. Zero hour was fixed at 6.20 a.m., and by 6 o'clock all ranks had breakfasted and were fortified by a stout issue of rum. In order as far as possible to conceal from the enemy the hour of attack there was no increase of our artillery fire immediately before the assault was timed to commence. Shortly after 6 o'clock three distinct lines of troops of the 2nd Battalion of Otago, which in conjunction with the 2nd Battalion of Auckland was to open the New Zealand Division's attack, had formed up in front of the new Otago Trench at intervals in depth of about 50 yards, and a fourth line was in Otago Trench itself.

Zero hour, 6.20 a.m., was the common signal for a mighty effort on the part of infantry and artillery. An intense and hurricane-like barrage of field artillery instantaneously broke out along the line ; the great howitzers in the rear, hitherto firing but intermittently, now burst forth in extreme violence, and the anxiously awaiting lines of infantrymen stepped forward as in one accord and moved straight to their task. But the advancing waves had not proceeded far before officers and men began to drop from the ranks, for heavy machine gun fire was coming from the left and from the front of High Wood. It had been strongly impressed on everyone that the leading waves must hug the barrage, but the pace of the barrage and the pace of an anxious infantry barely coincided, and even before Crest Trench had been reached two distinct halts had been made to allow of the barrage lifting. During these intervals men took snap-shots at machine guns which were observed on the line of Crest Trench. When it was possible to move forward again not a few in their eagerness worked their way through gaps in the barrage and were caught up in our own fire. On the left the 140th Brigade was temporarily held up outside High Wood, the result being a considerable and dangerous gap on our left flank, and from this quarter enemy machine guns and snipers enfiladed and swept our advancing waves with disastrous effect.

On the right of the Battalion the position was quite secure, and close touch was maintained with the 2nd Battalion of Auckland, which in turn was in touch with the 122nd

Brigade of the 41st Division on its right. Thus, with Otago and Auckland Battalions attacking on a combined frontage of approximately 950 yards, Crest Trench was stormed and its garrison quickly dealt with. Those of the enemy who chose to remain in it and confronted the Otago men hurled bombs and fired their rifles at the advancing infantrymen almost up to the last moment, and then threw up their hands and called for mercy. Two hundred or more of the enemy had previously elected to turn and run towards the shelter of Switch Trench in the rear, and a considerable number of them were shot down by our Lewis gunners in the third wave before they reached it. Crest Trench was in point of fact thus left lightly held, the leading wave quickly rushed it, fiercely brushed aside the enemy's foolish presumption of mercy to be bought so easily, and when Crest Trench was finished with there was a grim significance in the fact that the only enemy left alive in it were two stretcher bearers and two wounded men.

Sections from the fourth wave, now up in line, were left to mop up the trench, and the three leading waves swept on towards the more formidable Switch Line, a distance of about 250 yards ahead. Up to this stage the Battalion had suffered severely from the machine gun fire from the left previously referred to, but the 140th Brigade had now come up more into line and the trouble from that quarter diminished accordingly. On arrival at Switch Trench the four waves, according to programme, had merged into one, and when they jumped into the trench there was not much work left for the bayonet. Switch Trench had been strongly held by machine guns, but the speed with which the attack was delivered, and the manner in which it was pushed forward, prevented the enemy bringing these weapons into action once the barrage had forced him to run to cover. It was a case of point-blank rifle fire, a sudden rush, a liberal use of the bomb, and Switch Trench was clear of the enemy and in our hands. This was at 6.50 a.m., or half an hour after the attack had opened. The only prisoners taken were four German officers. Our slightly wounded were left as guard over deep dug-outs which, although already well bombed, possibly still contained lurking enemy.

The Battalion, in company with Auckland, then went forward a distance of 70 yards, and the siting and digging of a new line in front of Switch Trench was at once commenced. Major W. G. Wray and Captain D. E. Bremner, although both had been wounded, marked out the line along Otago's front. By midday, as the result of desperately hard work, the new line had been dug to an appreciable depth. The enemy's artillery had now determined our line of consolidation, and commenced shelling it with most destructive precision. This continued until well after dusk, and in places the new trench was completely blown in, necessitating a great deal of re-digging ; but our men, working with extraordinary vigour, had by evening dug into a depth of six feet over all. Following upon the capture of the objective one company of the 2nd Battalion of Canterbury came up and commenced the construction of strong-points and otherwise ensured the safety of the refused left flank from the possibility of attack from the direction of High Wood ; while the placing of four additional Vickers guns along the front gave still further security. During the night this Canterbury Company continued its task and connected up with the line of the 140th Brigade to the left.

For the purposes of the attack our artillery barrage in its various phases had proved wonderfully accurate and effective. The enemy's wire was practically smashed up all along the line, whilst his trenches were almost entirely demolished and in places quite obliterated. That the Germans up to the point when this avalanche descended upon them had lived with some degree of luxury was evidenced by the discovery of hot coffee, wine, and good cigars in some of the deep dug-outs—all spoils for the victors. Thus the first objective in our first attack on the Somme was carried and held. But our casualties were heavy. The Battalion went into action with 20 officers and 816 other ranks, and the losses for the day in killed, wounded and missing, were 15 officers and 445 other ranks; but the advance had been magnificently and determinedly carried out from start to finish. It was from the left flank that the Battalion suffered most ; and in view of the volume of machine gun fire which came from that quarter during the advance, and the fact that our left had not then been linked up with the right of the 8th Regiment of the 140th Brigade, and that High Wood had not at that stage been cleared of the enemy, Lieut.-

Colonel Smith, who had gone forward to personally reconnoitre the position, naturally for a time viewed the situation with a good deal of uneasiness. His left companies had suffered very severely. The 10th Company, after losing all its officers, was, for example, reduced to 36 men, and was commanded with much skill and judgment by Sergt. H. Bellamy. The arrival of the company of the 2nd Battalion of Canterbury, however, fortified the exposed left flank, and it was finally made quite secure.

At midnight on the 15th Otago was relieved by Canterbury, and the remnant of the Battalion marched back during the early hours of the morning to Savoy and Carlton Trenches. It rested there until 3.30 p.m. on the 16th, and during that interval men who had been wounded or got adrift in the confusion of attack were coming in from all quarters wet and weary beyond description. In the afternoon the Battalion moved up again to Worcester, Black Watch and Seaforth Trenches, with an effective strength of 17 officers and 466 other ranks ; and later in the evening took in hand the task of consolidating and making its position on the left flank secure against a threatened counter-attack from the direction of High Wood. The Battalion remained there over the 17th and the greater part of the 18th.

In resuming the narrative of the day's operations, it will be necessary in order to gain some fairly clear idea of the general course of the attack to remember that after a lapse of one hour from zero the troops of the 3rd (Rifle) Brigade were to advance to the assault and capture of the remaining objectives. At the appointed time the artillery barrage reopened with all its former intensity, and the men of the Rifle Brigade, passing through Otago and Auckland troops, now settled on the Switch Line, moved forward to the second objective, which was practically the trench system extending along and defending the south-western side of Flers village. Simultaneously, as these troops advanced from their assembly points, the 2nd Battalions of Canterbury and Wellington moved into the positions thus vacated. The Rifle Brigade, in face of heavy machine gun fire, captured the second line, then advanced to the assault of the third objective, and finally swept through the western edge of the village of Flers. About 1 p.m. advice had been received that an enemy counter-attack was developing from a point north-west of the village, and the 2nd Battalion of Wellington was ordered to move forward and meet it and afford support to the 3rd Brigade troops. The enemy was now heavily shelling the Switch Line and sweeping the areas between there and Flers village. The two leading Companies of Wellington, however, pushed on through Flers and beyond to the north-western side of the village. The capture of Flers was not actually in the New Zealand Division's programme, but to that extreme point, the north-western side, three platoons of 3rd Brigade troops had forced their way. The Wellington men were distributed along the shelter of the sunken road in rear, and a return was made to reconnoitre and search the village ; but so grim had been the earlier fighting there that only dead and maimed and dying men were found in the streets and among the shattered ruins. A continuation of the search along the road leading from Flers to Factory Corner, and to the right of the village, located two further platoons of 3rd Brigade troops. The Wellington troops were immediately called upon to fill the gap between these isolated right and left parties, and by connecting up the front the northern side of Flers village was secured. It was during this stage that one of the four tanks allotted to the Division, having nosed its way through the ruins, performed valuable work, lumbering along the Flers-Factory Corner Road and covering the infantry's task of consolidation with broadsides of machine gun fire and blasts from its forward gun. Later in the evening the position encircling Flers was made more secure by the arrival of additional men and machine guns, and before midnight the line was well dug in and protected by the cross-fire of Vickers guns. When a systematic search of the village was made, most of the cellars were found to contain enemy in numbers. Several prisoners had been taken when an enemy party came out with a machine gun and raked the clearing party, killing three and wounding four ; thereafter no prisoners were taken.

At the close of the day the XV. Corps consolidated on the line held, which was approximately that of the third objective. There was further grim work ahead for the morrow.

We may now turn to the 1st Battalion of the Regiment, which we had left in Fricourt Wood when the attack opened early in the morning awaiting developments and ready for any emergency. At 3 o'clock in the afternoon the Battalion moved up to Mametz Wood and again bivouacked. The 14th Company was then detached and ordered to proceed to Green Dump to act as ration carriers, and the Battalion was thus left with three Companies. Shortly after midnight it moved out from Mametz Wood and proceeding through Thistle Alley worked its way up to the allotted point of assembly, which comprised trenches prepared for the troops concerned in the attack of the 15th. Heavy rain, the darkness of night, and the strangeness of the surroundings did not tend to make this operation an easy one.

The general attack of the XV. Corps on Les Boeufs and Gueudecourt was to be resumed on the following morning, the 16th. The III. Corps on the left was engaged with the high ridge west of Flers and the village of Martinpuich. It was later discovered that bombing parties had reached the neighbourhood of Gird and Gird Support trenches on the right of Flers and found that they were lightly held. Further reconnaissances also pointed to Grove Alley being vacated. It was accordingly decided to suspend the heavy artillery bombardment of Gird and Gird Support trenches, and the 14th and 41st Divisions were ordered to push forward strong patrols and if possible occupy these lines. The New Zealand Division was to co-operate by guarding the left flank and occupying the line of Grove Alley originally allotted to it, which was on the left and in advance of the line then occupied. The 1st Infantry Brigade was ordered to carry out this operation, to move one Battalion up to near the third objective and concentrate the remainder of the Brigade between the Switch Line and the road leading thence to the south. It was decided that after this, the fourth objective, had been gained, further objectives would be attacked; the New Zealand Division's share in this extension of operations to be the capture of Goose Alley, stretching from Flers Trench to Gird Support and representing a front of approximately 1,750 yards, and joining up with the III. Corps. This actually meant for us swinging the attack round to the west from the northerly direction previously followed.

At 10.20 a.m. on the 16th the 1st Battalion of Wellington occupied Grove Alley with ease, and pushed forward patrols

123

in the direction of Goose Alley. By 10.45 a.m. the 1st Battalion of Otago, under the command of Lieut.-Colonel A. B. Charters, commenced to move forward to Switch Trench, and before 1 p.m. had reached and settled down there. In order to reach this position the Battalion had been forced to pass through a heavy barrage of fire, extending right along Switch Trench and from there back over the reverse slope to Tea Trench and its left extensions. The casualties incurred in effecting this change of positions for the attack were fairly numerous.

But the intended attack on Goose Alley, timed for 1 p.m. on the date mentioned, did not take place, owing to the attack of the 41st Division on the right not having advanced sufficiently far north of Flers. It was accordingly announced that the general attack would be renewed on the 18th, with the 55th Division in relief of the 41st, and the 21st Division in relief of the 14th. On the 17th it was notified that a further postponement to the 21st was necessary. But subsequently it was definitely postponed until the 25th owing principally to the severity of the weather and the ever-accumulating mud and accentuation of difficulties of movement and traffic.

During the night of the 16th-17th the 1st Battalion had moved up to Fat Trench in relief of the 4th Battalion of the 3rd Brigade, and the deepening and improvement of this line which was then effected materially assisted in keeping down casualties later. With the Battalion established in Fat Trench, the situation had continued fairly normal up to 1 p.m. on the 17th, when the enemy opened and maintained for some time a heavy bombardment of our left sector, occupied by 8th and 10th Companies. This intense bombardment of our lines was renewed at 3.30 p.m., and continued until 6 p.m., at which stage a message that the enemy was barraging Cough-drop Line necessitated steps being taken to watch the left flank closely in view of possible enemy action. There was a further resumption of this heavy shelling at 9 p.m., but it was not so severe over our area as formerly. The ultimate result of these periods of extreme artillery activity was an increasing toll of casualties and a necessity for constantly effecting repairs to our trenches.

At two o'clock on the morning of the 18th a message was received from Brigade that the Battalion of the

London Rifles on our left was making an attack on that part of Flers Trench and Flers Support adjoining the left of the line held by the 1st Battalion of Auckland and extending to Goose Alley, and that Otago Battalion was to take over the position when it had been consolidated. Previous to this, the 10th (North Otago) Company, commanded by Captain J. Hargest, had been in touch with the 8th London Regiment in Fat Trench, and because of the latter's numerical weakness had taken over about 200 yards of its line. When the 8th London troops attacked at 5.30 a.m. the Lewis guns of 10th Company, together with two Vickers guns under Lieut. R. B. Caws, were thrust forward in readiness to support their right flank, and for the material assistance thus given an appreciative letter of thanks was received from the G.O.C. 47th Division. The 8th (Southland) Company, commanded by Major S. Rice, now proceeded to take over the new line, but the enemy in Goose Alley harassed our men with bombs from the high ground at the junction of Flers Trench and Goose Alley, the locality of many grim struggles, and endeavoured to work their way down from it. It was therefore necessary to bomb the enemy back in the direction of Goose Alley and establish protective blocks. The work accomplished on this morning by our bombers, under Lance-corp. W. Murray, against almost overwhelming odds, was of a very gallant order. The enemy resorted to volley firing, and in addition to being more liberally supplied with bombs, had the advantage of position on the high ground. However, our party succeeded in accomplishing its task of establishing and maintaining a block, notwithstanding the fact that every bomber of the Battalion who had been engaged had become a casualty.

At 11 p.m. the Battalion was relieved by Companies of the 2nd Battalions of Otago and Auckland, and moved back to Carlton Trench, reaching there at 4.30 a.m. on the 19th. The weather was now extremely bad, and the floundering in the deep mud and ooze of the Somme made a change-over a most exhaustive process. A hot meal was served at Carlton Trench, and subsequently there was a slight improvement in the weather. But the troops were in the worst possible state of wretchedness and exhaustion. The period just completed, though it had passed without an actual attack being delivered, represented one of the very worst the Regiment had experienced. Incessant rain had fallen for 60 hours ; the men were standing or moving knee-deep in mud the whole of the time ; they were soaked in rain, and no hot food was procurable owing to the long distance to be covered from the dump. Furthermore, the effect of the enemy shell fire on congested trenches made the conditions simply appalling. On arrival at Carlton Trench, where the Battalion bivouacked over the succeeding few days, the state to which everyone was reduced was that of the deepest misery and exhaustion. Major Colquhoun at this time rejoined the Battalion, officers who had been left at the Rest Camp arrived, and the 14th Company returned from Green Dump, where it had been providing carrying parties. All available roads, such as they were, were taxed to the utmost by the constant stream of wheeled traffic with material of war for the artillery and front line, and with the heavy rain on top of all this, were in an almost impassable state. But repairs must be kept going ; new roads must be formed as the Army advanced ; and the demand for large working parties under these circumstances was inevitable. Still, the period represented a short respite of a kind and allowed for the gathering of new strength for a further effort before many hours.

When the 2nd Battalion of Otago moved up to Flag and Fat Trenches on the 18th in conformity with the relief of the 1st Brigade, the position on the left still remained obscure. The enemy was apparently determined not to be ousted from Flers Trench and Flers Support in the locality of Goose Alley, nor to be denied his hold on the junction of Drop Alley. The 4th and 8th Companies were sent up in support of Auckland troops who were endeavouring, though unsuccessfully, to push the enemy out by bombing attacks ; and in the interval 10th Company was concerned with the digging of a new assembly trench. It was imperative that a footing should be gained on the high ground in order to facilitate our further advance and the ultimate capture of the Gird trenches. On the 20th Canterbury troops made a most determined assault on the enemy at this point under cover of darkness in an endeavour to definitely settle the ownership of the disputed locality of Goose Alley and Drop

Alley. The attack, in which the fighting was of the fiercest order, was successful, but was followed by a well organised counter-attack up Flers Line, which drove back the bombing post and the garrison of the strong-point, regained the whole of Drop Alley and threatened the left and left rear. Rallying to the attack once more Canterbury overwhelmed the enemy in a fierce encounter, drove him off the crest, and finally held and consolidated the position against a further counter-attack launched on the evening of the 21st. Canterbury Regiment naturally suffered heavily in this bitter struggle ; but the ground was strewn with German dead, of whom it was estimated 300 had been killed in the fighting just concluded.

On the evening of the 21st there was an intense bombardment of all our lines. We were now in touch on the left with the 1st Battalion of the Black Watch, who had relieved the London Regiment, and at about 10 p.m. we were in turn relieved by the 4th Battalion of the 3rd (Rifle) Brigade, and companies went back independently to Worcester and Seaforth Trenches. On the 22nd welcome reinforcements arrived to the number of eight officers and 140 other ranks. The Battalion was being seriously weakened in strength, but in spite of the gruelling work, the heavy and almost incessant shelling, and the mud of seemingly unfathomable depths, there was no diminution of the fighting spirit. So it was, indeed, with the whole of the Regiment.

On September 24th the 1st Battalion moved out from Carlton Trench, *via* Turk Lane and Fat Trench, and the 2nd Battalion took up its quarters in the positions thus vacated. By 3 a.m. on the 25th the 1st Battalion had relieved Rifle Brigade troops in Flers Trench. The order of the day was quick reliefs, for it was only in this way that the hardships imposed by the weather and the unfavourable conditions generally could be successfully overcome. At 6 a.m. our trenches were heavily bombarded, and it was not until about 8.30 a.m. that the situation had quietened down. It was thought during this bombardment that the enemy was about to launch an attack, but no infantry action developed.

THE ATTACK RENEWED.

The time had now arrived for the resumption of the general attack by the Fourth Army. In the minor, though none the less desperate efforts of the preceding few days, we had gradually strengthened and advanced our positions, and had done much in the direction of asserting a valuable moral ascendancy over the enemy. The task allotted to the XV. Corps on September 25th was the capture of Gird Trench as far as its junction with the Gueudecourt-Factory Road, and the village of Gueudecourt itself. The New Zealand Division's share in this attack was the capture of Factory Corner, and the establishing of a line thence to the high ground running north-east from Flers Support across to Goose Alley over a frontage of 1,900 yards. This was to be carried out in conjunction with the advance of the III. Corps on our left, which was concerned with the capture of Flers Trench up to the High Wood-Thilloy Road, and finally joining up with the Reserve Army at Courcelette. The New Zealand Division was thus on the left of the XV. Corps, and on the gaining of the day's objective was to take over from the III. Corps on Flers Support as far north-west as its junction with Goose Alley. Three Battalions of the 1st Infantry Brigade were to be utilised for the New Zealand Division's part in the attack, namely, Otago, Auckland, and Canterbury, in order named from left to right.

The preliminary bombardment of the enemy's lines by the massed guns of all calibres had commenced at 7 a.m. on the 24th, but, as previously, in order to keep from the enemy any indication of the actual time of attack, there was to be no intensified bombardment immediately preceding zero hour. Grove Alley presented a rather serious obstacle to advancing troops owing to its great depth and width; but to overcome this difficulty steps were dug in the sides and duck-boards placed ready for facilitating the passage across. The attack really combined two stages, with the second part of which the 1st Battalion of Otago alone was concerned ; the intention being to push forward to the high ground beyond the lower portion of Goose Alley fronting the first objective. The attack was to be carried out with two companies, con- stituting four waves in the front line, namely, 10th (North Otago) Company, commanded by Captain J. Hargest, and 4th (Otago) Company, commanded by Temp.-Captain J. Herbert, both being led and directed by Captain Hargest, with 14th (South Otago) Company, commanded by Captain W.

LIEUT.-COLONEL A. B. CHARTERS,
C.M.G., D.S.O., (D.)

Ward, in support and 8th (Southland) Company commanded by Major S. Rice, in reserve. On the morning of the attack the enemy artillery had opened up very heavy fire along Flers Support. Zero hour was fixed for 12.35 p.m., and prior to that time the two leading waves had formed up in Grove Alley and the second two in rear.

Punctually to time the barrage of many guns broke out along the front, the great howitzers joining with unexampled violence in the chorus. Almost at the moment that our barrage fell, the fire from many light enemy guns grouped about Goose Alley ceased abruptly. The attack got well away, moving behind the barrage with such regularity as to resemble a practice movement on a grand scale. The road and low ground in front of Grove Alley having been safely crossed, the ascent of the ridge running up to Goose Alley was commenced ; but fairly heavy machine gun fire from the right front was encountered and a number of casualties sustained. A party of the enemy, numbering from 50 to 60, bravely counter-attacked over the crest of the ridge as our attack was actually in motion, but their attempt to get through our barrage was unsuccessful, and when our attacking troops passed over the ground a few wounded men and three smashed machine guns were all that was left of them. This enemy attack was delivered from about the junction of Goose Alley and the Flers-Eaucourt L'Abbaye Road, and was probably conceived with the object of covering the withdrawal of the enemy quick-firing guns previously referred to. On arrival at the crest of the hill it was found that Goose Alley, instead of being on the near slope, as was assumed, was about 200 yards down the forward slope, and in attacking down hill the men came under heavy sniping and machine gun fire from the direction of Eaucourt L'Abbaye, the sparseness of the line alone preventing many casualties. In Goose Alley itself the enemy was encountered in but limited numbers, and they were either bayoneted or surrendered.

The work of consolidation of the new line was immediately commenced, and Lewis gun posts were pushed forward to a distance of from 60 to 100 yards. Goose Alley, on the left of the newly-formed position, was found to be so blocked with the dead of friend and foe, the result of the desperate and bitter fighting which had waged round the junction of Goose

Alley and Flers Support during preceding days, that a new trench had to be dug in front. The supporting 14th Company was sent up to refuse the right flank, and dug in along the Flers-Eaucourt L'Abbaye Road, facing north-east, the line at this point now forming a pronounced salient at the apex of which a strong-point and block were established. The operation had proved eminently successful.

The 55th Division reported that it was in touch with Canterbury troops at Factory Corner, but the position there nevertheless for some time remained obscure. There was, indeed, a gap of about 500 yards between the right and the 55th Divisional troops, but this was ultimately adjusted by the 55th Division bridging it with strong-points. On the left everything had gone well, and we were in touch with the 1st Division. The day passed without change in the situation, though the enemy worried us in a desultory manner with heavy shells. Early in the afternoon Battalion Headquarters were blown out, and had to be moved forward to a new position in Flers Support. On the following day Battalion Headquarters again moved, on this occasion to Goose Alley, where a conference of Company Commanders was held in reference to further operations.

On the afternoon of the above attack, a warning order was received from Corps that in the event of the situation being very favourable the New Zealand Division should be prepared to receive orders to attack the line of Gird Trenches north-west of Gueudecourt and thence south along Goose Alley to the point where it was then held. As the 1st Battalion of Otago was on the left flank of the projected attack, Lieut.-Colonel Charters was ordered to form a defensive flank along the line of Goose Alley by constructing a line of strong-points facing north-west. The 55th Division on the right would at the same time attack from the Gueudecourt-Factory Corner Road northwards. The situation in Gueudecourt village, however, was not clear, and for that reason the attack intended for the 26th was postponed until the 27th. As a matter of fact, between four and five o'clock on the afternoon of the 26th the enemy was observed in considerable numbers advancing across the open from the direction of Ligny Thilloy and Le Barque with a view to attacking the 55th Division, east of Factory Corner. After covering some distance they were seen to conceal themselves in the corn and long grass, whereupon the area was promptly and, apparently, effectively searched by the 55th Field Artillery.

A BITTER EXPERIENCE.

The attack for the 27th, to which the 1st Infantry Brigade was committed, was timed to commence at 2.15 p.m., and at 7 a.m. the preliminary bombardment opened. The 1st Battalion of Otago was again on the left of the attack, and when the barrage came down deployed in the following order : 14th Company on the right ; 4th Company on the left ; 8th Company in support ; and 10th Company moving north along the line of Goose Alley on the left of the attack.

, Punctually to time and in good order the Battalion advanced to the attack, and with only a moderate number of casualties crossed the line of Factory Corner-Eaucourt L'Abbaye Road. From this stage the ground fell away abruptly and the attacking troops almost immediately came under a withering blast of fire from enemy rifles and machine guns posted along Gird Trench and Gird Support. The two leading Companies, 14th and 4th, valiantly endeavoured to press on against this hail of fire ; but it was only a question of distance when they were literally swept away by it. Every officer and almost every man became a casualty. The 8th Company, following in rear, now advanced into the breach. With equal gallantry the endeavour to reach Gird Trench was renewed, only to find that the protecting wire in the low lying ground was uncut. Here the attack withered away, and the few survivors, the remnant of three shattered Companies, took refuge in the shell-holes. A few of our men, joining up with the 1st Battalion of Auckland on the right, had succeeded in reaching Gird Trench.

In the meantime, 10th Company, advancing up Goose Alley on the left of the attack, found this enemy trench almost obliterated, an example of our artillery's incessant pounding. Posts were established at intervals of about 150 yards in order to form the left flank of the Division. On crossing the road, Goose Alley was found to be so utterly wrecked by shell fire that it practically ceased to exist. The required strength for a post pushed down the forward slope overlooking Gird Trench and there dug in.

It was now realised by Captain Hargest, commanding 10th Company, that the frontal attacking Companies had failed to gain their objectives ; had in fact been practically destroyed ; and as there were no officers it was decided to dig in on the line gained. Assuming command of the remnant of the four Companies, for 10th Company had also suffered heavily, Captain Hargest established a line which extended across to the right, thus forming a junction with Auckland, whose left Company had also received very severe punishment and had been equally unable to reach its objective. When darkness came down the line was further consolidated ; sergeants were placed in command of the various posts ; all the wounded that could be collected were brought into Goose Alley, and as many of the dead as possible were buried. Owing to the high total of losses in killed and wounded this was a bad day for the 1st Battalion. About one o'clock on the following morning a company of Wellington Battalion, together with a section of the 1st Trench Mortar Battery, came up and assisted to strengthen the position.

A further attack was contemplated with the object of capturing portion of the Gird system to right and left of Goose Alley, as well as an extension of Goose Alley itself. The attack, timed for 3 a.m. on the 28th, was to be carried out by Wellington troops, with the assistance of a tank, with the 55th Division on our right co-operating. On their way up to position of assembly so large a percentage of the troops intended for the operation was cut off by heavy artillery fire that when daylight broke it was decided not to persist in the attack. A reconnaissance subsequently made of the area covered by the junctions of Gird Trench and Gird Support with Goose Alley disclosed the fact that it was actually at the bottom of what might be described as a saucer, and practically untenable in itself. At a later hour a successful attack by troops of the New Zealand Division gave us possession of Gird Trench, Gird Support, and Goose Alley extending to the lip of the saucer, a distance of about 100 yards, and under cover of darkness the three trenches were junctioned.

The 1st Battalion's attack against the Gird system of

trenches and along Goose Alley on September 27th unquestionably represented the Regiment's most bitter and costly experience on the Somme. When the Battalion marched out of the line on the night of the 28th it was reduced to a strength of 113, which was considerably below that of a company. The fire encountered by the leading companies almost immediately after crossing the line of the Factory Corner-Eaucourt L'Abbaye Road was of a nature such as only those who had gallantly, though vainly, endeavoured to struggle through it could realise; and the line which the attack reached was only gained because of the extraordinary spirit of self-sacrifice of officers and men in face of overwhelming odds; Gird Trench, and Gird Support in particular having been densely packed with an enemy liberally supplied with machine guns. The problem presented by having to handle such a number of wounded called for the greatest exertions of the stretcher parties, who worked unceasingly throughout the night under almost insuperable difficulties of mud and distance. Many of the wounded succeeded in staggering back unaided, but there were others who were so sorely wounded as to be beyond the aid of the bearers when their turn came.

The 2nd Infantry Brigade took over the line on the night of the 28th, and it fell to the lot of the 2nd Battalion of the Regiment, then resting south of the Longueval-Bazentin Road, to relieve the 1st Battalion. The relief was apparently discovered by the enemy as it was being effected, and it was only the proximity of cover afforded by Goose Alley that saved the Battalion from the artillery fire that followed. During the night a communication trench was constructed in order to improve the junction with the 2nd Battalion of Auckland on the right. On the left we were in touch with the 2nd Battalion of the Rifle Brigade.

On the 29th the 1st Battalion of Otago had moved over to Mametz Wood, and was there afforded the rest so sorely needed.

The enemy, now obviously out of temper at being compelled to give ground at so many points, viciously shelled the locality of Goose Alley throughout the day following the inter-change of Battalions, and machine gun and sniping fire added to our casualties. This was maintained over the 30th, indicating on the part of the enemy a state of increasing nervousness and fear of further attacks. And, indeed, he had good grounds for alarm, for an attack, in which the New Zealand Division was concerned, had already been planned for Sunday, October 1st. This operation was directed towards sweeping the enemy out of his positions in the Gird system in the neighbourhood of Goose Alley, and attacking and capturing a line of trenches over a front of approximately 1,000 yards westward to a point known as the Circus. The 47th Division (of the III. Corps) on our immediate left, was co-operating, with Eaucourt L'Abbaye as its main objective. The New Zealand Divisional task was allotted to the 2nd Infantry Brigade, to which two Battalions of the 3rd (Rifle) Brigade were attached for the purposes of the attack. The Brigade was also responsible for the left flank, and for a communication trench running from the Circus south to the L'Abbaye Road. In the further allotment of tasks Otago and Canterbury were selected as the two assaulting Battalions, while Wellington Battalion was detailed to follow Otago as an immediate support ; Auckland meantime holding our front line in Gird Trench on the extreme right of the attacking Battalions.

A FINAL EFFORT.

At seven o'clock on the morning of October 1st a heavy preliminary bombardment of the enemy's defences over the Corps front was commenced. Zero hour was fixed for 3.15 p.m., and in order to deceive the enemy it was decided that at zero hour an additional and intense bombardment should be put down over his lines on a part of the front on which no attack was to be launched.

The 2nd Battalion of the Regiment assembled in Goose Alley for the attack, and under cover of an artillery barrage extending over a line parallel thereto, moved forward at zero hour to the assault in four waves, each perfect in line and interval, and with rifles at the slope. Almost immediately, 4th Company on the right, together with portion of 8th Company, came under heavy machine gun fire from the direction of Gird Trench. The 10th and 14th Companies on the left were at this stage advancing across a depression which afforded comparative cover, and thus escaped the gruelling fire which confronted the right companies. The 4th and 8th Companies had moreover a difficult manœuvre to execute. After advancing for a distance of about 200 yards to their front it was necessary to incline to the right and then eventually to change direction to that quarter; and despite the heavy fire encountered the movement was effectively carried out.

As the last Otago company went forward two companies of Wellington Battalion moved up Goose Alley and then forward in two waves in rear of and in support to Otago. Advancing to the crest of the ridge after changing direction, 4th and 8th Companies were seriously depleted in strength under the blasts of machine gun fire which swept their ranks. Every officer was a casualty, and non-commissioned officers and men were heavily hit. But with unfailing determination they pressed on, successfully reaching their objective and passing some distance beyond it. The terrific nature of our artillery barrage had so completely destroyed the enemy trench line that the objective was not recognisable; and soon afterwards the remnant of the attacking force were required to withdraw from under the line of our stationary barrage to what constituted the laid down objective, and there dug in with the supporting Wellington troops. In the meantime the two left companies of Otago, with equal determination, had pushed forward and past the Circus and established themselves along the road about 300 yards in advance of it, and there gained touch with the 19th London Regiment. It was near the Circus that Sergt. Donald Forrester Brown, of 10th (North Otago) Company, attacked and killed single-handed five enemy machine gunners and put the gun out of action. For his extraordinary courage and daring, and his equally worthy performance in the first attack on September 15th in rushing and knocking out enemy machine guns which were holding up the advance, this very gallant fellow was awarded the Victoria Cross. His death in action at a subsequent period of operations extinguished an heroic spirit and deprived the Regiment of a splendid soldier. Closely and actively associated with Sergt. Brown, and contributing to the success gained in the Battalion's opening attack, was Sergt. J. Rodgers, a soldier possesssing great courage and determination and equal to every emergency.

The 10th and 14th Companies had fared badly in the matter of losses. The first real opposition encountered was from a trench south of the Circus, where the enemy was finally either shot down or ran away. Touch had now been lost with 8th Company owing to the gaps created in its ranks and the dense smoke of battle which obscured the outlook. Furthermore, the extent to which the enemy trenches had been smashed by our artillery fire made it a difficult matter to determine the actual objective. The Circus was naturally thought to be a well defined point, but from a defensive point of view it had ceased to exist, and the men of Otago, together with those of the Wellington Company who had come up in support, pushed on to the ridge about 300 yards ahead and established themselves on what was certainly a very strong position, this step being taken as the result of a decision arrived at by the officers on the spot after a careful reconnaissance. Orders were subsequently received, however, to bring the flank back to the Circus in order to conform to the general line ; and at 10 p.m. Captain W. G. A. Bishop, M.C., succeeded in getting into touch with our right Companies and Wellington troops, and before daylight the whole position was consolidated and made secure by punctuating the front with strong-points and the aid of machine guns. The entire attack had been splendidly carried out under galling fire and consequent severe losses, its success being entirely due to the dash of the assaulting troops under conditions of a most exacting nature. The artillery's part in the attack was certainly gruelling work for the men behind the guns ; but even in spite of their devastating fire the enemy showed surprising quickness in getting his machine guns into action once the barrage had lifted. A very considerable number of the enemy were killed, and the prisoners taken totalled 200. Otago entered the attack with a strength of 19 officers and 314 other ranks ; and the casualties sustained in the operation and while holding the line on October 2nd amounted to four officers and 33 other ranks killed, six officers and 93 other ranks wounded, 49 other ranks being recorded as missing ; making a total of 10 officers and 175 other ranks.

On the right of Otago the 2nd Battalion of Canterbury sustained heavy casualties from rifle and machine gun fire while advancing across the open. On approaching the

SERGT. DONALD FORRESTER BROWN, V.C.

(*Killed in Action*).

LIEUT.-COLONEL G. S. SMITH, C.M.G., D.S.O., (D.)

enemy's trenches they were also subjected to heavy fire ; and severe fighting took place before they finally drove the enemy out and established themselves on the line of their objective. One minute before the attack was launched 36 oil mortars were discharged against the enemy from the front occupied by Canterbury, and 30 of these projectiles were observed to burst in Gird Support 400 yards away, covering the front with dense smoke and flame. When the trench was captured several groups, one of 20 and one of 15, of enemy dead were found badly scorched and charred by the oil flames. Some of the prisoners, as might have been expected, complained bitterly of the use of burning oil, and told of the terror excited by the fear of being caught by the flames. On the left of Otago men of the 19th London Regiment connected up at 5.30 p.m., but actually they were cut off from their own Division, the 47th, north of Eaucourt L'Abbaye ; and arrangements had to be made by the New Zealand Division for the temporary feeding of 80 men. The day of October 2nd, when Otago continued in line, was characterised by persistent and heavy shelling over a wide area. On October 1st an attack was launched against Eaucourt L'Abbaye and the enemy defences east of it, and by the evening of the 3rd the whole of the village had been wrested from the enemy.

At two o'clock on the morning of October 3rd the 2nd Battalion of Otago was relieved by the 1st Battalion of the 3rd (Rifle) Brigade. Darkness, the heavy rain, the appalling mud and the distance to be covered, made the relief operation a most trying one, and save for the hot meal which was issued on getting back, Carlton Trench offered little more in the way of comfort than any other part of the battle-field ; most of the men being destitute of ground-sheets or great coats. During the day the Battalion trekked down to Fricourt, six miles away, and there rested until 3 p.m. on October 6th.

In the meantime the 1st Battalion had moved up on the 2nd from Mametz Wood to Switch and neighbouring trenches in relief of the 4th Battalion of the Rifle Brigade as support Battalion. The holding of this position was quite a brief affair, for on the following day the Battalion was relieved by troops of the 124th Brigade of the 41st Division and went back through the ooze and mud to Pommiers Redoubt, where it bivouacked over the succeeding three days.

OPERATIONS REVIEWED.

An order for the relief of the New Zealand Division, less Artillery, by the 41st Division, was issued on October 2nd, and two days later this had been given effect to. The Regiment thereupon marched out of the Somme Battlefield and turned its back on the devastated region, bringing to a close its first great period of sustained fighting on the Western Front. For 23 days the Regiment had been heavily engaged in fighting of the most desperate kind. It had been pitted against and fought to a standstill the best and most seasoned troops of the German Army, and had acquitted itself in a manner that evoked widespread confidence and admiration. That the enemy regarded the retention of every yard of ground as a matter of the most vital importance, and stubbornly contested it as such, was proved by the contents of a captured German Order, dated September 25th, from which the following is an extract : " The guiding principle during the fighting on the Somme is that no sap-head or shell-crater will be abandoned without the express order of the Supreme Command of the First Army." But the express orders of the Supreme Command of the First German Army, however much they were respected, were found impossible of fulfilment because of the demands of our own irresistible infantry.

The methods of warfare employed in the Battle of the Somme were for the most part entirely new to our men, but they were assimilated and improved upon with an instinctive and ever ready initiative keenly alive to every emergency, backed by an unconquerable determination and a fighting spirit that never hesitated about paying the heavy toll so remorselessly exacted as the price of victory.

The toll levied in dead and wounded, in maimed and missing, and in personal sacrifice and suffering was heavy indeed ; but if the Regiment was at times temporarily broken in strength it was never broken in spirit. The appalling mud of the Somme Battlefield ; the exertion and terrible weariness of unceasing trekking to and from the line ; the prolonged and heavy fighting against a clever and stubborn enemy ; the rain and its accompanying miseries ; and the difficulties of transport, accentuated by the disappearance of roads and tracks and the congestion of a never-ending traffic which must feed the insatiable maw of the front line, all multiplied and heaped up what might be regarded as insurmountable difficulties and hardships ; but these were overcome with a determination and spirit that made our entry into the arena of the Somme the complete and sweeping success that it was. The gallant conduct in action of Company Sergt.-major Knox (4th Company, 2nd Battalion), who was awarded the Military Cross, was highly typical of the fine courage and leadership displayed by the senior non-commissioned officers of the Regiment throughout the operations.

In reading these only too brief records of the fighting on the Somme, the conclusion arrived at might be that on each occasion on which the Regiment went into definite action, it suffered almost annihilating casualties. Certainly our losses were very heavy, but this fact serves to illustrate the formidable and almost irresistible strength of the enemy defences, even after our stupendous array of artillery had dealt with them. The system of frontal or bludgeon attacks against an enemy strongly entrenched and fortified must invariably prove expensive, and the tasks to which the Regiment was committed on the Somme were of such a nature that less determined and less valiant troops might have faltered in pushing them home to a successful issue. Viewed in this light, and considering the fact that all objectives were ultimately gained, and at times a great deal more, it will be realised that heavy losses were the inevitable price of victory. For example, the general attack on September 15th, in which the Regiment made its debut on the Somme, was attended by considerably greater gains than in any single operation launched since the great offensive had opened ; and greater even than in the course of any subsequent operation. The New Zealand Division commenced its operations on a frontage of 950 yards, which was ultimately extended to 2,800 yards. It captured five miles of enemy front trenches, and five and a-half of subsidiary trenches, and effected an advance to a depth exceeding two miles.

A congratulatory message received from Sir Douglas Haig, Commander-in-Chief of the British Forces, ran as follows :—
" The New Zealand Division has fought with the greatest gallantry in the Somme Battle for 23 consecutive days,

carrying out with complete success every task set, and always doing more than was asked of it. The Division has won universal confidence and admiration. No praise can be too high for such troops."

General Rawlinson, Commanding the Fourth Army, wrote as follows :—" I desire to express to all ranks of the New Zealand Division my hearty congratulations on the excellent work they have done during the Battle of the Somme. On three successive occasions (15th and 25th September and 1st October) they attacked the hostile positions with the greatest gallantry and vigour, capturing in each attack every objective they had allotted to them. More than this, they gained possession of, and held, several strong-points in advance of and beyond the furthest objectives that had been allotted to them. The endurance and the fine fighting spirit of the Division has been beyond praise, and their success in the Flers neighbourhood will rank amongst the best achievements of the British Army. The control and direction of the Division during these operations have been conducted with skill and precision, whilst the artillery support in establishing the barrages and defending counter-attack has been in every way most effective. It is a matter of regret to me that this fine Division is leaving the Fourth Army, and I trust that on some future occasion it may again be my good fortune to find it under my command."

During these 23 days of fighting the Division had sustained the formidable total of over 6,700 casualties of all ranks. This was, of course, a severe blow, but it was gallant sacrifice freely given. The part which the Otago Regiment played in this grim business may be gained from the following list of casualties :—

1st Battalion.

	Killed.	Wounded.	Missing.	Total.
Officers ...	5	8	—	13
Other Ranks	46	277	64	387

2nd Battalion.

	Killed.	Wounded.	Missing.	Total.
Officers ...	5	24	1	30
Other Ranks	81	334	133	548

Grand Total .. 978.

The immediate result of these formidable casualties was reflected in the state of Companies, which, though they were 250 strong at the outset and had subsequently received reinforcements, were in some instances now reduced to a minimum of about 30 all ranks. Moreover, the few survivors were in a condition of almost pitiable exhaustion and weariness, and presented a woeful spectacle when contrasted with the extraordinary physical fitness and great buoyancy of spirits so evident when the Regiment marched down to the area of the Somme at the beginning of September.

When the Regiment once more turned its head to the north it left behind it many stout fellows who had paid the supreme price of devotion to duty, but in the hard realities of war, regrets, however keen, had quickly to give place to the serious affairs of the morrow.

As a test of strength the Battle of the Somme was convincing, if terribly expensive. The breaking of the weather in the middle of October so multiplied the difficulties of attack as to make it impossible to exploit the situation in such a manner as to reap the full benefits. The pressure on Verdun had been removed, the transfer of German troops from the Western Front had been prevented, and the enemy's strength had been considerably weakened. The concluding stages of the Somme Battle were slow and tremendously difficult, but at its close the British advance had extended down the forward slopes of the ridge, until from Morval to Thiepval the whole plateau and a considerable area of ground beyond had been wrested from the enemy. The general withdrawal of the enemy in March of the following year to the Hindenburg Line, which, branching off from the original defences near Arras, extended south-eastwards for a distance of 12 miles to Queant, and thence passed west of Cambrai towards St. Quentin, represented the final realisation of the fruits of the Somme Offensive.

CHAPTER III.

CORDONNERIE AND HOUPLINES.

WHEN the Regiment marched out of the Somme Battlefield on October 3rd, 1916, it withdrew behind the lines in order to rest and regain some of its lost strength and vitality, immediately prior to trekking north again. The 1st Battalion spent three days at Pommiers Redoubt, between Montauban and Mametz, and the 2nd Battalion marched back to the Base Camp at Fricourt. On October 3rd rain fell for the greater part of the day, and the succeeding days saw very little improvement in the general conditions. The intervening time was now devoted to reorganising the battalions, posting reinforcements to the various companies, cleaning equipment, and resting.

On October 4th a Divisional Order was issued that the New Zealand Division (less Artillery, which was to remain on the Somme for a further period) would be transferred from the Fourth Army to the Second Army, and temporarily was to be transferred from the XV. to the X. Corps from midnight 6th-7th October, and was to move to the Hallencourt area, thereafter entraining at specified points with a view to proceeding northwards.

The 2nd Battalion of the Regiment accordingly marched out from Fricourt to Dernancourt on October 6th, and entrained for Longpre. Then followed a march of eight miles to Erondelle, and during this stage of the journey the completely exhausted state of the men was very much in evidence. The 1st Battalion followed on October 7th. Leaving Pommiers Redoubt it marched to Albert, which was still being intermittently shelled by the enemy, and there entrained for Longpre, arriving there on the 8th, and thence marching to Airaines. On October 11th the 1st Battalion entrained at Longpre for Caestre, reaching there in the early evening and proceeding by motor lorries to Estaires, where reinforcements were received. On the same day the 2nd Battalion marched to Pont Remy, where it entrained for Bailleul, which was reached shortly before midnight. From this stage there was a march of ten kilometres to Strazelle. The Regiment remained at these two points over the succeeding two days, and on the 14th the 1st Battalion was transferred to billets near Bac St. Maur, and the 2nd Battalion to Armentieres.

Orders had now been issued for the relief by the New Zealand Division of the 5th Australian Division in the Sailly sector and the Houplines sub-sector. The 1st Infantry Brigade and the 3rd (Rifle) Brigade were to take over the Sailly sector and relieve the 15th Australian Brigade (Cordonnerie sub-sector) and the 14th Australian Brigade (Boutillerie sub-sector) respectively ; while the 2nd New Zealand Infantry Brigade was to relieve the 8th Australian Brigade Group (Houplines sub-sector), and was to be attached for tactical purposes to Franks's Force, a Composite Division commanded by General Franks, and comprising three brigades, one of which was now to be the 2nd New Zealand Infantry Brigade. Command of the new divisional sector was to pass on October 14th.

The Cordonnerie sub-sector taken over by the 1st Infantry Brigade was but a short distance south-west of Armentieres, and was overlooked by the high ground on which was situated, at a point about midway in the sector, the partially ruined village of Fromelles. It was against the ridge on which Fromelles stood that an attack by Australian troops had been directed a few months previously with such tragic losses, many of their dead still lying unburied in No Man's Land. The ground along which the front line breast-work of the Cordonnerie sector extended, and for a considerable distance to the rear of it, was exceedingly low lying and flat, and drainage, more particularly during the winter months, was a source of constant anxiety and labour. The sector when taken over from the 5th Australian Division was in a very neglected state of repair and defence, and although it could never be regarded as anything but a very quiet part of the line there were sufficient discomforts during the wet season, owing to the lack of decent accommodation and the flooded state of the

143

line and its approaches, to make it one of the most unpleasant. With the first heavy rainfall a great many of the sandbag shelters collapsed, and the duck-boards along the communication trenches were always more or less afloat. During the winter months conditions on the Houplines sub-sector were not very much better. Persistent hard work and sound organisation during the succeeding months of occupation of these parts of the Western line effected an appreciable though very gradual improvement in conditions. The breastworks were strengthened and a vast amount of wire entanglements constructed along the selected lines of defence, as well as some fairly substantial shelters for the garrisons of the front and support lines, while large numbers of men were kept constantly employed on the drains and waterways in the rear in order to clear the area of water ; but the fall was too negligible to produce any material improvement.

The portion of the Corps front for which the New Zealand Division was responsible extended over a length of approximately 5,600 yards. Within the area allotted to the Division the defensive system comprised the front breastwork, which was continuous ; the 70 yards line which was continuous but out of repair ; and the support line which comprised a series of small posts, joined laterally by a continuous fire trench and breastwork combined ; while slightly in rear of this line further posts existed. The subsidiary line consisted of a series of defended localities or posts, none of them of a very substantial nature. The normal distribution of troops in the Sailly sector was that to each of the two sub-sectors was allotted one infantry brigade, and in each brigade sub-sector two battalions were allotted to the front line system and subsidiary line, with two battalions in brigade reserve. In the forward system the garrison of the front line trench was reduced to a minimum, sufficient men, together with Lewis guns and a small proportion of Vickers guns, holding it so as to ensure the repulse of a surprise attack unaccompanied by bombardment ; the strength of the garrison approximating 150 men per 1000 yards. The defence of the system was thus organised in depth, and the governing principles on which action, in the event of hostile attack, were based were that no body of troops to whom a portion of a defensive line or post was entrusted would give it up under any circumstances ; while hostile penetration at any point was to be met by immediate counter-attack while the enemy was still disorganised and had not had time to establish himself.

On October 13th the front line of the Cordonnerie sector was taken over by Canterbury and Wellington troops, and on the following day the 1st Battalion of Otago relieved the 58th Australian Battalion in reserve. Three platoons of 4th Company occupied strong-points known as Winter's Night, Junction and Croix Blanche, in rear of the subsidiary line, the remainder of the Battalion being in billets still further in rear and within close range of Bac St. Maur. In the Houplines sub-sector, in accordance with the dispositions of the 2nd Infantry Brigade on being attached to Franks's Force, the 2nd Battalion of Otago was established as brigade reserve in billets at Armentieres, 4th and 8th Companies being billeted at Barb-wire Square, 10th Company at Tissage, and 14th Company at Lock House. During the several succeeding days the Regiment supplied working parties for the front and support lines of the two sectors. On October 20th the 2nd Battalion moved into the front line and took over from the 2nd Battalion of Wellington.

The Battalion remained in the line for a period of six days, the enemy displaying very little activity during the tour. The only incident of note occurred during the night of the 25th. At 8 p.m. one of our listening posts sighted a party of six Germans at a short distance from our wire. They were challenged, but no reply being received, were bombed ; subsequently machine gun fire was brought to bear on No Man's Land. Search failed to discover any further signs of the enemy, until at 8.20 p.m. a second and larger party were sighted approaching our wire. On being challenged they deployed and advanced on the listening post. One of the two men of the post ran back to give the alarm, when the remaining man shot one of the enemy dead, and after throwing bombs at the others withdrew to our lines. Lewis gun fire completed their dispersal, and later the body of the dead German was brought in and identification established. On the following day the Battalion was relieved and moved back to the subsidiary line. Here it was fitted out with the much improved small box respirator for protection against gas attacks. It remained in occupation of the subsidiary line until the close of the month, the daily routine consisting chiefly in supplying working parties under the direction of the Divisional Engineers.

The 1st Battalion of the Regiment commenced its initial tour of the front line of the Cordonnerie sub-sector on the afternoon of October 26th, when it relieved the 1st Battalion of Wellington in the left of the Brigade sector, extending from Mine Avenue to Devon Avenue. The enemy's attitude, generally speaking, remained passive, while our main activity was directed to battering down his front line and wire entanglements by means of concentrated trench mortar bombardments. The mortars employed were the heavy 68-pounders, the projectiles of which were commonly known as "plum puddings," and light Stokes, and by these means considerable damage was caused to the enemy's front line breastwork without, however, evoking any serious retaliation. These trench mortar bombardments became an almost daily performance, and from our point of view provided an inspiring spectacle ; but owing to the fact that the enemy, as subsequent investigations disclosed, was not holding his front line in any strength, our demonstrations must have occasioned him very little real concern, apart from the material damage sustained.

On November 8th the 1st Battalion was relieved in the line by Wellington troops after a fairly long tour, and moved back to billets formerly occupied in the locality of Rue de Quesnoy, near Bac St. Maur. On November 12th the Battalion relieved the 1st Battalion of Auckland in Brigade support, a series of five posts being occupied in the subsidiary line, with the strength of the garrison of each post at one platoon. On November 16th the Battalion moved into the front line system, 14th, 8th, and 10th Companies occupying the front and support lines in that order from right to left, one platoon of each company being in the front line and three in support, with the 4th Company in reserve. On the night of the 22nd a patrol led by Corporal G. Vincent, who was well supported by Pte. R. Bett, entered the enemy's trenches at a point known as the Tadpole, and examining it over some length found it unoccupied. This patrol definitely established the fact that the enemy, in consequence of the breached and broken state of the trenches as a result of our sustained trench mortar bombardments and the difficulties of drainage, was holding his front by means of isolated posts, and had presumably withdrawn the major part of his garrison to the higher and less disturbed area of Fromelles. The tour ended on November 24th, the Battalion returning to billets in Rue de Quesnoy and locality.

The 2nd Battalion had returned to the line in the Houplines sub-sector on the opening day of November in relief of Wellington, and continued in occupation there until the 7th. Two days later, when in billets at Armentieres, over 170 reinforcements arrived and were posted to the different companies. When the Battalion returned to the line on the 13th the tour then commenced proved by no means as uneventful as those that preceded it. On the 14th portion of the front line trench system was badly damaged by minenwerfer fire ; and on the following day at 5.20 p.m. the enemy commenced an intense bombardment of our front line, extending from Hobb's Farm to the River Lys. Minenwerfers were again largely employed by the enemy, resulting in serious breaching of the parapet. The bombardment was maintained for half an hour, and on ceasing the enemy, to the number of about 30, penetrated our line and worked along in the direction of 14th Company Headquarters and the entrance to our underground workings, where they appeared in some numbers. Five minutes afterwards they returned to their trenches on a given signal, leaving behind two demolition charges. Very considerable damage was occasioned to our trenches, which was increased by a second bombardment commencing at 6.5 p.m. and lasting until 6.20 p.m. Several huge craters were left in our lines and Irish Avenue was badly blown in. Our casualties, due mainly to the severity of the bombardment, were unfortunately heavy, amounting to nine other ranks killed, one officer and 25 other ranks wounded, and two other ranks missing. One of the raiders was shot by a company cook, and the body being left in our lines was identified as belonging to the 9th Bavarian Regiment. There were several aspects of this raid which, from our point of view, were considered as unsatisfactory. An inquiry held subsequently disclosed the fact, among other things, that the S.O.S. signal had not been put up, and that the wire between Company and Battalion Headquarters had been cut, and that no artillery support was available.

On the following night a raid was attempted against the enemy's lines. At 6.45 p.m. a party of ten other ranks under Lieut. W. Chapman left our trenches and advanced across No Man's Land in single file. On reaching the enemy's wire the party halted, and a reconnaissance was carried out over a distance of 70 yards. At one point the enemy's trench extended back in the shape of the letter V, with a distance of 50 yards from point to point. A machine gun opened fire from either extremity, and it was considered inadvisable to attempt an entrance over this locality. The wire over the area reconnoitred was thick and strong, our artillery fire having had little effect on it. The party accordingly returned to our lines.

On November 19th Otago was relieved in the line by Wellington, and moved back to the subsidiary line where it remained until the 25th, supplying working parties and carrying out a certain amount of training. On the 26th, the day following the Battalion's return to the line, the enemy heavily replied to a brief trench mortar "shoot," resulting in considerable damage to our trenches. During the next few days officers of the 10th Australian Brigade, 3rd Australian Division, visited the line in view of an early relief. This was commenced on the last day of November, when the Battalion returned to Armentieres as Brigade reserve.

There were occasions, particularly during the Regiment's earlier periods in France, when the S.O.S. call was sent out to the supporting artillery without there being sufficient justification for the expenditure of ammunition which it involved, simply because the purpose of the S.O.S. call was not fully appreciated at the time. The S.O.S. (Save our Souls) was a call from the infantry to the artillery for immediate assistance by covering with fire any portion of the front line which was being threatened or attacked. The call could be given by any officer on duty in the front line, and to that end every company, platoon and forward observing officer in the front line was required to carry at all times a message signed and ready to hand in to the signal office for immediate and priority despatch when an enemy attack appeared probable. Simultaneously with the handing in of the message the S.O.S. rocket was to be sent up, and the signal repeated at short intervals until it was clear that it had been observed and the necessary support was forthcoming. The sending out of the S.O.S. call had really to be decided upon by the officer on the spot, and there were occasions when it was considered that the situation could be handled without the support of the artillery, and if such did prove to be the case there was more merit in the achievement. If, on the other hand, the responsible officer failed to correctly appreciate the situation, and the enemy profited by the fact of the S.O.S. not being sent out, there were unpleasant consequences. But the making of a quick and accurate decision in this, as in all other questions, in time became a matter of intuition. It was laid down that on receipt of the S.O.S. message, or on observation of the S.O.S. rocket, or on the enemy heavily bombarding our front or No Man's Land, or when heavy rifle or machine gun fire was heard from the front and the enemy's parapet could not be observed, the batteries covering the front would open fire. The 18-pounders would place a shrapnel barrage as near to our trenches as safety permitted, gradually creeping forward over No Man's Land until it reached the enemy's front line trenches, when high explosive would be substituted wholly or in part for shrapnel, while howitzers would open fire on the enemy's front trenches. Fire would thus be directed and maintained until the situation was reported clear. In order to test the efficiency of the arrangements for obtaining immediate artillery support, it was open to battalion or company commanders of the front line, and this opportunity was on occasions availed of, to call for a test round at any time of the day or night, the time taken between the acceptance of the message and the arrival of the round being expected not to exceed 30 seconds. There were also circumstances under which requests could be made for the fire of our artillery to be directed to any special locality or target ; but in cases where the fire of the heavier howitzers was required, and the locality to which it was to be directed was in close proximity to our own lines, the limitations to the accuracy of guns and howitzers and the variations to be expected at different ranges had to be taken into account, in view of our garrison being brought within the danger zone.

An order issued on November 30th stated that gaps had been cut in the enemy's wire, and that during the night of November 30th-December 1st strong patrols were to be sent out along the whole Divisional front with the object of discovering the dispositions of the enemy's most advanced troops, and the condition and disposition of the wire in rear of his front line breastwork to the depth penetrated. If resistance was met with, no attempt was to be made to force an entry. Fighting was to be avoided, and the investigations were to be carried out secretly and silently so as not to allow the enemy to know that his lines had been entered. The capture of prisoners, it was pointed out, would probably do more than anything else to clear up the existing obscurity of the situation.

In conformity with this order patrols, each of one officer and 20 other ranks, went out over the front at midnight, some of them succeeding in penetrating the enemy's front line, and to a point 200 yards beyond. In only two instances were challenges received. The enemy's trenches were found to be so blown about as to be unrecognisable, representing merely a series of craters and shell-holes, emitting in places a strong smell, pointing to the presence of enemy dead. The conclusions to be drawn from the joint observations were that the enemy's forward trenches were too seriously damaged and water-logged for occupation ; that no attempt had been made to repair the damage done ; that the enemy had one or two small isolated posts stationed in his front line with ready exit available by means of communication trenches ; and that an appearance of holding the front line was simulated by firing flares from posts some distance in the rear. During the early hours of the morning an enemy patrol came over as far as our wire, indicating a certain anxiety on his part as to the meaning and purpose of our enterprise, while machine gun fire was for some time directed to one of our sally ports. The fact that the enemy had adopted the wise plan of getting out of the mud and going back to the higher and drier ground in rear for the period of the winter months, was now fully confirmed. It was, however, becoming increasingly evident that he was carrying out a considerable amount of constructive work in that more favourable tactical position.

Towards the close of November instructions were issued for the reorganisation of the New Zealand Divisional Artillery. The effect of this, it is interesting to note, was that the Divisional Artillery, then consisting of four Brigades, was converted into two Brigades, each of one six-gun howitzer battery and three six-gun 18-pounder batteries, the surplus batteries to form an Army Field Artillery Brigade of the same number of batteries and guns, and to be under the orders of the G.O.C. Army.

On December 2nd the 1st Battalion of the Regiment returned to the line in relief of Wellington, and continued to garrison the trenches until the 10th. The weather was now exceedingly wet and cold, hard frosts alternating with rain and snow. The issue of gum boots and frequent changes of socks considerably alleviated the hardships of the winter months; but nevertheless the parades of sick on returning to billets became increasingly large and for some time occasioned grave concern. The low-lying, fog-laden country of Flanders, and the never-ending mud doubtless contributed to this condition of affairs; but for the major portion of it the primary cause was to be found elsewhere. It was now that the severe strain and exposure to which the Regiment had been subjected during the course of the Somme fighting was making itself felt among those who had come through it, but had never properly recovered from the effects. Thus many had been reduced to a state which left them unable to withstand the severity of the winter months, and when this was realised a more generous policy in the matter of timely evacuations was decided upon and given effect to.

The 1st Battalion made another tour of the line before the close of December, and on the 23rd, when it was relieved, went out to new billets at Bac St. Maur, on the banks of the River Lys, and was then placed in Divisional reserve. The 2nd Battalion of the Regiment, on being relieved at Houplines and leaving Franks's Force at the close of November, had marched down to Bac St. Maur, and entering into billets there, commenced a course of training which extended over the succeeding three weeks.

On December 22nd Sir Douglas Haig, Commander-in-Chief of the British Army, paid a visit to the New Zealand Divisional area, and the Regiment was included in his tour of inspection. A fairly generous bill of fare was provided for Christmas Day, the first spent by the Regiment in France; and both Battalions having the good fortune to be out of the line the day passed very quietly. The general attitude of the troops in line on this occasion was one that could not have been mistaken by the enemy, and the deliberate harassment of his lines and billets throughout the day and night by the New Zealand Divisional Artillery must have convinced him that there was no goodwill or desire for fraternisation on our side of the line.

A Divisional Order was issued on December 28th to the effect that the 1st and 2nd New Zealand Infantry Brigades were to be reorganised as follows :—1st Infantry Brigade : To be comprised of the 1st and 2nd Battalions of Auckland Regiment, and the 1st and 2nd Battalions of Wellington Regiment. 2nd New Zealand Infantry Brigade : To be comprised of the 1st and 2nd Battalions of Otago Regiment, and the 1st and 2nd Battalions of Canterbury Regiment. It was notified that the reorganisation was to take effect as from January 1st, 1917. This, in brief, meant that where formerly the 1st Infantry Brigade was comprised of all 1st Battalions, and the 2nd Infantry Brigade of all 2nd Battalions, the 1st Infantry Brigade would in future comprise the four battalions which represented the North Island of New Zealand, and the 2nd Infantry Brigade the four South Island battalions. The system of distinguishing units by the wearing of regimental patches was at the same time extended, the patch of Blue and Gold (Otago Regimental colours) on a background of Black (Divisional colour), as worn by the 2nd Battalion of Otago from its formation in Egypt, being adopted by the 1st Battalion, with a distinguishing difference in the adjustment oı the two colours which ıormed the diamond-shaped centre of the patch.

In accordance with the reorganisation of the 1st and 2nd Infantry Brigades, the 2nd Battalion of the Regiment, on New Year's Day, 1917, marched out of its reserve billets in the Rue Petillon and took over the Cordonnerie sector in relief of the 2nd Battalion of Wellington. Relief was completed about 12 noon, and one hour later the enemy bombarded the whole area with projectiles of various calibre, including lachrymatory gas shells. Casualties amounted to one killed and six wounded, and the front line and communication trenches suffered badly. There was a recurrence of this hostility at 9 o'clock on the following morning, when about 60 minenwerfer shells were hurled against a front of about 100 yards, adding considerably to the damage of the previous day. By 11 a.m. the situation had quietened, but at 6 p.m. the area was subjected to further violent shelling for a period of over 40 minutes, and additional casualties resulted. Prompt retaliation by our artillery now followed, and a heavy fire was put down over the enemy's front and support lines.

There was reason for believing that on the occasion of the enemy's evening bombardment it had been his intention to raid our lines. A patrol drawn from Sergt. Travis's special party of scouts, while operating in No Man's Land, encountered an enemy patrol of considerable strength. This party they effectively bombed, and subsequently heavy rifle fire was opened up from the enemy's parapet. The hostile bombardment referred to commenced a few minutes after our special patrol returned, and the probability was that the enemy discovered in No Man's Land were moving into position prior to raiding. One outcome of this continued straffing was an immediate call for working parties from the reserve battalion in order to repair the damage to the defences. Comparative quietness prevailed over the remainder of the tour, although our own trench mortars were by no means inactive, and during the afternoons heavily pounded the enemy's forward system. On January 8th the 2nd Battalion was relieved by the 1st Battalion of the Regiment and moved back to reserve and billets.

During the 1st Battalion's occupation of the line there occurred two or three incidents which served to reveal outstanding individual merit. A small party which was acting as a cover to our wiring operations by night came under enemy machine gun fire. One of the party was killed and the remainder hurriedly driven in. At daybreak on the following morning Pte. J. D. Stark proceeded some distance across No Man's Land, and recovered the body lying there. He then made a return journey and collected the rifles lost by the covering party in its hasty retirement. Stark afforded a further demonstration of his utter disregard of danger when in broad daylight he walked across No Man's Land by way of challenge to an enemy sniper who an hour or so previously was responsible for a casualty in our lines. Remarkable as it may seem, he gained the enemy's line, floundered along in the mud under the shelter of the parapet over a consider

153

able distance, locating an enemy post at the foot of Delangre communication trench, and then as casually returned to our own lines without a shot having been fired at him. An early morning patrol comprised of Sergt. G. H. Seddon, Lance-corp. W. Hay, and Pte. F. W. Hamill, all of the 1st Battalion Snipers and Observers, traversed the lee side of the enemy's parapet over a distance of 700 yards, finally encountering, though still unobserved, an enemy sentry post. The post was apparently at the point of being relieved, and there being now too much daylight to accomplish anything beyond the extensive reconnaissance already effected, the patrol quietly and safely withdrew, one of the party minus his boots, which had been left fast in the mud.

The Regiment now completed its last period of garrisoning the line at Cordonnerie. The general defensive stability of the sector was considerably greater than when the Regiment first entered into occupation in October. A large number of shelters had been erected for the accommodation of the garrison, the front and support lines and communication trenches had been materially strengthened, and a very extensive system of wire entanglements had been completed over the forward area. In all of this work the Regiment had been hampered by the worst possible conditions of weather. On the 1st Battalion being relieved in the line, it proceeded to billets in the Rue de Quesnoy and neighbourhood, and eight days later, on January 24th, went back to Divisional reserve at Bac St. Maur. On the same day command of the Cordonnerie sector passed from the 2nd Infantry Brigade to the 3rd (Rifle) Brigade. The 2nd Battalion of the Regiment had meantime proceeded to billets in the area of Sailly.

CHAPTER IV.

BOIS GRENIER.

THE Regiment had now barely settled down in the belief that a period of pleasant rest was ahead of it, when on the morning of January 26th advice was unexpectedly received that the 2nd New Zealand Infantry Brigade was to relieve the 101st Brigade of the 34th Division, immediately adjoining the left of the New Zealand Division. This really meant an extension of the Divisional front to the north   The relief was to be completed by midnight on the 26th, and it fell to the lot of the 1st Battalion of Otago to forthwith get into marching order and take the road for the new area.

The sector to be taken over was known as Bois Grenier, and was situated approximately midway between the Sailly and Armentieres sectors. Otago went into the line direct after a long and vigorous march, and by 10.45 p.m. the relief of the 10th Lincolns was accomplished without hitch or interruption. The night was bitterly cold and the front line accommodation was of the most meagre description. On the following morning, the 27th, the enemy artillery raked our front line and communication trenches for several hours.

The new area was similar in many respects to the one held at Cordonnerie, the country being low-lying and flat, but as a result of the continued hard frosts was now very much drier under foot. The enemy's activity here was confined for the most part to exceedingly heavy minenwerfer " shoots," which in most instances were fortunately directed to a section of the line that was never actually garrisoned, and known as Jock's Joy. One result of minenwerfer fire was the existence of craters of extraordinary size and depth, there being few projectiles used during the war that were more effective for battering down or destroying defences in the shortest possible time. It will also be generally agreed that their moral effect was not inconsiderable.

The 2nd Battalion had followed the 1st Battalion on the 26th to the vicinity of Erquinghem and relieved the 11th Suffolks; 4th, 8th, and 10th Companies going into billets and 14th Company occupying a series of four posts in the subsidiary line. On February 3rd the 1st Battalion was relieved in the line by the 2nd Battalion, and on the 11th a further interchange was effected. Commencing on February 4th, a number of officers and non-commissioned officers of the 57th Division, which had recently arrived from England and was to relieve the New Zealand Division at an early date, were attached to the battalion in line in order to gain knowledge of the sector and the method of holding it. At this stage the low-lying country of Flanders was frequently enveloped in dense fog throughout the day, and while this fact afforded working parties protection from enemy observation, it proved exceedingly disconcerting to patrols, there being occasions when our patrolling parties, having completely lost their sense of direction, had found it necessary to lie out in No Man's Land until a late hour in the morning, when a momentary lifting of the fog revealed the relative positions of the lines.

The frosts experienced at this period were so severe and had been so continuous that the ground was frozen hard to a considerable depth; and although fatigue parties were despatched at an early hour every morning from the battalion in billets, it was practically impossible to make any impression on the ground with pick or shovel, and much of the time and energy so expended might have been better employed. This was the most severe and prolonged European winter experienced over a period of 30 years, and it exacted the last ounce of vitality to withstand it. For weeks in succession the sun failed to show itself through the dense fog, several inches of snow lay over the country-side, and the general outlook was depressing in the extreme. The only compensating feature was that while during the earlier months of the season almost the whole area of Flanders was under water and deep in mud, the ground was now dry and hard under the influence of the continued frosts.

On February 16th, betwen 8 and 8.30 p.m., the left group of the New Zealand Artillery, together with trench mortars, carried out a " dummy " raiding bombardment of the enemy's lines in view of a projected operation. The enemy's response was immediate and heavy, more particularly on the right of the Brigade sector, indicating that he was thoroughly alarmed ; but the damage to that part of the line held by Otago was inconsiderable. On February 19th the 1st Battalion was to have been relieved by the 2nd Battalion, but owing to the assumed capture of some of the members of a patrol which had entered No Man's Land at the apex of the Bridoux Salient on the right of the line held by Otago troops, the relief was postponed for a period of 24 hours. The 2nd Battalion of Otago thus took over the line on the 20th, and four days later the Regiment was relieved as a whole by troops of the 172nd Brigade of the 57th Division ; the 1st Battalion in reserve handing over to the 2nd-5th South Lancashires, and the 2nd Battalion to the 2nd-4th South Lancashires. Command of the Brigade sector passed on the following day. The 1st Battalion moved off to billets at Noveau Monde, and two days later proceeded to Nieppe ; while the 2nd Battalion, after spending a night at Sailly, marched to De Seule.

The Regiment, now in Divisional reserve, remained in these localities for a period of approximately three weeks, and spent a very profitable and enjoyable time in training, which was for the most part of a recreational order. Football matches were played, sports meetings held, and cross-country races run. The military side of training was not neglected, many useful lessons being learned on the area selected near Bailleul, particularly in regard to the new fighting organisation of a battalion ; Brigadier-General W. G. Braithwaite, Commanding the 2nd New Zealand Infantry Brigade, critically noting the operations.

On March 9th the Regiment paraded on the Bailleul-Nieppe Road for inspection by Major-General Sir A. Godley, who was accompanied by the Right Hon. Walter Long, Secretary of State for the Colonies. The morning was exceedingly cold and bleak, and on this account and because of the fact that everyone had to stand for an unduly long time under the weight of full packs, the occasion did not excite any particular enthusiasm. The period of rest and training finally came to a close, and although the weather was at times bad and the billets only passably good, the complete respite from the line and from fatigues was very welcome ; while the attempts, ultimately successful, of an enemy aeroplane to bring down in flames a British observation balloon over Nieppe, probably ranked first as a diversion for troops behind the line. On March 3rd Major D. Colquhoun left the 1st Battalion and proceeded to the United Kingdom for the purpose of organising and taking command of the 3rd Battalion of the Regiment about to be formed with the establishment of the 4th New Zealand Infantry Brigade.

On March 10th orders were issued for the relief by the New Zealand Division of the 36th Division in the area extending from St. Yves Avenue on the right to the Wulverghem-Wytschaete Road on the left, generally known as the Messines or Douve sector.

CHAPTER V.

MESSINES.

ON the morning of March 14th, 1917, the 1st Battalion of the Regiment marched out ot Nieppe, passed through Romarin and Neuve Eglise *en route*, and went direct into the line fronting Messines in relief of part of the 13th Royal Irish Rifles and the 9th Royal Irish Fusiliers. This was in compliance with an order for the relief by the New Zealand Division of the 36th Division in the Messines or Douve sector. On the tollowing day the 2nd Battalion of the Regiment lett De Seule, and by midday was established in Kortepyp Camp, near Neuve Eglise.

The sector thus taken over by the Regiment extended trom the Wulverghem-Wytschaete Road on the left to where the Wulverghem-Messines Road crossed our front line on the right. On the lett extremity, known as Slush Gap, the distance between the opposing front lines was less than one hundred yards ; but commencing almost at the right battalion boundary, the German line swung back at right angles across the valley of the Steenbeek, and thence following a course along the lower slopes of the opposite ridge, formed a deep re-entrant. Standing on the right extremity of the dominating ridge which overlooked our lines and far to the rear, was the gaunt skeleton of Messines ; away to the lett the village of Wytschaete ; and in the shelter of the valley to our leit rear a few battered buildings which marked the site ot the village of Wulverghem.

In taking over the new sector, 4th and 8th Companies occupied the front line with two platoons each, the balance of their strength in Fort Osborne and Surrey Lane and in Agnes Street respectively. The remaining two companies, 10th and 14th, occupied Forbes Terrace, S.P. 4, Fisher's Place and

159

Marine Terrace. The sector, generally speaking, was in a moderately good state of defence and repair; and along the partially sheltered reverse slope of the ridge on which the foremost line was sited, there were numbers of deep shelters in which the main garrison of the defences was quartered. The attitude of the enemy during the first few days of our tenure was such as to indicate that he had been accustomed to regard our side of the line with a great deal of complacence. This state of affairs was quickly altered by the aggressiveness of the Battalion sniping organisation, and it was only a question of time when a complete ascendency was gained over the enemy in this phase of trench-to-trench warfare. Our first period of holding the line in the Messines sector was comparatively quiet; but while the enemy artillery was only periodically active our own artillery carried out some effective early morning "shoots" at targets presented by working parties on the Messines Ridge. On March 22nd the 1st Battalion went back to billets and reserve at Kortepyp Camp, and the 2nd Battalion of the Regiment took over the line. On the following day the 1st Battalion moved across to Vuaxhall, Belfast and Hillside Camps a short distance off.

In the course of a Divisional memorandum issued at this date, it was pointed out that the enemy could concentrate sufficient reserves for an offensive on a large scale on the Western Front. It was thought probable that should the enemy attack the blow would fall on the Second Army in the neighbourhood of the Ypres Salient, extending as far south as Hill 63. It was also decided that an attack on Armentieres in strength, either as a diversion or to assist an attack on Hill 63, would require to be taken into account. It was further considered that the weight of such an attack would fall on the Ypres Salient, and as the position there was dangerously exposed, withdrawal on that front was more likely to be necessary than opposite the southern flank of the enemy's attack. The defence of Hill 63 and of Neuve Eglise in rear of it was therefore of the utmost importance, as they furnished a pivot connecting our front line system with the second line positions on which the troops holding the Ypres Salient might fall back. The defence of Armentieres, which to a large extent prevented Hill 63 from being outflanked from the south, was also important.

BRIG.-GENERAL W. G. BRAITHWAITE, C.B., C.M.G.,
D.S.O., (D.), [F.]

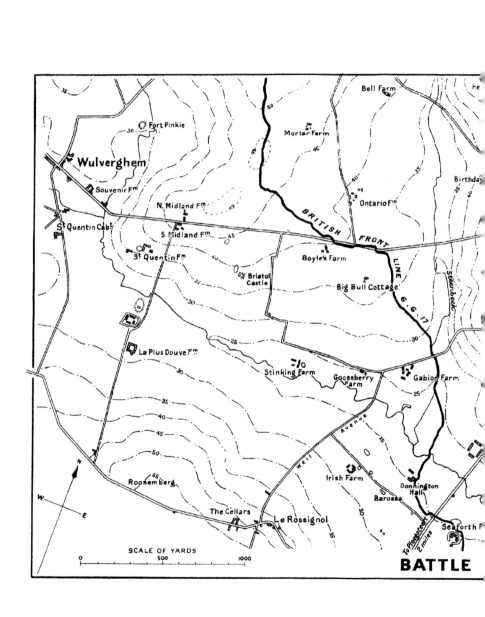

Bell Farm

He

Fort Pinkie

Mortar Farm

Wulverghem

Souvenir Fm

N. Midland Fm

Ontario Fm

Birthda

St Quentin Cab

S. Midland Fm

BRITISH

FRONT

St Quentin Fm

Boyle's Farm

Bristol
Castle

Big Bull Cottage

LINE 6.6.17

Steenbeek

La Plus Douve Fm

Stinking Farm

Goosberry
Farm

Gabion Farm

Avenue

N

Roosemberg

Irish Farm

Donnington
Hall

W

Barossa

E

The Cellars

Le Rossignol

Seaforth F

Well

To Ploegsteert
2 miles

SCALE OF YARDS

0   500   1000

BATTLE

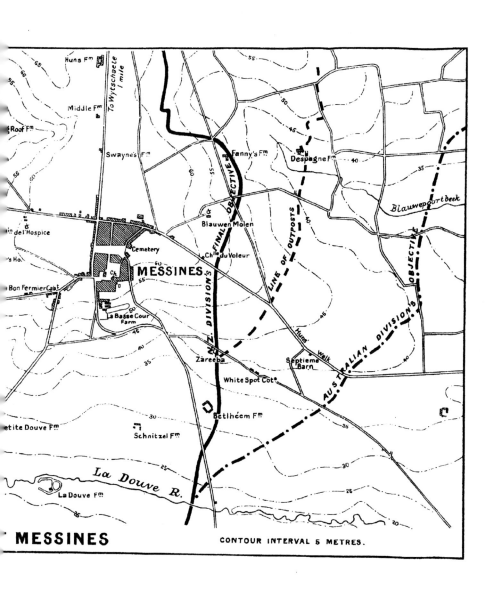

MESSINES   CONTOUR INTERVAL 5 METRES.

The 2nd New Zealand Infantry Brigade when in the line was tactically responsible for the front line from the River Douve to the Wulverghem-Wytschaete Road and for the subsidiary line and all the intervening area. The right Brigade was responsible for the defence of Hill 63 and of Ploegsteert Wood within the Divisional area. Maintenance and improvement of the trench system was an important consideration. Front line companies were to carry out two hours work per day, and companies of support battalions five hours per day, exclusive of time occupied in moving to and from work. Each Battalion in Brigade support was always to have one company ready to move at 15 minutes' notice throughout the night, with the remainder of its strength ready to move within three-quarters of an hour, in fighting order. In the application of the general principles of defence formulated, troops and Vickers machine guns were to be distributed in depth; the ground between front and subsidiary lines was to be organised so that it could be fought bit by bit; the front line was to be held by a minimum garrison consistent with safety; and finally, the placing of Vickers guns in the front line was to be avoided.

In keeping with the above policy, and for the purposes of establishing a reliable defensive system, it was found necessary to outline at once a considerable amount of constructive work, and in the allotment of working areas the 1st Battalion of Otago was made responsible for its front line, Surrey Lane, Midland Farm, and the Wulverghem Switch Line; while the 2nd Battalion was allotted its front line, Spring Walk, Northumberland Avenue, Durham Road, and part of the Wulverghem Switch. On the 16th a new subsidiary line, extending from Hill 63 to connect with the Wulverghem Switch at Wulverghem, was selected. Thus the Regiment was committed to a big programme of trench work immediately on moving into the Messines sector; and even at the outset the fatigue parties supplied by the battalion in reserve comprised as many as 450 men per day. Midland Farm, for maintaining the defences of which the 1st Battalion was responsible, was practically the mainstay of the front line system. It included a system of deep dug-outs and galleries connected with the trenches by stairways; the whole of the defences of this redoubt being such as to assure a protracted resistance.

At 4 o'clock on the morning of March 24th the enemy opened a terrific bombardment over the left of the sector occupied by the 2nd Battalion of the Regiment, the full force of his fire being directed over the locality extending from Spring Walk to the Wulverghem-Wytschaete Road and beyond, across Slush Gap and into the neighbouring Division's sector. The bombardment opened with heavy minenwerfer fire, followed by high explosive shell and shrapnel. The S.O.S. call was immediately sent to the 1st Field Battery by the officer on trench duty. Shortly afterwards the wire to the 15th Howitzer Battery and the direct wire to the Artillery Brigade were cut by the heavy shelling. Our artillery retaliation, however, was prompt in reply to the first call, and being on the correct sector gave immediate support to our infantry. About five minutes after the opening of the bombardment numbers of Germans moving in two lines in single file and estimated in strength at about 80, were observed advancing across No Man's Land. Our Lewis guns at once opened fire on them, and it appeared as if the attack might be beaten off. The enemy, however, succeeded in entering our front line between Durhum Road and Northumberland Avenue, and penetrated to a depth of about 100 yards. They were finally driven out by our Lewis gunners and bombers, who displayed great gallantry under a most intense bombardment. Between 5 and 5.10 a.m. the bombardment slackened off and a few minutes later ceased. Our casualties were 12 killed, 21 wounded, and one missing, believed buried. Three members of the Lewis gun crew of the left post were killed and one wounded, and the remaining man stuck to his post to the last.

Our front trenches suffered badly, and Spring Walk, Northumberland Avenue, and Durham Road were badly damaged. On the left the signal station was demolished and all wires cut, and the signallers had to be dug out, but were uninjured. The raiders did not escape punishment, and there was much evidence of blood on the outer side of the parapet. One wounded German was left in our lines riddled with bullets, and was sent back to the adjoining Division's dressing station on the Wytschaete Road. The preliminary bombardment was of a very heavy and destructive nature ; but the raiders could hardly claim to have achieved any permanent or material success. The enemy who penetrated the line at Slush Gap left behind several boxes of explosive, which suggested that they had aimed at reaching our underground workings.

On March 30th the 1st Battalion returned to the line in relief of the 2nd Battalion. While in reserve some of the companies had not been free from enemy shelling, apparently intended for batteries in the same locality, and it was during one of these occasions that 2nd-Lieut. F. C. Whittaker received wounds from which he subsequently died. On April 5th the Battalion was relieved in the line by the 8th Border Regiment of the 25th Division, and moved back to Kortepyp, command of the left sector passing to the 75th Brigade of the 25th Division on the same afternoon. The weather during this stage was still bitterly cold, and there were frequent heavy falls of snow ; and there was in addition the cheerless reflection that the long and dreary European winter was not yet at an end. On April 4th the 2nd Battalion shifted camp to De Seule. Although the two Battalions were now out of the line, practically the full strength of the Regiment was being directed to the prosecution of front line work either by day or night. The journey to and from the line was in itself an exhausting ordeal owing to the great distance to be covered ; the only consolation being that our back areas were at this time practically free from the attentions of enemy long range artillery, and undisturbed rest was afforded as a consequence.

It had long since become apparent by reason of the amount of preparation in progress behind our lines in the way of road and railway construction, the erection of dressing stations, the digging of gun-pits in forward positions, and the arrival of long range guns, that a big attack on Messines Ridge was imminent. All this evidence provided food for speculation ; and the work that was being carried out in the front line areas with so much energy was regarded with a special interest as being part of the attack preparations. On the night of April 13th an operation involving the construction of a great trench line in No Man's Land under the very nose of the German garrison was daringly undertaken and accomplished without incurring a single casualty. It was necessary to construct this trench as a stepping-off line for an impending attack owing to the depth existing between our front line and the enemy's from its point of intersection by the Wulverghem-Messines Road on the left and its meeting with the Steenbeek on the right ; and also in order to obtain improved alignment. The length of the new work was approximately 1,100 yards, and its greatest distance from our line 180 yards. There was a considerable amount of preliminary work to be done in the direction of patrolling and reconnoitring No Man's Land in order to obtain complete control of it, also in siting and taping out the trench ; and in this connection exhaustive and valuable work was performed by Lieut. C. H. Molloy, of the 1st Battalion.

Early in the evening of April 13th five officers and 400 men under the command and direction of Major J. Hargest, M.C., moved up to the line, and shortly after 10 o'clock went out into No Man's Land and commenced digging operations. In view of its proximity to the enemy's line, and the very large number of men employed, the operation was naturally regarded as a very hazardous and delicate one ; but it was so well organised and controlled by Major Hargest, and was prosecuted with such vigour that by three o'clock on the following morning it had been entirely completed and the whole party was clear of the area. The accomplishment of this task was always regarded as a remarkably fine performance. A strong covering party was furnished by the Wellington Battalion, but beyond certain desultory shelling the night was quiet and the enemy apparently unaware of what was going on. The existence of 1,100 yards of freshly constructed trench in No Man's Land doubtless occasioned surprise and interest in the enemy's lines on the following morning, and it was noticeable that during the day some of his artillery registered on it. The entirely successful completion of this undertaking, and the special reconnaissance performed by Lieut. Molloy, were the subject of a congratulatory message from Brigadier-General Braithwaite, which was read out on the following evening, when the last working party from the 1st Battalion during the month of April assembled prior to moving up to the line.

On the morning of the 14th an unlucky enemy shell struck a pile of trench mortar bombs at Ration Dump, alongside La Plus Douve Farm. A terrific explosion followed, and of a working party from the 2nd Battalion four men were killed and one wounded. Subsequently a German official communication stated that in consequence of the traffic observed for several days going to and from a building over which flew the Red Cross flag, they had shelled it and a loud explosion followed ; the implied suggestion being that the Red Cross flag was being used to conceal the presence of an ammunition dump. This was put forward as a counter-blast to charges made against the enemy at that time of sinking British hospital ships. As a matter of fact, there was a dressing station about 300 yards away over which the Red Cross flag flew, and the enemy was entirely wrong in his assumption that there was any connection between the dump at La Plus Douve Farm and the building which did duty as an advanced dressing station.

On the morning of April 16th the Regiment temporarily turned its back on the line and the strenuous work of trench construction for a period of intensive training, and set out for the Quelmes area, approximately 50 miles distant. During a three days' march there were occasional falls of snow and sleet. The 1st Battalion, after successive nightly halts at Sec Bois and Sercus, finally settled in the area of Esquerdes, while the 2nd Battalion, after halts en route at Strazelle and Eblinghem, entered the area of Leuline, Etrehem, and Hudethun. Here, under the direction of Brigade, a systematic course of training was commenced, and in ten days a great deal of strenuous and valuable work was accomplished. Attack practice figured largely in the syllabus, and it was in these exercises, aided by an exact model of the German defences over the Messines Ridge, that the real lessons were learned for the important operation to which the Regiment was shortly to be committed. During the course of manoeuvres visits or inspection were made by General Plumer, Commanding the Second Army, and by General Russell, Commanding the New Zealand Division, and there were frequent lectures and conferences for officers on matters of training and in relation to the concerted attack itself. On May 1st the Regiment commenced its return journey. The 1st Battalion was back at Kortepyp Camp on the evening of the 3rd, and the 2nd Battalion reached De Seule on the same day.

The storm clouds were now gathering on the horizon ;
the rumble of gun fire was growing louder and more insistent
day by day ; trench mortars had commenced the cutting of
the enemy's wire, and all the preparations for impending
attack were advancing under the eyes of an enemy from whom,
by reason of his dominating position, they could not well be
concealed. At 9.30 p.m. on May 5th the enemy opened a
heavy bombardment of our back areas. This was continued
for an hour, repeated at midnight, and again at 4 a.m. The
1st Battalion was compelled to beat a hasty retreat from
Kortepyp Camp to the adjoining fields, and later it was deemed
advisable to dig in there as a means of shelter. As it was
eight men were killed and eleven wounded, and the huts were
badly damaged. On the occasion of this unexpected bombardment the Division sustained a total of 106 casualties, and in
addition lost over 80 horses. Our artillery fired 2,500 rounds
on the enemy billets and back areas by way of retaliation,
and on the following night when the enemy repeated his performance, though with nothing like the same disastrous results
owing to the precautions taken, again replied vigorously.
The real punishment, however, was meted out on the night
of the 7th, when our artillery, in conjunction with the whole
of the formidable forces of the Second Army, opened out on
selected targets in the enemy's rear areas with five minutes'
intense fire, and at 11 o'clock repeated this very salutary lesson.

With the return of the Regiment no time had been lost
in resuming the front line labours on which it had been engaged
previously. A vast amount of preliminary work, such as
the construction of assembly trenches and approaches, still
required to be carried out, demanding the constant employment of units not actually engaged in garrisoning the line.
The control and direction of the whole comprehensive programme of work for which the 2nd Infantry Brigade was
responsible was entrusted to Major J. Hargest, of the 1st
Battalion of Otago. The construction of the Otira Assembly
Trench, 600 yards in length and traversed, was commenced
on the 9th, and a few days later the travel trench was opened
out and completed. On May 10th command of the Wulverghem
sector, the left portion of the New Zealand Divisional sector,
had passed to the 25th Division. On the 22nd the 1st Battalion moved to Hill 63, and the 2nd Battalion relieved the

1st Battalion of the 3rd (Rifle) Brigade in the front line between Currie Avenue and Medicine Hat Trail, with headquarters at McBride's Mansions. With the 1st Battalion fatigues continued to be the order of the day and night, cutting new trenches and improving others. The assembly trenches, although their construction involved a vast amount of labour, were only intended for disposing troops for a few hours prior to the commencement of attack.

Hill 63, where the 1st Battalion was now quartered, was like most other areas, not immune from enemy shelling, and on the 26th a direct hit on one of the huts killed two men and wounded another of 14th Company. As a result of the increasing intensity of enemy artillery retaliation, the casualties of the 2nd Battalion during its tenure of the line totalled three killed and 23 wounded. Patrols were out constantly over night in order to determine the attitude of the enemy. A patrol from the 1st Battalion, comprising ten other ranks under 2nd-Lieut. A. R. Cockerell, succeeded in penetrating to the enemy support line, and established the important fact that the enemy was holding the immediate front mainly by means of two great strongholds, the Moulin de l'Hospice on the right and Birthday Farm on the left. On the same night four artillery officers were taken out by this patrol for a distance of about 300 yards in order to determine the state of the Wulverghem-Messines Road for the passage of artillery.

The 2nd Battalion was relieved by the 1st Battalion of the Regiment during the afternoon of May 30th, and moved back to the slopes of Hill 63, to return daily or nightly to trench labours. On the early morning of June 1st Major W. G. Wray, M.C., was wounded by a shell which burst outside his quarters, and in consequence he was evacuated. During the afternoon and early on the following morning the enemy heavily bombarded our front line system, but all this was as nothing compared to the manner in which our own artillery was pounding the enemy and his defences. The Battalion's front line was being garrisoned at this stage by 4th and 8th Companies, with 10th Company at Petawawa Farm, and 14th Company at Red Lodge. The maintenance of nightly patrols with a view to announcing immediately any change in the enemy's dispositions and attitude towards

167

our ever-increasing artillery hostility and other indications of impending attack, was essential to the accumulation of an accurate intelligence in relation to the enemy, and in this important preparatory phase a large share of the work devolved upon 2nd-Lieut. C. F. Wilkie.

On the night of June 1st Major J. Hargest, accompanied by Sergt. T. Sounness, 8th (Southland) Company, penetrated a considerable distance through the enemy's lines. When within 50 yards of Uhlan Support, a party of 20 Germans emerged from a partially demolished structure in rear, and moving quickly in single file worked their way from shell-hole to shell-hole towards their front line. It was assumed that they were moving out to establish a series of listening posts, and in order not to be cut off, it was deemed expedient by our patrol to withdraw. The enemy's trenches were found to be battered almost beyond recognition, and no evidence of occupation was encountered over the front system. Scarcely a 1oot of ground remained that was not pitted or churned, some of the shell-holes being from ten to fifteen feet deep. It was in this inferno of unceasing shell fire and up-heavals of the earth's surface that the enemy garrison of the Messines Ridge lived for several days before the final blow overwhelmed them.

On June 2nd the 2nd Battalion took over the remaining portion of the Brigade sector, 10th and 14th Companies relieving troops of the 1st Battalion of Canterbury. The sector held now extended to Donnington Hall on the right. During the same afternoon the Corps artillery opened a violent bombardment over the Messines Ridge, with a practice barrage on No Man's Land, the enemy replying vigorously over our several communication trenches. Our casualties were one killed and six wounded; the precaution having been taken previously of withdrawing most of the garrison from the front line. On the morning of June 3rd Otago was relieved by Auckland troops, and marched back to the area of concentration at Canteen Corner. Here over the succeeding three days the Regiment was finally organised and equipped and rested before going into battle; an important side of this preparation being represented by lengthy conferences and discussions on the various phases of the *Magnum Opus*.

PREPARATIONS FOR BATTLE.

A brief study covering the period of the early part of 1917 will throw some light on the Allied situation then existing on the Western Front, and the relation which the Battle of Messines was to bear to the general scheme. In accordance with the plan of campaign adopted by the Allied Armies for the year 1917, a series of offensives were to be launched on all fronts, so timed as to assist each other by depriving the enemy of the power of drawing upon any one of his fronts in order to reinforce others. One of the fronts selected for these operations was Flanders, where an attack was to follow immediately upon one at Arras. The positions held by the Allies in the Ypres Salient since May, 1915, were under the direct observation of the enemy and at the mercy of his well-placed artillery. Their defence under such unequal conditions imposed a long and exhausting strain. It was maintained that our positions would be vastly improved by the capture of the Messines-Wytschaete Ridge, and of the high ground extending thence north-eastwards for several miles, and trending north through Broodseinde and Passchendaele. Subsequently, certain modifications were made in the general plan, due to unexpected military and political developments in the early weeks of the year, and to new proposals for action submitted by the French. The principle of the Spring offensive was, however, adhered to ; and it was agreed that if the full results hoped for from the combined British and French operations were not achieved in a reasonable time the main efforts of the British should be transferred to Flanders, as originally intended.

On April 9th the First and Third Armies, which were entrusted with the main British attack, opened the Spring Campaign with the Arras Offensive, and later the Fourth and Fifth Armies co-operated. At the close of six days fighting distinct successes had been achieved, measured in captures, ground gained, and the number of German divisions attracted to the area of the attack. Our front had been advanced four miles further east, and all the dominating features of the landscape, including the well-known Vimy Ridge, were in our possession. On April 16th the French followed with their main attack on the Aisne, and on April

23rd the British reopened the ball on a front of nine miles from Croisilles to Gavrelle. Obstinate resistance and strong counter-attacks at first stemmed the British tide, and the advance had to be renewed on the following day, this time with more definite success. The final attacks of the Arras Offensive were launched at Monchy-le-Preux and at Fresnoy, the former on April 28th, and the latter on May 3rd. The French attacked at Chemin des Dames on May 5th, and brought to a close the Spring Campaign and the first half of the Allied general plan. The Campaign had been successful at many points ; but it was not as decisive as had been hoped.

Attention was now directed to the development of the Northern plan of operations. The first phase of this, the Summer Campaign, was the delivering of a blow by the Second Army, which embraced the New Zealand Division, against the Messines-Wytschaete Ridge. The capture of this dominating geographical feature was an essential preliminary to the completion of the preparations for the offensive east and north of Ypres, which was to follow. Meantime activity was maintained on the Arras front in order to cover intentions. The immediate preparations for the Messines attack were as elaborate as those that preceded either the Somme or Arras Battles ; but in view of the manner in which the enemy overlooked us it was doubtful if our intentions were long concealed ; and as time advanced the only real uncertainty for the enemy was when the attack would actually be launched.

The preliminary work involved a big programme of road and railway construction, the assembling and registering of artillery, the establishment of forward dumps, the erection of dressing stations, and the problem of water supply. There was also the deep mining offensive, which had, in fact, been carried on for many months in face of stupendous difficulties of construction and the dangers of active counter-mining by the enemy. Along the original Second Army front there were 24 mines, which had involved the driving of 8,000 yards of galleries. Of these four mines were outside the front finally selected for the attack and one other was lost as the result of a mine blown by the enemy. This left 19 mines charged with over one million pounds of explosives as one of the terrible and unparalleled forces to be employed against the enemy in the Messines Battle.

A brief topographical explanation will assist the reader to visualise the situation and appreciate the task involved. The Messines-Wytschaete Ridge lay almost midway between the towns of Armentieres and Ypres. Situated at the eastern end of a chain of abrupt, isolated hills which divided the valleys of the Rivers Lys and Yser, it linked up with the rising ground which stretched north-east from Wytschaete to the Ypres-Menin Road, and then northwards past Passchendaele to Staden. The village of Messines, situated on the southern spur of the ridge, commanded a wide view of the Lys Valley and enfiladed the British lines to the south. Northwest of Messines was the village of Wytschaete, situated at the point of the salient and on the highest part of the ridge and commanding even more completely the town of Ypres and the whole of the British positions in the Ypres Salient. The Messines Ridge had many great natural advantages, and these the enemy during his long tenure had developed to the utmost. Messines and Wytschaete villages stood as the main centres of resistance, with numerous farm-houses and buildings, outwardly innocent looking shacks, as strong-points of great tactical strength. The German front line skirted the western foot of the ridge in a deep curve ; the second line system followed the crest of the ridge and formed an inner curve. The forward defences consisted of an elaborate and intricate system of well-wired trenches and strong-points, forming a defensive belt approximately 2,000 yards in depth. The many farms and woods were well prepared for defence, and the face of the ridge was liberally punctuated with strongly constructed and well concealed machine gun emplacements, with concrete dug-outs designed to protect the garrisons against the effects of our artillery fire. The enemy had fortified these naturally strong positions in a manner calculated by him to form an impregnable barrier to any attack on the part of the Allies.

A systematic bombardment of the enemy's elaborate trench system and defences and the cutting of wire had commenced on May 21st, and was intensified about seven days later. Night firing on a grand scale commenced on May 27th and 28th, when billets, headquarters and villages in the enemy back areas were shelled by long-range artillery, and a continuous barrage maintained over his communications in order to make it practically impossible for him to bring up supplies, to relieve or to reinforce the garrison of the Ridge. For ten days and before the assault was launched, our artillery carried out a most extensive and destructive programme of counter-battery fire. In this phase of warfare there was most determined retaliation by the enemy, and over the last few days a great artillery duel raged, in the course of which many of our guns were demolished and great dumps of ammunition blown up.

On June 3rd elaborate orders for the attack and capture of the Messines-Wytschaete Ridge were issued. The operation was entrusted to the Second Army, under the Command of General Sir Herbert Plumer, and the front selected for the attack extended from a point opposite St. Yves to Mount Sorrell inclusive, a distance, following the curve of the salient, of between nine and ten miles. The final objective was the Oosttaverne Line between these two points ; and the greatest depth to which the attack was to penetrate represented about two and a-half miles. The frontage allotted to the II. Anzac Corps, which embraced the New Zealand, the 3rd Australian, and the 25th Divisions, extended from St. Yves to the Wulverghem-Wytschaete Road.

The attack of the Corps was divided into two phases, as follows : 1st—The attack and capture of the Black Line, which extended across the forward side of the village of Messines ; 2nd—The attack and capture of the Green or Oosttaverne Line. The first phase was to be carried out by troops of three Divisions disposed side by side, namely, the 3rd Australian, the New Zealand, and the 25th, from right to left. The second phase was to be carried out by the 3rd and 4th Australian Divisions ; and to this end the 4th Australian Division was to pass through the New Zealand and 25th Divisions and capture the Green Line opposite the fronts of those Divisions. The New Zealand Division, being in the centre of the Corps front, was thus entrusted with the honour of capturing Messines Village. In the allotment of tasks within the New Zealand Divisional area, the 2nd Infantry Brigade and the 3rd (Rifle) Brigade were committed to the capture of the first and second German lines on the forward slopes of the ridge and the village of Messines itself. The two Brigades were to attack side by side, the 2nd Brigade

172

on the left and the 3rd Brigade on the right, the Brigade boundary being represented by a straight line drawn from a point in Hanbury Support, along the line of the Gooseberry Farm-Messines Road, and through the centre of the village. In the subdivision of the 2nd Brigade task the attack was to be carried out with two battalions in front, namely, the 1st Battalion of Otago on the left, and the 1st Battalion of Canterbury on the right, with the inter-battalion boundary represented by a line running from our new front line at Calgary Avenue to the road junction at Moulin de l'Hospice (inclusive to Otago), thence along the Wulverghem-Messines Road to the cross-roads on the north-western side of the village. The 4th (Otago) Company, commanded by Captain C. H. Molloy, on the right, and 8th (Southland) Company, commanded by Captain J. Thompson, on the left, were detailed to capture that portion of the objective allotted to the 1st Battalion of Otago ; and special parties from these two companies were detailed to deal with the two strong-points—the Moulin de l'Hospice on the right, and Birthday Farm on the left. The 10th (North Otago) Company and two platoons of 14th (South Otago) Company, the whole under Captain E. F. Selby, with Lieut. E. V. Freed in immediate command of the two 14th Company platoons, were committed to the capture of the enemy trenches between the Wulverghem-Messines Road and the left Divisional boundary. The Battalion reserve comprised the remaining two platoons of 14th Company, which were to follow the troops assigned to the second objective as far as the German front line, and there under cover await orders. Captain D. Rae was appointed Liason Officer to the Irish Brigade on the immediate left of the New Zealand Division.

After the capture of Oyster Reserve Trench, or Brown Line, by the 1st Battalions of Otago and Canterbury, a further advance was necessary in order to straighten out the line. The 2nd Brigade's main objective, the capture of Messines and the formation of a defensive line round the eastern side, was entrusted to the 2nd Battalion of Canterbury, to which was attached one company of the 2nd Battalion of Otago. This particular company, the 10th (North Otago), was responsible for straightening out the line on the left, and in its path was one of the enemy's formidable strongholds,

173

known as Swayne's Farm. The 2nd Battalion of Otago, less 10th Company, constituted the Brigade reserve, and if required was to be prepared to assist in the capture of the forward line of objectives within the Brigade area, or to move to any threatened point in the event of hostile counter-attack. The capture of the foremost line, known as the Black Line, the establishment of strong-points on the Black Dotted Line still further ahead, and the capture of enemy guns was to be carried out by troops of the 1st Infantry Brigade.

Owing to the tact that the German trench system swung forward sharply from our line of stepping-off, it was realised that the 25th Division on the immediate left of the New Zealand Division would be considerably in rear of our left flank when the general move commenced at zero. The left flank of the New Zealand Division would thus be exposed to the enemy until such time as the left Division of the Corps had advanced sufficiently far to effect a junction, which, according to the time-table of attack, was expected to take place when in line with Occur Avenue. Thereafter troops of the two Divisions would advance in close touch to the Black Line, when the three attacking Divisions of the Corps should be side by side. In thus leaving our left flank temporarily exposed there was an element of danger, but under the circumstances it was unavoidable ; and in order to reduce the attendant risks to a minimum protection was to be afforded by an artillery and machine gun barrage and by a smoke screen.

Twelve tanks were detailed to co-operate with the Division, and eight of these were allotted to the 2nd Infantry Brigade. All plans for the capture of objectives, however, were based on the supposition that no co-operation from tanks would be forthcoming, thus providing against any failure on their part to get forward with the infantry.

The arrangements for the participation of a stupendous array of artillery were most elaborate and complete, and included all the intricate details of barrages, creeping and standing, for the actual attack ; for counter-battery work, and the shelling of back areas and communications ; and finally for the pushing forward of guns once our objectives had been won, and then reopening on new lines and fresh targets. This meant an extraordinary concentration of artillery, from rows of 18-pounders established within a few hundred yards of our front line, to siege artillery and long-range guns mounted on rails and concealed in dummy houses. In addition to medium and heavy howitzers, the attack of the New Zealand Division was to be directly supported by nineteen 18-pounder batteries, representing 114 guns, and six 4.5 in. howitzer batteries, representing 36 howitzers. Immediately prior to the assault there was not to be any intensified bombardment, and artillery work was to be carried on as usual until zero as a precautionary measure against affording the enemy any indication of the hour of attack. From the German front line onwards the advance was to be protected and supported as follows :—(a) A creeping 18-pounder barrage moving in advance of the infantry with lifts of 100 yards ; (b) a standing 18-pounder barrage to ensure that the infantry as they advanced were not shot at through the creeping barrage ; (c) a standing barrage provided by 4.5 in. howitzers, which would lift when the infantry approached to within approximately 300 yards ; (d) a medium and heavy howitzer barrage which would lift when the infantry approached to within approximately 400 yards. These barrages were to be established on successive trenches and strong-points within the limits of safety of each gun or howitzer in such a manner that the whole of the area over which the infantry had to pass was kept under fire until the last possible moment. A new feature in attack in the way of barrages was to be provided by 144 machine guns along the Corps front, and of this number 56 were allotted to the New Zealand Division. In addition, eight Stokes mortars were attached to the various battalions as useful weapons for battering down or completing the destruction of any stronghold found to be still holding out.

The leading Battalions of Otago and Canterbury Regiments were to move forward on a two company frontage. The two leading waves were to be responsible for the capture of the first objective, the Blue Line ; the third wave for the second or Brown Line ; and the fourth wave in the case of Otago was to be used for straightening out the Brown Line on the extreme left. The 2nd Battalion of Canterbury, plus the 10th Company of the 2nd Battalion of Otago, was to follow the two leading Battalions on a two company frontage at a distance of not more than 50 yards, and the 2nd Battalion of Otago was in turn to move in rear of Canterbury, with its left on the Wulverghem-Messines Road, and form up in a position of readiness in the dead ground in the valley of the Steenbeek.

At eight o'clock on the evening of June 6th the 1st Battalion of the Regiment, under the command of Lieut.-Colonel A. B. Charters, paraded in full attack order ; an hour later the 2nd Battalion paraded similarly equipped. Lieut.-Colonel G. S. Smith at this stage temporarily handed over command of the 2nd Battalion to Major McCrae, and proceeded to Morbecque. The Regiment now moved off from its area of concentration, and commenced the march to the positions of assembly in the forward zone. The allotment of assembly positions was as follows :—1st Battalions of Otago and Canterbury Regiments, in the new advanced trench and Otira Trench ; 2nd Battalion of Canterbury Regiment, in Auckland and Canterbury Trenches ; 2nd Battalion of Otago Regiment, in Napier and Canterbury cut north of Calgary Avenue. The arrangement of positions was successfully accomplished and to time, although it had to be effected under very trying conditions. The enemy poured gas shells over our communication trenches throughout the evening and the early part of the night, which necessitated the wearing of gas helmets when moving through the affected areas. By 12.30 a.m. on June 7th all troops of the 2nd New Zealand Infantry Brigade were in position in their assembly trenches. The 1st Battalion of the Regiment was at fighting strength of 27 officers and 576 other ranks ; the 2nd Battalion at 26 officers and 772 other ranks.

Zero hour, the opening moment of the attack, was fixed for 3.10 a.m. on June 7th. The few preceding hours remained comparatively quiet, the intervening time being devoted to rest and sleep or sober reflection and thought. Four minutes prior to zero a section of machine guns opened its barrage, and although this might have led to confusion and alarmed the enemy, it apparently passed unnoticed ; and the morning being dark and misty, a premature forward move by some of the troops in the rear assembly trenches was not observed.

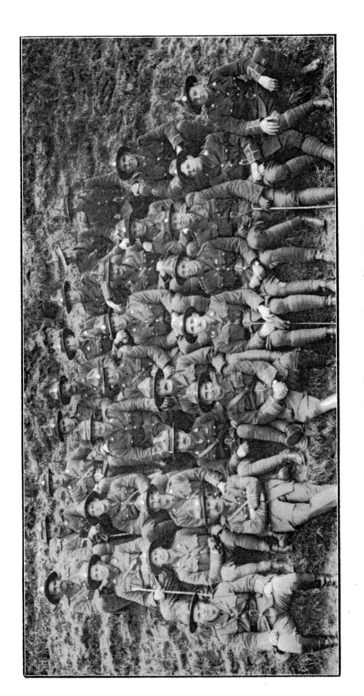

OFFICERS OF 1ST BATTALION, OTAGO REGIMENT.

(From a Photograph taken before Battle of Messines.)

THE ATTACK LAUNCHED.

Punctually to time the great series of underground mines were fired, the effect instantly being a premonitory heaving and trembling of the earth, as if Nature, in some mad freak of hideous sympathy with the prevalent human wickedness, was preparing to launch an assortment of horrors on her own account. Simultaneously with the rending of the blood-soaked Ridge, again to be the scene of desperate conflict, the dark and sullen sky, as yet untouched by the sleeping dawn, was suffused with a red glow as the fire of the massed artillery broke out along the line, its thunderous reverberations rolling over the distant spaces of the battlefield. The infantry were at once in motion, and in splendid unison were now sweeping over the foremost German defences.

The first trench system offered comparatively light resistance to our advance, and the attacking troops pressed on up the slopes of the Ridge to the assault of their main objectives. Within the hour the New Zealanders had captured Messines; before midday Irish troops had fought their way through Wytschaete; and then the attackers commenced to move down the eastern slopes of the Ridge. It was not long before our guns were being pushed forward. The final part of the Second Army's attack developed soon afterwards; by evening the advance had reached the approximate line of the final objective; and over 7,000 prisoners, 67 guns, 94 trench mortars, and 290 machine guns had fallen to the possession of the Second Army. The terrible and over-whelming destruction caused by the explosion of the underground mines, the pulverising blows of the artillery, and the rapidity with which the attack had been carried through by the infantry, left the enemy at the close of the day beaten and bewildered and the great stronghold of the Messines-Wytschaete Ridge in our hands.

The assaulting waves of the 1st Battalion of Otago Regiment, side by side with Canterbury troops, moved forward to the attack across No Man's Land at the appointed time. Seven minutes after zero, and before the enemy's counter-barrage came down, the whole of the 2nd Brigade troops were clear of the forward assembly trenches. The rapidity and ease with which this was accomplished, and the

177

subsequent comparative absence of indecision in the matter of assigned duties and direction were to be attributed to the frequent rehearsals of the attack during the period of training prior to the offensive. Moving in extended order, and closely following the barrage, the Otago Infantry crossed the valley of the Steenbeek and commenced the attack of the slopes in front. The German front line they had taken in their stride, and with almost incredible speed had captured and were consolidating the first objective. The two great strongholds, Moulin de l'Hospice and Birthday Farm, were surrounded and captured before the garrisons could do any material damage with their machine guns ; and in and around these localities five machine guns and 50 prisoners were taken and a number of the enemy killed. The two platoons committed to the capture of the Moulin de l'Hospice, in consequence of casualties to officers, were led to the final assault by Sergt. J. H. Wilson. A single machine gun had continued firing even up to the point when the position was surrounded, until it was finally put out of action by Sergt. J. Mason. Immediately this objective was gained consolidation was commenced over a line 80 yards in advance of the enemy strong-point ; and it was at this stage that Pte. C. A. Fitzpatrick on jumping into a shell-hole encountered an enemy machine gun which he forthwith attacked single-handed, bayoneting five of the crew and capturing the gun and one of the enemy.

The 10th Company and two platoons of 14th Company, under the command of Captain E. F. Selby, which were committed to Otago's portion of the second objective, moved forward and similarly quickly overwhelmed the opposition. Continuing their advance, they established themselves on a line approximately 200 yards in rear of Swayne's Farm, and there commenced consolidation. A machine gun now came into action from Swayne's Farm and threatened to interfere with operations. This new development was, however, countered by the arrival of one of the two tanks (the second having been ditched on the way up) detailed to co-operate with 10th Company and the two platoons of 14th Company. Captain Selby directed the tank commander's attention to the enemy opposition at Swayne's Farm, and the tank was headed straight for the redoubt, demolishing the superstructure and compelling the surrender of the garrison and large numbers of the enemy who had apparently collected there for shelter.

Consolidation on the line gained now continued without interruption ; but it was found necessary to construct and garrison about 100 yards of trench towards the left in order to connect up with the troops of the 25th Division, this actually being beyond the New Zealand Division's boundary. Lieut. Freed, in immediate command of the two platoons of 14th Company, had materially assisted with his formation towards the success of operations, though wounded early in the attack.

The suddenness of the assault and the fact that our attacking infantry had broken into the hostile defences almost at the moment the barrage lifted, afforded the enemy small chance of bringing his machine guns into action. Without our effective barrage and swiftly attacking infantry the German strongholds encountered, with their two or three machine guns and their garrisons varying in strength from 15 to 40 men, would have presented expensive propositions. Consolidation having been commenced over the new ground, it was not long before sufficient depth had been dug to afford comparatively good cover. Digging operations were vigorously pushed ahead throughout the day, and the positions strongly fortified against possible counter-attack. The two reserve platoons of 14th Company were directed to assist with the consolidation of the second objective, and Battalion Headquarters was established in a concrete emplacement on the Wulverghem-Messines Road, above the Moulin de 'Hospice.

On the right Canterbury troops had also made quick progress, capturing their first objective after meeting with inconsiderable opposition and securing 17 prisoners and three machine guns from the redoubt known as Au Bon Fermier Cabaret.

The 2nd Battalion of the Regiment (Major McCrae in command), less 10th Company, moved forward at zero from its assembly positions in artillery formation, and reached the position assigned to it at 3.16 a.m., where the troops dug in on a line named New Oyster Trench, and at 4 a.m. Battalion Headquarters was established there. The 2nd

Battalion of the Regiment constituted the Brigade reserve, and was to assist in the capture of the forward objective if required. Accordingly, at 5 a.m. the 14th Company, commanded by Captain Bremner, went forward to act as support to the 2nd Battalion of Canterbury, while No. 14 platoon joined in the mopping-up of Messines Village, afterwards assisting in conjunction with Nos. 13 and 16 platoons in the consolidation of New Oxonian Trench forward of Messines ; No. 15 platoon digging in as a reserve in rear of the village. One platoon of 4th Company received orders to construct a trench connecting Canterbury's left flank with the right flank of the 25th Division east of Swayne's Farm. This was accomplished by 2.30 p.m., though not without casualties, for fairly heavy shell fire was now being experienced. The 4th Company, commanded by Captain P. Spiers, advanced to reinforce the 2nd Battalion of Canterbury, but after halting and taking cover on the crest of the ridge found that its services were not required, and moved back to New Oyster Trench. Two platoons of 8th Company went forward and assisted Canterbury in the work of consolidation. By 6 p.m., the 4th, 8th, and 14th Companies had returned to New Oyster Trench, and by 10 p.m. had completed consolidation over a distance of 600 yards.

Under the command of 2nd-Lieut. (Temp.-Captain) J. Rodgers, M.M., 10th Company of the 2nd Battalion of Otago, which was attached to Canterbury and was entrusted with the task of capturing October Support from its junction with Oxonian Trench to the left Divisional boundary, carried out its task with the 25th Division in line on the left, and under heavy shell fire dug in about 200 yards in advance of its section of the Yellow Line. Practically no artillery fire had been encountered until the enemy's support line was passed, and no heavy fire until the objective was occupied. The earlier successful intervention of a tank had practically disposed of Swayne's Farm as a serious obstacle to progress, and there remained but a few stragglers to round up. The Distinguished Conduct Medal was conferred upon Company Sergt.-major J. C. Fothergill for his fine service during the period of consolidating the captured position. The same distinction was won by Pte. T. J. Beck, Battalion runner, who, though twice wounded, had remained on duty.

The 2nd Battalion of Canterbury, in clearing the village of Messines, was temporarily held up south of the Square, but the process of envelopment from left and right relieved the situation. Here a large number of the enemy were killed, several machine guns knocked out, and 180 prisoners taken. Opposition from enemy trenches in the cemetery was dealt with, and the capture of the Yellow Line was completed. The enemy's shelling of the forward area became increasingly heavy as the day advanced, and the gradual withdrawal of troops of the 2nd Battalion of Otago relieved the congestion and appreciably minimised casualties. At 8 a.m. Major McCrae had gone forward to the 2nd Battalion of Canterbury and found that unit's Commanding Officer, Lieut.-Colonel H. Stewart, badly wounded, and at his request assumed command until the arrival of Major Starnes shortly afterwards.

During the clearing of Messines our artillery had placed a " box " barrage round the village. The task of the 1st Brigade troops, following upon the capture of Messines, may be briefly described. Their particular operation was the establishment of the Black Line and the Black Dotted Line ahead, which was to serve as a jumping-off place for the 4th Australian Division in its attack on the foremost lines of the day's advance, the Green Dotted and Green Lines. Following in the wake of the 2nd and 3rd Brigade troops, they had established themselves on the Black Line by 5.30 a.m. Stubborn resistance was encountered at several points, and two 77 mm. guns, several machine guns, and many prisoners were captured. There was a pause in the attack for about three hours, and at 8.40 a.m. parties moved forward under cover of the barrage, captured one 77 mm. field gun, established posts on the Black Dotted Line, and sent out patrols to reconnoitre the ground ahead.

Shortly after 1 p.m. the enemy were observed from various points to be heavily massing for counter-attack, and soon were advancing in several waves along the whole of the Divisional front, preceded by an intense barrage over our forward lines. Similar reports of a counter-attack developing came from the 25th Division on the left. Our artillery barrage was immediately called for and brought down ; many machine guns joined in the firing and the counter-attack was effectively stopped and crushed.

At 3.10 p.m., following upon a further pause in the attack, the 12th Brigade of the 4th Australian Division advanced through the New Zealand troops on the Black Dotted Line. In this operation, representing a continuance of the day's battle, the Australians apparently met with much resistance and heavy fire from newly prepared gun positions, which the long break in the attack time-table had afforded the enemy every opportunity of establishing. The right Battalion was reported to have been held up by concrete machine gun emplacements, and later in the evening the left Battalion was reported to be on its objective. About 8.30 p.m. there were reports of a further enemy counter-attack, and during the evening several S.O.S. calls were received by the artillery, which opened up at S.O.S. rates; but beyond the enemy's heavy shelling it was doubtful if there was any real justification for the vast expenditure of ammunition which these calls involved. There were counter-attacks, both threatened and launched, at various points of the Australian front on the following day, when the enemy shelling was persistently heavy; while our aeroplanes reported considerable enemy movement over the back roads, all of it in a westerly direction. However, the forward line was definitely established by 10 o'clock on the morning of the 8th, and at 9 a.m. on the 9th the 4th Australian Division assumed command of the front held in advance of the New Zealand Division as far back as Messines and including that place. The New Zealanders then went into Corps reserve, and at midday the 2nd Infantry Brigade was ordered to commence dribbling its battalions back to billeting areas.

We now return to the troops of the Regiment. On the night of June 7th-8th arrangements were made for the 2nd Infantry Brigade to carry out within 48 hours a relief which involved holding the Purple Line and all ground west of Messines and east of the original No Man's Land. Accordingly orders were issued for the 1st and 2nd Battalions of Otago to remain in the trenches they were holding and complete consolidation. The headquarters of all battalions were moved back to their original places in the assembly trenches, whence it was much easier to maintain telephone communication with companies and with Brigade. Throughout the night the enemy artillery heavily pounded Messines and the trenches east and west of it ; the infantry over this area suffering severely, particularly from enfilade fire from the direction of Frelingien and Deulemont. During the early hours of the morning of the 8th, 10th Company of the 2nd Battalion of Otago was withdrawn from the 2nd Battalion of Canterbury, and rejoined its own unit in reserve. The 1st New Zealand Infantry Brigade was still holding the Black and Black Dotted Lines.

About 8.45 on the night of the 8th the enemy sent up the S.O.S. signal all along the line, evidently under the impression that we were about to make a further advance. The enemy's artillery barrage and our counter-barrage were intense ; but there was a certain wildness about the German shooting. This artillery duel lasted for about two hours, and finally as the fire of our guns slackened off, that of the enemy died down. About 11 p.m. a report was received from the 25th Division on the left that they were being attacked, and that a mixed force of New Zealanders, Australians, and English troops were falling back ; but the alarm was apparently occasioned by the fact that a relief was being effected to which the troops referred to belonged. Thereafter, there were no further alarms, and comparative quietness prevailed.

During the morning of the 9th arrangements were made for the 2nd Infantry Brigade, then in close battle reserve, to be relieved that night by the 4th Australian Brigade ; but at 2 p.m. orders were received to withdraw into Corps rest area without being relieved by other troops. Instructions were accordingly issued for Battalions to withdraw independently to the Waterloo Road area, and at 5 p.m. the 1st Battalion of Otago left its trenches and marched back to rest billets at Mahutonga Camp. The 4th, 8th, and 14th Companies of the 2nd Battalion had on the previous night commenced digging a communication trench from the junction of Oxonian Trench and October Support to connect with the extension of Calgary Avenue, and completed the work at 10 a.m. on the 9th. At 2.30 p.m. the Battalion moved back to Vauxhall Camp, arriving there late in the evening. Here over the succeeding days the Regiment secured that rest which it had so splendidly earned.

The extensive and careful preparations over the period immediately preceding the attack, the splendid unison in which all arms worked, the wonderful co-operation of a mighty array of artillery, and the incomparable work of the infantry, combined with the splendid leadership of officers and non-commissioned officers, made the Messines Battle a decisive and sweeping success. The operation was a set piece in which everyone knew his duty intimately and well ; an important factor in the execution of a scheme of attack so superlatively vital in its issue, so vast in the range of its unavoidable complexities and the multiplicity of its interdependent detail, and depending so largely for its success on the clock-like precision of responsive and cohesive action throughout the whole of the large force employed ; on its readiness in meeting and overcoming unexpected difficulties and beating down resistance ; on its intelligence, courage and dominating will power ; all of which were most brilliantly in evidence in this memorable combination of leadership and fighting man. Needless to say there was abundant reason for the elation which followed the capture of Messines and its dominating and seemingly impregnable ridge. The casualties suffered during the actual attack were not heavy. The initial blow dealt the enemy was so sudden and so overwhelming as to leave him little time for recovery before the infantry were upon him. It was subsequent to the capture of the Ridge, under the enemy's intensely heavy shell fire, that our casualties commenced to mount up. Enfilade artillery fire from the southeast proved particularly damaging to us, and with so many troops in a congested area heavy losses were inevitable. From about 250 casualties during the actual attack, the 2nd Infantry Brigade's list had increased to 900 before relief was effected on the evening of the 9th.

Twelve tanks were allotted to the New Zealand Division for the attack. It was intended that eight of these should co-operate with the 2nd Infantry Brigade, but were to work independently, each to have its particular objective laid down. Strong protest was made by Brigadier-General Braithwaite against the tanks being brought up too close over night, because of the danger of their noise of movement giving notice of our time of attack to the enemy. In this he was finally successful, although it was understood that the delay would prevent the tanks from getting up in time to assist the attacking troops in taking their earlier objectives. As anticipated, their work was of comparatively small value, as six of them never got out of No Man's Land.

The list of captures made by the 1st Battalion of the Regiment included 160 prisoners, two 77 mm. field guns, and nine machine guns. The prisoners captured during the operation seemed to have lost all power of effective resistance as a result of the terrific artillery bombardment they had been subjected to, and apparently submissively resigned themselves to the attack and the irresistible power behind it.

The losses sustained by the Regiment in the Messines Battle were as follows :—1st Battalion—Killed, three officers and 30 other ranks ; wounded, three officers and 189 other ranks ; recorded as missing, 17 other ranks. The officers who fell in action were : Lieut. N. L. Forsythe, and 2nd-Lieuts. C. F. Wilkie and A. J. Tiddy ; among the list of other ranks killed in action was Lance-corp. J. P. Egan, D.C.M., who as stretcher-bearer had rendered long and splendid service to the Regiment. 2nd Battalion—Killed, 24 other ranks ; wounded, five officers and 113 other ranks ; recorded as missing, five other ranks. 2nd-Lieut. (Temp.-Captain) J. Rodgers, M.C., M.M., who displayed fine qualities of leadership during the operation, subsequently died of wounds received in action.

CHAPTER VI.

ST. YVES.

THE Regiment remained at Mahutonga Camp, in the Waterloo Road area, resting and reorganising, until June 12th, when orders were issued for the 2nd Brigade of the New Zealand Division to return to the line, and take over the St. Yves sector, lying between Messines on the north and the Bois de Ploegsteert on the south, and bounded by the River Douve on the left and Westminster Avenue on the right. In compliance with this order the 1st Battalion entered into occupation of the trenches of the left sub-sector, extending from the Douve to Ash Avenue, and relieved the 36th Battalion of the Australian Imperial Forces. Since our leaving the line at Messines on June 9th the Australians had pushed forward to a line opposite the village of Warneton, and had there established a series of outposts. The system of trenches known as the Potteries, in the same locality, had been captured, and the general advance accomplished represented a distance of approximately half a mile beyond the Green Line, which was the final objective of the attack of June 7th.

The new sector taken over by the 2nd Infantry Brigade was divided into two sub-sectors, each held by one battalion distributed in depth. It comprised flat, undulating country, with a low spur lying between the River Douve and Ultimo Avenue, about 1,500 yards to the south, and extending from La Hutte through St. Yves to a point approximately 1,000 yards west of Warneton, which was held by the enemy. South of this spur, between the eastern edge of Ploegsteert Wood and the Armentieres-Warneton railway, the country was slightly lower and nearly flat, wet in places, and difficult to drain. East of the railway the ground fell gradually to the River Lys, with sufficient slope for the drainage of trenches in the vicinity. Along the western bank of the river the ground was marshy in places.

The dispositions of the 1st Battalion of the Regiment on entering the line were as follows :—4th Company holding the outposts in front of the Potteries ; 10th and 14th Companies in the support trenches; and 8th Company in Battalion reserve. During the course of a preliminary reconnaissance of the sector by Company Commanders, Captain D. Rae, commanding 8th (Southland) Company, was wounded, and evacuated. The 2nd Battalion of the Regiment, in Brigade support, was billeted at the Catacombs, a system of deep tunnels under Hill 63, on the northern edge of the Bois de Ploegsteert. On the afternoon of the day on which the line was taken over, the 4th New Zealand Infantry Brigade, which was in line on the right, and was then attached to the 3rd Australian Division, had found the German front and support lines south of St. Yves evacuated. These positions they occupied during the night, thereby straightening out our front over the old German support line and removing the salient of the Birdcage. On the 2nd Brigade taking over its part of the line on the night of June 12th, patrols were sent forward from various points in order to determine if the enemy still held the adjacent strong-points. These patrols moved out in the direction of Sunken Farm, Knoll 30, and Flattened Farm, and also down the River Douve. Owing to the early dawn not much information could be gained ; but there was something definite in the fact that the patrols were fired upon from Flattened Farm and Knoll 30. Later on a patrol was sent out in the direction of Trois Tilleuls Farm to the south, but returned without information ; though when another patrol was sent out it was fired upon when approaching this point. Patrols also worked along Ultra Support and Ultra Lane, but no enemy was encountered.

During the night battalions in the line consolidated and strengthened their front trenches and advanced posts, which had been handed over in a very poor state, especially those in the Potteries system, where we were supposed to take over five posts at a strength of 20 men in each, but where actually there were only three posts with a garrison of seven men in each. Certain points on our front occupied by detachments of the Corps Mounted Troops were also relieved by the 1st Battalion of the Regiment. As the Brigade sector had been taken over on a night of intense darkness and no previous knowledge of the ground existed, successful patrol work was exceedingly difficult, if not impossible.

On June 13th instructions were issued for the 2nd Infantry Brigade to advance its front to a depth of 1,500 yards, and to seize the enemy's forward posts, with the intention of eventually linking them up. This line was to run approximately from the road near La Truie Farm, and then north through Sunken Farm, to the Douve River, thus extending along the western side of Warneton Village and connecting with a similar advanced line thrown forward on our left by the 75th Brigade, and on our right by the 3rd New Zealand (Rifle) Brigade. The operation was to be carried out during the evening without the assistance of an artillery barrage. It was calculated that the undertaking was a comparatively simple one ; that it was merely a question of dribbling forward small parties unobserved by the enemy and seizing successive objectives on the way, each objective affording support and covering fire for the capture of the next. It was further presumed that the enemy had withdrawn his main strength. The task, however, was really beset with many difficulties, and was by no means as easy of accomplishment as was anticipated.

Late in the afternoon information was received that the 25th Division, on our left, had no intention of moving forward that day without artillery support, and that therefore the New Zealand Division was committed to the operation alone and without artillery support. It was accordingly undertaken, but was only partially successful. Troops of the 3rd (Rifle) Brigade on our right reached their objective, but those of the 2nd Infantry Brigade came under heavy fire from the enemy artillery, which doubtless, as the result of a reconnoitring visit from several low-flying aeroplanes, anticipated our advance. Instead of going forward at 9 p.m., Otago in consequence did not move until 11.30 p.m. The night was intensely dark, the troops committed to the attack did not know their country, and there was great danger of losing direction. This was actually what happened to Otago on the left. They completely lost their way, and finally arrived back at where they had started out from without accomplishing anything. Canterbury was in a sense more fortunate and did slightly better. Troops of that battalion occupied

Flattened Farm, and established a strong-point to the right of it, but considerably in rear of the intended objective. After weathering the enemy artillery barrage, heavy machine gun fire was encountered ; there were some mistakes in the matter of recognition of points, and when daylight broke and put an end to operations Canterbury had reached and was holding an exposed line approximate to Unchained Trench. The operation was a costly one and could certainly not be regarded as successful.

The original intention was that this undertaking should have been carried out by the two battalions of the 2nd Brigade which had suffered least during the attack on Messines. With this object the 2nd Battalion of Otago and the 1st Battalion of Canterbury had been placed in the Catacombs, prior to being brought up during the hours of darkness for the advance ; the 1st Battalion of Otago and the 2nd Battalion of Canterbury meantime holding the Brigade line. It had been further understood that the attack would take place at dawn, when the assembly could have been accomplished under cover of darkness. It eventually turned out, as already stated, that the attack was to take place in the evening, and it being impossible to assemble in daylight without announcing our intentions, the two battalions holding the line had perforce to be committed to the attack. Thus weariness was added to a certain unpreparedness.

On June 14th steps were taken with a view to making a second attempt on this advanced line. At half-past seven in the evening the operation was launched under a heavy artillery barrage. The objectives were the same as previously, excepting that Otago was detailed to deal with Sunken Farm in order to relieve Canterbury, who had suffered severely from the enemy's shelling on the previous night. The 10th (North Otago) Company, commanded by Captain C. Bryce, made an advance of approximately 800 yards, and established a series of three strong-points overlooking Warneton from the west. Subsequently, one of these strong-points, on the left, was evacuated by our garrison under the stress of heavy shelling, thereby leaving the right flank dangerously exposed until it was later restored. One platoon of 8th (Southland) Company, under 2nd-Lieut. A. R. Cockerell, captured Sunken Farm, and dug in about 50 yards beyond. To the right of

Sunken Farm, and now in rear of our outpost line, was a position which the enemy, apparently unaware of our new dispositions, about an hour later came out to reoccupy, but with disastrous results to themselves ; for being allowed to come within close range, they were shot down to the last man. Our casualties during the operation, due mainly to machine gun fire from the direction of the railway line west of Warneton, were two killed and 34 wounded ; but the advance, despite many adverse conditions, was carried out with dash and skill. Canterbury, on the right, encountered the enemy in considerable strength in places, and after brisk fighting captured Au Chasseur Cabaret, and La Truie Farm. The enemy retreated along the La Basse-Ville Road, and there vainly endeavoured to rally. The left strong-point established by Otago at a point adjoining the River Douve linked up with the 75th Brigade, which, now operating in conjunction, had also carried its objectives. The enemy still held the Warneton railway line, and occupied many of the houses in rear of it, but the pushing forward of posts had actually been successful along the whole Army front, and brought us up against the Warneton line. This was as far as it was then desirable to advance.

Over the succeeding 24 hours there was heavy enemy shelling, a great deal of which was directed to the Potteries system of trenches. Retaliation was asked for from our heavy artillery on several occasions, and but spasmodically granted. At about 9 p.m. on the 15th the S.O.S. signal appeared on our left, and our field batteries maintained an intense fire for an hour. No counter-attack developed. During the day our Sunken Farm outpost accounted for two enemy snipers and drove a third from his position. At 10.30 p.m. on the 15th the Battalion was relieved by the 2nd Battalion of the Regiment, after which companies moved back to the Catacombs for a rest.

Prior to effecting this relief the 2nd Battalion of the Regiment, after leaving the Messines Sector on the 9th, had enjoyed a period of rest at Vauxhall Camp. On the 11th Lieut.-Colonel G. S. Smith returned from Morbecque and reassumed command of the Battalion. On the evening of the 12th a move was made to the Catacombs under Hill 63, and on the following day 8th and 14th Companies commenced the construction of a communication trench in rear of the Potteries system, and on the succeeding night completed the work. The remaining two companies of the Battalion on the night of the 14th constructed a second communication trench towards the Potteries. When the 2nd Battalion proceeded to take over the line on the 15th, it came under enemy shell fire, and several casualties were incurred. The 8th (Southland) Company occupied the advanced posts, 14th (South Otago) Company the second outpost line, and 4th (Otago) Company the main line in rear. The 10th (North Otago) Company occupied the reserve trenches at Prowse Point, and acted as carrying party for the forward troops during the period of garrisoning the line.

A great deal of work was necessary in order to consolidate and strengthen our recent gains. A new support line extending over a considerable distance required to be constructed, existing trenches to be deepened, and the forward posts to be wired. The whole of the Battalion, less those who garrisoned the advanced posts and a small garrison in each company sector, was engaged on these works during the two following nights, the whole of the available strength of the 1st Battalion being similarly employed. The tour of the line, brief though it was, was exceedingly strenuous. On the day of taking over the line, the enemy artillery heavily shelled our advanced posts and trenches, particularly the Potteries system. Our own batteries had previously retaliated at intervals, but the enemy apparently was not disposed to slacken off. Accordingly, shortly after midnight a heavy barrage and counter-battery fire was opened by our artillery and maintained for 15 minutes. This proved fairly effective in silencing the enemy. Low-flying German aeroplanes also displayed considerable activity, searching out our forward posts and trenches and firing their machine guns on the garrisons. Our casualties over the period, in consequence of this repeated hostile activity, amounted to 13 killed and 33 wounded.

At this period there were circumstances which seemed to indicate a German withdrawal from Warneton and the River Lys. There was no intention of advancing our line beyond the railway ; but in order to maintain touch with the enemy it was deemed advisable to send out a patrol as far as the railway line. Accordingly Otago established a post which commanded the railway and overlooked the village of Warneton. Later on, however, it became evident that the enemy had not withdrawn from Warneton as anticipated, as he was observed to be constructing strong-points which must serve to protect the village.

The 1st Battalion moved out of the Catacombs early on the morning of the 18th, and before noon was established in Kortepyp Camp. The 2nd Battalion was relieved in the line by the 1st Battalion of Auckland on the same day, and by 5.30 the following morning the last company had reached and settled down in camp at De Seule.

The total casualties sustained by the Regiment between June 6th and June 19th, a period of great activity and many hardships, were 23 officers and 544 other ranks, made up as follows :—1st Battalion—14 officers and 289 other ranks ; 2nd Battalion—9 officers and 255 other ranks. This total included, of course, the casualties sustained in the Messines operations.

Events in the line following upon the Otago Regiment going into rest area may be briefly summarised. Patrols entered La Basse-Ville, and further south Pont Rouge on the night of the 18th-19th June was found to have been evacuated by the enemy ; but he was still holding and covering Warneton by a series of trenches and fortified shell-holes and hedgerows. By June 30th the New Zealand Division had handed over the front to the 4th Australian Division.

The Regiment now turned its attention to reorganising and training. On the 21st, as part of the 2nd New Zealand Infantry Brigade, it was inspected by the Corps Commander, Lieut.-General Sir A. J. Godley. Later there was an inspection by the Divisional Commander, Major-General Sir A. H. Russell, while a small detachment proceeded to Bailleul for inspection by H.R.H. the Duke of Connaught. The time spent during the tour in reserve afforded much desired rest, and an opportunity for attending to many necessary details which came under the comprehensive heading of interior economy. On the 28th the Regiment moved to a new camping area close to the Neuve Eglise-Wulverghem Road.

On July 5th Major J. Hargest assumed command of the 1st Battalion, Lieut.-Colonel Charters having temporarily taken over command of the 2nd Brigade. On July 12th the Regiment struck camp, the 1st Battalion proceeding to the Berquin area, and the 2nd Battalion to Doulieu near by. On July 15th Lieut.-Colonel G. S. Smith proceeded to the United Kingdom on leave, and Major J. McCrae assumed command of the 2nd Battalion. On the 17th, however, he was evacuated sick, and Major Hargest, of the 1st Battalion, filled the vacancy, Captain (Temp.-Major) E. S. McIntyre in turn taking command of the 1st Battalion, and continuing in charge when Lieut.-Colonel Charters left for the United Kingdom on leave. On the 18th the 2nd Battalion having vacated its billets in the Doulieu area moved to Romarin Camp, and on the following day the 1st Battalion marched to the Catacombs under Hill 63.

CHAPTER VII.

LA BASSE-VILLE.

On the successful conclusion of operations against Messines and fronting Warneton, the final dispositions for the main Allied offensive east and north of Ypres were entered upon. Although driven from the Messines-Wytschaete Ridge, the enemy still possessed direct observation over the Ypres Salient from the east and south-east, as well as from the north. By the middle of July preparations were well advanced for this, the Third Battle of Ypres. The front of the Allied attack decided upon extended from the Lys River opposite Deulemont northwards to beyond Steenstraat, a distance of over 15 miles ; but the main blow was to be delivered by the Fifth Army on a front of about seven and a-half miles, from the Zillebeke-Zandvoorde Road to Boesinghe, inclusive. Covering the right of the Fifth Army, the task of the Second Army (which included the New Zealand Division) was to advance a short distance only, the main idea being to extend the threatened area of attack, and by that means force a distribution of the enemy strength.

The attack was launched on the morning of July 31st, and on the greater part of the selected front the resistance of the German infantry was quickly overcome and good progress made. At the close of the day, after fierce fighting, the British Fifth Army had carried the German first system of defence south of Westhoek, and except at Westhoek itself, where they were established in the outskirts, had gained the whole of the crest of the ridge and denied the enemy observation over the Ypres Plain. Further north the enemy's second line of defence had been captured as far as St. Julien, and north of that again the British held the line of the Steenbeek to our junction with the French, who had gained all their objectives. Meanwhile the attack on the Second Army front had also met

194

with complete success. A period of stormy weather now intervened, quickly transforming the battlefield into a vast and almost impassable bog, and rendering the further immediate development of the offensive impossible. We now turn to the participation by the Regiment in the Second Army's share in this Battle of Ypres and the incidents leading up to it.

On July 15th orders were issued for the relief by the New Zealand Division of the 4th Australian Division in the La Basse-Ville Sector, east of the Bois de Ploegsteert. The relief was to be accomplished on July 18th and 19th, and the attached troops of the 4th New Zealand Infantry Brigade were to remain in the line. The Australian Division was holding the front with the 13th Brigade, of which two battalions were in the front line, and two in close support. The New Zealand Division was to hold the front with two Brigades, differently disposed, each having two battalions in line as far back as the subsidiary line inclusive ; the third battalion of each Brigade to be under Hill 63, and the fourth at Kortepyp and Romarin respectively. The 1st and 2nd Infantry Brigades were to carry out the relief, while the New Zealand Divisional Artillery was to remain in the line covering the Divisional front. The 2nd Battalion of Otago, in accordance with the above relief, took over from the 49th Australian Battalion on July 19th. The two front line Companies were 4th and 10th, with 8th and 14th Companies in support. Active patrolling was immediately commenced and carried out nightly without encountering any definite enemy movement, while working parties constructed a new front line trench and generally improved the system of communication trenches. On the 22nd Major W. W. Turner returned from leave and temporarily assumed command of the Battalion. On the 23rd the Battalion was relieved by the 3rd Battalion of Canterbury, and marched to Regina Camp, on the Ploegsteert-Romarin Road. Two days later a move was made to billets at Nieppe. Lieut.-Colonel G. S. Smith returned to his command on the 30th.

The sojourn, from July 19th to July 28th, which the 1st Battalion spent at the Catacombs, was not free from hard work nor from enemy shelling. On the 20th casualties were sustained numbering five killed, including 2nd-Lieut. G. Richardson, and eight wounded, including Major E. S.

McIntyre, who subsequently died of wounds. The death of Major McIntyre, who was at this stage temporarily commanding the 1st Battalion, occasioned deep regret in the Regiment. Captain W. F. Tracy now assumed command of the Battalion until Major Hargest returned from the 2nd Battalion on the 22nd of the month. Large working parties were supplied for the forward area until the 29th, when the Battalion relieved Canterbury in the line. On the same night a series of new forward positions were established. On the following afternoon and during the evening the enemy artillery displayed a great deal of activity, and our heavy batteries effectively shelled La Basse-Ville and Deulemont. The former village was, in fact, to be the objective of the operations planned for July 31st as part of the Second Army's contribution to the Fifth Army's attack further north, and previously referred to. La Basse-Ville had actually been in our hands for a brief period on the morning of the 27th. A company of the 2nd Battalion of Wellington attacked and cleaned up the village in the early hours of the morning; but the small garrison left there was at 5 a.m. forced to withdraw under the pressure of a heavy counter-attack. In the course of this operation the enemy suffered rather heavily; and it was also made clear that his tenure of the village was not to be a lengthy one.

A second attack by troops of the 1st Brigade against La Basse-Ville and the adjoining defence systems was timed for 3.50 a.m. on July 31st. In conjunction with this operation certain tasks were entrusted to the 1st Battalion of Otago, which were to be carried out on the night preceding the attack on the village, and included pushing out and establishing a post still further in advance of those secured on the previous night and overlooking the Lys River south of the Sugar Refinery. The object was to prevent the enemy crossing the river at or south of the Sugar Refinery and attacking the troops of the 1st Brigade once they had established themselves in La Basse-Ville. This was successfully accomplished during the night, when 2nd-Lieut. S. Cook and a party of 17 other ranks of 8th Company moved out through the front line and Vulture Post and established themselves as directed. An additional post was established further south near the railway line. The two support Companies were fully engaged effecting communication through the medium of trenches between the front line and the several posts.

The attack of the Fifth Army, and the minor operations of the Second Army, were opened on the morning of July 31st with the results already outlined. In conjunction therewith, and co-incident with a diversion by the 3rd Australian Division north of Warneton, an attack was delivered by North Island troops against La Basse-Ville, and notwithstanding considerable resistance the village was finally left in our possession. One effect of this operation was to draw heavy shelling over our trenches and forward posts in the early morning. There was also a great deal of shell fire throughout the day, so much so, in fact, as to result in the entire garrison of one of our left posts becoming casualties. Generally speaking, the system received a severe battering, and the casualties at the close of the day had mounted to eight killed and 13 wounded. Our own artillery was mainly occupied in countering the enemy fire on our left.

The weather at this stage was exceedingly bad, and the difficulties of maintaining forward communications were greatly accentuated by the rain and mud. It was not until August 2nd that the enemy's artillery fire had slackened off appreciably after the excitement of the few preceding days. Our patrols now covered a wide range of ground by night, down to the River Lys and up as far as La Basse-Ville, and nothing was seen or heard of the enemy; but low-flying hostile aeroplanes were active over our lines during the early mornings. On the night of the 3rd an inter-Company relief was effected, 14th Company relieving 8th Company, and 4th Company taking over the positions occupied by 10th Company; and as before the two supporting Companies carried out the exhausting work of maintaining supplies of rations and water to the front line garrison. Owing to the low-lying nature of the ground and the difficulties of drainage, the trenches and approaches were in places almost thigh deep in mud and water, all movement calling for the expenditure of a great deal of energy. On the 5th the enemy threw a considerable number of lachrymatory shells over our forward posts during the hours of darkness. Relief on August 7th was provided by Canterbury, and Otago marched out of the line at La Basse-Ville after a strenuous tour, 8th Company being quartered in the Catacombs, and the remainder of the Battalion in Regina Camp, on the Ploegsteert-Romarin Road. It was on August 7th that Brigadier-General F. E. Johnston, C.B., who had commanded the New Zealand Infantry Brigade on the Gallipoli Peninsula, and was at this date in command of the 1st Infantry Brigade, was killed in action by an enemy sniper.

The 1st Battalion was now in Brigade support, but ahead of it lay a heavy programme of front line trench improvement and construction work. As the result of a Divisional Commander's conference held on August 6th orders were issued for the consolidation of our line of forward posts, and the digging of a new trench system throughout the sector. The establishment of a new post or position required to be followed immediately by measures of consolidation if its security was to be maintained and the garrison provided against counter-attack or shell fire. Accordingly, there was a call for large wiring, digging and carrying parties, and on the night of the 14th the full strength of the Battalion was so employed. The wiring of the left front of the Brigade sector having been completed, the Battalion constructed a new front line trench from the Sugar Refinery to a post named Zero, approximately 700 yards south. The tape-line for this trench was laid by Lieut.-Colonel Charters and Captain S. C. Greer, who had proceeded ahead for the purpose, and under whose supervision the work of digging was carried out. This represented a highly successful undertaking, and special commendation was accorded the Battalion by the Brigadier on its conclusion. There was well-merited rest on the following day, and the same tranquillity might have been enjoyed on the 16th had not the enemy during the morning shelled the camp enclosure and caused casualties to the number of two killed and eight wounded. On the same day the Battalion shifted camp to Canteen Corner. Again at night there was a demand for 500 men for working parties, and for 350 men on the following night. Early on the morning of August 21st the Battalion marched out from Canteen Corner to the La Motte area, and reached its new billets at Cautescure, where a pleasant time was spent until the 27th. On the 28th the Battalion left Cautescure, and after marching to Caestre, entrained for Wizernes. On arrival there the journey was continued by road to Seninghem. The weather was anything but favourable, and the march was a lengthy one, but the Battalion stood the test well.

Towards the close of July, the 2nd Battalion of the Regiment was resting at Nieppe, and the first day of August saw it back in the line. This was in relief of the 1st Battalion of Wellington at La Basse-Ville, and consequent upon the 2nd Infantry Brigade taking over the right battalion front of the 1st Brigade, including La Basse-Ville. The 8th and 14th Companies supplied the garrisons of the forward posts. All reliefs had been completed by 11 p.m., but the men were wet through with the heavy rain which fell all day. A patrol from 8th Company was immediately sent out, but no enemy was seen or heard across the front.

Throughout the 2nd the forward garrisons had to contend with heavy shelling, but it was not until strong retaliation had been insisted upon that the supporting artillery subjected the enemy to an hour's bombardment. This had the desired effect for a time, though during the night the enemy resumed his activity. Our casualties for the day were six killed and 17 wounded. Rain continued to fall steadily, and the trenches and posts were in a wretched state. There was a recrudescence of hostile shelling early on the following morning, and although artillery retaliation on our part had a quietening effect for a time, the enemy continued to open out at intervals during the day. This involved a further casualty list of two killed and 21 wounded. During the evening, and again towards midnight, the enemy fire was particularly violent over our outpost and front lines. On the 4th the enemy was as aggressive as ever. At 2.30 p.m. a party of 30 of the enemy was observed to leave a building at the south-western corner of Warneton, but no action developed. A few minutes later, however, an advanced group of our left Company, holding a post across the Warneton railway line, was blown out, all excepting two of the garrison being casualties. The enemy's artillery now remained quiescent until 10 p.m., when a heavy bombardment of our posts commenced and lasted for an hour, accompanied by a gas-shell bombardment of St. Yves, Prowse Point, and Ploegsteert Wood. The casualties for the day were one killed, one missing, and 14 wounded.

During the night a patrol under 2nd-Lieut. C. B. McClure, and comprising Sergt. Travis and six others, reconnoitred the western bank of the River Lys. Along the line of the embankment were several dug-outs, in the locality of which were many enemy dead, evidently the victims of our shell fire. During the course of a search some papers and maps were secured from the body of a German who was either a Company Commander or Intelligence Officer, and on the return of the patrol to our lines these were taken to Brigade Headquarters by Sergt. Travis and were found to contain information of considerable value in reference to enemy dispositions and intentions.

Early on the morning of the 5th an intense box barrage was placed over our sector. The retaliation of our artillery silenced the enemy an hour later, but there was subsequent intermittent shelling, the casualties for the day totalling five killed and 12 wounded. When the Battalion was relieved on the night of the 5th it had completed a tour which was remarkable for sustained and destructive shell fire, to say nothing of the almost unceasing rain and consequent depths of mud. The fact of the New Zealand Division being on the right flank of the northern attack had contributed to persistent artillery activity, so much so that during the first fortnight of August the Division lost the equivalent of more than a battalion, almost exclusively from shell fire. In addition to these losses the wretched state of the trenches, caused by the almost incessant rain, resulted in a considerable number being evacuated on account of sickness.

On relief the Battalion trekked back to Le Romarin Camp, the last Company reaching there at 2.30 a.m. on August 6th. Then followed a period of rest of a kind, interrupted by stormy weather and frequent heavy demands for working parties. Over this period, extending to the 21st, some important work was accomplished, including the digging of several hundred yards of new front line and communication trenches. Heavy rain frequently interfered with or caused operations to be entirely suspended, but when the programme had been completed, the Battalion earned the congratulations of the Brigadier for its efforts. On the 17th a change of location was effected from Le Romarin to Canteen Corner. On the 22nd the Battalion again struck camp, and following in the wake of the 1st Battalion marched out to Puresbecque, in the La Motte area, and settled down to preliminary training in view of approaching events. On the 28th a move was made to Seninghem, which was reached at 2 a.m. on August 29th. Two days later training operations were resumed.

During the greater part of the month of August our heavy artillery had daily carried out concentrated bombardments of the enemy's back areas, this being mainly in connection with operations to the north. Much of this fire was directed to the village of Warneton, where several blockhouses were exposed, disclosing the enemy system, in evidence elsewhere, of stout concrete emplacements within the shells and under the cover of old buildings. There was frequent hostile retaliation over our own rear areas, including the locality of Hyde Park Corner, where reserve troops were invariably quartered. The relief of the New Zealand Division by the 4th Australian Division and the 8th Division was completed by August 27th.

The Regiment remained in training in the Lumbres area over the greater part of September. In the course of training operations particular attention was paid to practice in trench and open warfare, wood fighting, attack and counter-attack, and musketry. In view of the changed methods of defence adopted by the enemy, and his new system of shell-hole defences, the principle of extreme depth in attack was adhered to during practice operations, while the formations used were in the nature of " worms " rather than waves and lines. New enemy methods of attack or defence demanded the introduction of new counter-measures.

On September 14th, at a point half a mile east of Harlettes, the Regiment participated in a review of the New Zealand Division by Sir Douglas Haig, Commander-in-Chief of the British Forces, who expressed his appreciation of the smart and business-like appearance of the troops of the Division. Among those who were present on the occasion of this review was Mr. Winston Churchill.

201

CHAPTER VIII.

YPRES.

YPRES is a name that will always live for soldiers of the Regiment for its indelible memories of the fighting in October, 1917, on the slopes leading up to Passchendaele, and the weary winter months during which they held the line on the ridges in front of Westhoek and Zonnebeke. Ypres itself was but the ghost of a city when the Regiment first saw it. The famous Cloth Hall and the stately old Cathedral, with all their grace and mellow beauty, had gone ; in their stead were but naked ruins, enough, merely, to tell the eye what beauty had been theirs. The successive agonies that the town had endured since its streets first echoed to the crash of bursting shells had left no place whole or undamaged, and the gaunt ruins and deserted streets suggested some city of the dead. There was a very small population, purely military, which existed in cellars and dug-outs under the tumbled bricks, or in the more secure burrowings under the ramparts behind the town. It was very silent by day, but at night the cobbled Square woke to the rumble of transport and the tread of marching men as they went up to the line or passed back, weary and mud-spattered. The town was not shelled very often during the winter, but it was a place where few cared to loiter, so sinister was its quiet and so complete its desolation.

Behind the town the road ran past Chateau Segard, where Divisional Headquarters was located in a collection of Nissen huts, on to Dickebusch, within a mile or so of which were the Artillery wagon lines and the big camps where the Infantry Brigades were quartered while out of the line. It was all typical Flanders country, flat and featureless, and besides being bombed by clear nights was shelled on occasions with the high velocity gun with which the enemy swept the whole area right back to Poperinghe. Nearly all the traffic to the

202

forward areas went through Ypres and out by the Menin Gate on to the Menin Road; a fine thoroughfare in the days of peace, straight and broad and lined with tall poplars. Of the poplars only the ragged stumps remained; and the significance of the names which had been given to the corners and cross-ways on the road was evidenced by its battered appearance and the destruction on either side.

Forward of Birr Cross Roads, some distance up the Menin Road from Ypres, the whole countryside had been so completely devastated by weeks and months of shelling that it had become merely an expanse of shell-holes in which the water almost brimmed over on to the surrounding mud. It was a drear prospect; the drab coloured earth showed no single trace of vegetation, and where had been pleasant wood-lands were but the blackened and naked remnants. On every hand was evidence of the bitter struggles of the late summer and autumn, and derelict tanks lay scattered about the slopes like petrified monsters of some prehistoric age. The only things that seemed to have escaped destruction and to be still intact were the squat " pill-boxes " to take each one of which so much human life had been sacrificed. They were freely distributed all along the ridges, and as they afforded protection against everything but very heavy shells they were always occupied and sometimes contended for. The ground was so water-logged that it was impossible to dig good dug-outs unless they were properly engineered, and timbered and drained; they had been constructed in some places, the biggest of them, like those at Halfway House and Cambridge House, being down at the foot of the slopes on either side of the Menin Road; but they were damp and evil-smelling, and constant pumping was necessary to keep them habitable.

There were two means of communication to the forward zone—the plank road and the duck-board track; but off these footing was not to be had. The plank roads provided good going, but they showed up very clearly on an aeroplane map, and the enemy gunners knew their every turn and angle. Off the roads the duck-board tracks seemed to wind inter-minably until they disappeared from sight over the slopes or down into the valleys, where sometimes they traversed bogs formed by the choked and overflowing streams which had once trickled along the bottom. Over by the remains of Polygone Wood the Butte de Polygone, a big long earthen mound which had been covered with trees and foliage but was now bare and pitted with constant shelling, made the most striking landmark on the whole sector. Inside it was a perfect honeycomb of passages and dug-outs which were occupied by the headquarters of one of the Infantry Brigades in the line, the headquarters of Battalions, and a variety of individuals. The Butte was a hub from which tracks radiated in all directions, and the enemy shelled it at odd intervals during the day or night, so it was a place to be approached warily and entered with all possible speed.

Beyond all this was the forward zone, foul and waterlogged, tortured by shell fire, and forbidding in its every aspect. Across this waste the men of the Infantry, heavily burdened, and deep in thought, slowly struggled up to the front and support lines, where under the meagre shelter of those sinuous ditches they maintained their ground throughout the long months of a dreadful winter, contending against the inexpressible misery produced by the elements and the constant destruction wrought by the enemy. On that account alone the name of Ypres will always recall a long series of hardship and suffering ; but it is because of the unexampled bravery, and the agony endured along the tragic slopes of Bellevue in the heroic though unavailing struggle for Passchendaele that Ypres above all must ever stand as a place of revered but yet sinister memories.

It was on September 24th that the New Zealand Division, then in training in the Lumbres area, received short notice to relieve the 59th Division in the holding of the Saint Jean sector, situated in the ill-favoured Salient of Ypres. At 3.30 a.m. on September 25th the Otago Regiment, after hurried preparation, moved out from its training area and headed for the forward zone.

The route followed by the 1st Battalion lay through Renescure, St. Marie Cappel, and Watou, the Ypres North area being reached on September 28th. The 2nd Battalion proceeded through Hallines, Wizernes, and Arques to the Renescure area, thence *via* Staples to St. Marie Cappel, and *via* Terdeghem and Steenvoorde to the Watou area, which was reached on the 27th, the Battalion finding quarters at Hill Camp. From here the Battalion proceeded by motor-lorries to Goldfish Chateau, west of Ypres, and during the evening continued its forward move and entered into occupation of the old German front and support lines at Wieltje, north-east of Ypres. On the night of September 29th-30th the 2nd Battalions of Otago and Canterbury took over the front held by the 178th Brigade of the 59th Division. Prior to taking over the new sector, Lieut.-Colonel Smith and the Company Commanders made a tour of the line, and while engaged in this preliminary reconnaissance Captain L. M. Scott, M.C., was wounded. Otago relieved troops of the 6th North Staffordshire Regiment. The change-over was completed shortly before midnight, and attracted considerable machine-gun fire, the enemy having apparently detected the movement. The position taken over by the Battalion was on the extreme left of the Second Army Front, and the issued instructions were that it was to be held at all costs. Battalion Headquarters was established at Cornhill Farm. On September 29th the 1st Battalions of Otago and Canterbury marched from the Ypres North area and relieved two battalions of the 177th Brigade in the support line of the right sector of the 59th Divisional Front, Otago's frontage extending from the Wieltje Road on the left to Pommern Castle trenches (exclusive) on the right, with Battalion Headquarters at Bank Farm. On the following morning Otago relieved the 2nd-5th Leicester Regiment in the holding of the front line. The 2nd Infantry Brigade had now completed the taking over of the whole of the 59th Divisional front, and on the morning of October 1st the G.O.C. New Zealand Division assumed command of the Saint Jean sector. The 1st and 4th Brigades constituted the Divisional reserve, with two Battalions of each Brigade in the vicinity of the old German front line trench system as reserve to the 2nd Brigade.

The new sector represented the line reached in the renewal of the offensive on September 26th, in the Third Battle of Ypres ; and in view of the fact that it had been wrested from the enemy but a few days previously, the area presented every phase of the devastation caused by concentrated shell fire maintained over a period of several weeks. No regular or continuous trenches marked the line of the forward system ; the whole sector was in a badly damaged and water-logged condition, and the entire area and its approaches bore remarkable and gruesome evidence of the havoc created by the violence of modern warfare. The line taken over extended north-west and south-east, and was approximately 1,000 yards west of Gravenstafel.

Between five and six o'clock on the morning of September 30th the enemy's artillery assumed an activity which grew in intensity as our retaliatory fire developed, until their combined aggressiveness reached the stage of a fierce artillery duel. By 6.15 a.m. the enemy's guns had been silenced; but another form of hostile activity presented itself when enemy aeroplanes hovered over our lines almost continuously during the remainder of the morning. In fact, the whole day was marked by considerable aerial activity, during the course of which one of our aeroplanes was forced to land after an engagement with four hostile machines. Following upon the morning's outburst, our artillery continued intermittently active throughout the day and night.

On October 2nd orders were issued for the relief of the 2nd Infantry Brigade by troops of the 1st and 4th Infantry Brigades; on the following night the 1st Battalion of the Regiment was relieved by the 3rd Battalion, marching back to the old British front line by way of the Wieltje Road, and remaining there over the 3rd in reserve to the 1st Brigade. The 2nd Battalion of the Regiment was relieved at the same time by the 1st Battalion of Auckland. Relief was accomplished shortly before midnight, and after bivouacking for the night, the Battalion moved back to the Ypres North area and into Divisional reserve. Wieltje was persistently shelled by the enemy throughout the day of the 3rd. The same evening troops of the 1st and 4th Infantry Brigades took up their positions for the attack against Gravenstafel and the Abraham Heights, which was launched on the following morning. It was in this attack, dealt with elsewhere, that the 3rd Battalion of Otago Regiment was committed to its first big effort. The operation was extraordinarily successful. All objectives were captured and consolidated, 1,160 prisoners and 60 machine guns were accounted for by the two Brigades concerned, and the enemy suffered a very serious set-back. At 2.30 p.m. on the 4th the whole of the 1st Battalion of Otago was ordered forward to Capricorn Keep in close support to the 1st Brigade, which was threatened with a counter-attack. The Battalion was finally relieved at midnight by West Riding troops, and on the 5th moved to the Winnezeele No. 1 area. The Regiment now prepared to move back, and surplus fighting material was returned to stores. At noon on the 5th the 2nd Battalion marched to the Vlamertinghe-Reninghelst Road, from which point it was to proceed to the Winnezeele area. The lorries did not arrive until 8 p.m., the result being that the Battalion did not reach its destination until 3 a.m. on the 6th. The Regiment rested there over the day, and on the 7th moved to the Eecke area in order to be near the railway line in the event of the Division being called upon to exploit the success of the 49th Division in the operations of the 9th. The night of the 7th-8th was exceedingly wet and stormy.

PASSCHENDAELE.

Plans were now being prepared which were again to bring the New Zealand Division into the Ypres Offensive, following immediately upon the attack to be launched on October 9th. Orders were issued to the 2nd Infantry Brigade to hold itself in readiness to take over the line held by the right Brigade of the 49th Division, and for transport and advance and reconnoitring parties to be ready to move to the Brandhoek area, and thence to " Y " Camp, near Saint Jean. Prior to moving off a large number of officers proceeded to Poperinghe to inspect a model of the Passchendaele position which was to be concerned in the forthcoming attack. The Regiment followed its advance parties in motor-lorries, and reached the allotted point about midday. At 5 p.m. the 2nd Battalion assembled fully equipped, and moved forward to take over the sector held by the 148th Brigade on the right half of the Divisional front. The new sector extended from Peter Pan in the north to the Ravebeek in the south, and was approximately 2,000 yards due west of Passchendaele. Relief was completed by 2 a.m. on the 11th, and Battalion Headquarters and the Regimental Aid Post were established at Waterloo Farm. The 1st Battalion had left " Y " Camp an hour later, and during the night of the 10th took up positions in rear of the 2nd Battalion. Command of the new sector passed from the 49th Division to the New Zealand Division at 10 a.m. on the 11th.

The dispositions of the troops of the 2nd Infantry Brigade on the completion of reliefs were as follows:— The 2nd Battalion of Otago Regiment in the front line, with rear troops on the line Boethoek-Boetleer; the 1st Battalion of Otago next in rear on the line Delva Farm-Schuler Farm; the 1st Battalion of Canterbury on the line Capricorn Keep-Pommern Castle; the 2nd Battalion of Canterbury in the old German front and support line, south of the Wieltje Road. At 3 p.m. on the 11th a conference of Commanding Officers was held at the Capitol (advanced Brigade Battle Headquarters) in regard to the impending attack.

The success achieved in the British attack on October 4th against the enemy strongholds on the line of the ridge east of Zonnebeke had marked a definite stage in the operations entered upon. A line had been established along the main ridge for a distance of 9,000 yards from the starting point near Mount Sorrel. The breaking of the weather and the consequent difficulties of movement made it doubtful, however, whether the remainder of the programme could be accomplished before the winter finally set in. The state of the ground, as a result of the continued heavy weather and persistent shelling, was daily becoming worse, and was to prove a terrible handicap in regard to both our preparations and the attack itself. Nevertheless, the Ypres Offensive was persisted in. On the morning of October 9th the British renewed the assault on a front of over six miles, from a point east of Zonnebeke to the junction with the French north-west of Langemarck. On the left the French prolonged the area of battle to a point opposite Draaibank, and on the right of the British main attack minor operations were undertaken east and south-east of Polygone Wood. Only a measure of success was achieved, and at many points the losses were severe. Arrangements were immediately made for a renewal of the offensive on October 12th. On this occasion the attack was launched between the Ypres-Roulers railway and Houthulst Forest. It progressed along the spurs and higher ground, but the valleys of the streams which ran westward from the main ridge, and which were overlooked by formidable enemy defences, proved impassable. It was in this operation that the Regiment was to become tragically involved.

N.Z. Official Photograph.

Ruins of Ypres.

The obscurity which temporarily prevailed as a result of the unsatisfactory issue in the attack launched on October 9th, and the absence of any definite information on the situation until 3 p.m. on the following day, afforded New Zealand Divisional Headquarters but limited time in which to decide on the tape-line for the attack of the 12th; for the drafting and issuing of orders; for the commanders concerned to make the necessary vital preparations, and for artillery barrage tables to be formulated. There were other stupendous difficulties which the brevity of the warning seriously accentuated.

In accordance with orders issued on the evening of October 10th the offensive was to be renewed on the morning of the 12th by the Second Army (which embraced the New Zealand Division), together with the Fifth Army on our left. Attended by the measure of success which was hoped for, the operation was to place us in complete possession of the Passchendaele Ridge and the village of Passchendaele itself. The New Zealand Division, which had on its right the 3rd Australian Division, and on its left the 9th Division of the Fifth Army, was to attack with two Brigades disposed side by side, the 2nd Infantry Brigade being on the right and the 3rd (Rifle) Brigade on the left, with the 4th Infantry Brigade in Divisional reserve. The direction of the attack was north-easterly, and the width of the 2nd Brigade front approximately 750 yards. The right of the Brigade boundary, commencing at its base, followed the course of the Ravebeek, the western edge of Graf Wood, and the northern outskirts of Passchendaele village; the left boundary extended from Peter Pan (exclusive to the Brigade) in practically a straight line north-east to the Passchendaele-Westroosebeke Road about 250 yards beyond the Vindictive Cross Roads. The Brigade was to attack on a one battalion frontage in depth in the following order:—
(a) 2nd Battalion of Otago; (b) 1st Battalion of Otago; (c) 1st Battalion of Canterbury, with one company of the 2nd Battalion of Canterbury attached. The three objectives to be captured and consolidated were allotted in that order. Within the Brigade boundaries, the first of these, known as the Red Line, extended from the Ravebeek on the right across the Bellevue Spur to the left; the second, known as the Blue Line, was approximately 1,000 yards in advance of

the first objective; the third and final objective comprised the Green Dotted and Green Lines. The first of the two final lines was approximately 1,000 yards in advance of the Blue Line, and extended from the northern outskirts of Passchendaele village, at a point near the Westroosebeke Road, in the direction of Venture Farm on the left; the second followed a parallel course about 250 yards ahead.

At zero hour the 2nd Battalion of Otago, the leading assaulting formation, was to move forward to the attack on a three-company frontage; the 1st Battalion of Otago, in similar order, was to leap-frog the leading troops on the Red Line, followed by the 1st Battalion of Canterbury on a two-company frontage. When the 1st Battalion of Otago had reached the second or Blue Line, Canterbury was to push forward to the final objective. The 2nd Battalion of Canterbury (less one company detached) constituted the Brigade reserve, and was to follow in the wake of and if necessary assist the two Battalions of Otago. Provision was also made for sending forward 12 machine guns to assist in consolidating the final objective. Prepared and issued almost on the eve of the attack, these were the dispositions of the troops of the 2nd Brigade for an operation which, as a review of the situation will disclose, was already foredoomed to failure.

When the 2nd Battalion of the Regiment proceeded to take over the line from the Ravebeek to Peter Pan on the night of the 10th, a desperate state of affairs revealed itself. The whole countryside, under the continuous rain and heavy shelling, was rapidly approaching the state of a deep morass through which the relieving troops blindly floundered in the darkness of night until they reached the position which was only nominally a front line. There was overwhelming and gruesome evidence of the disastrous results of the British attack launched on the 9th. To say nothing of the dead, scores of men, wounded and near to death, still lay out over the country, unattended and without protection from the weather. The 148th Brigade, so heavy were its losses, had apparently found it impossible to cope with the task of clearing the wounded. At Waterloo Farm the congestion was such that many of the wounded were still lying above ground and in the open, and frequently enemy shells burst among or near them and put an end to their miseries. There

210

were probably 200 stretcher cases lying over the area, and it was doubtful if any of them had been fed until our troops provided them with rations on the morning of the 11th. The urgent necessity of clearing these wounded and the large number of stretcher cases at Waterloo Farm, and elsewhere, was pointed out to Brigade by Lieut.-Colonel Smith (Commanding the 2nd Battalion of Otago), in view of possible congestion on the 12th, and at the same time it was strongly advised that a large number of stretcher relays be held in readiness in connection with our own impending attack. This, serious enough in itself, reveals only one phase of the situation.

The enemy defences along the slopes and high ground of Bellevue Spur, which struck westward from the main Passchendaele Ridge, had not suffered materially from the attack delivered on October 9th. Rather was the enemy strengthened in his belief as to their impregnability. The seriousness of the position which confronted Otago on taking over the line overlooked by Bellevue Spur was disclosed, or rather confirmed, by an exhaustive reconnaissance made during the night of the 10th and the early morning of the 11th by that redoubtable fellow, Sergt. Travis. No Man's Land was a mass of shell-holes three parts filled with water, and scattered among them were broken wire entanglements. Overlooking this waste, and commanding approximately 1,000 yards of the valley and the country as far back almost as Korek, were many concrete "pill-boxes," or block-houses, hemmed in by wire. At least six of these were discovered along the front of the Battalion sector, four in front of 8th Company, and two in front of 14th Company. Parties of the enemy, numbering from 12 to 20, could be seen going towards two of the block-houses in front of our lines, suggesting that some of the garrison sheltered or slept in them by day and by night took up position in groups to form the front line. The enemy, who overlooked our lines from a gradually sloping spur, was distant only 100 to 150 yards from our forward posts, and the volume of machine gun and rifle fire at night would indicate that his positions were strongly held. The block-houses which the reconnaissance disclosed were still intact ; the belts of wire which surrounded them still uncut. The information obtained was despatched to Brigade by Lieut.-Colonel Smith at 5.30 on the morning of the 11th, and a request made that the fire of our heavy artillery should at once be brought to bear on them. Nothing followed; and so a further urgent request was made in the afternoon. After a lengthy period of time the heavy artillery opened out on the Bellevue Spur, but only briefly, and the damage done was negligible. This fatal remissness will be referred to later. At intervals throughout the day small parties of the enemy could be seen moving about in the village of Passchendaele, all dressed in fighting order. Under the Red Cross flag German wounded were being carried from " pill-boxes " opposite our front, there being six men to each stretcher, a grim forecast of events in our own line, where the ground was in an even worse state. At 4 p.m. a further report had been forwarded from the 2nd Battalion to Brigade Head-quarters in reference to the condition of the Ravebeek, No Man's Land, and the enemy's wire and block-houses.

It is now necessary to turn to the artillery side of pre-parations for the attack, and the difficulties which beset them. The New Zealand Field Artillery arrived in the Ypres zone during the latter part of September, when the whole of the area taken over at St. Julien was found to be water-logged and in a general condition of wreckage. Positions and communications called for the expenditure of unceasing labour to bring them to anything like the required condition. The Divisional Artillery took part in the attack delivered on October 4th, and when the Infantry were relieved continued in line. Orders were then issued for a readjustment of artillery groups, but in attempting to move forward many of the guns were stranded. Weather and traffic had made the one road for-ward to Gravenstafel, torn as it already was by shelling, practically impassable. Ammunition supply could be main-tained only by pack-mules, and stranded guns were hauled off the road and got into action where they were. The Divisional Artillery joined in the unsuccessful attack launched on October 9th, supporting the 49th Division. An endeavour was then made to move some of the guns to positions near Winnipeg-Kansas cross-roads, but was attended by only partial success. The roads were submerged in mud and strewn with the wreckage of transport and the mutilated bodies of men and horses, the result of the shelling of the previous night. These were some of the desperate conditions against which the Artillery had to contend. The result was that only a proportion of the guns were in position for the attack fixed for the 12th, and those that were got up in face of stupendous difficulties sank down to their axles immediately they commenced to fire, or before it. Adequate support from the artillery, so vital to the assaulting infantry, was in consequence not forthcoming.

The day preceding the attack was extremely, almost ominously, quiet. The great belts of enemy wire ahead were apparent to the most casual observer. At 3 p.m. final orders and instructions for the operation were issued by Brigade. In order to ensure that the leading waves should start in correct alignment and at a safe margin of distance from the creeping barrage, it was arranged to tape a line running from the Ravebeek on the right, where the Australian Division joined up, to Peter Pan on the left; all posts in advance of that line to be withdrawn a distance of 50 yards a quarter of an hour before zero. The laying out of this tape line was commenced by Major McCrae and 2nd-Lieut. Halliwell at 11 p.m. on the 11th, and completed about 4 a.m. on the 12th. Owing to the impassability of the Ravebeek, which ran at the foot of the Bellevue Spur, and the impracticability of effecting a crossing by the temporary duck-board bridge in reasonable time during daylight, this had to be done over-night; and three Battalions were thus assembled across an area which was approximately only 100 yards in depth, creating serious, though unavoidable, congestion. Actual assembly for the attack commenced early on the evening of the 11th, and was continued throughout the night, every unit being in position before daybreak on the 12th. In view of the state of the ground, it was decided that the three machine gun sections of the No. 2 Machine Gun Company, which were to be employed for purposes of assisting consolidation on the completion of the attack, should move up as far as possible during daylight on the 11th in order to reserve the strength of the crews for the following day. Accordingly, they moved forward and dug in on a line between Boethoek and Wimbledon. At 9 p.m. they pushed still further ahead with their 12 guns, the Otago section digging in about 400 yards in advance of Waterloo. Two light trench mortars of the No. 2 Trench Mortar Battery, detailed to support the attack, moved up on the afternoon of the 11th and assembled in shell-holes on the western slopes of Abraham Heights. Two other trench mortars which had succeeded in obtaining only 33 rounds were blown up by shell fire half an hour before zero, and had to be withdrawn. The night prior to the attack was fine at the outset, but during the early hours of the morning a heavy drizzle set in. The enemy was obviously jumpy during the hours of darkness, and used many flares.

The dispositions of the 2nd Battalion of Otago, which comprised the leading wave, across the Brigade frontage of approximately 750 yards, were as follows:—10th (North Otago) Company, commanded by Major W. W. Turner, on the right; 8th (Southland) Company, commanded by Lieut. G. B. Knight, in the centre; 14th (South Otago) Company, commanded by Lieut. J. O. Webber, on the left; 4th (Otago) Company, commanded by Captain H. S. Sanson, in support. Two companies of the 2nd Battalion of Canterbury were attached as a reserve of strength. The 1st Battalion of Otago, with one company of the 2nd Battalion of Canterbury attached, had previously moved up to the line Otto Farm-Gravenstafel Road, and at dusk on the evening of the 11th advanced to positions within 100 yards of the Ravebeek. Its dispositions were then as follows:—4th (Otago) Company, commanded by Captain G. H. Allan, on the right; 8th (Southland) Company, commanded by Captain R. H. Nicholson, in the centre; 10th (North Otago) Company, commanded by Captain S. C. Greer, on the left; 14th (South Otago) Company, commanded by Captain C. H. Molloy, in Battalion reserve.

The assaulting waves of infantry were to move forward to the attack behind the protection of artillery barrages, and normally, exclusive of heavy guns and heavy and medium howitzers, the operation would have been supported by 144 18-pounders, and 48 4.5in. howitzers. The difficulties of complying with the demands of the prepared programme of artillery co-operation were so great that there could not be ensured even the efficient support of anything approaching that number of guns—probably less than half.

The Headquarters of all four Battalions of the 2nd Infantry Brigade were established at Waterloo Farm an hour before zero, but owing to the severing of connections by shelling through-communication to Brigade Battle-Head-quarters at the Capitol was not obtained until about 10 o'clock on the morning of the 12th. For various reasons the preparatory signalling arrangements were anything but complete.

Throughout the night of the 11th-12th the enemy frequently shelled the Division on our right, using many gas-shells. The conditions affecting our infantry, about to attack in the morning, were the worst possible. The task of getting into positions of assembly, in face of darkness and over ground that was sodden and yielding and literally torn with shell-holes, and then lying over night in what was for the most part a morass, combined with a certain knowledge of the great difficulties of the task ahead, presaged a bad start for an attack at daybreak.

TRAGEDY AND HEROISM.

The hour of zero, 5.25 a.m. on October 12th, signalled the commencement of the tragedy of Bellevue Spur—a day of tragedy and heroism combined. The inadequacy of our artillery barrage, by reason of the conditions explained, was at once apparent, and its inaccuracy was responsible for wiping out many of our men while still in their assembly positions. On the left, for example, a number of men of 10th Company of the 1st Battalion were killed by our own shell fire when one hundred yards behind the starting tape. This, combined with the inevitable confusion created, prejudiced the success of the operation from the outset. Concrete block-houses and deep rows of uncut wire, from the security of which German machine gunners delivered a terrific volume of fire, confronted our infantry as they moved forward to the assault. The enemy was only too well prepared for an attack in which the elements and the deadly inefficiencies of the supporting artillery conspired to help him.

At the moment the attack was launched the enemy dropped an artillery barrage along a line about 50 yards on the western side of the Ravebeek and in the vicinity of Waterloo Farm. Simultaneously, from the block-houses and fortified shell-holes on the crest of Bellevue, there burst forth the most intense machine gun and rifle fire, which swept the ranks of the assaulting infantry with terrible effect from front and either flank. The advance was on the point of being immediately checked. The greater proportion of officers and men comprising the leading waves were shot down almost as they left their trenches. On the left 14th Company in particular made practically no headway. But there were groups of leaders and men who were to persevere even against this stress of fire, until they came up against great belts of uncut wire, in places 30 and 40 yards deep, and against concrete block-houses hemmed in and completely surrounded by barbed-wire entanglements. The artillery barrage in one of its lifts had completely missed the " pill-boxes " on the left of the advance.

Repeated gallant and desperate attempts were now made by officers and men to work round these strongholds from the flanks, or to approach them through gaps in the wire. A request for trench mortar assistance disclosed the fact that these weapons had been knocked out ; though Lewis gun fire and rifle grenades were brought to bear with effect on enemy machine gunners stationed in shell-holes outside. Increased machine gun and sniping fire, directed from known and concealed positions all along the crest, disputed every attempt at advance. On the right Major Turner, whose Company, the 10th, had made the most gallant efforts to get forward, personally succeeded in advancing some distance through the wire before he was shot down. To the left, 2nd-Lieut. C. B. McClure, accompanied by Pte. A. E. Greene, by crawling through the wire, achieved the temporary success of reaching a point within ten yards of two block-houses on the crest. At that stage he was wounded and his companion killed. Working his way back, Lieut. McClure gathered together several men with the intention of renewing the assault on these two " pill-boxes," but the whole of his party was almost instantly knocked out by a single shell. It was the concentrated fire of these two block-houses that practically smashed up a reinforcing company of 3rd Brigade troops as it moved forward in artillery formation, a distance of over 1,000 yards away to the left. To all this volume of machine gun fire was added that of enemy snipers posted in shell-holes and behind the stumps of blasted trees.

The 1st Battalion of Otago now pressed into the breach and renewed the struggle. Officers and men, temporarily unseen by the enemy, crawled through the belts of wire in an almost forlorn endeavour to get at the enemy block-houses and the machine guns which they sheltered. 2nd-Lieuts. J. J. Bishop and N. F. Watson had got so far forward as to be killed in the act of hurling bombs through the loop-holes. On the left 10th Company had all its officers either killed or wounded, and a small group dug in at Wolf Copse, away to the left. Only 28 other ranks of this Company were left unwounded. Captain C. H. Molloy pushed forward his reserve Company, the 14th, and was himself killed, as were also all his officers, excepting one who was wounded; and the Company was thenceforward ably commanded by Sergt.-major Bunbury. So, in succession, waves of infantry moved forward to the attack, but were unable to make any definite impression, and finally wilted away under the storm of fire. But away on the extreme right, after all this expenditure of gallant effort, it seemed as if a wedge was at last to be driven into the defences of Bellevue.

Following in immediate rear of the main advance, the 8th (Southland) Company of the 1st Battalion gained the first slope only to find that few men of the leading Companies were left. But it was also apparent that the trend of the general advance had been too much to the north, one result of this divergence being that the right flank was left completely exposed to the fire directed unrestrainedly from two " pill-boxes " established near the Ravebeek, and with an interval of approximately 100 yards between them. Captain R. H. Nicholson, commanding 8th Company, was killed almost as his Company commenced to move forward, and the advance was thereupon continued under the direction of 2nd-Lieut. A. R. Cockerell. It was at once evident to this officer that if the left of the attack was to achieve any measure of success, these two block-houses, so far quite unassailed, must be attacked and dealt with. But the force at his immediate disposal, at a nominal strength of two platoons, had progressed but an inappreciable distance when it was disorganised and had almost entirely disappeared under the fire encountered. A few more yards and its weight was spent. 2nd-Lieut. Cockerell now found himself alone and unsupported in this wilderness of shell-holes, in front the forbidding spectacle of enemy block-houses and broken trench lines still sheltering their garrisons, and to the rear seemingly none but dead and wounded men. Recorded in plain, unvarnished language, the experiences which befell this young officer as, undaunted by the peril of his isolation, he now went forward alone, must rank among the strangest set down in the pages of history. Continuing his advance, he was ultimately confronted by a short length of trench which extended across the front of the foremost block-house. Along this trench line approximately 40 of the enemy were established, but so rapid and so continuous had been their fire against the flank of our attack that their ammunition was completely expended, and when confronted and called upon to surrender they filed out of their post with hands above their heads and slowly trekked back as prisoners through our lines. A distance of but 20 yards ahead was the first block-house, into which those of the enemy who were without had rushed for shelter. Reaching this " pill-box " still unscathed, this single officer bayoneted six of the garrison as they emerged from it at the rear, and then forced the surrender of the remainder and sent them back as prisoners. Lieut. Cockerell was now joined by Pte. G. Hampton, of 8th (Southland) Company, who, carrying with him a Lewis gun, had struggled forward out of the confusion of 8th Company's shattered attack. With valorous determination both advanced to the attack of the second and larger block-house, approximately 100 yards distant. This concrete stronghold was found to contain a garrison of two officers and 30 men with two machine guns. Their guns had ceased to fire, the apparent reason, remarkable as it may seem, being that they also had expended their last round of ammunition, a further indication of the unceasing destruction directed against our troops from the time the attack opened until it had been effectively smashed. The whole of this garrison were also made prisoners, and the two machine guns destroyed. This represented a total capture of over 80 prisoners, two block-houses with their machine guns, and a length of enemy trench.

To the immediate right of the Regiment, troops of the 3rd Australian Division, when thrown into the attack at the break of day, had encountered the same withering blasts of fire, the same tremendous difficulties of uncut wire and barriers of destruction which the enemy's block-house system represented.

An Australian officer and six men who, almost in like manner had penetrated to a point far beyond the limits of their main advance, were now met with, and after a consultation this handful of resolute Colonials decided that the purpose of the attack could best be served by pushing forward and round to the rear of the defences of Bellevue. The first necessity was to establish a defensive point in the large block-house from which the enemy had last been cleared and to send a runner back in an endeavour to reach Battalion Headquarters and acquaint the Commanding Officer of the situation. Pte. Hampton was the first to attempt this almost forlorn task, but he had only covered a distance of 200 yards when the open space was swept by enemy fire and he was killed. Three Australians in turn as bravely endeavoured to make their way through, but each met the same fate. It was now agreed that it was impossible to get word back, and the garrison, reduced to two officers and three men, with one Lewis gun, directed all their energies towards consolidating the position. When darkness came down, Lieut. Cockerell, leaving the Australians in possession of the " pill-box," struggled back over what was now virtually No Man's Land to the rear, and there took command of and organised the remnants of the Battalion, now scattered along a line which was but a short distance in advance of where the attack had started from in the morning. For his extraordinary individual effort, and the very gallant work which he accomplished from the commencement of the attack until the Battalion was finally relieved, 2nd-Lieut. Cockerell was awarded the D.S.O., a rare Order for an officer of his rank.

The situation generally had remained practically unaltered. Canterbury troops had followed in the wake of Otago, and as they crossed the swamp and flood of the Ravebeek came under heavy shell and machine gun fire ; Lieut.-Colonel G. A. King, in command of the 1st Battalion, being killed within a few minutes of crossing the stream. Progress beyond the limits which Otago had reached over the main front of the attack was impossible against a hail of machine gun and rifle fire. Gaps in the enemy's wire had long since been discovered to be deliberate avenues for the fire of machine guns. The creeping barrage had ceased to be of any service to the attackers. Further advance was out of the question until the "pill-boxes" and wire entanglements had been effectively dealt with. Those of the attackers who were left alive had perforce to dig in where they were, or seek shelter in the shell-holes. Baulked of their first objective, they lay there throughout the day at the mercy of enemy snipers and machine gunners. Any attempt at movement was fatal, and nothing could be done until darkness came down and permitted the remnants of the infantry to be reorganised.

While this tragedy was being enacted, little or nothing of it was known at Battalion or Advanced Brigade Headquarters owing to the interruption of communications. The route between the front line and Waterloo Farm was heavily barraged by the enemy, and all attempts by runners to get through this difficult and shell-swept country to report the situation had failed. The absence of direct telephone communication between Waterloo Farm and the Capitol similarly left Brigade in the dark as to the situation. At 6.15 a.m. 2nd-Lieut. Halliwell, Intelligence Officer to the 2nd Battalion of Otago, was sent up to report on the position, and under great difficulties effected a reconnaissance of the line. A runner succeeded in getting through to Headquarters with a message which confirmed the fact that the whole advance had been held up. Information was at once despatched to Brigade Headquarters, and was received there at 7.20 a.m. Shortly afterwards Lieut.-Colonel Smith went forward himself to see what could be done in the direction of reorganising the remnants of the attacking troops and resuming the advance. After consultation with the remaining officers of Otago and Canterbury on the spot, the unanimous opinion expressed was that it was impossible to gain the crest of Bellevue under existing conditions, and that any attempt to renew the attack would be suicidal. There were now so few effectives left that a fresh attack, launched in broad daylight, could not have progressed. Individual effort was the utmost that could be expected. The only possible gap was by a road on the right, and this was covered by machine gun fire from either flank. Lieut.-Colonel Smith succeeded in getting back to Battalion Headquarters at Waterloo Farm, and there conferred with Lieut.-Colonel Charters (1st Battalion of Otago) and Lieut.-Colonel Mead (2nd Battalion of Canterbury). These two Commanders shared his opinion, and messages were sent forward by runners instructing the advanced elements to dig in where they were. Advice to this effect was despatched to 2nd Brigade Headquarters, to the 3rd (Rifle) Brigade, and the 10th Australian Brigade. Lieut.-Colonel Charters, with his Intelligence Officer, 2nd-Lieut. W. A. Stuart, had attempted to get forward to view the situation for himself, but was driven back by machine gun and sniping fire, his Intelligence Officer being wounded. The difficulties of maintaining communications were greatly accentuated by the large number of casualties among runners.

To the left, the 3rd (Rifle) Brigade had fared no better, except that it was in occupation of the Cemetery near Wallemolen, a position of some tactical importance. To the right, the 3rd Australian Division was at one time in possession of portion of the Red Line, the first objective, but although an attempt was made to continue the advance, the leading troops were finally obliged to fall back to positions approximately 300 to 400 yards in advance of their original front line. The 9th Division, on the left of the New Zealand Division, had also failed.

It was now suggested to Brigadier-General Braithwaite, Commanding the 2nd Infantry Brigade, that the barrage should be brought back to the Red Line, the first objective, in order to enable the attacking troops to make another attempt on the spur. In the meantime the Divisional Commander had arranged for the general advance to be resumed under the barrage at 3 p.m., with the intention of taking the first and second objectives only. The 1st Battalion of Otago on the right and the 2nd Battalion on the left were to capture the first objective, and the two Battalions of Canterbury Regiment the second objective after an hour's halt. Arrangements were being made to bombard with heavy artillery the whole of the block-house system west of the Red Line. Orders were accordingly received by Commanding Officers to re-organise their units preparatory to launching another attack.

The Battalion Commanders were still of the opinion that such an operation was impossible of achievement. If the heavy artillery was to deal with the enemy wire and block-houses, the infantry would require to be brought back to a position of safety. Heavy casualties had already been caused when attempts were made to reorganise, and any man who exposed himself was immediately knocked out. Lieut. Colonels Charters and Smith both telephoned and wrote to the Brigadier pointing out the exhausted condition of the men, the state of the ground, the heavy casualties, particularly among officers and runners, and the fact that our men were so close under the wire that they could not be extricated during the hours of daylight without incurring additional and abnormal losses ; also that reorganisation was impracticable, and that any attempt at a further advance that day would mean increased loss with nothing to show for it. Brigadier-General Braithwaite then communicated with Divisional Headquarters and advised the G.O.C. Division of the views expressed by the Battalion Commanders. At 2.10 p.m. the Brigadier was informed that the 2nd Infantry Brigade would not carry out the intended attack. In accordance with the original scheme for the resumption of the advance, the 2nd Brigade was to attack Bellevue Spur from approximately the south-west, and the 3rd (Rifle) Brigade was to co-operate from the north-west. The 3rd Brigade alone was now to resume the advance. Later, however, this order was also cancelled, and then finally it was definitely announced that no further attempt at advance would take place that day.

At 3.30 p.m. orders were received that the 2nd Brigade was to reorganise and take up a defensive position in depth on a two battalion frontage, with the two rear Battalions escheloned as far back as the Hanebeek. The 1st and 2nd Battalions of Otago Regiment were to hold the front line, with the two Battalions of Canterbury in Brigade support, one on either side of the Gravenstafel Road, their special duty being the defence of the Abraham Heights. The extrication and reorganisation of Battalions could only be accomplished under cover of darkness. The 2nd Battalion of Otago was to hold a line at least 150 yards in rear of the enemy's wire, and extending from the Gravenstafel Road to Peter Pan on the left, and the 1st Battalion from the Gravenstafel Road to the Ravebeek on the right.

After reorganisation, the strength of the 2nd Battalion of the Regiment was taken and revealed the fact that only 170 men could be accounted for. The strength of the 1st Battalion was even below that, being estimated at 160 all ranks. During the night additional numbers were reported to be mixed up with other units. The position along the front remained comparatively quiet throughout the night, except that at about 8 o'clock the S.O.S. rocket appeared on both the right and left, and the usual artillery activity followed. The greatest difficulties were experienced in getting water and rations to the line. Still further back, over the long chain of duck-boards which stretched from near Saint Jean forward to Otto Farm, and thence across the waste of country to the Battalion Dump at Gravenstafel, with everywhere deep craters and shell-holes into which pack mules frequently fell and never rose again, the rear supply system was maintained in face of almost insuperable difficulties and under the constant threat of enemy shell fire.

The second phase of the tragedy now presented itself. Hundreds of badly wounded men lay out over the front and in No Man's Land, exposed to the added miseries of mud and weather. The stretcher service, extended though it had been, was unequal to the task of dealing with such abnormal losses under conditions of movement presenting tremendous difficulties. Over 200 cases which had been carried down to Waterloo Farm had remained there throughout the day awaiting evacuation under intermittent shell fire, and several were killed. Others who had vainly endeavoured to struggle down from the line sank into shell-holes, and, weighted down by the appalling mud and the burden of their wounds, many of them never arose again. Such was the state of the ground and the distance to be covered that six men, working in relays, were required to each stretcher. The task called for more, but the men could not be spared. Representations were made for an additional large number of men, and during the night stretcher parties came up from the 4th Brigade and worked strenuously at evacuating the wounded. Throughout the night of the 12th-13th, 1,200 men of the 4th Brigade were so employed ; also all available men of the Divisional Artillery and the Army Service Corps. One Battalion of the 147th Brigade was also loaned to the Division for purposes of stretcher-bearing. The bearers of the Regiment, lurching and blundering with their burdens over this waste, had worked without the slightest regard for rest. But the task was by no means finished, and as darkness came down over the battlefield the stillness of the night was pierced by the agonised cries of the wounded, many of whom must have died before help could reach them. For them the Hell of Passchendaele was ended.

Arrangements were made at dawn on the 13th to organise bearer parties from the Canterbury Regiment, one half being detailed to cover the whole of the front and carry the remainder of the wounded down as far as the Regimental Aid Post at Waterloo Farm, and the other half from there to Bank Farm. These parties worked without interruption from the enemy until 5 o'clock in the evening, moving over No Man's Land as far forward as the German wire. The enemy was also engaged removing his dead and wounded under cover of the Red Cross flag, and thus a sort of armistice prevailed. It was during this period that a German medical officer admitted in course of conversation that they too had suffered heavily, a fact which was evidenced by the exertions of their stretcher-bearers. Close on 500 cases required to be carried from the Regimental Aid Post at Waterloo Farm to the Advanced Dressing Station at Spree Farm, on the Wieltje-Gravenstafel Road, a distance of about two and a-half miles, and so torn with shell-holes and deep in mud was the whole of the area that six and sometimes eight men, working in relays, had to be attached to each stretcher.

The congestion that resulted at Waterloo Farm can well be imagined. All attempts to relieve it were for some time unavailing, and by the early morning of the 14th there were still many cases there which had not been evacuated. All the available resources had been taxed to the utmost, and yet the situation was bad in the extreme, so bad as to impel the following message, despatched at 5.45 a.m. on the 14th, by Brigadier-General Braithwaite to the G.O.C. Division: " In spite of frequent appeals to every branch of the Staff, and the A.D.M.S. three times, the 75 stretcher cases at Waterloo which I asked the A.D.M.S. to arrange the removal of at 12 noon yesterday, are still lying there ; 40 of them have been lying out in the open under shell fire the whole night. I am powerless to do more than I have done. As ɛ last extremity I appeal to you personally." Further large stretcher parties were again immediately organised at the instance of Division, and by noon on the 14th Waterloo Farm was clear of cases.

2ND-LIEUT. A. R. COCKERELL, D.S.O., (D.)

The situation over the front on October 13th, the day following the attack, was quiet. The reorganisation of Battalions had for the most part been completed, and during the evening two companies of the 2nd Battalion of Canterbury were brought up to fill a gap existing between the left of the 2nd Battalion of Otago and the 3rd Brigade. Arrangements were now made to withdraw our advanced troops at dawn on the 14th to a distance of 600 yards from the enemy's " pill-box " system in order to allow of those defences being systematically bombarded by heavy artillery. This was effected, and on the bombardment ceasing the original line was restored. When darkness set in that night the Regiment was relieved by troops of the 4th Brigade, and, exhausted and depleted in numbers, slowly trekked out of this area of death and desolation.

The casualties sustained by the Regiment in the course of these operations reached a total of 22 officers and 787 other ranks, made up as follows :—1st Battalion : Killed, 7 officers and 98 other ranks ; died of wounds, six other ranks ; wounded, six officers and 230 other ranks ; missing, 56 other ranks. 2nd Battalion : Killed, five officers and 85 other ranks ; wounded, four officers and 241 other ranks ; gassed, six other ranks ; missing, 65 other ranks. The following were the casualties among the officers of the Regiment :—1st Battalion : Killed, Captains R. H. Nicholson and C. H. Molloy, 2nd-Lieuts. W. A. French, N. F. Watson, T. R. B. Macky, J. J. Bishop, and A. L. Smith ; wounded, Captains S. C. Greer and G. H. Allan, 2nd-Lieuts. C. H. Fyffe, W. A. Stuart, F. J. Traynor, and A. Martin. 2nd Battalion : Killed, Major W. W. Turner, Lieut. K. G. Smith, 2nd-Lieuts. G. B. Knight, N. Tompsett, E. M. Ryburn, A. S. Coatman ; wounded, 2nd-Lieuts. C. B. T. McClure and S. D. MacPherson. In respect of the large number of men who at the first estimate were officially recorded as missing, this did not imply that they had become prisoners of war, but that after the battlefield had been cleared there was no direct evidence afforded of their death.

The casualties incurred by the New Zealand Division in the Passchendaele operations were approximately 2,730. The 2nd Brigade's proportion of this number was 54 officers and 1,529 other ranks, this being inclusive of the losses sustained by the No. 2 Machine Gun Company and the No. 2 Light Trench Mortar Battery. The number of prisoners who were received through the lines of the New Zealand Division was three officers (including one battalion commander), and 89 other ranks.

Seldom, if ever, has an attack operation in which the Regiment has been concerned been marked by so many individual acts revealing high courage and determination. When officers were shot down, non-commissioned officers and men alike showed remarkable qualities of leadership; no fewer than five senior n.c.o.'s, namely, Company Sergt.-majors T. A. Bunbury and A. L. Hibbs, and Sergts. W. D. Evans, I. D. Guy, and E. C. Jacobs, being singled out for special honour in being awarded the Distinguished Conduct Medal.

In the course of his report on the operations which aimed at the capture of the Passchendaele Ridge, Brigadier-General Braithwaite, Commanding the 2nd New Zealand Infantry Brigade, attributed the failure of the Brigade to reach its objectives to the following causes:—" (a) Enemy uncut wire :—This held up the whole of the advance on the Brigade front, and although plainly marked on the map, had been left practically untouched by our artillery fire. In some places it was 50 yards in depth. The attention of the Artillery Liason Officer was called to this by the Brigade-Major and myself on the day previous to the attack, and the co-operation of the heavy artillery asked for, but without any apparent result. All gaps in this were completely covered by machine guns in ' pill boxes.' (b) ' Pill boxes ' :—These also had not been properly dealt with by our artillery, as they were all practically undamaged and fully manned with numerous machine guns, which caused our troops severe casualties. (c) Enemy snipers :—These were extremely active when once our barrage lifted from the enemy's system of trenches. Their shooting was most accurate, and appeared to be specially directed on those in authority. (d) Weakness of our artillery barrage :—Everyone is agreed as to the poor and inadequate barrage. It is understood that owing to the difficulty in communications, only about one third of the guns were able to get up into position. The 108th Field Artillery Brigade only managed to get eight out of their 18 guns up, and they were supposed to have been rather fortunate. The barrage itself was remarkable for its weakness and inaccuracy, many casualties among our troops being caused by our own shells. This was the result of want of proper registration, as some batteries did not register until zero hour. It has also been reported that some of the heavy batteries were not informed that an attack was to take place, being under the impression that it was a practice shoot. (e) Communications : —These were in a very bad state owing to the weather. The Artillery had much difficulty in moving their guns forward, many guns becoming absolutely bogged on the way, and consequently were unable to be brought into action. (f) Signal Communications :—These were far from satisfactory, as owing to the heavy shell fire and the rough ground, service wires could not be maintained between the Brigade and the Battalion Headquarters. In fact, the whole operations appeared to have been far too hurried, sufficient time not having been given to preparations by the Artillery, or to the proper construction of roads, tracks and approaches, and signal communications." In conclusion, Brigadier-General Braithwaite paid a high tribute to the gallantry and devotion to duty displayed by all ranks during the operations.

In his review of the operations, Major-General Sir Andrew Russell, G.O.C. New Zealand Division, gave expression to some salient points. The direct cause of failure, he stated, was the strong and continuous wire entanglements. The formidable nature of the entanglements in Bellevue was not known until the 11th, when a patrol report fully disclosed it ; and it was not known to Division before for the reason that it had only taken over command of the sector a matter of a few hours before zero. This information 24 hours earlier would have been invaluable. Continuing, General Russell stated : " When the success of the attacking infantry depends on good artillery support, provision for moving forward the guns and stable platforms for them is essential, otherwise the conditions of success are absent. In the operations of the 12th the barrage was inadequate."

At a conference of Commanding Officers held subsequent to the Passchendaele operations, General Russell, referring to the fact that the Division had had no definite and timely information in regard to the state of the enemy's wire and defences across the Divisional front, stated, in effect, that even if the position had been known earlier, and it had been possible to make representations to G.H.Q. on the subject, he doubted if the likelihood of the non-success of one Division would have effected any alteration in the programme already determined upon in respect of the fronts of two Armies.

CHAPTER IX.

POLDERHOEK CHATEAU.

FROM the tragic area of Bellevue the Regiment moved back on the night of October 14th into Divisional support. The 1st Battalion took up a position on the line Delva Farm-Schuler Farm, south of the Gravenstafel Road, with headquarters at Pommern Castle. The 2nd Battalion was established on the same line, but north of the Gravenstafel Road and with headquarters at Corn Hill. As long as the Regiment remained there, it was to be in readiness to move forward at half an hour's notice to the line Berlin-Calgary Grange, with the 1st Battalion south of the Gravenstafel Road and the 2nd Battalion north of it. This provision was in view of the 4th Brigade being compelled to move its supporting battalions to repel counter-attacks, in which event Otago would become responsible for the defence of the Abraham Heights. But there were no counter-attacks to contend with, and on the 15th the Regiment secured some respite. On the following day it was relieved by the 1st Battalions of Wellington and Auckland Regiments, and thereupon marched back to camp quarters near Saint Jean. The Regiment remained at this point until the 20th, and was rested, reorganised, and refitted.

On October 17th Lieut.-Colonel G. S. Smith, C.M.G., D.S.O., commanding the 2nd Battalion of Otago, proceeded to La Motte, and thereafter to the United Kingdom on duty, which, in accordance with the practice then recently introduced, afforded the complete change which a continuous and exacting period as commander of a front line Battalion demanded. By this departure for England, Lieut.-Colonel Smith, it so eventuated, was, for reasons of health, to definitely terminate his service with the Otago Regiment in the Field, dating from the commencement of the Gallipoli Campaign, during the course of which he shared with ability and distinction in many of the major operations with which the Regiment was vitally concerned. Command of the 2nd Battalion was now taken over by Major J. McCrae.

During the early morning of October 21st the Regiment moved out of camp at Saint Jean, and entrained at the Ypres railway siding. On reaching Wizernes, the 1st Battalion proceeded by motor-lorries to Harlettes, and the 2nd Battalion by road to Affringnes and billets. On the 23rd the 2nd Battalion marched to the Selles area.

On November 1st Lieut.-Colonel Charters assumed temporary command of the 2nd New Zealand Infantry Brigade, and on the 12th presented medal ribands to those officers and other ranks whose gallantry during the Passchendaele operations had been recognised in the conferring of Awards. The 1st Battalion was now under the command of Major W. F. Tracy, M.C.

Following upon the issue of orders for a return to the Ypres area, the Regiment moved on November 13th. On reaching the Chateau Segard area, the 1st Battalion proceeded to Brewery Camp, and the 2nd Battalion to Cafe Belge Camp.

On November 23rd the Staff of the 2nd Infantry Brigade had proceeded to Zillebeke, and from there to the Headquarters of the 118th Brigade at Stirling Castle, where arrangements were made for temporarily taking over from that unit the front line of the sector extending from the Reutelbeek on the north to the Scherriabeek in the south, and fronting Polderhoek Chateau. The new sector was immediately south of the Reutel and Noordemdhoek sectors and, incidentally, about four miles south of Passchendaele. On the night of the 14th-15th the New Zealand Division had relieved the 21st Division in its holding of the line from the Reutelbeek in the south to Noordemdhoek in the north, the Otago Regiment, as part of the 2nd Brigade, being then in Divisional reserve at Chateau Segard. On the night of the 25th-26th, as previously indicated, the Division entered into possession of the sector immediately to the right, the 2nd Battalion of Canterbury occupying the front line.

Preparations were now being advanced for launching an attack by troops of the 2nd New Zealand Infantry Brigade against the enemy stronghold known as Polderhoek Chateau, standing on the high ground overlooking our line and situated at a point about 1,000 yards north of Gheluvelt, which was also within the enemy's lines.

Following upon the attempt against the Passchendaele Ridge on October 12th, arrangements were made for continuing operations, though of a more limited nature, over the same area. On October 25th Canadian and English troops attacked on a front extending from the Ypres-Roulers Railway in the south to a point beyond Poelcappelle in the north. On the right, the Canadians attacked on both sides of the Ravebeek, which included the area of the enemy defences with which the Regiment was concerned on October 12th. The defences of Bellevue Spur had over the intervening period been subjected to the concentrated fire of heavy artillery, but even with this preparation still presented a formidable obstacle to success, and it was only after a second attack had been delivered in the afternoon that the enemy's resistance was beaten down. In a subsidiary attack launched at the same time to the south Polderhoek Chateau was captured, only to be wrested back by the enemy the same day.

On November 25th the 1st Battalion of the Regiment marched out of Brewery Camp, and proceeded to Walker Camp, south-east of Ypres. The projected attack against Polderhoek Chateau was to be delivered by the 1st Battalions of Otago and Canterbury. This made it necessary that they should train in conjunction, and on November 30th a combined practice attack was delivered over ground which was a facsimile of the real objective. Meanwhile our heavy artillery was actively engaged pounding the defences of Gheluvelt ; while 18-pounders and 4.5in. howitzers concentrated on Polderhoek Chateau ; but it was noticeable that many of the shells fell short. A practice barrage over the area of the Chateau and vicinity, in which short shooting was again reported, drew heavy retaliation. There was further considerable artillery activity on the 29th. A second practice barrage was carried out on the 30th, and on this occasion many direct hits were registered on the Chateau buildings. Towards the close, however, the shooting deteriorated in accuracy, and a number of shells fell so far short of the mark as to cause casualties in our own lines. During the period over which this concentrated artillery fire was being maintained, every effort was made by the troops in line to prevent the enemy repairing damage done to his wire.

231

Operation Orders for the attack on Polderhoek Chateau and grounds were issued on December 1st. The assault was to be delivered on December 3rd with two Battalions of the 2nd Infantry Brigade in line, namely, the 1st Battalion of Otago on the left, and the 1st Battalion of Canterbury on the right. The number to be thrown into the attack by each Battalion was two officers and 100 other ranks per Company. The Brigade boundaries were approximately defined by the Reutelbeek on the north, and the Scherriabeek on the south. The first objective, the Red Dotted Line, was represented by a line running north and south immediately to the east of the Chateau. The second or final objective, the Red Line, was at its deepest point 200 yards ahead, and aimed at encircling the whole of the grounds and ruins and at the same time covering the southern and south-eastern flanks. Each Battalion was to attack in depth, two companies being in the front line, one in support for dealing with any counter-attack that might develop, and one in reserve. The front line companies were to attack in two waves, with an interval of depth of 50 yards between each wave. The first wave was committed to the task of capturing and clearing the enemy's trenches and block-houses as far as the Red Dotted Line inclusive, on which it was to consolidate. There was then to be a pause of ten minutes in the advance of the barrage, after which the second wave was to pass through the first wave, clear the Chateau grounds between the two objectives, and finally establish and consolidate the Red Line. The assaulting troops were to be dressed in the lightest fighting order.

In addition to the artillery barrage which was to support the attack, arrangements were made for the operation to be covered by a barrage of machine gun fire, by trench mortars, including the 6in. Newtons, which were used for the first time, and by a discharge of gas by 4in. Stokes mortars. At the same time Becelaere and Gheluvelt were to be kept under the fire of heavy artillery and machine guns. In the light of recent events, every precaution was adopted to ensure adequate stretcher-bearing and first-aid arrangements. In this connection the 2nd Battalion of the Regiment, in Brigade reserve near Ypres, was to have 400 men in readiness to be sent forward as stretcher-bearers if called upon.

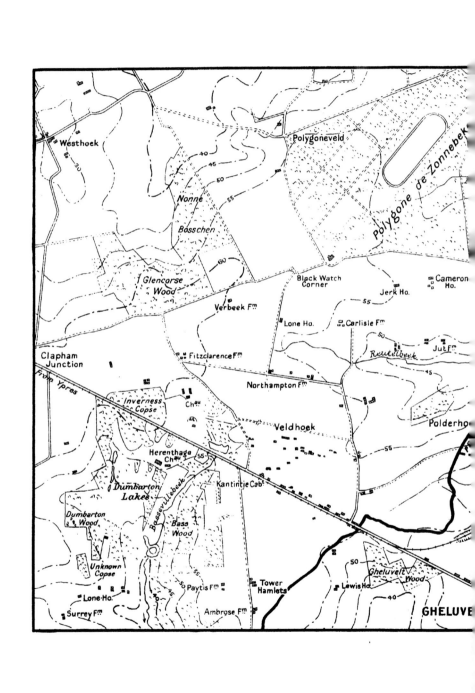

Westhoek

Polygoneveld

Polygone de Zonnebek

Nonne

Bosschen

Glencorse
Wood

Black Watch
Corner

Jerk Ho.

Cameron
Ho.

Verbeek Fᵐ

55

Lone Ho.

Carlisle Fᵐ

50

Jut Fᵐ

Reutelbeek

Clapham
Junction

From Ypres

Fitzclarence Fᵐ

45

Northampton Fᵐ

Inverness
Copse

Chᵃᵘ

Veldhoek

Polderho

55

Herenthage
Chᵃᵘ

55

Dumbarton
Lakes

Kantintje Cab'

Dumbarton
Wood

Bossvillebeek

Bass
Wood

50

Unknown
Copse

55

Gheluvelt
Wood

Paytis Fᵐ

Lone Ho.

Tower
Hamlets

Lewis Ho.

40

Surrey Fᵐ

Ambrose Fᵐ

GHELUVE

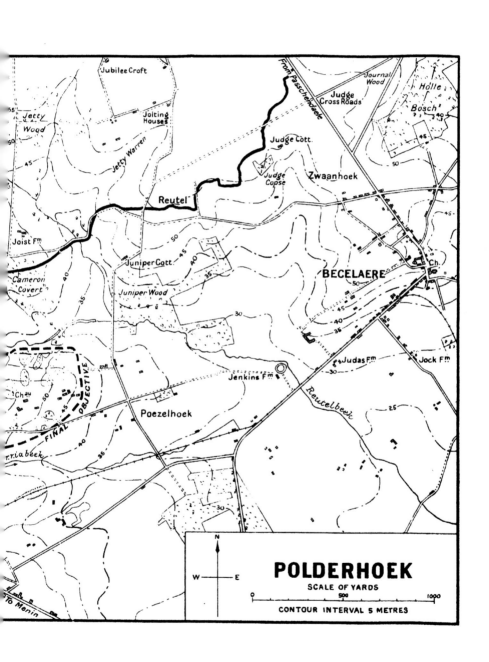

Jubilee Croft

Jetty Wood

Jetty Warren

Jolting Houses

Reutel

Joist Fm

Cameron Covert

Juniper Cott.

Juniper Wood

FINAL OBJECTIVE

Chau

Poezelhoek

Polygonabeek

To Menin

From Paschendaele

Judge Cross Roads

Judge Cott.

Judge Copse

Zwaanhoek

Journal Wood

Holle Bosch

BECELAERE

Ch.

Jenkins Fm

Judas Fm

Jock Fm

Reutelbeek

POLDERHOEK

SCALE OF YARDS

0   500   1000

CONTOUR INTERVAL 5 METRES

N
W — E

The two leading Companies of the 1st Battalion of the Regiment selected for the assault were the 10th (commanded by Captain C. Bryce) on the right, and the 4th (commanded by Captain J. N. Hines) on the left. The 8th Company (commanded by Lieut. D. McAuley) was to be in support, and the 14th (commanded by Captain J. P. Hewat) in reserve.

The troops of Otago and Canterbury Battalions who were to lead in the attack moved up and took over the front line system west of Polderhoek Chateau on the evening of December 1st, and relieved the garrison of the 2nd Battalion of Canterbury, who on their first occupation of the front a few days previously had found that considerable constructive work was required as a preliminary to assembly and attack. On the evening of December 2nd the support and reserve Companies of Otago and Canterbury Battalions were moved up, and the front line temporarily taken over with the object of moving the assaulting Companies into and familiarising them with their assembly positions. By daylight on December 3rd all troops had been withdrawn to their positions of assembly, with the exception of Lewis gunners and snipers of the counter-attacking Companies, who were left in the forward trenches with instructions to fire freely on all enemy movement in order to maintain a normal atmosphere. These elements were gradually withdrawn, and by 11.50 a.m. the front line was vacant of troops.

The dispositions of the 2nd Brigade troops immediately prior to the attack were as follows :—1st Battalion of Otago : Two Companies in Chord Line and in Chord travel trench, one Company in Timaru front and travel trenches and support line, and one Company at Clapham Junction. 1st Battalion of Canterbury : Two Companies in Chord Line and Chord travel trench, one Company in Timaru front and travel trenches and support line, and one Company at the Tower. 2nd Battalion of Otago : In dug-outs at a point about 750 yards E.S.E. of the Lille Gate, Ypres. 2nd Battalion of Canterbury : At Walker Camp.

Zero hour was fixed at 12 noon on December 3rd. The enemy wire entanglements had been destroyed by our bombardments of November 28th and 30th, a fact which had been confirmed by exhaustive patrolling.

SUCCESS DENIED.

By a set of circumstances, in the course of their development curiously alike those which marked the tragic failure of Passchendaele, the attack against Polderhoek Chateau was from the outset destined to fall short of its mark. The fixed starting line of the artillery barrage for the operation was 150 yards in advance of that on which the foremost infantry were assembled. By some fatal miscalculation or influence a considerable part of the entire weight of the barrage fell across the area occupied by the first waves of the assaulting troops. The immediate outcome was that the two leading Companies, 4th on the left and 10th on the right, became seriously involved in the destructive fire of our own artillery. The losses incurred were at once severe. To move forward was accepted as the quickest method of escaping our own fire, because more appeared to be falling to the rear than to the front. Captain Hines, commanding 4th Company, accordingly gave the order to advance, and 10th Company on the right almost immediately followed suit. But the irregularity of the barrage was such that some distance had to be covered before it was cleared, and by that time casualties, now increased by enemy machine gun fire, were so heavy as to seriously prejudice the success of the attack. It was during this stage of the advance that 2nd-Lieut. F. Marshall, of 4th Company, was killed, and that Captain Hines was wounded, though he continued to lead forward his Company. Approximately 150 yards beyond our old front line the second wave merged into the first. Captain Bryce, commanding 10th Company, was at this moment severely wounded, and while making his way back was killed. Command of 10th Company was taken over by Lieut. H. Digby-Smith.

Intense machine gun fire was now being directed to practically every point of the attack from the enemy blockhouses and the locality of the Chateau, and from the commanding ground of Gheluvelt to the right. The enemy's artillery barrage, which had opened out four minutes after zero, had added to the destruction. Reinforcements were sent forward to fill the gaps and press on with the assault, but they came under the same heavy fire as they moved up, and, suffering badly, were unable to make any impression

when thrown into the breach. Continuation of the advance
was seriously threatened, and despite many individual efforts
of gallantry and leadership, it was not long before it was
definitely held up.

But despite all this intense fire and the initial disorganisation and certain inevitable confusion caused by short
shooting, there were determined elements of both attacking
Companies who had succeeded in penetrating to a point
which brought them abreast of the Chateau, and in some
instances even beyond it. On the right, Lieut. Digby-Smith
and a handful of men reached a position which was actually
in advance of the Chateau ruins, but were forced to withdraw
for a short distance, and there hung on until blown out by
shell fire. On the left of the attack a small proportion of
4th Company's strength had pressed on until they also were
abreast of the main Chateau buildings, and in a position which
gave them observation to the rear. Further advance was
impossible against the heavy machine gun and sniping fire
which the enemy, in considerable force, directed from the
shelter of the ruins, from fortified shell-holes, and from a
trench about 60 yards in length sited to the left rear of the
Chateau. Our artillery barrage had some time since out-
stripped the infantry, and the smoke barrage was on the
final line of the attack. Captain Hines was now wounded
a second time and could only be carried out under cover of
darkness, one of the stretcher-bearers being killed on the
journey. Command of this advanced group, numbering 12
in all, was taken over by Sergt. J. H. Wilson, M.M., who
organised the party in shell-holes and set up a definite and
determined stand against the enemy. Snow had now commenced to fall. Throughout the afternoon repeated attempts
were made by enemy parties to cross the swamp of the
Reutelbeek and envelop this small post from the left flank,
but on each occasion they were shot to pieces at close range
by the fire of the one Lewis gun possessed by the garrison.
All of these attacks were delivered with great persistence
and bravery by troops of an obviously fresh Division, which,
there was reason to believe, was newly arrived from the
Russian Front. By dusk the supply of ammunition, most
of which had been collected from the dead, had almost given
out, but there were sufficient bombs left to successfully beat

off two attacks made during the night. It had been apparent towards evening that the enemy was being reinforced from the direction of Becelaere. as large parties could be observed moving along the ridge towards the Chateau.

During the night Lieut. McAuley reached the post, and its disposition in relation to the other advanced elements of the Battalion was ascertained. Thereafter digging operations were commenced across the front, but it was not until the early morning of the 5th that Sergt. Wilson and his small party were relieved from the position, which, isolated and unsupported, they had so gallantly held for practically two days and nights.

In view of the check received and the situation prevailing over the front, orders were issued by Brigade at 5.20 p.m. to consolidate the ground gained, but in a later message, timed 5.35 p.m., emphasis was laid on the urgent necessity of capturing under darkness the line of block-houses on the right of the Chateau, and the Chateau itself, an enveloping movement from the north being suggested. In reply to this communication, both Battalion Commanders, Major Tracy (Otago) and Lieut.-Colonel Mead (Canterbury), strongly urged that any attempt at further advance was inadvisable on account of the heavy casualties, which now amounted to 50 per cent. of the total strength and included many officers and senior non-commissioned officers; the activity and alertness of an enemy who had been reinforced at dusk, the uncertain situation on the left flank, and the necessity of keeping in hand a force to counter any attempted enemy action. In this view they were supported by Lieut.-Colonel Charters, who was stationed at forward Brigade Headquarters and had himself reconnoitred the situation. It was therefore reluctantly decided to abandon the offensive and consolidate the line held, which was approximately from 200 to 250 yards in advance of the original front line.

During the night of the 4th-5th the advanced line held by Otago was taken over by 8th and 14th Companies, from right to left, and the remnants of 4th and 10th Companies moved back to the locality of their original assembly positions. The consolidation of the line was now advanced to such purpose that by the morning of the 5th an almost continuous trench had been constructed across the Brigade sector.

The attack, while certainly failing to achieve its objective, had resulted in the gaining of certain high ground which commanded the Chateau to such an extent as to seriously embarrass the enemy's occupation of that stronghold.

For every success registered and for every failure admitted, there are certain definite causes which contribute to or influence the result. In this instance the misdirected fire of the supporting artillery was both demoralising and damaging. The Officer Commanding the 2nd New Zealand Infantry Brigade, in the course of a report on the Polderhoek operations, expressed the opinion that the main cause of failure was inadequacy of training. Though several days were devoted to practice over ground specially marked out, all reports served to show, he stated, that the men were not " intensively " trained to the necessary standard. They started off with considerable élan, and there was no lack of natural courage and grit once a line was formed and the course of action obvious. But a large proportion were reinforcement drafts, quite unfamiliar with hostile shelling or our own barrage fire. When the experienced officers and other ranks became casualties, many falling in the most gallant efforts to push forward, the new hands, " already to some extent demoralised by the short shooting of one 18-pounder battery," were at a loss and failed to show the necessary qualities of dash, determination and readiness for self-sacrifice which were indispensable factors for success. A glaring instance, he continued, was shown by the troops of the right Battalion leaving their assembly trenches too soon, by their returning to them, and on their starting forward again by their pressing into our own barrage. " All competent observers lay stress on this lack of training, and there is no question but that this is the main reason for the failure." Two further contributing causes were advanced as follows :—" (1) The mutually supporting block-houses were mostly undamaged by our artillery. The volume of machine gun fire from in front and from Gheluvelt was heavy. (2) The isolated nature of the attack drew intense artillery and machine gun fire, and its limits were still more clearly defined by the smoke barrage. It merits consideration as to whether a further attempt should not be part of a joint enterprise to include an attack on Gheluvelt, and possibly Becelaere."

Little further need be added to the above observations, save, perhaps, to emphasise the disadvantages of an isolated attack against a position the strength of which, great in itself, was not tactically confined within its own boundaries. There was little doubt but that the enemy regarded Polderhoek Chateau as an extremely important point. He had fortified the position with innumerable " pill-boxes " and machine guns. The Chateau itself, by reason of the unceasing artillery poundings to which it had been subjected, was on the surface little more than a pile of bricks and rubble, but underground it was capable of sheltering a numerous garrison. The existence of this stronghold, at such close range and over-looking our defences to the north, was no doubt regarded as a menace to the safety of our line, and there were sound arguments for its seizure. But any such undertaking must have revealed the tactical importance to the enemy of Gheluvelt, immediately to the south and across the swamp of the Scherriabeek. An isolated attempt on Gheluvelt with Polderhoek Chateau in the way would doubtless have proved a dangerous undertaking ; and the same might reasonably have been said of an attempt on Polderhoek with Gheluvelt in the way.

The casualties which the 1st Battalion of the Regiment sustained in the Polderhoek Chateau operations were as follows :—Killed, two officers and 43 other ranks ; wounded, seven officers and 153 other ranks ; missing, 26 other ranks ; total, 231. The officers killed were Captain C. Bryce (commanding 10th Company) and 2nd-Lieut. F. Marshall (4th Company). Lieut. C. D. Gabites, of the 2nd Light Trench Mortar Battery, and formerly of 8th Company, 1st Battalion, also fell in action. Every officer of the Regiment who went into the attack became a casualty, and at the same time the Battalion lost some of its best senior non-commissioned officers. Among the latter were Sergt. J. Hoff and Sergt. J. Guthrie, two Main Body soldiers, who were killed in the van of the attack. For his splendid work throughout the operations in maintaining the Battalion Signal Communications under the very greatest difficulties over an area swept by heavy fire, Sergt. G. Hayton, M.M., was awarded the Distinguished Conduct Medal.

It remains to be stated that the New Zealand Divisional Artillery was not in line for the Polderhoek attack.

At 8.30 a.m. on the 4th enemy troops had been observed assembling to the east of Polderhoek, but were dispersed by artillery fire. At 6 a.m. on the 5th an attack was delivered on the Brigade front by approximately 80 of the enemy, but was effectively and sanguinarily repulsed by Lewis gun and rifle fire. During the same afternoon our trench system was subjected to a heavy hostile bombardment, in the course of which 10th Company suffered severely. At the same time abnormal enemy movement was reported in the vicinity of Becelaere, to the north-east of Polderhoek, and our artillery developed an intense fire over the area in which this movement was observed. Enemy shelling ceased about 4.30 p.m., and no further attempts at attack developed. During the evening the Battalion was relieved by the 2nd Bedfordshire Regiment, and marched out of the line and back to Howe Camp, near Ypres, in Brigade support. On December 6th command of the Polderhoek sector was handed over to the 30th Division, and the Reutelbeek became the southern Divisional boundary.

Within almost a week of the date on which command of the Polderhoek sector passed from the New Zealand Division, the enemy had counter-attacked heavily and regained the ground won by the Regiment on December 3rd.

During this period the 2nd Battalion of the Regiment had not been inactive. On November 20th it vacated the Cafe Belge Camp in the Chateau Segard area, south-west of Ypres, and proceeded to Mic-Mac Camp, within easy marching distance. Three days later four officers and 200 other ranks proceeded to the area of Polygone Wood and completed 400 yards of communication trench from the Butte to the new support line. On the 26th, 4th Company relieved one company of the 3rd (Rifle) Brigade at Clapham Junction, on the Ypres-Menin Road; while the remaining Companies of the Battalion proceeded to dug-outs south-east of the Lille Gate, Ypres, in support to the 2nd Battalion of Canterbury. Over the several succeeding days there was a steady demand for large working parties, who were engaged carrying material and ammunition from Hooge Crater to points on the Menin Road, to Veldhoek, and to the front and support

239

lines of the Polderhoek sector; while others were engaged burying mules, the unfortunate victims of the enemy's systematic shelling of the routes which our transport followed. On December 2nd, 4th Company returned from Clapham Junction. On December 3rd, the day on which the attack was delivered against Polderhoek Chateau, the Battalion was required to furnish a party of 400 men in order to maintain the stretcher-bearing service between Clapham Junction and Hooge. In consequence of the non-success of the Polderhoek operation, orders were received for two companies to be despatched to Clapham Junction, there to be held in close reserve. The companies detailed moved off in the afternoon, and remained at that point until the 5th. Those who were engaged on stretcher-bearing returned to camp on the 4th, after performing heavy and continuous work throughout the night. Additional numbers were required for carrying water and rations for the front line garrison.

On December 7th orders were issued that the New Zealand Division would on the night of the 9th-10th extend its front for a short distance northwards, and that on the same date the 2nd Infantry Brigade would relieve the 3rd (Rifle) Brigade in the sector extending from the Polygonebeek on the right to the new northern boundary. The dispositions of the Brigade on relief were as follows :—2nd Battalion of Otago on the right, 1st Battalion of Canterbury in the centre, 1st Battalion of Otago on the left ; 2nd Battalion of Canterbury in support. The 1st Battalion of the Regiment moved into the line *via* Westhoek Road, 8th Company occupying the forward trenches on the right and 14th Company on the left, with 4th Company in support and 10th Company in reserve. The 2nd Battalion, moving into the line *via* Chateau Wood Road, had 4th and 8th Companies disposed in the front line from right to left, with 14th Company in support, and 10th Company in reserve. The Headquarters of the 1st and 2nd Battalions were established at the Butte.

From a defensive and constructive point of view the new sector presented every conceivable weakness. The erection of wire entanglements along the front and the construction of support and switch lines were works of first importance. There was necessity for a readjustment of the forward and subsidiary systems, while communication trenches required to be deepened to permit of safe passage to and from the front line.

During the afternoon of the 10th the enemy heavily bombarded parts of the front, and to this outburst our heavy artillery retaliated with counter-battery fire. The weather, previously dull and showery, was now fine and clear. A salvo of 5.9in. shells directed to Wattle Dump during the early morning of the 12th, while rations were being delivered, caused casualties to the number of four killed and eight wounded, including two company quartermaster - sergeants wounded and one killed. There was a great deal of artillery activity on the 13th. Our artillery carried out a concentrated shoot at 9 a.m., and repeated the performance at 7.30 p.m. During the night of the 13th-14th the 1st Battalion of the Regiment established three posts in advance of the forward line ; while the 2nd Battalion continued to push ahead with the construction of the new front line undertaken at the commencement of the tour, an attempt to connect between the two Companies on the night of the 14th being unsuccessful owing to the trench filling with water. On December 15th the Regiment was relieved by troops of the 4th Infantry Brigade. The 1st Battalion moved back to Halfway House and Railway Wood, and the 2nd Battalion to dug-outs near the Lille Gate, Ypres.

During this period of occupation of the line, complaints had been made of short shooting by the supporting artillery at certain points over the Brigade front. The New Zealand Divisional Artillery maintained that its guns were not in action at the times stated, and when the New Zealand group fired alone on the S.O.S. line, as a test on the 16th, the results were such as to make its contention appear justified. However, several conferences were held at this period at which the questions of short shooting, artillery registration, liason, test shoots, and other matters were fully and profitably discussed.

The Regiment remained over the next several days in the camp areas taken over on the 15th. Lieut.-Colonel J. B. McClymont arrived and took over command of the 2nd Battalion of the Regiment on December 19th; on the following day Major McCrae left on extended leave to the United Kingdom.

Unusual movement of enemy infantry was observed between the 14th and the 26th of December at points immediately north and south of, and opposite the Divisional sector. On the first mentioned date, an attack was delivered against the 30th Division opposite Polderhoek Chateau, and the front trench occupied. A counter-attack delivered at night, our machine guns co-operating, restored the line; but a further attack by the enemy left it in his possession. On the 20th there was a threatened attack under cover of fog south of the Scherriabeek, and the New Zealand Divisional Artillery was called upon to fire on the S.O.S. line. On the 22nd abnormal movement in the vicinity of Gheluvelt was dispersed by artillery fire; while attacks were threatened on the Reutel sector on the 25th, and on the Passchendaele sector on the 26th; and though the artillery was required to respond to S.O.S. calls, no definite infantry actions developed.

On December 22nd the Regiment returned to the sectors previously occupied. All available energies were again directed to the erection of wire entanglements, the improving of lateral communications, and the strengthening of the defences generally. During the afternoon of the 24th the sector held by the 2nd Battalion was subjected to a sustained bombardment, resulting in casualties to the number of six killed and 20 wounded. Snow commenced to fall in the evening and the weather became bitterly cold. The observance of enemy movement and unusual machine gun fire at 2.30 a.m. on the 25th suggested the probability of a raid along the 2nd Battalion frontage, and in response to the S.O.S. signal the artillery put down heavy fire. A patrol of three men then reconnoitred the front, and there gained contact with the enemy, one of whom Pte. H. Boreham succeeded in capturing and bringing back to our lines. It was admitted by the prisoner that he was one of a party detailed to demolish a " pill-box " on our front, and as a precautionary measure this block-house was on subsequent nights occupied by a post of seven men.

There was a rather curious encounter with the enemy on the evening of the 26th on the front of the 1st Battalion. A patrol under 2nd-Lieut. E. Newton, while operating near the Cemetery, was fired on from a distance of about 40 yards. Our men lay down and returned the fire, but the cold was so extreme that after they had been in that position for some time they were unable to use their rifles. Two of the enemy approached the party, evidently under the impression that it was out of action. The officer in charge threw a bomb, which did not explode. The enemy threw a bomb in return, and that also failed to explode. The Germans thereupon returned to their post, but later came out and were observed by the sergeant of the patrol, which had now shifted its ground, to lift one of our men and carry him into their own lines. It was assumed that this man had been killed when the enemy first opened fire.

The Regiment was relieved in the line on the night of the 27th by troops of the 4th Brigade, and thereupon moved back by road and light railway to Walker Camp.

This closes the account of the operations of at least two Battalions of the Regiment for the year 1917, but before entering upon another stage of the Great Adventure, there remains one event to be chronicled. On December 22nd Brigadier-General W. G. Braithwaite, C.B., C.M.G., D.S.O., Commanding the 2nd New Zealand Infantry Brigade, was evacuated to hospital on account of ill-health, a departure which finally involved his severance from the New Zealand Division after a long association commencing with the earliest days of Gallipoli. It was during the course of the Campaign on the Western Front that Brigadier-General Braithwaite became intimately known to the Regiment. In his capacity of Brigade Commander he exhibited a deep and sincere consideration for the well-being of everyone under his command— a feeling that was reciprocated by a certain affectionate regard, a warm admiration for personal gallantry, and an outspokenness that was oft-times staggering in its directness. His vigorous and uncompromising declarations under all circumstances, and the great force and genuineness of character which uniformly distinguished him, combined to make him one of the striking and outstanding figures in the Division, and assured for him a lasting place in the roll of those whose memories will long be cherished by the Regiment.

CHAPTER X.

THE 3RD BATTALION.

AT the beginning of 1917, the steadily accumulating strength of New Zealand Forces in the United Kingdom, comprised of reinforcements from the Dominion and of men who had been evacuated from hospital after service on the Peninsula or in France, led to the formation and establishment in the Field of an infantry Brigade additional to the three which the New Zealand Division then embraced.

The inception of this, the 4th New Zealand Infantry Brigade, dated from March 15th, 1917. Its formation was determined in London, where a staff was assembled, and appointments made to the commands of the units of which it consisted. These included the 3rd Battalions of the Otago, Canterbury, Wellington, and Auckland Regiments. The Brigade command was given to Lieut.-Colonel H. E. Hart, D.S.O. In the selection of commanding officers for the various Battalions, command of the 3rd Battalion of Otago Regiment was given to Major D. Colquhoun, with promotion to the rank of Lieut.-Colonel. Previous to this Major Colquhoun had for a considerable period occupied the position of Second-in-Command of the 1st Battalion, and was a well-known and highly popular officer of the Otago Regiment.

On March 26th the Brigade staff and commanding officers proceeded to Codford; on March 29th the 3rd Battalion of Otago Regiment came into being. The Brigadier-General then arrived and took over command as G.O.C. Troops, Codford Area. On the same day a draft of 570 n.c.o.'s and men were transferred from the Command Depot to the new Brigade; on March 30th a draft of 66 officers and 870 other ranks arrived from the New Zealand Infantry Reserve Group, Sling Camp; on April 3rd, 19 officers and 737 other ranks; and on April 24th a final draft of 925 other ranks, drawn mainly from the 20th, 21st, and 22nd Reinforcements. Among the officers and non-commissioned officers of the new Battalion of the Regiment were many soldiers of proved ability, who had been specially selected and sent across from France in order to furnish the required stiffening ; and these, with the large number of " old hands " included, provided a very valuable leavening.

The 3rd Battalion of the Regiment now had a strength of 20 officers and 580 other ranks. Major J. B. McClymont was appointed Second-in-Command to Lieut.-Colonel Colquhoun, and the Company Commanders at that date were Captains F. K. Waring, M. H. R. Jones, M. Watt, and K. S. Caldwell, with Lieut. D. S. Chisholm as Adjutant.

With a view to expediting and ensuring that the training of the Battalion was on sound lines, officers and non-commissioned officers were despatched to various schools of instruction in the United Kingdom ; while the services of special instructors from the Command Schools at Hayling Island and Aldershot were secured for training in musketry, and in Lewis and Vickers guns. With the preliminary work of organisation and equipment completed, training operations were carried on at high pressure.

On April 30th, as a unit of the 4th Brigade, the Battalion marched from Codford to Sling Camp, near Bulford, to participate in a review by His Majesty the King of the New Zealand Forces in England. The march proved a rather exhausting experience for unseasoned troops, owing to the excessive heat and the long distance travelled. The Review was held on the Bulford Fields on the following day and was a pronounced success, His Majesty the King, in a special message, expressing his appreciation of the appearance displayed by all ranks. At the close of the review General Sir Ian Hamilton briefly addressed the troops. This was his first renewal of acquaintance with the New Zealanders since the Gallipoli Campaign, and it was natural that he should receive an ovation marked by extraordinary warmth. The Hon. W. F. Massey and Sir Joseph Ward, then on a visit to England, also delivered brief addresses. The return journey to Codford was commenced early on the morning of May 2nd, when the Battalion was strengthened by the addition of several officers and about 300 men from Sling Camp.

Training was continued under excellent weather con ditions, and the standard of efficiency appreciably advanced. On May 10th the 4th Brigade was inspected by Field-Marshal Viscount French, who expressed himself as confident that the troops would uphold the best traditions of the New Zealand Division.

On May 25th orders were received for the 4th Infantry Brigade to move over-seas. In the early hours of the morning of May 28th, the 3rd Battalion of the Regiment, at a strength of 35 officers and 928 other ranks, entrained at Codford, and commenced the first stage of its journey to the Western Front. The whole unit had detrained at Southampton Docks by 12 noon, and at 6 p.m. departed by transport for France. Le Havre was reached in the early hours of the following morning after an uneventful passage. Disembarkation was effected and the Battalion marched to the Rest Camp. There it remained until May 31st, when it entrained and proceeded to Bailleul, which was reached on June 1st. The Battalion went under canvas, and on the following day was inspected by General Sir H. Gough and Lieut. - General Sir A. J. Godley.

The new Battalion of the Regiment had arrived in France in time to witness the launching of the great Messines Battle, and although its participation in this operation was not active, it nevertheless played an important role in rear. In accordance with operation orders the 4th New Zealand Infantry Brigade was to be held in Corps reserve, and was to carry out specified tasks under the direction of the C.E., 2nd Anzac Corps. In this connection, the 3rd Battalion of the Regiment was to be employed on the repair and reconstruction of the Wulverghem-Messines Road, following immediately upon the attack launched on the morning of June 7th, and was to work under the orders of the O.C. 3rd Tunnelling Company, Canadian Engineers. Previously, five officers and 135 other ranks had been detached for traffic control duties in the Corps area, while during the several days prior to the Messines Battle working parties were being supplied for various undertakings. At this stage the enemy's long range guns were periodically shelling the town of Bailleul; but the Battalion camp escaped damage.

On June 6th all working parties were withdrawn prior to moving forward, and on the following morning, when the Second Army launched its great attack against the Messines Ridge, the Battalion sat quietly by waiting until midday, when it moved off, and at 4.15 p.m. reached and bivouacked near Boyle's Farm, on the Wulverghem-Messines Road and immediately in rear of our old front line. The available strength was now divided into three shifts, and at 5.30 p.m. the first section commenced the task of putting the Messines-Wulverghem highway, so long in disuse, in a state of repair. Without interruption, save when it was necessary to shelter during periods of enemy shelling, this work was advanced with great vigour until the 10th, when parties were withdrawn and marched back to Bailleul.

LE BIZET.

On June 9th preliminary orders were issued for the 4th New Zealand Infantry Brigade to take over the front held by two battalions (Royal North Lancashire troops) of the 57th Division during the night 10th-11th June, the 4th Brigade to come under the command of the G.O.C. 3rd Australian Division. The 3rd Battalions of Auckland and Canterbury Regiments were to occupy the line from right to left, with the 3rd Battalion of Wellington in support; while the 3rd Battalion of Otago was to find all Corps working parties. The sector to be taken over by the 4th Infantry Brigade on this, the first occasion of its holding a part of the line on the Western Front, extended from the River Lys on the south to Westminster Avenue on the north, and was immediately south of Messines.

On June 12th it was discovered that the enemy had retired from his forward system of trenches along the Brigade front. The line thus vacated was occupied without opposition, and incidentally the trenches were found to be in a much better state of repair than our own. Further slight advances followed; and on the night of June 13th-14th the front occupied by the 4th Brigade was materially shortened as a result of the New Zealand Division extending its sector to the south, and the 2nd and 3rd Brigades taking over the line as far south as the Warnave River. This left the 4th Brigade holding a front from the Warnave River to the Lys.

In the meantime, the 3rd Battalion of Otago had met all requirements of Corps in the matter of working parties. These were maintained until the 18th, when the relief of parties was commenced and the Battalion concentrated in its area at Bailleul in readiness to move. Camp was struck on the morning of the 19th, and the Battalion set out for Brune Gaye. On the following day company commanders reconnoitred the Le Bizet sector, lying between the Lys and the Warnave, which the Battalion was to occupy in the course of the next few days.

On the night of the 22nd-23rd June the Battalion carried out the ordered relief, and thus entered into possession of front line trenches for the first time. This was in relief of the 3rd Battalion of Wellington, and the change-over was successfully accomplished by 2 a.m. on the 23rd, although the road approaches were under shell fire as the Lewis gun limbers were moving up.

The Le Bizet sector lay to the south of the Bois de Ploegsteert, with Armentieres still further to the south. The main geographical and tactical feature of the sector was the River Lys, which ran practically parallel to the front and separated the German defences from ours. The Lys was from 20 to 30 yards broad, normally six or seven feet deep, and liable to flood on its western bank. To a certain extent its presence modified some of the conditions of trench warfare, and security of our position and complete check of the enemy depended largely on active patrolling. The forward area of the sector was low-lying and in several places water-logged. Across the river, to where the enemy had retired only since the Battle of Messines, were the villages of Frelinghien on the right and Deulemont on the left, both strongly held by the enemy.

The dispositions of the Battalion on taking over the sector provided for the 4th, 8th, and 14th Companies occupying the front line and supports, with 10th Company in reserve. The 4th Company was opposite Frelinghien, 8th Company in the locality of the Brickfield, and 14th Company opposite Deulemont. On the left of the Battalion were troops of the 3rd (Rifle) Brigade ; on the right the 171st Brigade. The

Officers of 3rd Battalion, Otago Regiment.

LIEUT.-COLONEL D. COLQUHOUN, D.S.O., (D.)

Battalion remained in occupation of the Le Bizet sector until the close of the month, a period of eight days, and apart from the periodical activity of enemy artillery, conditions were for the most part normal. The main activity of the garrison was directed to patrolling the western bank of the Lys and countering possible enemy aggression.

On the afternoon of June 26th a small patrol which was operating along the river bank from a point near Frelinghien bridge, was fired upon by the enemy from the opposite side. The n.c.o. in charge of the patrol was severely wounded in the thigh, whereupon Pte. E. Grieve, who accompanied him, proceeded to assist him to a place of safety. He persisted in his task until it was accomplished, although it was necessary to cover a considerable distance, the enemy meanwhile firing heavily on the retreating party. For this worthy action, Pte. Grieve was recommended and awarded the Military Medal.

The Battalion was relieved in the line on June 30th by the 3rd Battalion of Canterbury, having acquitted itself creditably in the line, and having effected a great deal in the way of trench improvements. By way of familiarising the Battalion to some extent with general conditions of the line, and in view of the fact that it was to take over a front line sector for the first time, the work carried out immediately prior to and during the Messines operations had certainly proved of great value.

On being relieved the Battalion proceeded to billets at Les Trois Tilleuls, near Pont de Nieppe, and there embarked on a programme of training. At this period enemy night-flying aeroplanes were active and frequently dropped bombs over the billeting area.

On July 16th the Battalion moved up to Brune Gaye, and from there supplied all working parties for the line. On the 24th the Battalion returned to the line; 10th, 8th, and 14th Companies occupying the front system, and 4th Company being in reserve. This was the sector which the Battalion had previously occupied, and it was noticeable that a still further improvement had been effected in the state of the defences.

In order to assist in the operations of the Second Army, which in turn were designed to further the offensive of the Fifth Army set down for July 31st, orders were issued at this stage for the maintenance of increased activity in the patrolling of No Man's Land, and the display of special interest in the River Lys; also for digging short fire trenches which might suggest the construction of posts to cover a projected crossing of the Lys. All this was given effect to; and as part of the harassing and disturbing programme to which the enemy was subjected, increased artillery fire of a suggestive nature was maintained; while small forward posts, commanding and threatening the bridges over the Lys, were established by the Battalion on our left. Furthermore, at midnight on July 30th, a special company of Royal Engineers carried out a heavy gas projector bombardment of Frelinghien. The enemy gas alarm was sounded, but there was no retaliation, and the actual damage occasioned was not known. By these and other means the threatened area of attack in what was known as the Third Battle of Ypres was increased.

On August 1st the Battalion was relieved in the line and returned to billets. Owing to the bad weather conditions and the discomfort of the billets, improved accommodation had to be sought at Pont de Nieppe. The Battalion returned to the line on August 9th. The weather, previously unsettled, had now improved, and there was a corresponding increase in artillery activity on both sides. Our back areas shared in these attentions of the enemy, and as a consequence the Divisional baths at Pont de Nieppe were forced to close and many of the civilians found it desirable to leave the area. During the course of the shelling of the front line the enemy discharged a number of mustard-gas shells over the centre company's sector, presumably by way of retaliation for a light trench mortar bombardment of his machine gun positions in Frelinghien on the previous evening.

On August 16th the artillery in immediate support fired 5,000 rounds, mainly gas shells, in connection with operations being conducted further north, the enemy retaliating on our lines with heavier shelling than usual. On the 17th the Battalion was relieved and went back to billets for the periodical rest. A good deal of constructive work had been accomplished during the tour; while the increase in artillery activity was exemplified by the fact that the casualties amounted to four killed and 10 wounded. At this stage the civilian population was ordered to leave Pont de Nieppe owing to the continued enemy shelling.

A warning order was now issued that at an early date the 4th Brigade would be relieved entirely in the sector then occupied ; but the projected move was subsequently postponed, and a week later the Battalion was again in the line. On this occasion portion of the sector on the left was taken over by the 3rd Battalion of Canterbury Regiment, and the reduced frontage was held by 4th and 8th Companies, with 10th Company in support, and 14th Company in reserve. The continuance of fine weather led to considerable aerial activity over the forward and rear zones. The relief of the New Zealand Division along this front was carried out on August 27th by the 8th Division, but the 4th Infantry Brigade remained in the line and temporarily came under the comma ndof the latter Division. On the closing day of the month the Battalion was relieved by troops of the 2nd Middlesex Regiment, and moved back to hutments and tents at Canteen Corner.

On September 1st the Battalion transport left Nieppe by road for the new Brigade area at Henneveux, and on the following day companies entrained at Steenwerck, and proceeded to Wizernes, detraining there and continuing the journey by road and motor-lorries to the Surques area. On the following day a move was made to Cremarest, where the Battalion finally settled down in billets, the transport arriving the same evening after a trek of three days. The Battalion was now committed to a complete course of training, the value of which was enhanced by the peaceful nature of the surroundings. The weather was fine and warm, and training was continued without interruption. Particular attention was paid to attack practice in view of pending operations. There was an inspection by General Sir A. H. Russell, who was accompanied by Sir Thomas Mackenzie. The period of training, which was valuable in both a military and physical sense, terminated with a Brigade practice attack in the presence of General Godley.

On September 25th the Battalion set out for the Lumbres area. The Eecke area was reached two days later, and from this point a party of officers made a reconnaissance of the line east of Ypres. The Battalion had covered a considerable distance by road, and while the comparative ease with which the march was accomplished, notwithstanding the warmth of the weather, proved the effectiveness of training operations, the two days rest which followed were greatly appreciated. The march was continued to a point two miles west of Poperinghe, where the Battalion entered Forth Camp.

Orders were now received to move to the Ypres North area and the old British and German front line systems, Saint Jean sector. Less transport and cookers, Companies moved out at noon on October 1st, travelling by road and then by 'bus to Vlamertinghe, thence winding slowly in the evening light through the desolation of stricken Ypres, and finally reaching and bivouacking over the appointed area.

GRAVENSTAFEL.

The first stage of the Allied attack in the Third Battle of Ypres, launched on the morning of July 31st, extended over a front of 15 miles, from the River Lys opposite Deulemont (at which point the 3rd Battalion of Otago was then holding the line) northwards to beyond Steenstraat ; but the heaviest weight was thrown against the enemy by the Fifth Army on a front of about seven and a-half miles from the Zillebeke-Zandvoorde Road on the south to Bœsinghe in the north, east and north-east of Ypres. At the close of the first day's fighting between these two points, the enemy's foremost system of defence south of Westhoek (east of Ypres) had been carried ; north of this point the enemy's second line had also been captured as far as St. Julien ; and north of that again the attacking troops held the line of the Steenbeek to the point of junction with the French. Stormy weather now broke over the battle area, desperate conditions of rain and mud preventing any serious development of the offensive for several days. On August 16th the second attack was launched east and north-east of Ypres.

On the left of the British attack, practically the whole of that part of the Langemarck-Gheluvelt line, which formed the final objective, was gained ; but in the centre and on the right the main enemy resistance was encountered, and, save for a few small gains, the situation south of St. Julien at the close of the day was unchanged. Minor operations followed, but owing to the state of the ground it was September 20th before the third main attack, planned to penetrate to an average depth of approximately 1,000 yards, could be launched. On this occasion the left of the Second Army was extended northwards, and the assault upon the whole of the high ground which was crossed by the Menin Road entrusted to it. The attack of the Second Army penetrated to Veldhoek, and to the western side of Polygone Wood; while to the north the Fifth Army, operating cn both sides of the Ypres-Roulers Railway, reached the points of its objective along the Langemarck-Gheluvelt Line.

Persistent and heavy counter-attacks were now delivered by the enemy, but on September 26th the advance was renewed by the two Armies north and south of the Menin Road. The outcome of this attack was that the whole of Polygone Wood was cleared, the village of Zonnebeke was captured, and numerous strong-points north and south of the Wieltje-Gravenstafel Road wrested from the enemy. Again the enemy was not slow to deliver a series of determined counter-attacks. On the morning of October 4th the British reassumed the offensive, the selected front of the principal attack, which was directed against the main line of the ridge east of Zonnebeke, extending from the Menin Road north-wards for a distance of about seven miles. It was at this stage of the protracted series of operations conducted during the closing months of 1917 against the deep enemy defences east and north-east of Ypres, that the 3rd Battalion of Otago Regiment was committed to its first offensive action.

The two Armies concerned in this operation were, as before, the Second and the Fifth; and along the Second Army front the attack was to be delivered with two divisions disposed side by side; the 3rd Australian Division on the right and the New Zealand Division on the left, with the 48th Division of the Fifth Army on our immediate left. The task of the New Zealand Division was entrusted to the 1st and 4th Infantry Brigades, each attacking on a two battalion frontage. The 4th Brigade, disposed on the right of the Divisional front, was committed to an advance of approxi-mately 1,700 yards, with a frontage of 800 yards; the operation also including the capture of the village of Gravenstafel, and a small subsidiary spur running in a north-westerly direction from the main Passchendaele Ridge, known as the Abraham Heights. The first of the two objectives into which the advance was divided was approximately on the line Boethoek-Gravenstafel-Abraham Heights Spur, which was to be captured by the 3rd Battalions of Otago and Auckland Regiments, from left to right ; while the second or final objective, the capture of which was allotted to the 3rd Battalions of Wellington and Canterbury in the same order, extended across the northern edge of Berlin Wood. Special mopping-up parties were to be detailed by each of the assaulting Battalions, and in the case of Otago Battalion these were to deal with Otto Farm and Wimbledon, and the dug-outs in that locality.

The attack programme provided for five barrages to take the infantry forward, to break up counter-attacks, and to protect the infantry when on their objectives ; these being constituted as follows :—(a) 18-pounder creeping barrage under which the infantry advanced ; (b) 18-pounder and 4.5in. howitzer ; (c) machine gun ; (d) 6in. howitzer ; (e) 60-pounder and 8in. and 9.2in. howitzer. The depth effected by these barrages was over 1,000 yards, and in addition to the above, the super-heavy guns and howitzers were to engage special points of enemy defence. Arrangements were made for a total of 64 machine guns to barrage the Divisional front ; and exclusive of heavy guns and heavy and medium howitzers, the attack was to be supported by 180 18-pounders and 60 4.5in. howitzers. After the capture of the first objective there was to be a halt of one hour and a-half before the 3rd Battalions of Wellington and Canterbury Regiments moved forward to the capture of the second or final objective.

The 3rd Battalion of the Regiment, quartered in the area of the old British and German front lines, completed all details of equipment during the day of October 2nd, and Company officers visited the front line and made a reconnaissance of the country. On the same evening the Battalion moved forward and took over the front line from the 1st Battalion of Otago, which had been in occupation since the morning of September 30th, relief being completed by 10 p.m. Otago troops on the left and Auckland troops on the right were now holding the 4th Brigade front, each on a two-company frontage escheloned to a depth of 500 yards, the remaining two companies escheloned to a further depth of 600 yards. The 10th Company occupied the front line below the Abraham Heights, and two platoons from 4th and 14th Companies were established at the Kansas Cross Roads, with the remainder of the strength on the slope behind, and 8th Company at a point known as Gallipoli, to the right rear. The 3rd Battalions of Canterbury and Wellington were located in the old British and German front line systems and in the Ypres north area to the rear. The weather was still holding fine, but the general devastation of the Ypres area, the countless shell-holes and the yielding mud accentuated the difficulties of transport and movement. During the day of October 3rd two trial barrages were put down by the supporting artillery. On the occasion of the first, at 7.30 a.m., there were several short bursts ; on the second occasion, at 1.45 p.m., further " shorts " fell on the support line.

On the night of October 3rd the positions of assembly for the attack, from 200 to 300 yards in rear of the existing front line, were arranged and taped out by Captain M. Watt (14th Company) and Captain N. H. Arden (4th Company), as also were the approaches for a distance of 300 yards.

Zero hour was 6 a.m. on October 4th. Rain fell overnight and the morning broke cheerless and drizzly, with the sky heavily overcast. The early stages of the night had passed fairly quietly, save for intermittent shelling, but after midnight enemy artillery fire gradually increased in intensity, until at about half an hour before zero it assumed the fierceness of barrage fire and extended heavily to the south. This, it was subsequently learned, was the preliminary to an attack in force which the enemy was about to launch in an endeavour to regain the positions wrested from him during the British attacks of September 26th, and which our own attack but briefly anticipated. An hour and a-half before zero all companies had reached their assembly positions, and under increasingly heavy shell fire awaited the moment of attack. The two front line Companies selected for the assault were, from right to left—4th, commanded by Captain N. H. Arden, and 14th, commanded by Captain M. Watt ; 8th Company, commanded by Captain E. H. Sharp, was detailed for mopping-up purposes, and in that capacity was to assist the leading Companies ; whilst 10th Company, commanded by Captain C. M. Littlejohn, constituted the Battalion reserve. Fifteen minutes before zero hour the troops of 10th Company who had been holding the forward line were withdrawn and rejoined their Company in reserve.

At 6 a.m. our artillery broke out in thunderous concert with the enemy's guns, and moving behind a splendid barrage the Battalion advanced to the assault. The attack, once launched, moved forward without check until the main enemy resistance was encountered, consisting of " pill-boxes," machine gun emplacements, and fortified shell-holes along the slopes of Abraham Heights. The locality of Otto Farm, the first enemy stronghold, fell to the determined attack of one section of 8th Company, and yielded 33 prisoners. Forward of this point the quagmire of the Hanebeek rendered progress exceedingly difficult, many of the attacking troops sinking almost to their thighs in the slime and filth. Van Meulen Farm and dug-outs constituted one of the main defensive points of the ridge, and with strongly emplaced machine guns and a considerable garrison, offered a resistance which eventually broke before a determined attack organised and personally led by Captain N. H. Arden, resulting in the capture of over 50 prisoners and machine guns. On the objective being gained, Captain Arden, who had been wounded early in the advance, went forward to determine the most suitable line for consolidation, and was there grievously wounded, dying a few moments after he had given his instructions. In the death of Captain Arden the Regiment lost a brave and capable officer. Command of 4th Company was now taken over by Lieut. M. Rohan.

Four minutes after zero hour enemy machine guns opened fire on the line of Kansas Cross Roads-Douchy Farm, and three minutes later an artillery barrage to meet our attack fell along the same line, causing considerable casualties among the 3rd Battalion of Wellington. Otago troops thus escaped the enemy's retaliatory barrage ; but as the attack advanced came under the fire of machine guns emplaced along the ridge. Despite this fire and the resistance which the several strongholds offered, all objectives were speedily gained. The proximity of enemy localities at certain points had necessitated the advance being carried a further distance ahead. The battered ruins of Gravenstafel Village, standing on the crest of the ridge and strongly held by the enemy, confronted 14th Company, and it was essential that they should be cleared. Considerable opposition was encountered in the course of this operation; but it was overcome, and Captain Watt then withdrew his Company to the defined line of consolidation, which was approximately 100 yards down the reverse side of the slope. The Battalion now dug in under the continued fire of the enemy, and connected up with the 3rd Battalion of Auckland on the right and with troops of the 1st Infantry Brigade on the left. On the left flank of the Battalion, one platoon of 14th Company consolidated about 70 yards in advance of the remainder of the Company, joining up with troops of the 1st Battalion of Wellington. The right of 14th Company rested on the Gravenstafel Road, while the right flank of 4th Company was about 40 yards in advance of the line taken up by the 3rd Battalion of Auckland. Between the left flank and the Gravenstafel Road a gap of about 150 yards was bridged by a trench constructed by the attached mopping-up parties.

On the capture of the first objective, the 3rd Battalions of Wellington and Canterbury passed through the line held by Otago and Auckland troops, and forming up under the protective barrage waited until it lifted again at zero plus 130 minutes. Immediately on gaining the Abraham Heights spur a considerable volume of machine gun fire was encountered from the main ridge. At 9.30 a.m. the final objective of the attack was reached by these two Battalions, and touch established with the 10th Australian Brigade on the right; but it was not until later that a junction was effected with the left Battalion. Strong enemy opposition was met with at several points; and when the work of consolidation was commenced it was seriously hampered by machine gun and rifle fire from " pill-boxes " in the direction of Waterfields and from the main Passchendaele Ridge.

The New Zealand Division had on this day achieved a remarkable success. It had gained all its objectives, and captured 1,160 prisoners (covering four enemy divisions) and a considerable number of machine guns. The 3rd Battalion of Otago Regiment, as its share in the operation, had also achieved substantial and decisive success, which was the more remarkable by reason of being the Battalion's first offensive effort. The Battalion's casualties totalled six officers and approximately 150 other ranks; on the other side of the scale, the captures included over 250 prisoners and eight machine guns. The sodden and yielding nature of the ground, while seriously impeding advance, had certainly minimised casualties from shell fire, the shells generally burying themselves well below the surface before bursting. The majority of the casualties sustained were due to machine gun fire. Sergt. D. Sterritt's worthy performance in taking charge of his platoon, though wounded, and consolidating under heavy shell fire was rewarded with the Distinguished Conduct Medal.

The attack apparently left the enemy thoroughly disorganised; the only counter-attack threatened having been destroyed at the outset of its assembly near Kronprinz Farm, on the left of the Divisional front.

The ground gained as a result of these operations now afforded excellent observation on to the northern end of the Passchendaele Ridge.

Intermittent though somewhat scattered enemy shelling continued until 4 a.m. on the 5th, when it abated considerably and the situation remained normal over the day. Consolidation of the ground gained and improvement of communications were vigorously prosecuted, and when the time arrived on the night of October 5th-6th for relief of the Battalion by troops of the West Riding Regiment, of the 49th Division, all work was well advanced. Across the Divisional front, two practically continuous trenches had been dug, the construction of communication trenches was well in hand, and duck-board and mule tracks had been pushed forward from the old lines. The single road forward leading to Gravenstafel, which fed the Division for all purposes, was in a bad condition from shelling, which seriously retarded the forward transport of guns and material.

Command of the new Saint Jean sector passed from the New Zealand Division to the 49th Division on October 6th.

On being relieved on the night of October 5th-6th the Battalion trekked back to point of bivouac near Goldfish Chateau. On the 6th the Battalion marched to Vlamertinghe, and from that point proceeded in 'buses to Steenvorde. From there a cold and miserable journey was continued to Eecke, which was reached at 2 a.m. on the 7th, and billets secured in the town. Opportunity was taken by the Commanding

Officer, Lieut.-Colonel Colquhoun, to address all ranks and compliment them on the splendid work accomplished during the course of the operations just concluded.

RETURN TO THE LINE.

Orders were now received for the 4th New Zealand Infantry Brigade to relieve the reserve Brigade of the 49th Division in the Saint Jean sector, command of which passed from that Division to the New Zealand Division at 10 a.m. on October 11th. The Battalion accordingly set out for the forward area, and on detraining at Ypres, marched to the locality of the old British and German front line systems. On October 12th, the day of the tragic attack launched against the Bellevue Spur by the 2nd and 3rd Brigades, the Battalion first occupied positions in the area of Capricorn Keep and Spree Farm, and later moved up into support on the western slopes of Abraham Heights. At this point heavy gas shelling was experienced. Following upon the Passchendaele operations large parties were supplied for stretcher-bearing.

In compliance with orders for the relief of troops of the 3rd (Rifle) Brigade in the line, the Battalion moved up during the evening of the 14th and took over advanced positions held by the 3rd Brigade after the Passchendaele attack, extending approximately from the Cemetery on the left to Peter Pan on the right. The front line Companies were 8th and 10th, with the remaining two Companies disposed over the support and reserve positions, and with Battalion Headquarters established at Kronprinz Farm. It was impossible to accommodate the Battalion in the positions held by the 3rd Brigade, which had been seriously reduced in strength as a result of the Passchendaele attack, it being found necessary to extend the line some distance to the right towards the sector held by the South African Brigade. There was inconsiderable artillery fire during the night, but on the following day the enemy disclosed activity which increased until the whole of the forward area was swept by an obviously largely augmented artillery strength ; while low-flying enemy aeroplanes persistently harassed the trench garrisons. Meantime our own heavy artillery had proceeded with the bombardment of the block house system of the Bellevue Spur. Thus conditions were far from settled, and continued so until the night of the 17th, when the Battalion was relieved and moved back into support on the western slopes of Abraham Heights.

The next move was to reserve positions in the old British and German front line area, where a certain amount of rest was assured. Early on the morning of October 22nd the Battalion proceeded to the Ypres entraining station, and from there by rail to Wizernes, which was reached at midday. From this point the Battalion marched to comfortable billets at Haut Loquin, Rougemont, and Reberques. On October 22nd command of the sector held by the New Zealand Division had passed to the 3rd Canadian Division, and by October 25th the whole of the Division was back in training areas. On the 26th it was announced that Lieut.-Colonel Colquhoun, Commanding the 3rd Battalion of the Regiment, had been awarded the D.S.O. in recognition of the splendid success which his command had achieved in the operations of October 4th.

The opening days of November saw the Battalion still out of the line. The weather at this stage was anything but favourable, but not bad enough to interrupt a prescribed programme of recreation and route marches. On November 6th the Battalion, with transport complete, was inspected by Brigadier-General Hart, Commanding the 4th Infantry Brigade, and at the close of the inspection medal ribands in connection with awards for gallantry in the field were presented to several men. The period of rest and training came to a close on November 11th, when the Battalion moved by road and train to Brewery Camp, near Dickebusch. A halt was made there until the 16th, when the reserve quota proceeded to the details camp, and the Battalion marched out of Brewery Camp to Zillebeke Bund dug-outs. From this point large parties were detailed for carrying material from Birr Cross Roads to Brigade Headquarters at the Butte, at the northern extremity of Polygone Wood.

Orders had previously been issued for the relief by the New Zealand Division of the 21st Division on the front extending from the Reutelbeek on the right to Noordemdhoek on the left, east of Polygone Wood, and accordingly the 4th Infantry Brigade on the night of November 14th-15th relieved that Division in the left sub-sector. On November 21st the Battalion moved into the line in relief of Wellington troops on the right of the Brigade sector. The two front line Companies were 4th and 8th from right to left, with 10th Company in support, and 14th Company held in reserve for counter-attacking purposes. Heavy rain fell all night and considerable work was required to effect drainage of the trenches. There was intermittent enemy shelling throughout the 22nd and the 23rd, and on the latter date our artillery carried out a test barrage, followed by harassing fire, the enemy retaliating over our back areas during the night. The weather now improved slightly, the resulting increased visibility producing considerable aerial activity on both sides.

On the morning of November 24th our artillery resumed its programme of harassing fire, drawing a vigorous reply from the enemy over our front and support lines. Artillery duels of more or less violence continued at intervals throughout the day, and casualties were much above the normal. The following day was appreciably quieter, although our own artillery subjected the enemy to brief concentrated " shoots." This performance was repeated on the 26th, and on this occasion the response was heavy indeed, the front line, the Menin Road, and Hooge Crater receiving considerable attention. On the same day an inter-company relief was effected, and in addition a portion of the right sub-sector held by the 3rd (Rifle) Brigade was taken over by the Battalion. On the 27th our artillery delivered concentrated fire over the area of Polderhoek Chateau, this being repeated with increasing intensity over the succeeding days, apparently with considerable damage to the enemy defences and the infliction of many casualties. The last day of the month was one of constant and furious artillery duelling, commencing with a heavy barrage which was put down in response to an S.O.S. signal sent up on the right, followed by an intense bombardment of the enemy defences over the whole of the Divisional front. On December 1st the Battalion was relieved in the line and journeyed back to Mic-Mac Camp, where comparative rest was enjoyed in Divisional reserve over the succeeding fortnight.

At midday on December 15th the Battalion left camp and marched to Ouderdom, proceeding thence by light railway to Hellfire Corner, and in compliance with an order for the relief by the 4th Brigade of the 2nd Brigade, took over support positions in the Polygone Wood sector. Just prior to this Major McClymont had proceeded to the 2nd Battalion ; Major K. S. Caldwell, who had for some time commanded 8th Company, being appointed Second-in-Command. On the 22nd Otago moved into the front line in the sector opposite Cameron Covert. The weather was now bitterly cold, and hard frosts alternated with falls of snow. Intense artillery activity continued, and Christmas Day, with the Battalion in the line, was no exception to this order of things. The unusual enemy movement observed at various points along the Divisional front and north and south of there, and the appearance of the S.O.S. signal as a warning of attempted enemy attacks, led to frequent intense bursts of artillery fire from our side, invariably provoking retaliation from the enemy; it was not until the Battalion had been relieved on December 27th and moved back as support battalion to the Brigade in line that a return to settled conditions followed. At 11 o'clock, British time, on the night of December 31st, our artillery saluted the New Year, and incidentally the enemy, by firing salvoes of one, nine, one and eight rounds in succession.

As from January 1st, 1918, the Regiment came under the XXII. Corps, the II. Anzac Corps being now no longer in existence. At the same time the II. Australian Corps was formed, and the New Zealand Division was merged into the XXII. Corps.

On the night of January 2nd the Battalion relieved the 1st Battalion of the 3rd Brigade in the Cameron Covert, or Becelaere sectoi. The 10th Company and one platoon of 4th Company occupied the front line ; 14th Company was in support, and 4th and 8th Companies were in reserve. This period in the line did not witness very great activity, save for intermittent shelling. On relief the Battalion moved back to Birr Cross Roads and there entrained for Howe Camp, which was reached shortly after midnight. The weather was still exceedingly cold, and there were several rather heavy snow-falls. From Howe Camp the inevitable working parties were supplied. The Battalion remained there until January 17th, when Companies moved independently to Belgian

Chateau Camp, in accordance with the relief of the 1st Brigade as the Corps Working Brigade.

A successful reunion of officers of the 4th Infantry Brigade was held at Poperinghe on February 2nd, and at this function the 3rd Battalion of the Regiment was well represented.

THE BATTALION DISBANDS.

The time was now approaching when the 3rd Battalion of the Regiment was to cease to exist as such, under orders of the G.O.C., N.Z.E.F. ; a decision arrived at in consequence of the impracticability of maintaining four New Zealand Brigades in the Field at the required strength with the reinforcements coming to hand. On February 7th the 4th Brigade terminated its existence as an infantry unit of the Division, and came to be known as the New Zealand Works Group, Headquarters then being at Hoograaf. Thus the 3rd Battalion of the Regiment, the foundations of which were laid in England in March, 1917, brought to a close its comparatively short though highly effective career as an active infantry unit of the Regiment and of the New Zealand Division on the Western Front.   •

From the reinforcements thus made available, and from those passed as trained by the New Zealand Reinforcement Wing at Abeele, temporary units, representative of each Battalion, were formed for work under Corps. Lieut.-Colonel Colquhoun now proceeded to the 2nd Battalion of the Regiment, remaining there for a period of two months, and then leaving for New Zealand on a tour of duty. Shortly afterwards the four Works Battalions were reorganised into three Battalions corresponding to the three Brigades of the New Zealand Division, and this arrangement was given effect to at midnight on February 20th. The name " New Zealand Works Group " was altered to that of " New Zealand Entrenching Group," and the three Battalions were similarly known as Entrenching Battalions—1st, 2nd, and 3rd. Drafts were to be forwarded periodically to the Division from the Entrenching Group, such drafts to be assembled at the New Zealand Reinforcement Camp for completion of equipment and for necessary training prior to going forward.

The gradual absorption of officers and non-commissioned officers of the 4th Brigade into the 1st, 2nd, and 3rd Brigades followed, and 200 other ranks were almost immediately transferred to the two active Battalions of Otago Regiment.

At midnight on February 20th, 1918, all rolls of the 3rd Battalion of Otago Regiment were closed ; and approximately 600 other ranks transferred to the New Zealand Entrenching Group.

CHAPTER XI.

1918.

WITH the dawn of a new year, 1918, the military horizon failed to reveal any sign which might be construed as promising from the point of view of the Allies. The fogs of winter hung with depressing weight over the battlefield ; the guns still boomed their unsatisfied challenge over the incarnadined and tortured wastes ; and mud was everywhere so deep and movement in consequence so difficult and restricted as to force the great Armies to a complete standstill. It was as yet too early to forecast the startling *denouement* which the advent of spring was to witness. Of this and the subsequent rapid and decisive march of events which the year 1918 produced, the succeeding chapters of the History will proceed to speak.

On January 6th orders were issued for the relief by the 2nd Infantry Brigade of the 3rd (Rifle) Brigade in the left sub-sector of the New Zealand Divisional front. The 1st Battalion of the Regiment was to take over the Noordemdhoek sector, and the 2nd Battalion the Reutel sector, both lying immediately to the east of Polygone Wood.

In accordance with these orders, the Regiment reached the front line on the evening of January 8th, the 1st Battalion occupying the extreme left of the Divisional frontage. The state of the two sectors was such that all the available strength had to be employed in the hope of effecting an improvement. Heavy snow made the conditions infinitely worse, and the lack of shelters was keenly felt. Following upon an almost immediate thaw, the trenches were reduced to a state impossible to describe. There were further heavy falls of snow ; large areas of country became completely inundated ; the trenches were either flooded or fell in, and many of the avenues were waist deep in mud. The Ypres area was living up to its winter reputation.

The Regiment was relieved on the 14th, whereupon the 1st Battalion moved back to dug-outs at Halfway House and Railway Wood, and the 2nd Battalion to Otago Camp.

After such an arduous tour it was unfortunate indeed that there should have been an immediate and insistent call for working parties. Exceedingly heavy weather continued, and there was great difficulty in meeting the daily demand for men, owing to the large number who were medically classified as "excused duty," or "light duty." A number of men were also suffering from the various stages of trench feet ; a state of affairs which was not to be wondered at.

On January 20th the Regiment returned to the line, the 2nd Battalion being now under the command of Major J. Hargest, who temporarily succeeded Lieut.-Colonel J. B. McClymont, evacuated sick. The trenches were in an even worse condition than formerly ; but any improvement by drainage could not be hoped for until there was a return of fair weather. Shortly after midnight on the 20th the enemy heavily shelled our support and reserve areas, and following upon this the S.O.S. signal appeared on the right. Our artillery responded and the enemy fire died down. About 6 o'clock on the evening of the 21st a party of the enemy moved across the front of one of the forward posts occupied by 14th Company of the 2nd Battalion. They were immediately engaged, and when a party under Sergt. J. T. Clearwater moved out and reconnoitred the area one wounded prisoner and a heavy machine gun were secured. At 1.30 on the following morning the enemy was encountered in considerably greater strength. A total of approximately 100, in four parties, attempted a raid on the left of the line held by 8th Company of the 2nd Battalion, under cover of a preliminary bombardment. Only one of the four parties succeeded in getting through the wire, and none of them reached our trenches, the attack being beaten off by Lewis gun, rifle fire and bombs, aided by the artillery and machine gun barrages which came down promptly in response to a call from the line. In this action the combined bombing efforts of Sergt. Travis and Sergt. A. Maclean, the latter of whom remained at his post though severely wounded, assisted very materially in effecting the repulse of the raiders. There were eight enemy dead in front of our wire, and our casualties numbered one killed and three wounded.

There was a slight improvement in the weather on the 23rd, and consequently improved observation ; but after his experience of the previous night the enemy was not disposed to show himself. On the 24th our artillery carried out a destructive shoot on the right of the Brigade sector, Lewis gunners and snipers standing by in anticipation of obtaining favourable targets, but without their materialising. Subsequently Sergt. Travis and some of the members of his special patrol party moved out and examined the area to which the artillery fire was directed. During the evening an enemy relief was plainly visible in the bright moonlight, and considerable fire was brought to bear on it. The Regiment was relieved in the line on the 26th, and the 1st Battalion moved back *via* Wattle Dump and Westhoek Road to Manawatu Camp, and the 2nd Battalion to Otago Camp. Much useful work had been accomplished during the tour.

The two Battalions remained at their respective camps until the close of the month; and though a certain demand for working parties had to be complied with, there was time available for parading to the baths established at the Moat. Very close attention had to be devoted to all incipient cases of trench feet. Major McCrae had now returned from leave, and assumed command of the 2nd Battalion. On the last day of the month orders were received which involved a move into Divisional reserve, and within two days the Regiment was settled down at Walker Camp, where it remained over the succeeding week.

On February 7th several officers reported on loan from the 3rd Battalions of the Auckland and Wellington Regiments. This was the beginning of the end of the 4th New Zealand Infantry Brigade. A few days later a large number of other ranks reported at rear Battalion Headquarters as reinforcements from the 3rd Battalion of Otago.

Orders were now received for the Regiment to return to the line. On February 8th the 1st Battalion moved up to Polygoneveld into support positions in relief of 3rd (Rifle) Brigade troops, while the 2nd Battalion left Dickebusch siding, and after detraining at Birr Cross Roads, proceeded *via* Westhoek and the Butte to the front line of the Reutel sector. At this time it was announced that the 20th Division would take over the Cameron Covert sector, to the south of Reutel, from the New Zealand Division, and that the latter would extend its northern flank to a point opposite Broodseinde. While in support the 1st Battalion provided carrying parties for the front line troops, and during the same period erected over 3,000 yards of double apron wire entanglements in front of Patoka trench, Papanui switch, and Otaki support. The 2nd Battalion, minus the garrison, was similarly engaged, the state of the defences offering plenty of scope for surplus labour. On the 12th enemy artillery displayed marked activity, sudden bursts of fire being delivered to points where any movement disclosed itself. On February 13th Lieut.-Colonel Colquhoun, D.S.O., arrived from the now disbanded 4th Brigade, and took over command of the 2nd Battalion.

While reconnoitring No Man's Land during daylight on February 15th, Pte. A. Macdonald, one of Sergt. Travis's special patrol party, was fired on by an enemy sniper. Returning and moving further along our line, he succeeded in picking up the post from which the shot had been fired, and then alone moved into No Man's Land with the object of attacking the position. Macdonald, who subsequent to moving out was joined by Sergt. B. W. Croker, reached the post unobserved. Peering through the loop-hole of a steel plate, he discovered that the position, which comprised a fortified shell-hole with a covering of " elephant " iron, was occupied by five of the enemy. Closing the loop-hole again he threw two bombs into the post, and then jumped in among the enemy. The n.c.o. in command, refusing to be taken prisoner, was killed, and the remaining four of the garrison successfully brought back to our lines. The very daring of this action assured its success, and for this fine effort Pte. Macdonald was awarded the D.C.M., and Sergt. Croker the M.M.

The 1st Battalion now moved into the front line from support, and the 2nd Battalion on relief trekked back to dug-outs in Albania Woods. The dispositions of the 1st Battalion on taking over the forward area were as follows :—
4th and 10th Companies in the front line from right to left ; 8th Company in support, and 14th Company in reserve. The weather over the succeeding few days was considerably better, with a corresponding improvement in the state of the trenches. On the morning of the 17th a special patrol of two n.c.o.'s left our right post and set out to reconnoitre the ground and approaches to a derelict tank and " pill-box "

near Juniper Wood. The patrol reached the tank and remained in it for half-an-hour. Five enemy dead were counted, apparently the result of our shelling during the previous weeks. There were no obstacles in the way of wire entanglements to contend with, and there was a well-beaten track from the tank to the " pill-box."

During the 18th artillery activity was much above the normal. Between 10 o'clock at night and the early hours of the following morning, the enemy poured a heavy concentration of gas shells over the area of the Butte de Polygone, with disastrous results to the personnel of the 2nd Brigade and Battalion Headquarters established there. The mustard gas used probably did not reach the height of its activity until influenced by the warmth of the morning sun ; but the fact remained that during the day the extraordinary total of 14 officers and 162 other ranks of the Division were evacuated as gassed cases, a large proportion of whom belonged to the Headquarters establishment of the 1st Battalion of Otago.

During the night of the 19th-20th a successful raiding operation was accomplished by the 1st Battalion. The party committed to the task comprised 30 other ranks from 4th Company, under the command of 2nd-Lieut. W. O'Connell, and had previously received special training at the Brigade School. The objective was a portion of the enemy's line at the northern edge of Juniper Wood, including the derelict tank and " pill-box " previously referred to. Heavy rain had fallen, and No Man's Land was in an extremely wet and muddy condition. Rapid movement was therefore almost impossible. The raiding party moved out into shell-holes about 30 yards in front of our parapet in readiness to carry out the plan of attack, which was to rush the derelict tank and then move in a northerly direction towards and slightly beyond the " pill-box." Our artillery maintained a heavy bombardment of other sectors of the line in order to mislead the enemy as to the location of the raid, while at the same time light trench mortars briefly bombarded the objective. The raiding party, on the trench mortars ceasing fire, rushed forward to their task, leaving a Lewis gun and section on the right flank to prevent their being cut off. The derelict tank was reached and surrounded, and five of the enemy secured as prisoners, but one of them was immediately shot by Pte. Stark, who was not officially one of the raiding party. The mud was so bad and the going so heavy that the party detailed for the "pill-box" did not reach their objective within the allotted time. They were within 30 yards of it when the recall flare was sent up; and as the orders were that once identification had been secured the raiding party was to withdraw on the signal being given, the officer in command of the operation gave instructions for the party to return. Casualties were confined to one n.c.o. slightly wounded by a fragment of trench mortar shell.

The 2nd Battalion, which since the 15th had been supplying carrying and salvaging parties, on the 21st relieved the 4th Battalion of the 3rd (Rifle) Brigade in the Noordemdhoek sector. On the 22nd the 1st Battalion of the Regiment was relieved by the 4th Battalion of the Duke of Wellington's West Riding Regiment, and thereupon moved back to Manawatu Camp. On the same evening the 2nd Battalion was relieved by the 7th Battalion of the West Riding Regiment, and proceeded *via* Westhoek to the Ypres infantry barracks where it received an additional strength of over 270 other ranks from the Reinforcement Camp, from the 3rd Battalion of Otago, and from the 2nd Brigade Training School. The 1st Battalion also received drafts totalling about 150 men from the same sources. On the 23rd the 1st Battalion entrained at Ypres *en route* for Caestre, where it detrained and billeted the same night. The 2nd Battalion followed suit, and after detraining at Caestre, marched to Hondeghem, which was reached after midnight.

On February 24th command of the New Zealand Divisional sector was handed over to the 49th Division, and the New Zealand Division passed into Corps rest area.

With the Regiment out of the line, and clear of the pestilent salient of Ypres, the first few days had necessarily to be devoted to interior economy, refitting, and reorganising. Continuous fighting under the worst possible conditions of ground and weather, such as had been experienced in the Salient over the preceding few months, had produced a state of complete exhaustion, and training of a judicious and progressive nature was required to stimulate and restore impaired vitality of mind and body.

A tragic affair occurred in the 2nd Battalion lines on March 3rd. Captain R. J. Hill, M.C., and 2nd-Lieut. D.

McLean, M.M., were fatally shot without apparent reason by a private of the Battalion Transport, who, presumably insane, subsequently shot himself. A funeral service held in the Hondeghem Cemetery on the following day was attended by representatives of each Company and of other branches of the Division.

On March 5th Major McCrae left the 2nd Battalion on a tour of duty to the United Kingdom, and on the 7th Lieut.-Colonel Charters was evacuated suffering from the effects of gas poisoning. Major Hargest thereupon assumed command of the 1st Battalion.

In order to carry out a course of musketry it was necessary for the Battalions to proceed to Moulle, where several days were profitably devoted to rifle and Lewis gun range practices, open warfare and tactical schemes, and anti-gas training.

On March 22nd the Regiment's period of rest and training, pleasant and beneficial though it had been, came to an abrupt termination. The expected German offensive—the great Battle of St. Quentin—had opened against the Third and Fifth British Armies.

CHAPTER XII.

BATTLE OF ST. QUENTIN.

It is necessary to briefly review the situation which obtained on the Western Front at the beginning of 1918. Russia had ceased to exist as an active belligerent Power on the side of the Allies, and the transfer of German and Austrian Divisions from the Russian to the Western Theatre of War had already commenced. This gave the enemy a definite numerical superiority. The American Army to come was in a mere stage of development. Consequent upon these events, the British Army set itself a policy of defence ; but there were certain considerations which tended to limit this defensive policy. In January, 1918, after protracted deliberations, the British relieved the French of about 28 miles of front, and with this extension to the right the British Army was holding a front which stretched over a distance of approximately 125 miles. The exhausting operations conducted at the close of 1917 had seriously drained the strength of the Army, and when the German blow fell in March, 1918, it would seem that the British Army was still deficient of the necessary reserve of strength.

Certain it was that the enemy was about to launch a formidable offensive. Frequent air reconnaissances indicated that communications by road and rail were being extended, and that great ammunition and supply dumps were being established in rear of the whole enemy front from Flanders to the Oise. In his Despatch covering events of that period, Sir Douglas Haig, Commander-in-Chief of the British Armies, stated that on the 19th March his Intelligence Department reported that the final stages of the enemy's preparations for an offensive on the Arras-St. Quentin front were approaching completion, and that from information obtained it was probable the actual attack would be launched on March 20th or 21st. "On our side," he added, "our dispositions were as complete as the time and troops available could make them."

The Armies holding the front affected were the Fifth and the Third. The front of the Fifth Army, at that stage commanded by General Sir H. Gough, extended from the junction with the French, just south of Barisis, to north of Gouzeaucourt, a distance of about 42 miles. The Third Army, under the command of General the Hon. Sir Julian Byng, held a front of approximately 27 miles, from north of Gouzeaucourt, to south of Gavrelle.

The great German Offensive was launched on March 21st on a front of about 54 miles; and on March 28th extended northwards until from La Fere to beyond Gavrelle about 63 miles of our original front were involved. According to estimates, a total of 73 German divisions were engaged against the Third and Fifth Armies and the right of the First Army, and were opposed in the first instance by 22 British infantry divisions in line, with 12 infantry divisions and three cavalry divisions in close reserve. Additional reserves were hurriedly collected from other parts of the front, once the enemy's intentions became known. Before the end of March a further eight British divisions had been brought south and committed to the battle, and by April 9th an additional four divisions had arrived.

The opening of the German attack was signalled at 5 o'clock on the morning of March 21st by a bombardment of terrible intensity with gas and high explosive shells from guns of all calibres directed along the front and back areas of the Fifth and Third Armies from the Oise to the Scarpe River. Heavy bombardments on other parts of the Western Front broke out simultaneously. Shortly after 9 o'clock the infantry assault had been launched along the whole of the selected front. Following upon this terrific artillery preparation, and under cover of a dense fog, great masses of German infantry swept forward to the attack, completely overwhelmed the British foremost defences and advanced field guns, and by midday had reached the first line of battle positions on almost the whole front of the attack. The most desperate resistance was unavailing against this avalanche. Attack followed upon attack, and a break-through by the enemy at one point imperilled the position and compelled a withdrawal at another. The offensive was renewed with equal determination on the 22nd, and despite heavy losses inflicted on the enemy at short range, the British had again to give ground under the weight of the onslaught. By the evening of the second day of the battle, the enemy had penetrated to the third zone of defence at several points. The whole of the resources at the command of the Fifth Army had already been committed to the fight, and a withdrawal to the bridgeheads east of the Somme was inevitable.

On the morning of the 23rd the Fifth Army Commander, in order to avoid almost certain defeat by committing his exhausted divisions to an engagement with fresh and vastly superior numbers, decided to continue the withdrawal to the west bank of the Somme. Retractions were also necessary on the front of the Third Army; and at the junction of the two Armies the position became critical. One result of these retirements was that divisions and brigades lost touch, and with the enemy, now flushed with success, maintaining an incessant pressure, the rearward movement continued. The days of the 24th and 25th were equally disastrous. On the 24th the III. Corps (the right Corps of the Fifth Army) passed under the command of the French Third Army, and French troops were coming rapidly to its assistance. On the 25th the situation over the front of the Third Army had improved, and there were hopes that the enemy would be stopped north of the Somme and the line of the Ancre held. South of the Somme there was more cause for anxiety. The troops had reached a state of almost complete exhaustion; and it was not to be wondered at that serious demoralisation and disorganisation had set in.

On the night of the 25th orders were given that in the event of the enemy continuing his attacks in strength, the divisions affected should fall back to the approximate line Le Quesnoy-Rosieres-Proyart, and the Fifth Army link up with the right of the Third Army at Bray. The enemy did resume his assaults on the morning of the 26th, south-westwards and westwards from Nesle, also about Hattencourt, in the neighbourhood of the St. Quentin-Amiens Road, and at Herbecourt. The withdrawal accordingly commenced and the new line was taken up. North of the Somme the situation was becoming more settled, although a dangerous gap existed between the V. and IV. Corps of the Third Army, over the area between Hamel and Puisieux. It was into this gap that the New Zealand Division, which had travelled by rail and forced march from the north, was thrown, definitely arresting the enemy's advance about Colincamps and Beaumont Hamel, and then quickly hurling him back from the high ground which gave him observation far to our rear. It was on the 26th of March that General Foch assumed supreme command of the Allied Forces on the Western Front.

On the 27th, again attacking in great strength against the greater part of the Fifth Army front and against the French, the enemy continued to gain ground. An unfortunate retirement to beyond the Bray-sur-Somme-Albert line on the previous day precipitated a withdrawal further south, and the great railway junction of Amiens, towards which the German wedge had been driven to a depth of over 40 miles from the starting point, became imperilled. At the close of the day of the 27th the approximate line held at this point was the defence of Amiens. On the 28th the enemy renewed his attacks with great violence, notably from Puisieux to north-east of Arras, which represented an extension of the original front so far as the northern flank was concerned. While gaining ground at many points, the Germans failed to achieve the dramatic successes of the preceding days. The great force was expending itself, and the resistance was becoming more durable. Two further efforts, the first on April 4th, south of the Somme, and the second on April 5th, north of the Somme, were no more successful. The stupendous Battle of St. Quentin was at an end.

ORDERED SOUTH.

On March 21st the New Zealand Division, then in XXII. Corps reserve, received orders to be prepared to move south as G.H.Q. Reserve. On the 23rd orders were issued for the Division to commence entraining at Hopoutre, Godewaersvelde, Caestre, and Cassel, to detrain at St. Pol, Frevent, and Petit Houvin, and then to concentrate in the Third Army area at Le Cauroy, 12 miles east of Arras, and to come under the command of the XVII. Corps. Early on the morning of the 22nd the Regiment left Moulle, and returned in motor lorries to its former areas, the 1st Battalion to Caestre, and the 2nd Battalion to Hondeghem. Shortages in ammunition and equipment were at once made up, and final preparations completed for the move. On the 24th the original movement order was cancelled and the Division was diverted to the Fifth Army area. This involved detraining at Corbie, Edgehill, and Mericourt, and concentrating in the Bray area, under the command of the VII. Corps, but still in G.H.Q. Reserve. The 1st Battalion, commanded by Major J. Hargest, M.C., entrained with first line transport at Caestre at 11 p.m. on the 24th ; the 2nd Battalion, commanded by Lieut.-Colonel D. Colquhoun, D.S.O., after marching from Hondeghem, entrained at the same point by 3.30 a.m. on the 25th. Departure was made immediately entraining was completed.

The fluctuations of battle and the ever-changing situation necessitated fresh orders, and at 1 a.m. on the 25th the detraining stations were altered to Hangest, Ally, and St. Rock, in consequence of the railway to Amiens being damaged ; and the concentration area to Mericourt l'Abbe, Morlancourt, and Dernancourt. Packs and blankets were to be left at or near the detraining stations under a guard ; ammunition was to be brought up to 220 rounds per man ; and that for Lewis and Vickers guns up to the maximum carrying capacity of the limber teams. The Regiment detrained at Hangest after a cramped and cold journey of 16 hours. The 1st Battalion formed up on the road, and after marching as far as Picquigny all surplus gear was dumped. The Battalion moved forward again in battle order of dress in the direction of Amiens, and when darkness set in, halted and slept in abandoned motor-lorries drawn up on the roadside. The 2nd Battalion, also in fighting order, moved out of Hangest at 8 p.m., and bivouacked for the night near Brielly, with the sky for a covering.

At a late hour on the night of the 25th further orders were received that the Division was to march by the Hedauville-Mailly Maillet-Puisieux Road, and fill the gap between Hamel and Puisieux-au-Mont, the Division to come under the IV. Corps of the Third Army. Orders were accordingly at once issued to direct all troops and transport of the Division to Hedauville, which was to be the new concentration area.

The Regiment was on the move again early on the morning of the 26th, and before midday passed through the outskirts of Amiens, headed by its Regimental Bands. The sweeping and destructive nature of the German advance and the startling depths to which it had penetrated, had some time since become tragically evident. Throughout the previous night there had been a constant stream of motor-lorries and ambulances speeding westward with refugees and wounded men ; and on this day the roads were choked with the swell of guns and transport, the stragglers of broken regiments, peasants with their primitive wagons conveying a few cherished effects and their sobbing women ; others, old men and women and children, struggling woefully along on foot, anon glancing back in terror at their burning homes and the smashing of high-explosive and incendiary shells among the ruins—a human stream driven to none knew where by the fury and the ruthlessness of war.

The 1st Battalion, continuing its march through Pont-Noyelles and Franvillers, reached the area of Hedauville at 8 p.m., and awaiting battle instructions, bivouacked in the open without covering through a bitterly cold night. The Battalion had accomplished the gallant performance of a 27 miles forced march without a single man falling out, which must stand as a record for the Division. The 2nd Battalion, after reaching Pont-Noyelles, completed the journey to Hedauville by motor lorries, and was also compelled to pass the greater part of the night lying in the open fields. At 11.30 p.m. orders were received to be in readiness to move at 1 a.m. on the 27th.

New Zealand Divisional Headquarters had opened at Hedauville at 1.30 a.m. on the 26th. At 2 a.m. a conference was held and a plan for an attack on Serre decided upon.

The 1st Battalion of the 3rd Brigade was to move at 8 a.m., and take up an outpost position on the Englebelmer-Auchonvillers Ridge, and secure the right flank of the main advance of the 1st and 2nd Infantry Brigades, which were to bridge the gap between the left of the 12th Division at Hamel and the right of the 62nd Division at Puisieux-au-

Mont. The objective of the 2nd Brigade extended from Hamel, inclusive, where touch was to be gained with the 12th Division, northwards through " Y " Ravine to a point about 1,000 yards north-east of Beaumont-Hamel. That of the 1st Brigade was firstly a prolongation of that line due north for a distance of 1,000 yards; and secondly a line extending from in rear of the first line north-west to Serre where it was to be further extended to get into touch with the 62nd Division at Puisieux-au-Mont. In the event of the enemy being met in greatly superior numbers, his advance was to be checked, and the Brigades concerned were to manœuvre so as to gain and hold the line Colincamps-Hebuterne. To assist in this movement the 3rd (Rifle) Brigade was to be prepared to occupy a line in continuation of that held by its 1st Battalion on the Englebelmer-Auchonvillers Ridge. The definitely affirmed principle on which these operations were based was that whatever the development of the enemy offensive, the New Zealand Division was to set itself as an impassable barrier to the German onslaught. How valiantly and with what splendid determination it gave effect to that principle will be realised in the course of the succeeding passages.

At 8.30 a.m. the 1st Battalion of the 3rd Brigade moved forward from Hedauville, and at 10 a.m. reported Englebelmer and Auchonvillers to be occupied by various British troops. An hour later contact was made with the enemy 500 yards east of Auchonvillers, where German patrols were engaged and driven in. The left flank of the advanced guard encountered the enemy in considerable strength at the sunken road south of the Sugar Factory; and although the right and centre platoons of the left outpost company succeeded in establishing posts after slight opposition, fighting continued on the left. At 11.45 a.m. the left platoon became hotly engaged with superior numbers of the enemy, some 300 of whom had taken up a position extending from Euston Corner on the left, past the Sugar Factory, to Kilometre Lane on the right, with additional troops advancing along the Serre Road. The villages of Martinsart and Mesnil were found to be occupied by troops of the 12th Division; while troops of the 17th Division held the Auchonvillers-Hamel Road near the latter village.

By 12 noon on the 26th five infantry battalions and two machine gun companies had assembled at Hedauville. The motor-lorry arrangements had proved inadequate throughout; and as with the 1st Battalion of Otago, several units had to march the whole distance from the detraining station. The result was that the concentration of the Division was greatly impeded; and units had to be sent into action irrespective of the Brigade to which they belonged. At 12 noon the 2nd Brigade, less two battalions, followed by the 1st Brigade, less three battalions, and the 2nd Battalion of the 3rd (Rifle) Brigade, moved forward from Hedauville through Mailly Maillet, and proceeded to put into execution the plan of attack above referred to.

Further enemy penetrations necessitated slight alterations in the original plans; but the attack was not launched on the left until 4.30 p.m. Fourteen whippet tanks, which had reached the vicinity of Colincamps on the previous night, successfully operated on this flank. On the right the attack reached its objective, but on the left it was held up by heavy machine gun fire from the ridge overlooking Colincamps. There was also a gap between the left flank and the right of the 4th Australian Brigade, which on the evening of the 26th had been ordered to fill the breach between Colincamps and Hebuterne to the north. A total of 50 prisoners and 16 machine guns were captured during the operation; our casualties amounted to 150, of which the majority were walking cases. The night was spent in consolidating the ground gained and in maintaining touch with the enemy.

By 6.30 p.m. on the 26th further battalions of the Division had arrived at Hedauville after stiff marching. Orders were now given for troops to move at 1 a.m. on the 27th, to close the gap along the Sugar Factory-Hebuterne Road, and connect with the Australians, attached to the 62nd Division, at Hebuterne. Accordingly, at one o'clock on the morning of the 27th the 3rd (Rifle) Brigade, less three battalions, with the 2nd Battalions of Otago and Wellington, and one Machine Gun Company, moved out from Hedauville, Otago troops leading. This force proceeded through Mailly Maillet to Colincamps, where the 2nd Battalion of Otago Regiment put out a screen covering the eastern side of Colincamps and the remainder of the Brigade. At dawn the 2nd Battalion of Wellington on the right and the 3rd Battalion of the Rifle Brigade on the left moved forward to close the breach referred to between the 1st New Zealand Infantry Brigade at about Euston Corner and the 4th Australian Brigade at Hebuterne.

Opposition from enemy machine guns was immediately met with; though there was no shell fire. On the left the advance was rapidly pushed home, the objective reached at 6.30 a.m., and touch gained with the Australians on the outskirts of Hebuterne. On the right, however, heavy machine gun fire was again met with from the ridge in front of La Signy Farm and overlooking Colincamps; but the centre being unable to advance further, dug in on a line 300 yards west of the Sugar Factory-Hebuterne Road. In the course of these operations 42 prisoners were captured. During the day the enemy delivered four successive attacks against the line at various points. Three of these were effectively driven off, though not without difficulty; and the fourth, the last of the day, necessitated a slight retraction immediately north of Euston Corner. There was considerable movement of hostile troops across the Divisional front; and it being fully expected that the enemy would renew his attacks in the morning, orders were issued for preparations to meet such a contingency.

On the afternoon of the 27th four 18-pounder batteries and one 4.5in. howitzer battery of the New Zealand Divisional Artillery had arrived in the area, and after concentrating at Hedauville moved into position near Mailly Maillet.

The 2nd Battalion of the Regiment, having effected its purpose in the attack launched on the morning of the 27th was during the evening withdrawn from the front of Colincamps, and occupied the newly-constructed Purple Line in rear in a series of posts, with Battalion Headquarters in the orchard near Courcelles.

HOLDING THE LINE.

On the morning of the same day the 1st Battalion of the Regiment moved forward from its point of bivouac near Hedauville, through Mailly Maillet, and took up a line in

LIEUT.-COLONEL JAMES HARGEST, D.S.O., M.C., (D.), [F.]

N.Z. Official Photograph.

Lewis Gunners of the Regiment in Support Position near Mailly Maillet.

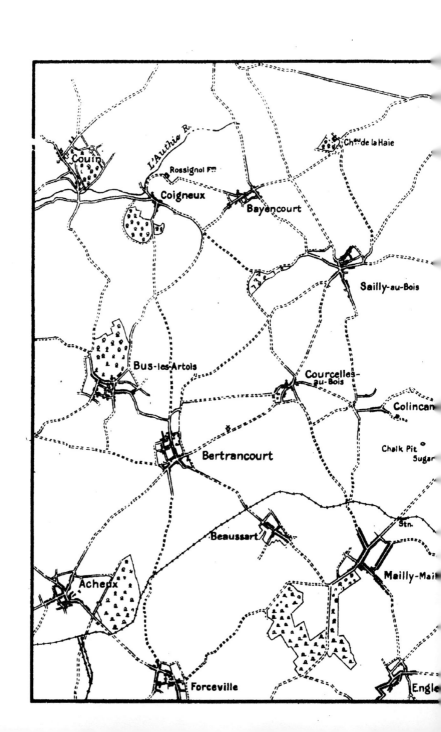

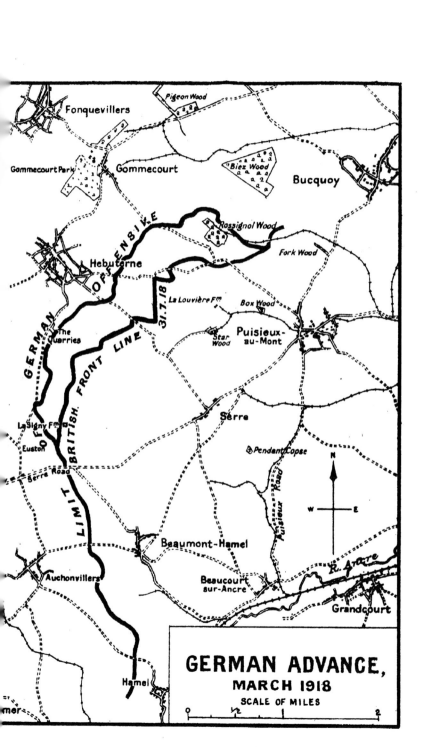

Fonquevillers

Pigeon Wood

Gommecourt Park

Gommecourt

Biez Wood

Bucquoy

Rossignol Wood

GERMAN OFFENSIVE

Hebuterne

Fork Wood

La Louvière F^m

Box Wood

31.7.18

LIMIT BRITISH FRONT LINE

The Quarries

Star Wood

Puisieux-au-Mont

Serre

La Signy F^m

Pendant Copse

Euston

Puisieux Road

Serre Road

N

W E

Beaumont-Hamel

Auchonvillers

Beaucourt sur-Ancre

R. Ancre

Grandcourt

Hamel

GERMAN ADVANCE,
MARCH 1918
SCALE OF MILES

0   ½   1   2

relief of the 1st Battalion of the Rifle Brigade, extending along the ridge in front of Englebelmer and Mailly Maillet, and along the east and north-east of Auchonvillers, representing a total frontage of approximately 3,000 yards. These positions were maintained over the 28th, when the enemy artillery, apparently searching for our batteries which had now taken up positions in the villages in rear, became much more pronounced in its activity. It was during this shelling of Colincamps that the Headquarters of the 3rd (Rifle) Brigade were destroyed, and Brigadier-General Fulton and Major R. G. Purdy were killed and others of the Staff wounded.

Minor attacks were made during the day by the left Brigade in line of the Division; the main success achieved being the capture of the Quarries, immediately south of Hebuterne, a position which commanded a field of fire in a south-easterly direction for a distance of about 3,000 yards. At all points of the line tested the enemy was found to be holding it in strength; and considerable movement was reported to be still taking place across the Divisional front. The weather, hitherto fine, now showed indications of breaking; and in view of the fact that great coats and blankets had been dumped during the forced march from the north, the prospect was not very cheerful.

On the morning of March 29th orders were issued to the 1st Battalion of the Regiment to relieve the 2nd Battalion of Canterbury in the front line of the left sub-sector of the 2nd Brigade. Relief commenced at 9 p.m., and was completed by one o'clock the following morning. The position taken over extended north and south, with Auchonvillers in the immediate rear and the site of the village of Beaumont-Hamel to the front. The trenches comprised those of the old British front line before the Somme Offensive of 1916, which though in a moderate state of repair when first taken over, reached a deplorable condition when the weather broke. The front line and communication trenches then fell in badly, and drainage was difficult or impossible. Sentries stood at their posts for two and sometimes four hours during the night thigh-deep in mud and water, and when relieved, indifferent to all else but sleep, crawled exhausted into filthy, shallow holes scooped out of the slime of the parapet. With the exception of one or two dug-outs which were in a dangerous state of collapse, the system contained no shelters. **Wrapped** in an old bag or blanket or dead German's ground-sheet, unshaven, and caked with mud and filth, men lumbered heavily along the trenches by night or lay huddled in these holes in the ground, more resembling beasts than human beings. The written impressions of a French correspondent during a visit by night to a front line trench fairly describe the conditions obtaining in this unwholesome place. " A sinuous ditch bottomed with mud, and foul with human refuse. There are holes in its sides from which as you lean over there comes a foul breath. Misty, shadowy things are emerging from these side caverns, and moving about in shapeless bulk like bears that shamble and growl. They are the squad." With the substitution of the word platoon for squad, the description stands.

So passed several days, with no change in the outlook, except with the rum issue in the early morning, when for a space of five or ten minutes more optimism, more pugnacity, and more grim humour were exhibited than in the whole of the preceding 24 hours. The ration carrying parties, drawn from the support platoons, soon found it impossible to struggle along the communication trenches, and finally took a course over the open. The trenches on the enemy's side were obviously in the same terrible state; and for a time it seemed as if a mutual understanding existed on the point that ration parties would not be fired upon from either side, until this limited form of armistice was abruptly terminated when a German carrying some sheets of iron attempted to avail himself of the same privilege, and was shot by one of our sentries.

At two o'clock on the afternoon of the 30th a minor operation was carried out by troops of the 1st Infantry Brigade, one Battalion of the 3rd Brigade co-operating, with a view to improving the line and gaining better observation. The objective aimed at was the line of the hedge from near the Serre Road on the right to a point about 1,000 yards to the left, which was also the line of the ridge overlooking La Signy Farm. The flanking Battalions were to conform to the movement. The main attack met with instant success; and it was only over a short stretch on the left that the enemy held his ground behind heavy machine gun fire. This pocket was cleared on the following morning, and the new front, affording good observation over a wide stretch of country, was consolidated. The captures in this highly successful operation were 290 prisoners, five light minenwerfer guns, and the extraordinary total of 110 machine guns. Over 200 enemy dead were counted on the front attacked. Our casualties amounted to 43 killed and 100 wounded. The presence of such a surprising number of machine guns over the front attacked served to indicate one of the phases of the tactics employed by the enemy during his offensive; which was to push forward machine guns with great boldness to successive commanding points, and under cover of their sustained fire, allow the infantry to filter through and encircle their objective. The attack on the 30th was delivered behind a protective barrage, and almost immediately our artillery had opened fire considerable numbers of the enemy left their trenches and scampered over the face of the ridge in rear of their line. These were engaged by Lewis gun and rifle fire from Otago's sector, and there was little doubt that many casualties were inflicted. At 6.15 p.m. the enemy opened a heavy bombardment over our sector, evidently in retaliation for the 1st Brigade's success.

At this stage there were several changes in commands. On the 28th Lieut.-Colonel D. Colquhoun, D.S.O., proceeded to the United Kingdom on duty, prior to leaving for New Zealand. On the 30th Major W. G. A. Bishop, M.C., left the 1st Battalion to take over command of the 2nd Battalion. Captain R. Fraser assumed command of 8th Company, *vice* Major Bishop; Captain J. P. Hewat was wounded and evacuated, and command of 10th Company fell to Captain D. J. Walls. Major Hargest, commanding the 1st Battalion of Otago, was a few days later granted the temporary rank of Lieut.-Colonel.

Our artillery was now becoming more firmly established along the Divisional front, and as the difficulties, at first very acute, of obtaining adequate supplies of ammunition were overcome, hostile movement was subjected to harassing fire. On the other hand the enemy was undoubtedly utilising captured British guns as well as the great ammunition dumps that had been left in his possession; immediate and unpleasant proof being afforded of the effectiveness of our own artillery weapons. Some of these abandoned guns could still be observed on the ridge in front, repeated efforts by the enemy to get them away to a less prominent position being ultimately successful.

On April 1st, the last day of the Battalion's tour, a daring daylight incursion into the enemy's lines was carried out by Major Hargest and Corporal R. Marshall, of 8th Company. This patrol proceeded out from the left of 8th Company's sector, and worked its way for a distance of 300 yards along a communication trench leading to the enemy's lines. A number of other communication trenches were successfully reconnoitred, until a block was reached. Here an enemy sentry was caught unawares and shot. The patrol then moved a considerable distance further ahead, and finally returned safely to our lines after having accomplished a daring and useful reconnaissance of the enemy's area.

On being relieved by night by the 2nd Battalion of Canterbury, Otago moved out of this area of mud and filth to support positions in front of Auchonvillers, Englebelmer, and Mailly Maillet, previously occupied. The extreme darkness of the night, the heavy going, and the unfamiliar country, made the relief an arduous operation, and daylight had broken before some of the companies had settled down. Under such conditions the carrying out of a relief was more to be dreaded than the actual garrisoning of the line. During the strenuous tour just completed, the 1st Battalion sustained casualties to the number of two killed and 34 wounded.

Throughout this period the 2nd Battalion had been contending with the same difficulties of mud and movement, and enemy activity. On March 29th it moved from the Purple Line and relieved the 1st Battalion of the 3rd Brigade as reserve to the 2nd Brigade, the companies being disposed in bivouacs in rear of Englebelmer. On the night of the 30th the Battalion relieved the 1st Battalion of Canterbury in the front line between " Y " Ravine and Hamel, on the extreme right of the Divisional sector. The conditions there were no better than those experienced by the 1st Battalion. The trenches were deplorably muddy, there was an almost entire absence of shelters; and owing to the great length of front held the posts were very scattered, even with the four companies in line and one platoon of each in close support.

The enemy frequently harassed the garrison with trench mortar fire; and although the tour was comparatively brief, it was by no means free of hardships. On the night of April 3rd, when the reorganising of the Divisional front on a two-brigade frontage was commenced and part of the northern extremity near Hebuterne was taken over by the 4th Australian Brigade, the Battalion was relieved and moved back to positions at Englebelmer. There was a considerable increase in enemy artillery activity on April 4th. The village of Englebelmer was consistently shelled, and companies were forced under stress of casualties to quit some of their bivouacs. This was but a prelude to much more furious events.

THE ENEMY HELD.

At 5 o'clock on the morning of April 5th the enemy commenced an artillery bombardment which must rank as one of the heaviest and most sustained the Regiment ever experienced. It extended along the whole Divisional front; and from guns of all calibres shells were poured down over the forward, support and rear positions as far back as Bus-les-Artois and Bertrancourt, almost without interruption from early morning until the late afternoon. It furiously searched every known and likely forward position, and in the back areas batteries and villages and roadways were pounded by guns of the heaviest calibres. Its extraordinary depth and intensity indicated an attempt by the enemy to renew the progress which had been so abruptly stayed a few days previously. It was not long before these attacks developed. At 8.15 a.m. reports were received from the 3rd Brigade that the enemy was attacking from the right of the Serre Road to the left boundary south of the Quarries. The attack was beaten off; but when renewed at 10 a.m. the enemy succeeded in capturing a short length of trench east of La Signy Farm, and the Farm itself, the small garrison of three sections of Rifle Brigade troops who comprised this advanced post being overwhelmed. At no other point did the enemy make any progress, and he suffered very severely from our artillery and machine gun fire, his casualties being estimated at 500 killed. Prisoners captured on the front of the left Brigade stated that their ultimate objective was Colincamps, also that many new batteries had been brought up for the attack. At 2 p.m. an attack was made against the right of the Divisional sector, but similarly failed, the only party of Germans who reached our line being taken prisoners. Under cover of this sustained bombardment attacks were launched by the enemy during the day along the whole Army front; but nowhere did he achieve more than very local successes. This may be said to have signalled the termination of the great German drive in the Battle of St. Quentin.

The positions occupied by the Regiment in support had to weather the storm of this extraordinary and relentless artillery bombardment, and a large number of casualties were sustained among both officers and men. During the afternoon an enemy two-seater aeroplane was brought down by Lewis gun fire directed from one of the posts occupied by 4th Company of the 1st Battalion, and the pilot and observer made prisoners. Rain commenced to fall late in the afternoon, after which the situation became comparatively quiet.

On April 6th the 1st Battalion of the Regiment received orders to return to the front line and take over the sector previously occupied. As the relief was about to commence, the S.O.S. signal appeared on the left and was repeated along the line. All movement in respect of reliefs was delayed for one hour. No infantry attacks developed, although there was a considerable amount of shelling. In consequence of a misunderstanding some of the relieving troops did not reach the line until a late hour on the following morning. Heavy rain fell almost continuously throughout the night, and the approaches and trenches were in an even worse state than formerly. The tour lasted until the 10th, and during that time the weather was exceedingly stormy, and the conditions under which the garrison maintained the line indescribably bad and exhausting. There were periodical bursts of shelling over our front and support lines, but on the whole not much damage was done. Our own artillery displayed considerable activity over the same period, directing sudden bursts of fire to the enemy's forward and back areas. On the night of the 10th the Battalion was relieved by Canterbury and returned to its old positions of support in front of Auchonvillers, Englebelmer, and Mailly Maillet.

The 2nd Battalion of the Regiment took over its former front line sector, from " Y " Ravine to Hamel, on the night of the 7th. Enemy activity on the 8th was confined to trench mortar fire, but on the following day, between 10 a.m. and 12 noon, the front and support lines were heavily bombarded with high explosive and 77 mm. shells, and during the afternoon low-flying aeroplanes patrolled the system apparently with the object of determining the damage done. Finer weather and improved observation on the 10th disclosed considerable movement of enemy troops and transport over the back areas, suggesting that a relief was in progress. On the night of the 13th the Battalion was relieved by the 1st Battalion of the 3rd Brigade, and after a long and exhausting journey, at 3 o'clock on the following morning reached its bivouac area in rear of Beaussart and south of Bertrancourt. On the 13th the 1st Battalion moved back to the Purple Line, where it occupied a series of posts extending from Sailly-au-Bois in the north to Courcelles in the south.

The period of exceptional activities in which the Regiment had been engaged as a result of the startling German advance was now at an end. The general situation on the Divisional front had become more settled : and the decisive check which the enemy received on April 5th when he attempted to renew his advance after a terrific artillery preparation, was gradually followed by conditions approaching those of trench-to-trench warfare. The new positions taken up had of course to be established, and new defensive lines constructed in the rear ; but as far as the front line defences were concerned the continued broken weather and the consequent deplorable state of the trenches made anything in that direction impossible. The period of rest and training completed in the areas of Caestre and Hondeghem had enabled the Regiment to resist some of the worst conditions of warfare in a remarkable manner, following upon its forced march from the north. Continuous standing in water-logged trenches threatened a serious state of trench feet ; but the number of such cases evacuated was actually comparatively few. Casualties from enemy action were, however, heavy, as indicated by the fact that between March 27th and April 5th the total incurred by the 2nd Battalion of the Regiment was 11 killed and 59 wounded, while the 1st Battalion suffered to an even greater extent. The penetration by the enemy to such a great depth over the fronts of two Armies naturally created serious dislocation of the main lines of supply, and the service had to be maintained under the very greatest difficulties. Any shortages of rations experienced by the Regiment, at least over the first several days of the period under review, were met when in support by drawing upon the poultry and vegetables, to say nothing of the contents of the well-stocked wine cellars, left behind by the civilian population in its flight; and oft-times the menu was one of chicken and champagne, topped off with some of the finest liqueurs,—surely great fare under such conditions.

During the period from March 24th to April 14th the New Zealand Division captured a total of 430 prisoners, 127 machine guns, and five trench mortars. The Division's casualties amounted to : Killed—29 officers and 482 other ranks ; wounded—97 officers and 1,748 other ranks. This high total affords some indication of the severity of the period.

The Division received the congratulations of the Commander of the IV. Corps for its " courage and endurance." In a communication dated March 28th, General Harper expressed his confidence that the troops of the Division would continue to hold the line against all attacks, and that confidence was not misplaced. For the operations subsequently carried out the Division received the congratulations of the Commander of the Second Army (in which it was formerly incorporated), General Godley (Commanding the XXII. Corps), and General Monash (Commanding the 4th Australian Division).

The Regiment remained but a short time in reserve, but during that period every opportunity was availed of to restore lost vitality. Baths were improvised by the 1st Battalion at Sailly-au-Bois, and by the 2nd Battalion at Bertrancourt ; the luxury of a hot tub after five weeks of filth and weariness being something to be remembered. Equipment and clothing were cleaned and repaired, and all possible rest afforded. The new lines of defence constructed along the rear of the Divisional front were reconnoitred by officers and n.c.o.'s, and every opportunity taken to become familiar with the country. Throughout the 15th considerable enemy

BRIG.-GENERAL R. YOUNG, C.B., C.M.G.,
D.S.O., (D.), [F.]

movement was observed at points fronting the Divisional sector, while from the 37th Division on our left similar activity was reported. Special precautions were adopted in view of a possible attack; and on the morning of the 16th our artillery directed heavy fire over the areas where the enemy concentration had been observed. About this time several officers of the 14th Division of the French Army arrived and effected a reconnaissance of the Purple Line; and at a later date a considerable force of French troops, embracing some of the crack Regiments of that Army, arrived in the area in rear.

CHAPTER XIII.

LA SIGNY FARM.

ON April 17th, the 1st Battalion of the Regiment relieved the
2nd Battalion of Wellington in the front line sector extending
over a length of about 1,200 yards from Waterloo Bridge,
left of the Serre Road, along the hedge line overlooking La
Signy Farm to the northern boundary, south of Hebuterne.
The dispositions were as follows: 8th and 14th Companies
in the front line from right to left, and 4th and 10th Companies in support in the same order. Battalion Headquarters
was established in the sunken road near Euston Corner.
It was at the latter point that, prior to our taking over the
line, an extensive dump of trench mortar ammunition had
been exploded by enemy shell fire. There was still a great
deal of ammunition and explosive there and in the vicinity,
and further explosions occurred at a later date. The front
line trenches of the new sector were shallow, and extending
towards the enemy's lines were several old communication
trenches which were either eventually filled in or were utilised
for establishing advanced bombing posts. On the left company sector there were two such posts approximately 250
yards in advance of the main line, and garrisoned by a strength
of one platoon. The weather at this stage was fine, and as
soon as the trenches were drained it was possible to proceed
with the improvement of the defences all round. There
was little or no wire in front, which was a matter demanding
immediate attention, while the trenches required deepening and
traversing. All this called for the expenditure of much
time and labour; but it was a fortunate circumstance that
the enemy was apparently anxious for peace and quietness
and consequently work was not interrupted to any extent.

During the early evening of the 18th three of the enemy were observed approaching a forward post occupied by 14th Company, evidently having lost direction. On being fired upon, two effected their escape, but the third was chased and captured. The prisoner explained that his battalion was further north, but that his party had lost its way when carrying rations to the front line. The outcome was that one of the party and some of the rations fell into our hands. Enemy artillery fire on the 19th was confined to spasmodic bursts. Our own artillery heavily engaged enemy battery positions in the locality of Pendant Copse and Miraumont.

At 8 o'clock on the morning of April 20th a party of five other ranks from 14th Company, under Lance-corp. J. Frew, carried out a most effective raid into the enemy's lines to the left of La Signy Farm. Working down an old communication trench, they reached a block 60 yards in advance of our forward post, and there surprised and captured first the German sentry and then four others who were asleep in the post. The five prisoners were sent back to our lines with an escort, and the remainder of the party advanced along the enemy trench to a suspected machine gun post at the Mound. No Germans were encountered there, but further along a superior force was met with, and unobserved the party of three returned to our lines without being fired upon. At 4.30 p.m. the same day a bombardment by heavy and light trench mortars was opened over the locality visited by the morning's patrol, and a further patrol of eight men under Sergt. J. R. Lyall, M.M., left our lines with the object of determining the damage done to the enemy post, and if possible, capturing its occupants. The bombardment unfortunately broke down at an early stage, and the patrol, on approaching its objective, found the garrison very much alert and "standing to." Our men engaged them with bombs, the enemy vigorously replying. Sergt. Lyall was wounded, and as the enemy was being reinforced, the patrol withdrew under cover of Lewis gun fire and rifle grenades from our post behind. At least six casualties were known to have been inflicted on the enemy. The Mound and adjoining trenches were effectively bombarded again on the following afternoon with 6in. trench mortars, and when three men subsequently went out and examined the position they found that it was badly battered, that the enemy had evacuated it and was occupying a trench some distance off.

Early on the evening of the 22nd the Battalion was relieved by the 2nd Battalion of Canterbury, and moved back to support, occupying a series of posts about 1,000 yards behind the front line, north and south of Colincamps and astride the Serre Road. During the tour just completed, over 1,200 yards of wiring had been erected, and a considerable length of trench deepened and traversed.

A Divisional Order was issued on April 21st announcing that the right sub-sector was to be handed over to the 12th Division, which was coming into line on the right. At the same time the New Zealand Division took over the Hebuterne sector on the left from the 4th Australian Brigade, temporarily attached to the 42nd Division, which had on the 15th relieved the 37th Division. These new dispositions were complete by the night of the 24th-25th. On the 26th the New Zealand Divisional Lewis Gun School was established at Louvencourt, parties being periodically despatched there from the Regiment for instruction.

On April 17th the 2nd Battalion of Otago moved up to positions of Brigade reserve west of Colincamps, and from there supplied parties for the improvement and extension of the defences of the Purple Line and switches. On the 22nd it proceeded into the front line sector immediately south of that recently occupied by the 1st Battalion. Considerable work confronted the garrison owing to the lack of stability of the system, which the periodical fire of light and heavy minenwerfer did not tend to improve. During the night of the 23rd a wounded German was brought in, and early on the following morning a party of about fifteen of the enemy attempted to rush one of the forward posts. They were beaten off with rifle fire and bombs, leaving one of their number dead in front of our wire, while evidence was afforded of further casualties. On the 25th there was considerable artillery activity. Our 8in. howitzers heavily pounded La Signy Farm, in conjunction with the heavy trench mortars, the enemy retaliating over our forward system.

A remarkable incident occurred at this period, when two horses attached to a wagon broke away from the rear of the enemy's lines, and galloping down the Serre Road, came to an abrupt halt in front of our wire. The enemy at once opened fire, but Corporal McDonald went out and cut the animals free, when they crossed our lines and continued along the Serre Road to the Sugar Factory, where they were caught and despatched to the transport lines. The horses were in fair condition, and the harness new but inferior in quality. The limber, which contained timber for the construction of dug-outs, had presumably been drawn up in readiness for unloading when the animals were started by the firing of our 6in. Newton trench mortars. It was at first stated that the wagon was loaded with minenwerfer shells, and this, it was humorously suggested, was merely the method adopted by the enemy of delivering them in bulk.

On being relieved the Battalion moved back to support positions near Colincamps, and on the last day of the month withdrew to the Purple Line, with Battalion Headquarters at the Windmill, on the high ground east of Bertrancourt.

The 1st Battalion continued in support positions in the locality of Colincamps until April 27th. On the 25th the area occupied by 10th Company was subjected to a bombardment with 5.9in. and 4.2in. howitzer shells, presumably intended for batteries in that locality, and a few casualties were sustained. On the evening of the 27th the Battalion returned to its old sector overlooking La Signy Farm, 4th Company being on the right and 10th Company on the left, with 8th Company in support and 14th Company in reserve. The tour was a brief one, and except for a certain amount of enemy trench mortar activity was uneventful. On the night of the 30th April the Battalion was relieved by the 1st Battalion of the 3rd Brigade, and trekked back to Divisional reserve at Rossignol Farm, in rear of Bayencourt.

The Regiment remained in reserve until May 6th, on which date the 2nd Infantry Brigade relieved the 1st Infantry Brigade in the left sub-sector of the Divisional front, adjoining Hebuterne, and immediately north of the previously held sector. On that evening the 2nd Battalion of Otago relieved the 1st Battalion of Wellington in the front line ; the 1st Battalion of Otago moving from Rossignol Farm and relieving the 2nd Battalion of Wellington in the locality of Sailly-au-Bois ; the four Companies being disposed around the eastern and north-eastern edges of the village.

Heavy rain on the night of the 6th-7th had caused the front line trenches to become badly water-logged; but the perfect weather on the succeeding days and the almost complete state of inactivity on the part of the enemy afforded every opportunity for draining and improving the system. Enemy artillery activity was for the most part confined to bombardments directed to the villages of Hebuterne and Fonquevillers, and on the night of the 11th gas shells were poured into the ruins of the latter place for a period of about four hours. On the night of the 12th-13th the 2nd Battalion handed over the sector to the 1st Battalion of Canterbury, and proceeded into support positions on the western side of Hebuterne; while the 1st Battalion of the Regiment relieved the 2nd Battalion of Canterbury in the front line sector on the right of Hebuterne. The two forward companies were the 8th and 14th from right to left. The activities of the support and reserve companies were mainly directed to improving the defences of Fort Grosvenor, a tactical point near the front line.

At this period it was notified by Division that enemy identification was urgently required. Although the 2nd Battalion of Otago had been relieved from the front line, Sergt. " Dick " Travis at once volunteered to go out through Canterbury's lines and secure the necessary prisoners. This Canterbury consented to only after one of its own patrols had failed to meet with success. Sergt. Travis was now afforded his opportunity, and after a remarkable encounter with the enemy, achieved striking and instant success. At 7.45 p.m. on the 14th, when it was still daylight, and accompanied by Ptes. H. Melville, R. V. Conway, A. D. D. Clydesdale and N. Thomson, he set out for the enemy lines. Leaving from the Warrior Street junction, in front of Hebuterne, he and his party succeeded by the skilful use of cover in reaching the enemy position aimed at without being observed. The post, which contained a machine gun and seven of the enemy, was rushed, and the garrison, who were lying in their shelters without a sentry, were taken completely by surprise. One of the enemy showed fight and had to be shot, and the patrol commenced its return to our lines with the remainder of the prisoners. The commotion, however, had roused a neighbouring post, which immediately rushed to give assistance, and the patrol experienced the utmost difficulty in getting away with its unwilling prisoners. Sergt. Travis covered the withdrawal by exchanging shot for shot with the fresh enemy numbers, and in the course of the melee two of the prisoners were killed by their own men. The four remaining prisoners were eventually got to cover, and the whole party safely reached our lines after a most thrilling experience, the prisoners secured affording the identification required. This was a typical example of Sergt. Travis's ability to strike the enemy swiftly and effectively.

On the morning of the 18th a raid was also made into the enemy's lines by a patrol from the 1st Battalion. As a preliminary to this operation active patrolling had been carried out nightly with a view to determining points at which prisoners might be secured. Two such areas were marked down, and it was decided to carry out two silent raids during the early morning. A party from 14th Company was to raid an enemy post in the locality of Jena trench, but was prevented from accomplishing its object by machine gun fire directed from several points. The other objective selected was a machine gun post in Home Avenue, and failing that a point further to the left. A party from 8th Company, comprising 12 other ranks under Sergt. P. McGregor, moved out from our lines at 1.30 a.m., and proceeded down Home Avenue, leaving a covering party of four in rear. As there was not sufficient darkness to carry out the first operation, the raiders moved back along the Avenue, and then crossed north to Jean Bart sap. Here it was decided to lie quietly during the early hours of the morning and wait until the enemy had breakfasted and retired to sleep. On commencing active operations, the trenches west of the sunken road were first searched and found to be unoccupied ; the party then crossed the road and pushed further along Jean Bart to a single bivouac which could just be observed. On the flap of the shelter being raised, four Germans were discovered asleep inside. They were immediately secured, and the party thereupon returned to our lines along Jean Bart, and reached it safely with their prisoners.

On the same evening the Battalion was relieved by the 4th Battalion of the 3rd Brigade, and moved back to the Purple Line as part of the garrison of that system, held by the Brigade in reserve. The Battalion here occupied a series of posts between Sailly-au-Bois and Beaussart, and in rear of Colincamps, with Battalion Headquarters established at the Windmill on the Courcelles-Bertrancourt Road. It remained in these positions until the 24th of the month, carrying out a few minor fatigues, and generally enjoying the warmth of sunshine and the refreshing greenness of the landscape. In the meantime the 2nd Battalion of the Regiment had experienced a fair amount of shelling in and around the village of Hebuterne. On the 18th of the month it was relieved and moved back to Rossignol Farm, in rear of Bayencourt.

It was at this period that the wearing of the small box respirator by all ranks, however employed, for periods of time ranging up to one hour, was instituted under Divisional Orders in view of the contingency of a sustained enemy gas bombardment. Considerable inconvenience and discomfort attended these practices at the outset, but after a time it was found that the gas mask could be worn continuously for an hour with comparative ease, the knowledge of which afforded a feeling of confidence which was valuable in itself.

On May 24th the 2nd Infantry Brigade was relieved in the Purple Line by the 63rd Brigade, and on completion of relief moved forward and took over the right sub-sector of the Divisional front from the 1st Infantry Brigade. This brought the 1st Battalion of the Regiment (relieved by the 4th Battalion of the Middlesex Regiment) to a system of posts with a frontage of about 3,000 yards extending along the front of and around the village of Colincamps, and in support to the La Signy Farm sector ; while the 2nd Battalion of the Regiment took over the front line from the 1st Battalion of Wellington to the right of the above-named sector. The tour thus commenced by the 2nd Battalion was not without incident. On the 25th considerable enemy movement was observed, and several targets were engaged by our 6in. Newton trench mortars. On the 26th the Division in line on the left carried out a successful raid against the enemy's trenches, and in response to the S.O.S. call the enemy placed down a fairly heavy barrage, which extended to the left of the Battalion sector. There was considerable shelling over the whole area during the day, and in the early hours of the

N.Z. Official Photograph.

The Windmill near Courcelles.

following morning the Divisional front and the villages of Hebuterne and Sailly-au-Bois were subjected to heavy and sustained gas shelling. This was part of a general bombardment by the enemy over a great length of front, and synchronised with his attack between Laon and Rheims. The gas used was mainly phosgene ; but owing to the precautionary methods adopted, our casualties were slight.

During the early morning of the 29th the enemy attempted a raid against one of our forward posts, occupied by 4th Company to the right of La Signy Farm, but was driven off, apparently with losses. Our casualties numbered six. During the afternoon, our 6in. Newton trench mortars, a most destructive form of weapon, " shot up " the post from which the enemy was believed to have launched his raid.

On the closing day of the month a small patrol led by Sergt. Travis, and including Sergt. Swainson, Pte. Conway and Pte. Ballantyne, left our lines at 7.30 p.m. from near Waterloo Bridge for an enemy post about 300 yards in front. The party worked its way down the shelter of an old communication trench, and when about 25 yards from the post was held up by a stout wire block. Getting out of the trench the raiders crawled to within ten yards of the unsuspecting enemy, and then suddenly swarmed over the post. The two sentries, completely surprised, threw up their hands when ordered, on which an old dug-out close by was investigated and found to contain several of the enemy. They poured out of their shelter and a desperate melee followed. Three were shot dead ; others succeeded in escaping, and Sergt. Travis and his party proceeded to make back to our lines with their prisoners. Further numbers of the enemy, now thoroughly aroused, rushed up from the rear and immediately opened fire with bombs and rifles. The party was obliged to make for the shelter of Newgate Avenue, Sergt. Travis deliberately covering its withdrawal. During this development one of the prisoners made his escape ; but there was good reason for believing that he was subsequently caught by our Lewis gun fire. The party had now gained the communication trench, but while hurrying along with his reluctant prisoner, a German officer, Sergt. Travis narrowly escaped disaster from the explosion of several bombs attached to a trip-wire. The party finally reached our lines in safety with two prisoners. This dramatic invasion created considerable stir in the enemy sector, and a party of Germans, two of whom were officers with revolvers drawn, were subsequently observed to enter the post in a belated investigation of what was for them a costly espisode.

At this stage the Regiment had attached for experience several officers from the 74th Division, recently arrived from Palestine. The month closed with considerable artillery activity on our part, in the course of which a great deal of damage was caused to the enemy's defences.

Early on the morning of June 1st the S.O.S. signal appeared to the north and south of the Divisional sector, which was then repeated over a wide area. Our own artillery joined in the general response, but no enemy attack developed. On this occasion there was certain short shooting across the front, resulting in several casualties in our lines. During the evening the 1st Battalion of the Regiment relieved the 2nd Battalion of Canterbury in the La Signy Farm sector. At the same time the 2nd Battalion of the Regiment completed its tour of the front line, and moved back to the defences of Colincamps. Casualties during the period had amounted to five killed and 25 wounded.

The opening days of the 1st Battalion's tour in the line were quiet and the weather perfect. Frequent daylight reconnaissances of the enemy's lines were being carried out by Pte. Stark, until when single-handed he rushed an enemy post near La Signy Farm and was grievously wounded; his adventurous career thus abruptly terminating for a time at least. The Battalion completed the construction of a number of solid dug-outs for platoon and company headquarters, and the general defences of the sector were materially strengthened.

On the afternoon of June 5th Corporal Moir and Lance-corp. Falls, of 10th Company, left our trenches for the enemy lines, and surprised and entered a German post to the left of La Signy Farm. The enemy sentry was engaged perusing his correspondence, and paid the penalty of his remissness by being captured, along with one other German. A shower of bombs assailed the party as it commenced the return journey, and Lance-corp. Falls was wounded and one of the prisoners killed. The remaining prisoner was safely brought in to our post at Central Avenue. At 10 o'clock on the following morning a second party from 10th Company raided the enemy's lines at a point still further to the left, and met with remarkable success. The raiding party, which comprised Sergt. Scott, Corporal Stewart, and four other ranks, worked its way along the shelter of a hedge line, crossed the wire entanglements, and then suddenly jumped into an enemy post. Two Germans were surprised and captured. A search of some bivouacs 15 yards further along the trench yielded an additional five prisoners. The party then made its way back and reached our lines without casualties, and with only a single shot being fired at it. The effect produced on the German *moral* by these several incursions into his lines in broad daylight by parties of the two Battalions, and the impunity with which his garrisons were being carried off, can well be imagined, to say nothing of the information and identification which the prisoners afforded. During the afternoon of the 6th, following upon information obtained from the prisoners, a bombardment by 4.5in. howitzers and heavy trench mortars was directed against the enemy posts, and considerable material damage occasioned at points where machine guns were reported to be located.

Relief of the New Zealand Division by the 42nd Division was now at hand. On the morning of June 5th General Sir Andrew Russell, accompanied by the G.O.C. 42nd Division, inspected the front line system, expressing his pleasure at the state of the defences and the bearing of the garrison. On the 6th several officers and n.c.o.'s of the 10th Middlesex Regiment visited the line in view of the pending relief. The change-over was commenced the same evening, and was preceded by a sudden burst of enemy shelling, which lasted for some time and delayed the approach of the relieving troops. As soon as the sector had been handed over, the 1st Battalion started a weary march back to the locality of Authie. The 2nd Battalion of the Regiment, on being relieved in the defences of Colincamps by a battalion of the Lancashire Fusiliers, had already moved out to the Bois du Warnimont, overlooking Authie Valley. The camps occupied by the two Battalions comprised tents and shelters, established among ideal surroundings.

A PERIOD OF REST.

A long period of rest was now ahead of the Regiment. The New Zealand Division, having been relieved by the 42nd Division, was reserve Division of the IV. Corps, and the 2nd Infantry Brigade, concentrated in the Authie-St. Leger area, constituted the Divisional reserve. The particular rôle of the New Zealand Division while in reserve was to restore any part of the Purple Line penetrated by the enemy. The opening days of the rest period were devoted to interior economy, and thereafter general training was commenced. The weather continued perfect for all outside operations, and at the close of each day opportunity was afforded of attending a performance by the Divisional Entertainers, visiting the camps of other units of the Division and renewing acquaintances, or resting in the cool shade of the woods ; while the opening of a Club at Authie provided a gravitating point for officers. Thus delightful mid-summer weather, the rare freshness and beauty of the surroundings, the excellent country available for every phase of operations, combined with the pleasant relaxations of the evening, contributed to one of the most profitable and enjoyable periods of rest and training that the Regiment had experienced in France. In the routine of work, attack practices over open country, wood fighting, night operations and musketry received particular attention ; while in view of the increased issue of Lewis guns to each Battalion, a large number of additional men required special training in the use of this weapon.

One of the several practice attacks carried out over open country was witnessed by General Sir Julian Byng, Commanding the Third Army, accompanied by his Staff, and in the course of an address to the assembled officers at the close, he expressed his admiration of the way in which the New Zealand Division had filled a gap in the line at a critical period in the great German attack in March. It was realised, he said, that the existing front line system was weak, but the Purple Line was to be held at all costs, and, he continued, " it is to troops such as you that we look to restore it in the event of a break-through."

On June 16th the New Zealand Divisional Horse Show was held on the high ground overlooking St. Leger; and forgetting for a moment its inevitable military aspect, it was an easy matter for a spectator to imagine that he was attending one of the big Summer Shows in far-off New Zealand. In the general organisation and direction, ring management and stewardship, there was much that would have set many people in New Zealand with long experience of shows thinking deeply. There were the same thousands of interested spectators; light and heavy gun and transport teams showed fine condition and evidence of expert preparation, and the jumpers and hurdlers included some of the British Army's best horse flesh, even if the horsemanship displayed by some of the riders from outside the Division was not up to Colonial standard. During the afternoon an enemy aeroplane appeared high overhead, as if to emphasise the almost forgotten fact that the war was still in progress; and later, as the troops were leaving the area of the show ground, several high velocity shells, apparently directed to the locality, burst well beyond and did no damage. Not the least memorable part of the gathering was the opportunity afforded of renewing acquaintances, for it was rarely that the different units of the Division were brought so closely together. The transport of the 1st Battalion of Otago, having been placed first at the 2nd Infantry Brigade Show, was selected to represent the Brigade at the Divisional Show, and secured second place. On June 23rd the New Zealand Divisional Military Tournament was held on the same grounds, the 2nd Battalion of Otago securing second place in the Guard Mounting Competition. The Divisional Band Contest followed on June 27th, involving quite a round of festivities.

By the late afternoon of June 22nd the 2nd Battalion of Otago Regiment had left the Bois du Warnimont, and taken over support positions in the Purple Line between Beaussart and Sailly-au-Bois, until then occupied by the 4th Battalion of the 3rd Brigade, with headquarters at the Windmill. On the same day the 1st Battalion of the Regiment took over the vacated camp in the Bois du Warnimont, and continued along practically the same lines of routine as had obtained during the preceding few weeks.

On June 25th an order was issued for the relief by the New Zealand Division of the 57th Division in the Gommecourt-Hebuterne, or centre, sector of the IV. Corps front; the New

Zealand Division also taking over the northern portion of the front occupied by the 42nd Division. The new Divisional front then extended approximately from the southern side of Biez Wood south to a point immediately beyond Hebuterne, and comprised the forward system, the Purple system or main battle positions, the Chateau de la Haie switch and the Fonquevillers switch, the Red Line, and the Bayencourt switch.

On taking over positions in the Purple Line on June 22nd the 2nd Battalion of the Regiment was committed to supplying working parties for the various defences of the sector, which continued until July 2nd, when it was relieved by a battalion of the Lancashire Fusiliers and moved back to Rossignol Farm, in rear of Bayencourt. Here it was established for several days under very comfortable circumstances of living.

On the morning of July 2nd the 1st Battalion of Otago participated in the review of the 2nd New Zealand Infantry Brigade by the Hon. W. F. Massey and Sir J. G. Ward, who were then paying a visit to the Division in France. The ceremony took place on the outskirts of the Bois du Warnimont, the assembled troops being briefly addressed by the two Ministers.

On the same afternoon the 1st Battalion of the Regiment left the Bois du Warnimont and took over positions in trenches in the Chateau de la Haie switch, near Sailly-au-Bois. The system extended round the south and east sides of Sailly, thence north to the Chateau, comprising a frontage of about 3,500 yards. The weather continued exceedingly fine, and there was no interruption to works of improvement, the construction of new systems of defence rendered necessary by the recent German drive still being vigorously prosecuted. These operations included the construction of deep dug-outs at selected points, and the opening up and development of the vast system of chalk pits under the village of Sailly, a place with great ramifications of tunnels and passages capable of sheltering a very considerable body of troops if occasion demanded it.

CHAPTER XIV.

BATTLE OF THE LYS.

THE terrific and costly struggles which the Battle of St. Quentin involved had barely ceased when the British Forces were called upon to withstand the shock of a further great enemy offensive. On this occasion the weight of the German attack was directed against what might be called the northern zone of operations on the Western Front; and while the area affected was not as extensive as before, the driving force behind it was not less formidable and the fighting that ensued not less violent and sanguinary. The Battle of St. Quentin may be said to have ended on April 5th; on April 9th the Battle of the Lys had opened.

The opening phase of this second German attack was launched against the northern portion of the front of the First Army, to the east of Laventie, ground familiar to the Regiment because of its occupation of that portion of the Flanders front during the winter months of 1916. The battle immediately spread to the north and south, until the area affected extended from the northern flank of the Ypres Salient to a point opposite Bethune in the south, a distance of roughly 30 miles. After protracted and bitter fighting, lasting from April 9th until the beginning of May, the British front was rolled back, at the extreme point of penetration, to a depth of approximately 12 miles, resulting in the envelopment and occupation by the enemy of such familiar places as Merville, Estaires, Armentieres, Ploegsteert Wood, Bailleul, Messines, Wytschaete, and Kemmel Hill, and forcing a considerable retraction of the line about the Ypres Salient.

While neither Battalion of the Otago Regiment was concerned with this new offensive, being then actively engaged away to the south, the 2nd New Zealand Entrenching Battalion became deeply involved in certain of its stages. This formation was comprised of reinforcements for Otago and Canterbury Regiments, and was established, along with the 1st and 3rd Entrenching Battalions, under the New Zealand Divisional Wing, which in turn was incorporated in the organisation of the 2nd Army under the name of the 2nd Army Entrenching Group. In the two Otago Companies of the 2nd Entrenching Battalion were men who had at one time or another been active members of either the 1st, 2nd, or 3rd Battalions of the Otago Regiment in the Field, while others were reinforcements who would sooner or later in the ordinary course of events have been drafted to the Regiment.

The activities of the Entrenching Battalions were directed to the construction of rear defences, road formation and repair, tunnelling, cable-laying, etc. Some of this work was of a very heavy nature; but throughout the whole course of operations, and whatever the conditions, the Entrenching Battalions established a high and lasting reputation for their great working ability.

Towards the close of January, 1918, the receiving centre for all New Zealand reinforcement troops arriving in France, originally and up to that date established at Etaples, had been transferred to Abeele, west of and in the area of Ypres, where it was commanded as formerly by Lieut.-Colonel G. Mitchell, Otago Regiment. When the German offensive was launched in March, 1918, the Entrenching Battalions were employed in the back areas of the Ypres Salient. On March 27th and 28th the 1st and 3rd Entrenching Battalions were ordered south, their destination being the area of Famechon and Pas, rear of the New Zealand Division's new sector.

At the same time the detachments of the 2nd Entrenching Battalion employed around Westhoek Ridge were recalled to Abeele. Reorganisation was effected, platoons strengthened by the inclusion, among others, of men of the 30th Reinforcement draft, which had arrived at Abeele a few weeks previously, and the formation established as far as possible on a fighting basis. On April 11th, two days after the German attack in the northern zone was launched, the 2nd Entrenching Battalion received warning orders to hold itself in readiness to move. At 5 p.m. on April 12th the formation, commanded by Captain (Temp.-Major) J. F. Tonkin, moved out of camp prepared for action, and headed for Meteren, with orders to report to the 33rd Division.

The journey to Meteren encountered the extraordinary traffic which the tide of a rear-guard battle promotes and swells—the hurried forward march of supporting troops, the columns of motor-lorries and ambulances, the passage of artillery and transport, and, unforgettable above all else, the stream of civilian refugees fleeing from the threatened destruction.

Passing through and beyond all this extraordinary movement, the 2nd Entrenching Battalion arrived at the outskirts of Meteren. Orders were received to dig in behind the village, but it was not long before the several platoons of the Battalion were drawn upon to reinforce the defensive line taken up by English troops about Meteren.

On April 15th the enemy attacked and enveloped the town of Bailleul. At daybreak on the 16th the sweep was continued in strength against Meteren. The 2nd Entrenching Battalion at once became heavily involved. At this stage half the strength of the 1st Otago Company of the Entrenching Battalion was disposed along with Canterbury mainly to the right of Meteren ; the 2nd Company of Otago and the remaining strength of the 1st Company were disposed with English troops to the left front.

There were wide intervals of distance between the several posts which constituted the general line. For that reason mutual support was somewhat difficult. But the whole situation on the left was soon to be seriously complicated and imperilled by a set of circumstances over which the Otago troops had no control. With the fall of Bailleul and the anticipated continuation of the enemy's advance towards Meteren, it was notified that the English troops still further to the left would probably retire down the valley. In that case the New Zealand troops on the left of Meteren were to conform by withdrawing to the newly constructed switch trench in rear of the village. The withdrawal by the English troops did eventuate during the night ; but they failed to advise the adjoining posts of their action. Before day-break on the 16th the garrisons of our advanced positions were notified by their own Headquarters that it was expected that the enemy would attack, in which case a withdrawal was to be effected, while at the same time endeavouring to check the hostile advance.

The German attack, preceded by heavy machine gun fire, developed about daybreak. The enemy, meeting no resistance on the left, immediately exploited his initial success. It was not long before our positions were under fire practically from three sides. The opportunity for effecting a withdrawal had now passed. The platoon of the 1st Company of Otago, commanded by Sergt. T. Sounness, endeavoured to get clear by forcing its way along the Bailleul-Caestre Road, but failed. The two platoons of the 2nd Company, now heavily pressed by the enemy, their ammunition practically expended, and all avenues of escape closed, decided that in the circumstances their only alternative was to comply with the demand for surrender. Thus three platoons, or a total of 210 other ranks, fell to the enemy as prisoners. Only two men had succeeded in getting through, one a lance-corporal who was despatched by Sergt. Sounness with a message indicating the position and asking for assistance, and the other a private of the 2nd Company.

This was the single instance in the whole of the campaign where any considerable numbers of New Zealanders were taken prisoners. Had timely warning been received of the withdrawal of the supporting English troops, this loss must have been averted. Even had the general line been maintained at its original strength, it could have offered an appreciable resistance to the enemy, or at least have withheld his advance sufficiently to permit of an orderly withdrawal. On the other hand, it must be admitted that a large number of the troops concerned in this unfortunate affair were entirely new to action ; the formation suffered from a shortage of experienced leaders, and ammunition supply had in many instances been seriously reduced on the journey from Abeele to Meteren because of an impression that the Battalion was going to construct trenches, not occupy them. But even allowing for these considerations, it is doubtful if experienced and better prepared troops would have fared differently in the same situation. The disaster might have been delayed, though not wholly averted.

The majority of those who had the grave misfortune to become prisoners of war in the Meteren operations were for some time subjected to the cruellest and most inhuman treatment. For a definite period they were confined in the

" Black Hole of Lille," an underground chamber of the fort on the outskirts of Lille town, where the conditions of confinement were indescribably bad. It was sufficiently clear that this was a deliberate and calculated form of German torture, intended to break the spirit of prisoners before sending them out to work in gangs.

The troops of the 2nd Entrenching Battalion established to the right of Meteren withstood the attack at that point and inflicted severe losses on the enemy; but the collapse of the line to the left and the fall of Meteren ultimately forced a withdrawal. Subsequent to the enemy's occupation of Meteren, half the strength of the 1st Company of Otago, which linked up with Canterbury on the right of the line, was forced to withdraw to new positions in rear of the village. From this point Lieut. J. R. Leys (commanding the 1st Company of Otago) and 2nd-Lieut. J. McGregor (platoon commander) moved out with a small party with the object of destroying an enemy machine gun post a short distance to their front. The position proved to be too strongly held, and although the party succeeded in reaching its objective and made a gallant attempt to overwhelm it, the enterprise was unsuccessful. 2nd-Lieut. McGregor was killed, and Lieut. Leys mortally wounded at the moment of shooting down one of the crew of the gun. Lieut. Leys had at one time commanded 8th Company of the 3rd Battalion of Otago Regiment.

On the following morning, on relief, the troops marched out to Berthen, and from there proceeded to Abeele, where the remnant of the 2nd Entrenching Battalion was assembled. From Abeele the Battalion entrained for Rubrouck, in the Ypres area, where the New Zealand Reinforcement Wing was now established, and was reorganised and reinforced from surplus strength.

After a period of considerable activity in the locality of Dickebusch, the 2nd Entrenching Battalion departed from Rubrouck, commencing on May 14th, for the Famechon-Pas area, where the New Zealand Entrenching Group now became established.

The casualties of the 2nd Entrenching Battalion in the Meteren operations totalled two officers and 40 other ranks killed, nine officers and 139 other ranks wounded, and 210 other ranks officially reported as prisoners of war. For fine qualities of leadership displayed during the difficult period of the Meteren operations, Sergts. W. P. Morrin, M.M., and W. J. Pauling were recommended and awarded the D.C.M.

CHAPTER XV

ROSSIGNOL WOOD.

THE activities of the Regiment were shortly to be centred in the locality of Rossignol Wood, which lay within the enemy's lines to the north-east of Hebuterne.

On July 9th the 2nd New Zealand Infantry Brigade relieved the 1st Infantry Brigade in the left sub-sector of the Divisional front, which extended from a point opposite Bucquoy in the north to near Hebuterne in the south. This brought the 1st Battalion of Otago to support positions on the eastern outskirts of the sorely battered village of Gomme-court, with a frontage of about 1,700 yards, comprising old trench systems provided with very deep and spacious German dug-outs. At the same time the 2nd Battalion of the Regiment moved into the Gommecourt reserve trenches to the right. The system taken over was in a neglected state ; and there was in consequence a steady demand for working parties from the two Battalions for the strengthening of existing trenches and the construction of new lines. Practically the whole of this work required to be carried out under cover of darkness, as the enemy enjoyed many advantages in respect of high ground and observation.

On July 15th a minor operation was carried out by the New Zealand Division, resulting in the general line being advanced a short distance in front of Hebuterne and in the vicinity of Rossignol Wood. This was succeeded by con-siderable activity on both sides, and when it fell to the Regi-ment to relieve Canterbury in the front line of the left Brigade sector on the night of the 17th, the situation was still very unsettled. The inter-battalion boundary was at Green Street, at the northern point of Rossignol Wood, where by means of a series of posts held by the two Battalions in con-junction a footing was maintained on the edge of the Wood.

The enemy was very close at this point, being established in Rossignol Wood in concrete "pill-boxes," with blocks constructed across the old communication trenches which connected the opposing lines. To the left the front extended along Railway Trench for about 250 yards to the south-west of the Wood, with further to the left a line of outposts about 300 yards in advance of Bass Trench, fronting the enemy's main line of resistance to the south-east.

It was soon to be disclosed that one effect of the minor operation carried out by the Division on the 15th was to force the enemy to the conclusion that his retention of Rossignol Wood was undesirable or impracticable. About midnight on the 19th several explosions were heard from the interior of the Wood, subsequent investigation disclosing the fact that the enemy had blown up his concrete "pill-boxes" prior to evacuation. At an early hour on the 20th a reconnaissance was effected by Sergt. Travis, when it was definitely learned that the enemy had evacuated the Wood entirely. All posts were now advanced and preparations made for regaining touch with the enemy and determining the extent of his withdrawal.

On the left the 1st Battalion proceeded to push forward patrols from the outpost line in front of Bass Trench to the sunken road west of Fork Wood, at the same time extending the move in a south-westerly direction to Railway trench in order to gain touch with the right Company, the 14th, a party from which was pushing up from Railway trench to make good the high ground in the vicinity. Further parties operated in the direction of the south-eastern fringe of Rossignol Wood. Similarly, the 2nd Battalion of the Regiment had established posts on the south-western edge, and patrols were pushing forward in the direction of Owl trench, with Auckland troops co-operating still further to the right. The trenches east of the Wood were found to be filled with wire, which forced the patrols on to the top and retarded their progress. Furthermore, trenches east and south-west of Rossignol Wood were strongly held by the enemy, who offered considerable resistance to any attempt at advance beyond the limits of his deliberate withdrawal overnight. Thus there were several bombing encounters at close range, and minenwerfer fire was employed by the enemy to dislodge our patrols. The enemy appeared to be holding the lines of Moa and Shag trenches in strength; while the sunken road running at right angles to the head of Railway trench was also strongly manned. This was evidently his selected line of resistance; and it was found a difficult task to persuade him to retire beyond it. Intermittent fighting continued throughout the greater part of the day, and a fairly large number of casualties were inflicted on the enemy across the front of operations; our own casualties being comparatively light. The enemy left behind some material, including one minenwerfer gun.

The line established at the close of the day, the result of gruelling work in a hot sun, was well in advance of Rossignol Wood on the southern and eastern sides. During the night a new trench was cut by the 1st Battalion from the junction of Auckland and Railway trenches to a point about 200 yards to the right, thus giving access to the new line from right to left without having to pass through Rossignol Wood. During the afternoon there was increased artillery fire over Rossignol Wood and the new ground; also a certain amount of machine gun fire from Fork Wood and the high ground in the vicinity. Artillery fire developed considerably during the night and continued for some time; our own artillery retaliating strongly.

On the 21st both Battalions carried out inter-company reliefs. With the 1st Battalion, 14th Company on the right of the front line was relieved by 10th Company, and 8th Company on the left by 4th Company. With the 2nd Battalion, 10th Company relieved 4th Company in the front line; 14th Company went into support; 8th Company remained at Salmon Point; and 4th Company moved back to reserve. On the 22nd slight improvements were made in the general line, and our patrols were again active in front of the newly won ground.

A review of the new positions showed that it was highly desirable that the line should be advanced still further, which would secure the higher ground, afford improved observation and field of fire, and at the same time effect a more complete clearance of Rossignol Wood. A minor operation to effect this purpose was decided on and set down for 5 p.m. on the 23rd. Meanwhile preparations were commenced for establishing forward dumps and continuing the Biez switch through Rossignol Wood. Heavy shelling of the area continued at intervals, causing considerable interruption to parties journeying to and from the line. Stormy weather now intervened, flooding the trenches and approaches, and compelling the postponement of the operation for 24 hours. The attack was originally to have been carried out under a light trench mortar barrage, with the 1st and 3rd Brigades of the New Zealand Field Artillery and the Corps heavy artillery co-operating; the 37th Divisional Artillery creating a diversion by bombarding Bucquoy on the left, and establishing a smoke barrage in that locality.

At the revised time, 5 p.m. on July 24th, under a brief light trench mortar bombardment only, the two Companies of the Regiment committed to the operation, 10th Company of the 1st Battalion on the left and 10th Company of the 2nd Battalion on the right, advanced to the attack. The enemy being busy with his evening meal was taken completely by surprise; there being also evidence that he was on the point of being relieved. His resistance was accordingly weaker, and his posts were either rushed or bombed in quick succession. On the left of the attack, the first post yielded two prisoners and a machine gun to the 1st Battalion; while further ahead at the junction of a communication trench with Shag trench another post was encountered and bombed, the enemy being driven out, leaving one killed. The left platoon met with temporary opposition from a machine gun position in Shag trench, from which quarter 2nd-Lieut. A. M. Rhinesmith and his orderly were shot down on entering the trench. Right parties, working from the flank, drove the post out; the enemy abandoning a machine gun in his flight. The left attacking platoon, after establishing a block in Railway trench, worked its way across the open to the sunken road and rushed a position, which we then took over and established a block at the junction of the sunken road and Railway trench. A number of the enemy were killed, and three prisoners, two machine guns, and a quantity of equipment captured. The assault over the left portion of the selected front had thus achieved distinct success.

On the right of the attack, the bombing parties of the 2nd Battalion found the garrison equally disconcerted by the

SERGT. L. A. BERG, D.C.M., M.M.

SERGT. G. HAYTON, D.C.M., M.M.

CORPL. T. J. BECK, D.C.M., M.M.

PTE. H. MELVILLE, D.C.M., M.M.

SERGT. RICHARD CHARLES TRAVIS, V.C., D.C.M., M.M., [F.]

(*Killed in Action.*)

suddenness of the assault. Several enemy were killed and a number escaped down the communication trenches, which they insistently but unsuccessfully endeavoured to hold by bombing. A patrol with a Lewis gun pushed along Slug Street until Hawk trench was reached ; the ground being gained yard by yard and at some cost to the enemy. From this point a bombing party and several scouts, headed by the redoubtable Sergt. Travis, bombed their way along Hawk trench for a distance of about 250 yards, driving the enemy before them. Finally, running short of bombs and encountering the enemy in great numbers, a temporary block was constructed and the enemy held until permanent barriers could be established. An attempt to cut the party off from the left of Hawk trench was frustrated and the enemy beaten off.

Severe fighting marked this stage of the operations ; and standing out above it all was the splendid gallantry, determination and resourceful daring of Sergt. Dick Travis. It was his crowning effort on this day that won for him the coveted Victoria Cross. An extract from the official narrative of events will show the stuff he was made of :—

> " A bombing party on the right of the attack was held up by two enemy machine guns, and the success of the whole operation was in danger. Perceiving this, Sergt. Travis, with great gallantry and utter disregard of danger, rushed the position, killed the crew, and captured the guns. An enemy officer and three men immediately rushed at him from a bend in the trench and attempted to retake the guns. These four he killed single-handed, thus allowing the bombing party, on which much depended, to advance."

It was estimated that approximately 50 of the enemy were killed during the course of the operations. The captures amounted to four prisoners (all identifications being of the 73rd Fusilier Regiment, 111th Division), six machine guns and two trench mortars. The greater portion of the trenches captured were in good order and contained dug-outs and shelters. We were now afforded direct observation into Puisieux. In the actual operations our own casualties were light, but they increased considerably when the enemy artillery retaliation came down 14 minutes after zero on Rossignol Wood and adjoining trenches, and along the valleys. During the night the enemy maintained almost uninterrupted artillery fire over our area, the majority of the shells falling in rear of the new front line.

At daylight on the 25th a heavy barrage descended over the sector occupied by the 1st Battalion, and about 10 o'clock in the morning this was repeated with increased activity and over a much wider area. The fire from this concentration of artillery, embracing guns of various calibres, was of exceptional severity, and for close on an hour swept over the front and forward positions of the 1st and 2nd Battalions. No infantry action developed and the fire gradually died down. At 3 p.m. there was a further outburst. At 7 p.m. the enemy artillery broke out in still greater fury; and on this occasion heavy machine gun fire was added. The enemy was observed massing in the valley to the south of Rossignol Wood, and as an attack appeared imminent the S.O.S. signal was sent up by the 2nd Battalion; but it was some time before artillery support was forthcoming. Following upon this intense preparation the enemy launched an attack across the front of the two Battalions of the Regiment. The assault against the 1st Battalion was delivered by two distinct parties. The left party, consisting of one officer and 20 men, took as its objective the post commanded by Lieut. H. Holden at the junction of the sunken road and Railway trench. After working down the shelter of the communication trench the enemy crossed over the open, but were immediately met with Lewis gun and rifle fire and successfully beaten off, a number being killed. The right assaulting party of about one officer and 25 other ranks similarly worked their way down the old communication trenches, and on their barrage lifting divided into three sections. When within 60 yards of our line they commenced throwing stick bombs, at the same time advancing on the post. The garrison of this section of the line, commanded by 2nd-Lieut. A. Macdonald, at once assailed them with Lewis gun fire and bombs, and beat them off with deadly effect. Our artillery barrage came down at this juncture and added to the destruction.

Along the front of the 2nd Battalion of the Regiment
the enemy attacked in much greater strength. Here again,
after taking advantage of the cover provided by the several
disused saps, they advanced over the open as their barrage
lifted from our line, and delivered their assault in three
sections, each at an estimated strength of 40. On the right
flank the enemy overwhelmed the garrison and penetrated
the line. At all other points the assault was most effectively
smashed. The platoons held in readiness in Moa trench
were at once organised for counter-attack against the invasion.
Under the command of Lieut. C. F. Atmore they advanced
against the enemy, supported by a small party under 2nd-
Lieut. E. Malcolm, which crossed over the open and went
straight to its objective with the bayonet. This combined
counter-stroke was driven home with such determination
and skill that the whole of the enemy who had penetrated
our trenches were either killed or wounded, allowing the line
to be firmly re-established. The determined leadership
of Lieut. C. B. McClure, M.C., throughout the two days'
operations had contributed largely to the success achieved.

Altogether about 30 prisoners, the majority of whom
were wounded, were left in our hands ; and along the front
of the 2nd Battalion, where the weight of the attack fell,
close on 60 enemy dead were counted. In addition to the
casualties inflicted by the trench garrisons, the enemy when
retreating undoubtedly suffered from our artillery fire.

Subsequently enemy troops were reported to be massing
in the locality of Fork Wood, east of Rossignol Wood, a
development which was effectively dealt with by our heavy
artillery. This was followed by a brief period of retaliatory
shelling, directed mainly to High Street, after which the
situation became entirely normal. Had the bombardment
and counter-attack opened but a few minutes later the Regiment would have been caught in the middle of a relief ; a
process involving a dangerous congestion of troops in the
forward system. Fortunately there was time to despatch
orders to the approaching relief to stand fast until the situation had cleared. When relief was accomplished an hour or
two later the Regiment handed over to the incoming troops
of the 3rd Brigade a system of trenches in many places completely flattened out by the weight of the bombardment.

The enemy's casualties in the concluding operation were clearly heavy ; our own losses, due to the exceptional severity of the several bombardments directed against our lines, were by the close of the day also severe. Among the morning's total was 2nd-Lieut. C. A. Kerse, of the 2nd Battalion, who was killed by shell fire ; and among those who fell later in the day, Lieut. D. J. Beechey, also of the 2nd Battalion, who was bayoneted when valiantly holding his ground at the point where the enemy penetrated our line.

The Regiment had on this day suffered one other loss, the tragedy of which left it overwhelmed with grief. Sergt. Richard Travis, after a long series of exploits of unexampled daring and courage, and at the moment when the greatest of all military honours had been conferred upon him, had been struck down in the storm of the morning's bombardment. The hero of countless gallant deeds had passed across to the silent legion of unreturning and honoured dead.

CHAPTER XVI.

SERGT. RICHARD TRAVIS.

In the years still distant, and in the nearer times, when men who have fought side by side in the Great War foregather and, in reminiscent mood, go back in memory to those days of storm and stress, of great peril and blood-stirring adventure, the name of one man of the Otago Regiment will always be spoken of with pride and admiration, touched with something akin to reverence for the gallant spirit, around which centre stories of personal daring and adventure mediaeval rather than modern in the flavour of romance which they exhale.

This was Sergt. Richard Travis, V.C., D.C.M., M.M., Croix de Guerre, a man of striking and outstanding personality even among the bravest of the brave men by whom he was surrounded. He was in truth the knight-errant of the Regiment, steeled and modernised. His forays into enemy territory, attended by his small but carefully chosen band of men-at-arms; his swift and dramatically sudden surprises in enemy strongholds and trenches; his desperate single-handed encounters against many—the number of the enemy in these affairs never troubled him—his summary and terror-inspiring methods; his unfailing resource and lightning changes of attack in seemingly hopeless emergencies; his killings and capturings and forced surrenders—these things became merely the normal programme of events in the daily and nightly fighting life of this remarkable man.

His escape from death and his immunity from wounds of a serious nature in this life of observer, sniper, scout, patrol leader and raider, extending over a period of two years, with all its attendant and thrilling adventure, and his death ultimately within his own lines, suddenly and tragically struck down at the height of a bombardment by a chance missile,

317

is curiously and pathetically suggestive of the waywardness and eccentricity of Fate—or was it in accordance with an ordered and settled design inexorable and relentless in its operation ?

Sergt. Travis was New Zealand born. He enlisted from Ryal Bush, Southland, in August, 1914, joining the Otago Mounted Rifles Regiment, and left New Zealand with the Main Body. His Regiment having been temporarily detained in Egypt at the moment when the New Zealand Infantry sailed from there on their great adventure, his restless spirit revolted against the prospect of comparative quietude however brief, and he made an unofficial departure to the busier and more congenial theatre of the Peninsula Campaign.

With the close of that campaign and the return of the New Zealand Forces to Egypt, Travis, with many others of the Mounted units, transferred to the infantry, joining the 2nd Battalion of Otago Regiment, and being posted to 8th (Southland) Company ; with that Battalion of the Regiment he fought until his career closed.

He first came into notice when the Regiment, in the middle of 1916, entered into occupation of its first sector on the Western Front at Armentieres, establishing a reputation as scout, sniper, patrol leader and raider ; and when the Regiment became engaged in the stubborn fighting of the Somme offensive his daring exploits, distinguished by the highest qualities of courage and resource, gave him a distinct and special value in the rôle he had made his own.

When the Regiment headed north again and settled down in Flanders for the winter he was promoted Sergeant, and given command of the sniping and observing organisation of the 2nd Battalion, and in that capacity gathered round him a small band of men whose special function was night patrolling of No Man's Land and of enemy territory generally. These men were carefully chosen, and being closely associated with Sergt. Travis in many of his exploits, it is fitting that the names of the original members should be recorded. They were Ptes. T. Barber, H. Boreham, A. Campbell, J. McGregor, J. Nicholson, T. Powelly, and R. Fitzgerald. Mainly by reason of casualties the personnel of the party changed from time to time ; but so long as the organisation continued Travis remained the master-hand and the directing mind. Of this party Nicholson, a very worthy fellow, was killed prior to the Messines Battle when on the point of leading out a raiding party; Barber was killed at Passchendaele; and Clydesdale, who joined later, was also killed. Other men were Miller, Macdonald, and G. Fitzgerald; all of the right mettle and always ready for any adventure.

The last of the many reports bearing on remarkable achievements sent in by Sergt. Travis dealt with events of the day at Rossignol Wood on July 24th, the occasion when he gained the Victoria Cross. The report was as follows: " A few seconds before 5 p.m. several Stokes bombs thrown in enemy entanglements in front of blocks. At 5 p.m. our trench mortars put up a perfect barrage on enemy's forward posts for one minute. Our bombing parties rushed the trench and found the enemy very much shaken. Some ran down communication trenches, while remainder were killed, except those who were sent to the rear. Fifteen dead bodies counted and two machine guns captured in forward positions. On several occasions enemy tried to hold c.t.'s with bombing parties, but the ground was gained yard by yard. We reached objective about two minutes past 5 p.m.; but bombing party and several scouts bombed up Hawk trench for a distance of about 250 yards. As we were running short of bombs we had to establish a temporary block, and hold the enemy until we put permanent blocks across saps. Huns tried to cut us off from the left of Hawk trench, but were beaten off with their own bombs. Very heavy casualties inflicted on enemy in Hawk trench. Total for the day about 50 killed (including two officers) and six machine guns captured. Had our party had enough bombs they could have gone to Berlin." It was on the following day that Sergt. Travis was killed.

The body of this gallant fellow was carried out of the line, and in the falling rain of the late afternoon of July 26th was buried in the little cemetery above Couin by the Rev. D. C. Herron, M.C., padre to the 2nd Battalion of the Regiment. The death of no other soldier could have stirred men to such deep sorrow or caused such an acute sense of real loss. Full military honours and a long procession of all ranks, including the Divisional Commander, were the last tributes paid to his memory. As representatives of the

Regiment returned through the valley below Couin the soldiers of English Regiments came out of their billets and cheered them—a estimony of their admiration for the gallant New Zealander who had just been laid to rest.

In the records of the 2nd Battalion of the Otago Regiment in the Field, dated July 26th, 1918, these words are written of Sergt. Richard Travis : " His name will live in the records of the Battalion as a glorious example of heroism and devotion to duty."

British 9·2in. Naval Gun in Coigneux Valley.

CHAPTER XVII.

IMPORTANT EVENTS.

FOLLOWING hard upon the Battle of St. Quentin, the enemy had opened the Battle of the Lys on the morning of April 9th and made substantial progress ; on May 27th a formidable attack was launched against the French Sixth Army on the Aisne, forcing the line of the Aisne River along a wide front and finally reaching the Marne in the centre of the attack ; on July 15th there followed a further great drive east and south-west of Rheims, in which the crossing of the Marne was again effected. All this was startling evidence of the ability of the enemy to embark on fresh offensives and prosecute them with great vigour and strength, notwithstanding the enormous expenditure of effort which the Battle of St. Quentin had involved.

But more startling still, and more damaging and dramatic in its consequences, was the great counter-stroke launched by Marshal Foch on July 18th between Chateau Thierry, at the apex, and Soissons, on the northern flank, against the deep German salient which resulted from the Battle of the Aisne two months previously. From this master stroke might be said to date the turning point of the War, and the commencement of a sequence of events, following in rapid succession, which signally and completely changed the whole complexion of the conflict.

The British Forces had now almost entirely recovered from the shock sustained in March and April, and the American Army was growing rapidly in numbers and efficiency. The sweeping successes which attended Marshal Foch's counter-offensive, and the fact that the German reserve of strength had been largely drawn upon in these several great attacks, presented overwhelming argument in favour of a broad Allied scheme of offensive. The first phase was the Battle of Amiens. The plan of operation decided upon was to strike in an easterly and south-easterly direction, with the primary object of gaining the line of the outer defences of Amiens and thereby disengaging the main Paris-Amiens Railway. The attack was then to be pushed forward in the direction of Roye, with the object of capturing the railway junction of Chaulnes, which would have the effect of cutting the communications of the enemy forces in the Lassigny and Montdidier areas, south-east of Amiens.

The attack by the Fourth Army was launched early on the morning of August 8th, on a front of over 11 miles, the Australian Corps operating in the centre, the Canadian Corps on the right, and the III. Corps on the left. Over 400 tanks supported the attack. One hour later the French First Army advanced on a front of five miles between Moreuil and the British right. The success achieved in this five days' battle was represented by the capture of close on 22,000 prisoners and over 400 guns, the complete disengaging of Amiens and the converging railways, and the penetration of the enemy's defences to a depth of 12 miles. This deep advance, combined with the operations of the French on the right, compelled the immediate evacuation by the enemy of considerable territory to the south. August 8th, the day on which was accomplished the delivery of this swift and decisive stroke, has been referred to by Ludendorff as "Germany's Black Day."

There followed a series of great battles and enforced enemy withdrawals north and south, in which, in three months of continuous fighting, our Armies advanced without check from one victory to another until the enemy was finally overwhelmed and fell back in utter confusion and disorder.

GOMMECOURT.

On being relieved in the line at Rossignol Wood on July 25th the Regiment marched back to reserve, the 1st Battalion to Couin Wood, and the 2nd Battalion to Rossignol Farm, above Coigneux village. These positions were maintained until, in the opening days of August, the 2nd Infantry Brigade relieved the 1st Infantry Brigade in the right sub-sector of the Divisional front, which extended between Gommecourt and Hebuterne.

The Regiment now moved into new positions. The 1st Battalion was disposed along the valley between Sailly-au-Bois and the Chateau de la Haie, and in the eastern edge of the village itself; the 2nd Battalion in support trenches at Hebuterne village.

At this stage the Regiment received a complement of selected troops, about 100 to each Battalion, from the American Expeditionary Force; these being merged into the different Companies with a view to obtaining a knowledge of the line and its conditions under the guidance of experienced troops.

For several days the activities of the Regiment were confined to trench construction and improvement; while the 1st Battalion, by reason of being further back from the line, found it convenient to carry out modified training. On August 7th Major Hargest assumed command of the 1st Battalion on Lieut.-Colonel Charters proceeding to the United Kingdom on leave.

On the night of August 10th-11th the 1st Battalion relieved the 2nd Battalion of Canterbury in the line to the east of Gommecourt as the left front line Battalion of the right Brigade. The two forward Companies were 14th and 8th from right to left, with 4th Company in support and 10th Company in reserve. A Composite Company, formed of men surplus to the establishment consequent upon the additional strength given to the Battalion by the inclusion of 100 Americans, took up its quarters in Patricia trench, in Gommecourt Park, and was made responsible for the major portion of the work carried out in the front line area.

The new sector extended across the front of Hebuterne and the southern extremity of Gommecourt, and was immediately south of the sector at Rossignol Wood previously occupied. From the slopes of the high ground of the front line back to Battalion Headquarters in Gommecourt Park there was still remarkable evidence of the grim and protracted struggles which were waged round the Gommecourt salient during the Somme Offensive of 1916—trees riven and blasted by shell fire, derelict tanks, the ground pitted with great shell-holes, densities of heaped-up wire entanglements, wooden crosses, and even trenches still lined with grinning skulls and bones and the litter of broken paraphernalia of war. And perhaps more remarkable still, as exemplifying the almost impregnable nature of the defences of the salient, were the maze of deep trenches still undestroyed, the belts of wire still intact, the iron-plated machine gun loop-holes which commanded every approach, and the scores of dug-outs of extraordinary depth and size.

AN ENEMY WITHDRAWAL.

Following upon the Battle of Amiens, warning advice was issued of a probable withdrawal by the enemy opposite the New Zealand Divisional front. Patrols were commanded to display added activity in maintaining touch with the enemy in order that any attempt in this direction should be detected immediately. Demolitions were reported to have been carried out in Albert; abnormal movement in rear of the enemy's lines strengthening the belief of an intended withdrawal at certain points as the result of the deep penetration of the line further south in the Battle of Amiens.

Across the front occupied by the 1st Battalion of the Regiment the enemy was holding an outpost line extending along the high ground of Louviere Alley, about 300 yards in advance of our line. On the morning of August 13th these posts were still occupied, and enemy movement was observed throughout the day. At 4.45 a.m. on the 14th, however, a patrol from 14th Company, under Sergt. W. A. McMillan, which had been out over night, discovered that the enemy had evacuated his positions along our front. This patrol and a party from 8th Company which had moved out at 3.30 a.m., pushed over the ridge and down the reverse slope towards the railway line in the direction of Star Wood ; but still failed to gain contact.

Upon receipt of information at Battalion Headquarters disclosing this important development, Major Hargest immediately put into operation the plans which he had prepared for exploiting to the utmost such a contingency. The reserve Company, the 10th, under the command of Lieut. K. Scott, M.C., at once moved up from its position in rear and occupied the line Kaiser's Lane, Fritz Avenue, and the eastern edge of Box Wood. The remainder of the Battalion conformed to the advance. Fighting patrols were pushed

2ND-LIEUT. J. H. WILSON, M.C., M.M., BAR TO M.M.

2ND-LIEUT. P. T. MOIR,
D.C.M., M.M.

2ND-LIEUT. W. P. MORRIN,
D.C.M., M.M.

out and gained contact with and actively engaged strong enemy rear-guards at several points beyond Kaiser's Lane. It now became clear that the enemy was carrying out a withdrawal of his forces over the Brigade front; but the real extent of it was as yet difficult to determine. With the Battalion organised and established on the line of Kaiser's Lane and adjoining trenches, about 750 yards in rear of the Serre-Puisieux Road, an advance of considerably over 1,000 yards had already been accomplished. Our patrols continued to maintain active touch with strong enemy rear-guards; but the advance of the Battalion was temporarily embarrassed by the fact that the troops of the left Brigade were apparently at this stage unaware of the enemy's withdrawal. On the immediate right of Otago, and on the 2nd Brigade front, was the 2nd Battalion of the 317th U.S.A. Regiment, attached to the New Zealand Division, and on the left the 1st New Zealand Brigade. To the left of the New Zealand Division, the 37th Division had made little or no progress, owing to the fact of Bucquoy, which was the northern pivot of the enemy's withdrawal, being strongly held.

At 4 p.m. one Company of the 2nd Battalion of Canterbury passed through the line held by the 1st Battalion of Otago, with the intention of establishing posts in the trench system beyond the Serre-Puisieux Road. The reason for this was not quite clear, because Otago was still strong and full of fight; and moreover the movement occasioned delay and temporary loss of touch with the enemy. At 6 p.m. the Canterbury Company was held up by strong machine gun and rifle fire from the left. Two further Companies of Canterbury Regiment were then moved forward; the objective being gained only after encountering and breaking down considerable opposition. The line was now firmly established in advance of the Serre-Puisieux Road, with patrols operating to the front. The first serious shelling of the day was experienced about 8 p.m., when the enemy put down a heavy barrage between Kaiser's Lane and the Serre Road.

During the night Otago moved forward and relieved Canterbury in the newly advanced positions. The dispositions of the Battalion at that stage were: 8th Company on the right and 10th Company on the left, occupying the trench system west of the sunken road, and thence by a line of posts on the western edge of Puisieux village. The right flank was refused and held by posts established in the trenches immediately south-east of Serre village. The 14th Company was disposed in Kaiser's Lane in support, and 4th Company in Louviere Alley in reserve; with the Composite Company located in Snuff Alley and supplying ration and water carrying parties for the front line troops.

The day's operations had resulted in an important and substantial advance well conceived and executed with dash and initiative under conditions which closely resembled those of open warfare. They were the prelude to a series of events which were to have far-reaching results. In the important preliminary phase the 1st Battalion of the Regiment had specially distinguished itself; in the first place by its early discovery of the withdrawal, and in the second place by the rapid and effective manner in which it forced the enemy beyond the limits of his deliberate retirement. The Commander of the IV. Corps, in the course of a congratulatory message to the Division, referred to this operation as "Another example of splendid initiative." It was Major Hargest's sound dispositions and personal leadership that contributed so much to the success achieved.

A high bank and trench on the eastern side of the sunken road was held by the enemy apparently in strength, and from this quarter was encountered considerable fire. On the morning of the 15th the enemy was forced out of this position by fighting patrols, leaving a machine gun in our possession. At this stage the 1st Battalion of the Regiment was holding practically the whole of the 2nd Brigade front; the 2nd Battalion of the 317th U.S.A. Regiment having side-slipped to the right owing to the 125th Brigade of the 42nd Division not being in line. This position was adjusted during the day by that Brigade capturing Pendant Copse, when touch was restored. At night the 2nd Battalion of Otago moved up from its support area at Hebuterne and relieved the Americans in the right Battalion sector; and subsequently both Battalion fronts were readjusted. In the meantime the activity of the enemy's artillery was increasing, and barrages of varying intensity were periodically directed along the Serre-Puisieux Road, Kaiser's Lane, and the valley of Star Wood.

On the evening of the 15th an endeavour was made to determine the enemy's position in relation to Puisieux. A search of the village pointed to the fact that it was not occupied. Early on the following morning, however, it was clear that the enemy had returned and was established among the ruins in some force, particularly in the locality of the church, now a pile of bricks and rubble. A hostile covering party was encountered at the road junction on the southern side of the village; and at 6.30 a.m. a strength of one platoon under 2nd-Lieut. R. E. Fyfe worked forward under cover, and at a given signal assaulted and drove the enemy from the southern outskirts of Puisieux. Seven prisoners and two light machine guns were captured; while a number of Germans were shot down by Lewis gun fire directed from the flanks. This operation was quite brilliantly conceived and executed, and was subsequently quoted with approval by General Sir Julian Byng at the Third Army Senior Officers' School.

Throughout the 16th there were periods of intense artillery activity. Our own artillery had rapidly conformed to the forward movement commenced on the 14th; batteries being now established in positions which two days previously had been occupied by the front and support line infantry garrisons. Forward roads, long since in disuse, were being repaired and made fit for wheeled traffic.

Active patrolling was continued over the front, and the closest contact with the enemy maintained. An attack against a post held by 14th Company of the 2nd Battalion was most decisively beaten off. One officer and six other ranks were taken prisoners; and one officer and five other ranks killed. A post immediately to the right, held by the neighbouring Division, was raided at the same time; one other rank and a Lewis gun falling into the hands of the enemy. The persistency of our patrols finally drove the Germans from Puisieux and its environments, and by midday on the 17th the village was under hostile artillery fire. On the same evening the 2nd Battalion of Otago was relieved by the 3rd Battalion of the 317th U.S.A. Regiment, and moved back to reserve positions, on the following night, the 18th, being withdrawn to the Chateau de la Haie switch north-east of Sailly-au-Bois.

Supported by a considerable weight of artillery, the enemy launched an attack at dawn on August 18th against our positions at Puisieux and along the slopes of the Serre Ridge, occupied by 10th Company, under command of Lieut. K. Scott, M.C. The assaulting party numbered approximately 100 men, including a proportion of what were technically known as storm troops, which had been brought for the purpose from as far afield as Douai. The enemy were apparently completely unaware of our dispositions ; for they manœuvred into a position which gave every advantage to our infantry. The immediate result was that the majority of the attackers were shot to pieces by the concentrated fire of Lewis guns and rifles, and the few who succeeded in reaching our lines surrendered. The captures totalled ten unwounded and three wounded prisoners and three light machine guns. The unexpected destructiveness of our fire was exemplified by the fact that the bodies of two officers and 25 other enemy ranks were found dead in one group, and seven in another. The *moral* of our troops at this period was extremely high ; as was demonstrated by the fact that immediately the attack was launched the front line garrison swung forward of its own accord with the object of destroying the enemy's flanks and rear.

After this very severe lesson the enemy remained quiet during the remainder of the day. At nightfall the Battalion was relieved by the 2nd Battalion of the 3rd (Rifle) Brigade, and moving back to Rossignol Farm, now a considerable distance in rear, settled down as one of the units of the Brigade in reserve.

N.Z. Official Photograph

A Corner of Puisieux-au-Mont.

CHAPTER XVIII.

TURN OF THE TIDE.

WHILE the Regiment was thus temporarily retired from the scene of active operations, in which it had played such a leading part, preparations were being speedily advanced for the launching of a great offensive movement. The Third Army had been ordered to press back the enemy towards Bapaume without delay, and to make every endeavour to prevent his destroying the system of road and railway communications in rear. In compliance with this order, the 37th Division was to attack and capture the high ground east of Bucquoy and Ablainzeville, further north; and following upon this operation, the 5th Division and the 63rd (Royal Naval) Division were to be ready to push forward to the line Irles-Bihucourt. The New Zealand and 42nd Divisions were to co-operate in the first phase with artillery and machine gun fire, at the same time advancing their fronts to a general line extending along the eastern edge of Puisieux-au-Mont and the high ground to the immediate south; and in the second phase by advancing to conform with the 5th Division to the general line extending along the western side of Miraumont. The attack was to contain all the elements of surprise; every effort being made in assembling troops to maintain secrecy.

A readjustment of the New Zealand Divisional sector completed on the night of August 19th-20th, resulted in the 3rd (Rifle) Brigade holding the Divisional front, with the 1st Infantry Brigade in support; the 2nd Infantry Brigade being concentrated in reserve positions. In accordance with this readjustment, the 2nd Battalion of Otago had on the evening of the 18th moved into the Chateau de la Haie switch, north-east of Sailly-au-Bois, and on the 19th the 1st Battalion moved from Rossignol Farm to a bivouac camp on the northern outskirts of St. Leger. On the 20th the Regiment was fitted and equipped as for battle, and at an early hour on the following morning, in compliance with concentration orders affecting the 2nd Infantry Brigade, the 1st Battalion moved forward to Bayencourt and bivouacked in the orchards in the outskirts ; while the 2nd Battalion had moved across overnight to the eastern edge of Sailly-au-Bois.

Lieut.-Colonel W. S. Pennycook arrived from the United Kingdom on August 20th, and took over command of the 2nd Battalion of the Regiment; Lieut.-Colonel J. B. McClymont proceeding to England on duty.

FALL OF BAPAUME.

The Third Army, Commanded by General Sir Julian Byng, launched its attack on the morning of August 21st. The morning broke wet and misty, and it was well on to midday before the sun penetrated the heavy fog, which, though favouring the opening stages of the attack, was calculated to cause loss of direction to troops moving over new ground. The 3rd (Rifle) Brigade, representing the New Zealand Division, gained its furthest objectives, nightfall finding it on a line well over 1,000 yards to the east of Puisieux-au-Mont, with patrols pushed forward to a point approximately midway between Achiet-le-Petit and Miraumont. The general line reached by the Third Army approximated to that of the Arras-Albert Railway, and over 2,000 prisoners were sent to the rear.

The way was now clear for the launching on August 23rd of what was regarded as the main attack by the Third Army and the Divisions of the Fourth Army north of the Somme ; with the remaining Divisions of the Fourth Army south of the Somme co-operating by pushing forward and covering the flank. The front to be affected extended over a distance of 33 miles from the junction with the French, north of Lihons, to Mercatel. With the launching of this great sweep immediate and important successes were achieved ; and on the succeeding days the pressure was maintained and the battle continued. On the New Zealand Divisional front stubborn opposition was met with at the outset in the locality of Beauregard Dovecote, near Miraumont, and the high ground north-east of it ; but by the 23rd the line occupied was in advance of the Albert-Arras Railway.

The Regiment had continued in bivouac over the 22nd, passing the time for the most part in pleasant idleness, but ready to move at one hour's notice. Batches of prisoners were periodically coming down from the line ; but otherwise there was little or no indication of the development of events along the front. On the 22nd a reconnaissance was made by the Commanding Officer and the Company Commanders of the 1st Battalion of the forward area and its approaches. On the 23rd, following upon an order for the concentration of the 2nd Brigade in the area immediately south of Bucquoy and west of the railway line, the Regiment moved towards the line of battle. The 1st Battalion passed over familiar ground, through Hebuterne and Puisieux-au-Mont, and after encountering a certain amount of gas shelling in the latter stages of the march, reached some old trenches, until recently occupied by the enemy, near Bucquoy, where it settled down for the night under temporary shelters. Rain commenced to fall shortly afterwards. The 2nd Battalion of the Regiment had followed a parallel course further north, skirting the northern side of Rossignol Wood and the southern side of Biez Wood, and also experienced slight trouble from the effects of enemy gas shelling.

With the resumption of the general attack on the 24th orders were issued for the New Zealand Division to assault and capture Loupart Wood and Grevillers to the east of it ; the 37th Division of the same Corps (the IV.) operating on the left, with Biefvillers as its objective. The 1st Infantry Brigade was entrusted with the first stage of the New Zealand Division's task ; the 2nd Infantry Brigade was to move in support, and finally push through the 1st Brigade to the capture of the final objective, which was represented by Bapaume and the high ground to the east of it.

The attack was launched at 4.30 a.m. The 1st Brigade made rapid progress on the left until Grevillers was reached, when heavy machine gun fire was encountered and the advance temporarily checked. By 7 a.m. the village was reported to be in our hands. On the right, strongly placed enemy machine guns in the southern edge of Loupart Wood required the co-operation of two extra tanks before the Wood could be reported clear. On the left the 37th Division had met

331

stiff opposition in its advance on Biefvillers, and was temporarily held up in rear of the village.

The 2nd New Zealand Infantry Brigade (commanded by Brigadier-General R. Young, C.M.G., D.S.O.) had now moved forward to its point of concentration near Achiet-le-Petit. At 8.30 a.m. the 2nd Battalion of Otago on the right and the 2nd Battalion of Canterbury on the left advanced on a line between Grevillers and Biefvillers to the continuation of the attack and the capture of the final objective. Otago moved forward in artillery formation until the western outskirts of Grevillers were reached. At that point the Battalion extended, its right flank resting on the northern edge of the village. The line of Grevillers was gained after certain opposition had been dealt with ; but the foremost troops had barely cleared the village when machine gun fire assailed them from the front and from either flank. The destructiveness of this fire caused the formation of the leading waves to become somewhat disorganised. The 10th Company, held in reserve, was pushed forward to fill the gaps. The trenches which fronted the eastern side of the village and gave observation towards Bapaume on the ridge beyond were gained and occupied ; but the growing intensity of the machine gun fire and the heavy nature of the shelling threatened the progress of the main advance. In the meanwhile the 2nd Battalion of Canterbury, on the left, had been temporarily held up, as Biefvillers was not clear of the enemy as reported. The most advanced elements of Otago had succeeded in penetrating along the road and railway line as far as the outskirts of Avesnes-le-Bapaume, some of them actually reaching as far as the Bapaume-Albert Road, to the right of Bapaume. Lieut.-Colonel Pennycook (commanding the 2nd Battalion) and Lieut. H. S. Sanson (Assistant-Adjutant) had now gone forward to personally reconnoitre this advanced situation. But the enemy, apparently more reassured since our main advance had been checked, or appeared to be, now delivered a counter-attack against the left flank of our foremost position. This was preceded by a process of infiltration, by which the enemy succeeded in massing strongly against our left. Then by intense rifle and machine gun fire, delivered at close range, they overwhelmed and practically wiped out the whole of our advanced elements ; though actually they made no attempt to follow up their success. It was under this severe fire that Lieut.-Colonel Pennycook and Lieut. Sanson were shot down, their bodies being recovered on the following day when the advance was taken up by the 1st Battalions of Otago and Canterbury. Lieut.-Colonel Pennycook's command of the 2nd Battalion of the Regiment was thus tragically cut short within a few days of his arrival from the United Kingdom. It might be suggested that he had gone much further forward than in his capacity of Battalion Commander there was actual necessity for him to have done ; but certainly under the heavy fire which he encountered when the enemy attacked he displayed fine coolness and self-possession until his end came.

The obviously increasing strength of the enemy west of Bapaume and in the locality of the railway line and Avesnes, made impracticable any further advance for the time being, and the Battalion was forced to hold on and dig in where it was, which was in front of Grevillers. Over the left of the 2nd Brigade front the 2nd Battalion of Canterbury reached Biefvillers, a few of the enemy remaining there up to the last moment and then making their escape in the direction of Sapignies, to the north-east. As with Grevillers, Biefvillers came under the heavy fire of enemy artillery almost as the enemy were driven out. The most advanced troops of Canterbury, as was the case with Otago, had been forced to withdraw from the approaches to Avesnes ; the general line occupied by the troops of the 2nd Brigade concerned in the attack finally extending across the eastern side of the villages of Grevillers and Biefvillers. The right flank of the attack was secured by troops of the 1st Infantry Brigade ; but touch had not been gained with the Division on the left. The continued heavy shelling of the area occupied and of the two villages increased the number of casualties already incurred ; the total losses sustained by the 2nd Battalion of Otago being six officers and 105 other ranks.

It was now decided that the attack should be renewed on the following morning, August 25th, by the other units of the 2nd Brigade, namely, the 1st Battalion of Otago and the 1st Battalion of Canterbury. On the morning of the 24th Otago had moved by stages to a position across the railway line and south of Achiet-le-Grand, digging in on the reverse slope of the ridge, where it remained throughout the day.

At this stage all roads forward were choked with the movement of troops, of artillery, tanks, armoured cars, ammunition and supply limbers, and the varied machinery and accessories of war, presenting at once an extraordinary panorama of all the elements and phases incident to the launching of a great offensive, and at the same time reflecting the stupendous nature of the organisation entailed. Already long rows of 18-pounders, almost wheel to wheel, with 4.5in. howitzers and the heavier artillery in rear, conscious of their might and with a splendid contempt for the necessity of concealment, periodically burst into violent fire, as if to emphasise to the enemy how close at hand were defeat and disaster. Towards evening a great number of German aeroplanes flew low over this vast concentration of men and artillery, emptied their machine guns into passing targets and showered bombs over the forward area.

Orders for the following day's operations were changed frequently during the night. It was finally decided that with the 1st Battalions of Otago and Canterbury operating side by side, the 63rd Division co-operating on the left, the objective assigned to Otago would be firstly the line of the Bapaume-Arras Road; secondly a line extending from the village of Favrieul to the Bapaume Cemetery, including Monument Wood. Otago was thus disposed on the left of the 2nd Brigade front. At 2 a.m. on the 25th the Battalion, under the command of Major J. Hargest, commenced to move forward to its point of assembly in the trenches surrounding Biefvillers. During the concluding stages of this operation the enemy subjected the village and its approaches to a considerable amount of gas and high explosive shelling; notwithstanding which assembly was completed in good time. The dispositions for the attack involved 4th Company, commanded by Captain E. V. Freed, M.C., on the right, and 8th Company, commanded by Major L. M. Scott, M.C., on the left, as the two leading Companies ; with 14th Company in close support ; and 10th Company in reserve.

The assault was delivered at 5 a.m., being supported by an effective artillery barrage. The enemy was almost immediately encountered in considerable strength ; but the extreme density of the morning fog permitted many of the attacking troops to reach unobserved within point-blank range of the German machine guns, which constituted the first line of real resistance. The crews, huddled round their guns and uncertain of the development of the action, realised too late that the attacking troops were upon them. An extraordinarily large number of machine guns, sited so as to threaten any advance east of Biefvillers, were with their crews thus completely knocked out before half the distance between that village and the Bapaume-Arras Road had been covered. Without check, the leading Companies topped the crest of the rising ground, gained the Bapaume-Arras Road and then proceeded to advance beyond it. But from that point an intense volume of machine gun fire burst upon them ; and as the fog had now lifted and casualties were severe, further progress became impossible. Four heavy tanks, which were late in arriving, now lumbered through our advanced line with the intention of clearing the machine gun nests in the locality of Monument Wood and the Bapaume Cemetery, but had only progressed a short distance when they were knocked out in quick succession. The final line established by 4th and 8th Companies was astride the Bapaume-Arras highway, commencing from a point on the northern edge of the town. An armoured car which had previously exchanged several bursts of fire with our own troops owing to a misunderstanding, now attempted to penetrate along the road leading into Bapaume, but failed to achieve any definite object beyond revealing some of the enemy machine gun strength which held the town.

The Battalion's casualties during this operation were heavy, particularly those of the right Company, the 4th, which lost over 50 per cent. of its initial strength, including its commander, Captain E. V. Freed, M.C., who was shot down when in the van of the attack. Captain Freed was a fine type of soldier, very determined, and indifferent to all danger where his purpose was to be achieved. Although mortally wounded and nearing the end he had insisted on being carried to Battalion Headquarters when on the way out to the Dressing Station in order to report the situation. There was a high percentage of casualties among the senior n.c.o.'s of the Battalion, and in this list was Sergt.-major W. Schaumann, of 4th Company, who was killed at the extreme point of the morning's advance.

Over the right of the 2nd Brigade front, Canterbury was at the close of the attack established against the western outskirts of Bapaume; and still further to the south troops of the 1st Brigade had materially advanced the general line. The original intention of waging a direct assault against the enemy stronghold of Bapaume was now shaping in the direction of envelopment from either side.

During the afternoon the Companies of the 1st Battalion of Otago were reorganised and dispositions readjusted in view of a further operation planned for the evening. The intention now was to advance the line across the Bapaume-Favrieul Road, and at the same time effect the capture of Favrieul village. The two Companies committed to the attack were the 14th (commanded by Captain T. Sim, M.C.), and the 10th (commanded by Captain S. C. Greer) from right to left. The operation, preceded by a furious barrage in which the heavy artillery played an important part, was attended by complete and immediate success. On the right 14th Company, after meeting with resistance at one or two points, hunted the enemy from the cover of an extensive dump which lay across the track of the advance, and quickly reached its objective. On the left 10th Company was entrusted with the difficult task of clearing the southern part of Favrieul and the wood on the western side of it. This it effected with great dash. Early in the operation casualties occurred among the officers; and when Captain Greer was forced to retire wounded, 2nd-Lieut. J .A. Miller took over the command and with his Company gained the objective set it. Unlike the morning's attack, the casualties were comparatively light. Troops of the 2nd Battalion of Canterbury now pushed through Otago and established a line of outposts on the high ground adjoining the Bapaume-Beugnatre road. The situation on the left of the 2nd Brigade front was somewhat compromised during the evening by a withdrawal of elements of the 37th Division, which was concerned with the capture of the northern part of Favrieul; and it was found necessary to send forward one platoon from 8th Company to make the position secure. During the night there were indications that the enemy was endeavouring to filter back to the Bapaume Cemetery; but with the assistance of troops of Canterbury Battalion the right flank was strengthened and these attempts frustrated.

N.Z. Official Photograph.

Bapaume.

The captures effected over the day of the 25th by the 1st Battalion of Otago totalled 270 prisoners (including a Regimental Commander and his staff, and a medical officer, who assisted for several hours in dressing our wounded), large quantities of small arms and artillery ammunition, an extensive engineering dump, one 77 mm. field gun, five anti-tank rifles, four light trench mortars, and over 40 machine guns. The number of enemy dead left across the ground gained was very considerable. Our casualties totalled seven officers and 211 other ranks.

The successful operations of the Regiment on the 25th were largely instrumental in determining the ultimate fate of Bapaume. On the 26th General Sir Andrew Russell, G.O.C. New Zealand Division, visited the headquarters of the 1st Battalion of Otago, and personally offered his congratulations on the success achieved.

The 2nd Infantry Brigade was now in support to the New Zealand Division, and the Regiment accordingly remained in the area between Bapaume and Grevillers over the succeeding few days. Opportunity was afforded for reorganising Companies and posting reinforcements ; there was also work to be done in the direction of salvaging the battlefield of abandoned material, and in burying the dead. The men of Otago who fell in action on the 25th found their last resting place on the summit of the morning's advance, adjoining the Bapaume-Arras highway, and on the northern outskirts of the town.

Early on the morning of the 26th troops of the 3rd (Rifle) Brigade had passed through our foremost line, and in conjunction with the 1st Infantry Brigade continued the advance. An event of unusual interest on this day was the dropping by aeroplanes in our forward areas of several boxes of small arms ammunition, attached to parachutes. The town of Bapaume was still occupied by the enemy, who continued to direct machine gun fire on all observed movement from the summit of the terraced fortification on the southern side of the town and from other points of vantage. The 3rd Brigade continued the advance beyond the Bapaume-Beugnatre Road to the north-east ; but attempts to advance on the southern flank of the enveloping movement continued to meet with strong opposition. During the night of the 28th-29th

Bapaume was violently bombarded by our heavy artillery, and on the morning of the 29th fighting patrols went through the town and found that the enemy had abandoned it. The steady advance of the enveloping movement north and south, combined with a terrific artillery outburst overnight, had evidently forced the enemy to make a quick decision. With but a percentage of the casualties which a direct assault must have involved, Bapaume had fallen, and was occupied by the New Zealand Division. Battered and crumbling from the repeated blows of two Armies, its streets choked with debris and enemy dead lying in its main thoroughfares, this once prosperous town presented a grim and pathetic spectacle of almost entire destruction. It was in March, 1917, that Bapaume was occupied by the Australians during the period of the more deliberate German retreat to the Hindenburg Line, to fall into the enemy's hands again a year later in the course of the great sweep westwards against the Third and Fifth Armies.

THE ADVANCE CONTINUED.

The advance eastward now continued. On the same day as Bapaume was occupied, our troops penetrated along the line of the Cambrai Road for a distance of about a mile. On the northern flank no appreciable progress had been registered, while to the south troops of the 1st Infantry Brigade were in touch with the enemy along the road leading to Beaulencourt. On August 30th Fremicourt and the ridge east of it were taken at small cost to ourselves ; but the line was later retracted to the eastern edge of the village. Over the right of the Divisional front a substantial advance was also made by the 1st Brigade and Bancourt captured ; but the fact of Riencourt, on the neighbouring Division's front-age, being still occupied by the enemy, left the right flank badly exposed. At 5 a.m. on the last day of the month of August, practically the whole of the New Zealand Divisional front was counter-attacked by the enemy. The attack was preceded by an intense artillery bombardment, and was supported by six tanks. The enemy failed to seriously dis-turb our line, and two tanks and about 50 prisoners remained in our hands.

On September 1st the 1st and 3rd Brigades advanced the line still further to the east of Bancourt and Fremicourt ; and the same night the 2nd Brigade received orders to take over the whole of the Divisional front in relief of the other two Brigades. The Regiment was once more on the move. Passing round the outskirts of Bapaume, which was being intermittently shelled and bombed, the 2nd Battalion proceeded to take over positions east of Bancourt. The dispositions of the Battalion were 4th and 8th Companies in the front line, 10th Company in support, and 14th Company in reserve. The 1st Battalion of the Regiment was to be in reserve, and moved up a comparatively short distance to the area west of Fremicourt, where the night was spent in old trenches and shelters.

The general advance was to be continued on the following morning, September 2nd, under an artillery barrage. On the right of the New Zealand Division, the 42nd Division was to attack Villers-au-Flos and the spur in front, with exploitation towards Barastre and Haplincourt Wood as a second objective. On the left the New Zealand Division was to co-operate with the 5th Division, which was attacking Beugny and Delsaux Farm, and the high ground east of Beugny.

The assault was launched at dawn, and as far as the Otago Regiment was concerned, 4th Company of the 2nd Battalion was entrusted with the initial stages of the operation. A trench approximately 400 yards to the front was found to be strongly held by the enemy ; but by the time it had been dealt with the artillery barrage was too far ahead to be caught up. There was stubborn fighting at this point, and losses on both sides were severe ; the main enemy resistance being in the nature of machine gun and rifle fire from the vicinity of the Bancourt-Haplincourt Road and hutments. On the left, Canterbury had also met with stiff resistance ; the advance being similarly temporarily checked. Otago consolidated on the position gained, and at 1 p.m. a second attack was launched behind the protection of an artillery barrage. The assault, carried out by 8th Company, two platoons of 4th Company, and one of 10th Company, was vigorously delivered against the enemy positions in the sunken road and around the shelter of the huts, and was on this occasion entirely successful. At 6 p.m. Canterbury improved the general situation in an attack launched behind artillery fire, Otago at the same time taking advantage of the opportunity to straighten its line. The enemy, who had held out during the day, now surrendered freely, having evidently been brought to the limits of their resistance. The captures effected by the 2nd Battalion over the day totalled 200 prisoners, one enemy tank, about 60 machine guns, three trench mortars, tank rifles and other material. Our own casualties were fairly heavy, but light compared with those of the enemy.

The New Zealand Divisional front now extended from a point immediately west of Haplincourt in the south, to the Fremicourt-Lebucquiere Road near Delcaux Farm in the north. The night remained quiet, except that the enemy's bombing aeroplanes passed almost continuously overhead. The glare from extensive conflagrations behind the enemy's lines suggested that a wide retirement was in progress. Early on the morning of the 3rd patrols discovered that Haplincourt had been evacuated. Fires were now burning in Lebucquiere, Velu, and Bertincourt, still further to the east. The 2nd Battalion of Otago at once pushed forward to regain touch with the retiring enemy. No resistance was encountered until the outskirts of Bertincourt were reached, at which point the enemy engaged our advanced troops with the fire of 77 mm. field guns directed over open sights from the locality of Ruyaulcourt. Lewis guns were brought into action, but the enemy succeeded in getting his artillery out of reach. A line was established along the Ytres-Cambrai Railway, extending across the front of Bertincourt. Velu Wood, on the left, had been cleared, and by nightfall the 1st Battalion of Canterbury was also on the line of the railway, and in touch with the 5th Division on its left. To the right of the New Zealand Division, the 42nd Division had not advanced sufficiently at this stage to be in line. Patrols were pushed forward to Ruyaulcourt, which was found to be held, though lightly, and posts were established by the Battalion for the night well in advance of the main line. Throughout the hours of darkness the enemy harassed our infantry with blue-cross gas shells.

Meanwhile, the 1st Battalion of the Regiment had kept pace with and in rear of the general advance, taking up successive positions, first on the high ground east of Bancourt, and then in the valley west of Haplincourt, astride the Haplincourt-Bancourt Road. In the afternoon the Battalion was in position just west of Bertincourt, from which point no further advance was made that day, the 3rd.

Orders were now issued for the advance to be resumed at 7 a.m. on September 4th. The most distant objective aimed at, in conjunction with the flanking Divisions, was represented by the trench systems east and north-east of Havrincourt Wood. Approximately, the line of advance laid down for the New Zealand Division was across the Canal du Nord, and through the villages of Neuville-Bourjonval and Metz-en-Couture, and the southern half of Havrincourt Wood. North of Ruyaulcourt the waterway of the Canal du Nord ran into a deep tunnel and then followed a course underground for a distance of 4,500 yards, to a point south of Ytres. It therefore did not present any obstacle to our advance.

In compliance with orders for a general advance on the morning of the 4th, it was decided that advanced guards, acting as fighting patrols, should precede the main body, and that in the event of heavy resistance being encountered, our troops were not to undertake any operation calculated to involve casualties, but were to await artillery support, behind which the advance would then be continued. At 6.30 a.m. the 1st Battalion of Otago, in artillery formation of platoons, with patrols well in front, moved forward round the right flank of Bertincourt. The order of battle was as follows : 8th and 14th Companies in front, 10th Company in support, and 4th Company in reserve. One section of artillery, one section of Vickers guns, and four light trench mortars accompanied the Battalion. At 7 a.m. the line held by the 2nd Battalion of the Regiment was passed through, the first enemy resistance met with being from the deep chalk pits to the right of Ruyaulcourt, and from the southern side of the village itself. Our patrols pushed ahead, and a line extending along the west and south of Ruyaulcourt was gained. Touch was maintained with Canterbury on the left, but there was a gap of 1,000 yards on the right to where the 42nd Division could be seen moving from Ytres in the direction of Neuville-

341

Bourjonval. Rather heavy machine gun fire was now being encountered from the forward side of Ruyaulcourt; our patrols were accordingly withdrawn and the area briefly searched by the supporting artillery. At 9.15 a.m. the patrols commenced to push forward again, and on the left gained ground in face of slight opposition. On the right 14th Company met more determined resistance. Lewis gun fire was brought to bear on its centre, and the position then rushed, nine men and a machine gun being captured.

Neuville, to the south-east of Ruyaulcourt, was still occupied by the enemy. In front of these two villages was the more formidable barrier of Havrincourt Wood. Its greatest depth following the line of our advance was about 3,500 yards, and with the trees bearing dense foliage it afforded the enemy excellent cover and shelter, while the tallness of the timber assured facilities for maintaining observation over the approaches. It was realised that the enemy would not be readily dispossessed of his hold over this extensive wood; and heavy machine gun fire from its western side and the sunken road in front strengthened this belief.

There were indications that the enemy was filtering back to Neuville in increasing numbers. Two platoons of 10th Company were now astride the Ruyaulcourt-Neuville Road; while further to the left Canterbury had continued its advance into the valley between Ruyaulcourt and Havrincourt Wood, and by a flanking movement had succeeded in clearing some of the trenches on the western side of the Wood.

At 7.15 p.m. two platoons of 10th Company, with a Company of the 42nd Division co-operating, resumed the advance behind an artillery barrage of considerable intensity. The village of Neuville was cleared of the enemy, and the line established on the northern and eastern sides of it. Platoons of 8th and 14th Companies now pushed forward and occupied portions of Ponder trench, north-east of Neuville. At nightfall the Divisional line extended approximately along the eastern side of Neuville, and skirted the western front of Havrincourt Wood, touch being gained with the 37th Division on the north, and with the 42nd Division at Neuville on the southern flank. The Battalion's casualties for the day numbered 20 wounded, and the prisoners 45.

During the following day, the 5th, brief patrol encounters improved our position at one or two points. Warning orders were now issued for an operation which aimed at establishing, in conjunction with the 42nd Division, the line of Pestle-Proud trenches extending along Green Jacket Ridge between Neuville and Metz-en-Couture; the Neuville-Hermies Road running parallel with the western edge of Havrincourt Wood; and the spur to the east of Ruyaulcourt. At the same time orders were issued for a readjustment of the IV. Corps front. This meant that there were to be two Divisions in line, the New Zealand Division holding the right sector on a three-battalion frontage; the 37th Division the left sector; the 42nd Division to participate in the attack set out for the evening of September 5th, and then to be withdrawn.

The attack was launched as arranged at 5.30 p.m. behind a heavy artillery barrage. The 8th, 10th, and 14th Companies of the 1st Battalion of Otago gained and consolidated their objectives, operating in conjunction with the 2nd Battalion of Canterbury. During this attack, 2nd-Lieut. W. Junge, of 10th Company, was fatally shot when engaged in clearing a trench of Germans who had ostensibly surrendered. He had rejoined his Battalion only five days previously from England after receiving his Commission, previous to which he had enjoyed a fine reputation as a senior non-commissioned officer. The prisoners captured during the day's operations numbered 103, while many more were diverted to the neighbouring Division on being sent back. Our casualties numbered 49.

In accordance with the readjustment of the Corps front previously referred to, the Battalion was now to side-slip to the right. The 8th and 14th Companies were relieved by troops of the 2nd Battalion of Canterbury, and 4th Company took over positions in front of Neuville. The relief by 4th Company, effected under a heavy bombardment, was seriously complicated by the fact that the troops of the 42nd Division were not holding the line claimed, and that elements of the enemy had filtered back.

The morning broke quiet, and there were indications of further withdrawals by the enemy. After a brief fight, a machine gun and infantry post on the high ground overlooking Neuville was surrounded and rushed by a party from 4th

Company, 25 Germans, including one officer, being captured. Arrangements were immediately effected by Lieut.-Colonel Hargest for maintaining touch with the enemy and exploiting success. Patrols from 4th and 10th Companies pushed down to and occupied Proud and Pestle trenches, overlooking Metzen-Couture, many more prisoners and machine guns being swept up by 4th Company on the way. On the left, our patrols discovered that enemy parties were still in occupation of the western edge of Havrincourt Wood, though numbers of them had been observed moving back carrying full packs. Late in the afternoon our troops had penetrated the Wood to a considerable depth. Over the interior there were several extensive clearances as a result of the enemy's activities in the direction of timber getting ; but the density of the trees and undergrowth in other parts demanded cautious movement in order to avoid anything in the nature of surprise.

Our advanced troops, moving in the form of a screen, had by 6 p.m. penetrated the village of Metz, into which the enemy was directing spasmodic bursts of 77 mm. shell fire. Prior to this German batteries were observed hurriedly withdrawing from the valley in rear of Metz towards Gouzeaucourt. Quotient Avenue, on the eastern side of Metz and overlooking Winchester Valley, was occupied by 4th and 10th Companies. At this stage enemy artillery could plainly be seen firing from Dead Man's Corner on the high ground of Trescault Ridge. But within a few minutes these impromptu gun positions were entirely obscured by bursting shells and clouds of smoke and debris, and when our "heavies" ceased fire there was no evidence of the presence of German artillery.

The Battalion had barely settled in its new positions when Lieut.-Colonel Hargest, with unflagging energy, decided to push on and across the valley to the lower slopes of the more formidable Trescault Ridge, occupied by the main enemy's strength. This was effected by 4th Company, which gained touch on the right with the 1st Battalion of Canterbury. On the left, 10th Company was in position on the high ground on the western side of Winchester Valley, and adjoining the southern edge of Havrincourt Wood. The 8th Company was in support in Quotient Avenue, and the 14th Company in reserve in Quibble trench, west of Metz. These were the

Captured German Tank.

N.Z. Official Photograph.

BERTINCOURT

N.Z. Official Photograph.

Heavy Artillery moving Forward.

N.Z. Official Photograph.

German Prisoners passing Havrincourt Wood.

final dispositions for the night. The prisoners for the day totalled 72, while the material captured comprised 26 machine guns and one 5.9in. howitzer. Our casualties numbered six. The night remained quiet except for intermittent machine gun fire from near the eastern edge of Havrincourt Wood and the slopes of Trescault Ridge.

The 7th was a day of much individual effort and very little material progress. Our advance had now reached what might be regarded as the outer defences of the great Hindenburg System. The Trescault Ridge confronting us was the first of a long series of commanding heights fortified with a labyrinth of trenches and strong points, the former not always deeply dug, but the whole deliberately sited and the defences stiffened by long and deep belts of wire entanglements. Moreover, the enemy now appeared to have reinforced his front with a fresh Division; as his resistance wherever it was tested throughout the day proved to be much more active and determined.

From the early morning our patrols persistently endeavoured to penetrate the enemy strength along the upper slopes of the Ridge; but although Gouzeaucourt Wood on the right was eventually cleared by Otago and Canterbury patrols working in conjunction, elsewhere the dense wire and the enfilade rifle and machine gun fire directed from behind it, prevented our making any appreciable headway. The enemy positions were intermittently shelled throughout the day; but at nightfall the Battalion had to be content with establishing outposts on the lower slopes. The enemy artillery fire was gradually becoming more deliberate, our forward positions, Winchester Valley, and the village of Metz all receiving very considerable hostile attention.

During the early evening of September 8th the 1st Battalion was relieved in the line by the 3rd Battalion of the 3rd (Rifle) Brigade, and marched back through Metz and Neuville to trenches and shelters in the locality of Bertincourt and Ytres.

When the 1st Battalion of the Regiment took up the running from Bertincourt on September 4th, the 2nd Battalion remained in trenches on the outskirts of the village and in advance of the railway line. On the evening of the 5th orders were received to move to trenches in the vicinity of Ytres and Neuville. Over the 9th the 2nd Battalion strength was employed clearing the battlefield of dead, friend and foe, and on the following day a party of 300 men was supplied for trench digging. The 1st Battalion was by this time settled in comfortable hutments in the locality of Ytres and Bertincourt.

On September 11th the 2nd Infantry Brigade, now in support, was relieved by the 1st Infantry Brigade and passed into Divisional reserve. The Regiment accordingly moved further back. The 1st Battalion marched to Barastre and entered dilapidated hutments on the outskirts of the village, while the 2nd Battalion was transferred to Haplincourt. The accommodation available at the latter point was so limited that Battalion Headquarters was established in a " house " the front part of which only was left standing, and moreover was liable to fall over at any moment. Still, there was nothing new in this experience; for frequently maps had been studied and decisions arrived at with no better shelter than that provided by a shell-hole.

In the interval the New Zealand Division continued its advance against a stiffening opposition and against much more formidable country. The enemy was apparently holding the trench system on the ridge from Trescault southwards to a point near Gouzeaucourt in considerable strength, and with newly arrived troops. On September 9th an attack was launched in conjunction with the 17th Division, the objective of the New Zealand Division being the high ground east of Gouzeaucourt Wood, the sunken roads in the locality of Dead Man's Corner, and thence along the Trescault Ridge to the left to a point in advance of Havrincourt Wood. Strong opposition and heavy machine gun fire were met with. Over the right of the Division's attack, African Support was gained ; Dead Man's Corner remained in the enemy's hands, and on the left, despite a heavy counter-attack, the objective was won and held. Seventy prisoners were taken, some of whom confessed they had not had a full meal for four days, a fact which apparently did not cause them to fight any the less stubbornly. Throughout the remainder of the day the enemy gas-shelled the forward area, and on the 10th, under cover of a heavy bombardment, attacked our positions in African Support, but was repulsed.

On September 12th troops of the 3rd (Rifle) Brigade again took part in a general attack, the objective being the Trescault Spur. The attack was launched at 6.30 a.m. behind an effective artillery barrage, and quickly reached the first line of the objective. Thereafter the enemy fought most stubbornly along the whole front, launching three vigorous counter-attacks against our advanced elements. The day's operations, however, had produced 490 prisoners and an appreciable advance in our line. At 1.45 a.m. on the 15th a strong enemy counter-attack, supported by liquid fire, was launched against the African trench junctions, and the garrison driven back to African Support.

The 5th Division had now commenced to relieve the New Zealand Division, and on September 15th command of the front had passed to the former Division.

A German Intelligence Summary, dated July 17th, 1918, captured during the course of the operations just concluded, contained full and accurate information bearing on the composition of the New Zealand Division. It included a complete illustration with colours of the distinguishing patches of the different Regiments, all of which were correct with the exception of those of the 1st Battalions of Otago and Canterbury Regiments, which apparently were unknown. The document also contained the following appreciation of the New Zealand Division : " A particularly good assault Division. Its characteristic is a very strongly developed individual self-confidence or enterprise typical of the Colonial Englishman, and a specially pronounced hatred of the Germans. A captured officer taken at the end of April did not hesitate to boast of this while in the prisoners' cage."

CHAPTER XIX.

THE HINDENBURG SYSTEM.

In the whole of the sweeping operations in which the Regiment had become engaged since its discovery of the first German withdrawal on the morning of August 14th, the tactics employed were almost essentially those of open warfare. Trench-to-trench fighting had suddenly given place to a war of movement. Within a month the Division had advanced to a depth of close on 20 miles. Many villages of size and a great area of country had been liberated. The whole machinery of war, the cogs of which had long been stationary, was working swiftly and with telling effect. The enemy, now withdrawing everywhere, had been thrown off his balance. On the one side, terrific artillery barrages delivered by guns massed almost wheel to wheel, the infantry, flushed with victory, exerting relentless pressure or in full pursuit, an ever-increasing toll of prisoners and enemy dead, piles of booty, and, as a spectacle never to be forgotten, a bewildering and enormous stream of men, guns, tanks, ammunition supply, transport, and all the vast essentials of a great Army, ceaselessly rolling eastward; on the other side retreat, stubborn rear-guard actions, counter-attacks to save time and artillery or in a vain endeavour to snatch back a vital position, the abandoning of guns and material, the blowing up of roads and bridges, disorganisation, and the lowering *moral* that comes of defeat. It was the *debacle* of March over again, but with the positions reversed.

After those strenuous days and nights of battles and pursuits, the New Zealand Division, on being relieved by the 5th Division, withdrew to Corps reserve for a brief rest. On September 14th the Regiment marched back to the area of Bihucourt, where it was established in huts and underground shelters. Later, several officers and over 100 other ranks were received by each Battalion as reinforcements, and training, principally in open warfare tactics, was proceeded with. During the night of the 17th a heavy thunderstorm broke over the camps and flooded the underground shelters. The 2nd Infantry Brigade was held in readiness as the leading unit of the Division to move at two hours' notice, in the event of sudden counter-attack by the enemy and support being required. On the evening of the 18th, during a performance by the Divisional Entertainers at Bihucourt, the announcement was made that the enemy had heavily attacked the 37th Division north of Havrincourt Wood, and the entertainment was abruptly closed in order that units should at once prepare to move. Advice was subsequently received that the attack had been repulsed, and after standing to for some time the Regiment was ordered to stand by at half-an-hour's notice until the following morning.

While the Regiment was in the Bihucourt area, several changes were effected in Battalion commands. Lieut.-Colonel Charters, C.M.G., D.S.O., had returned from the United Kingdom, where he had been on leave, and reassumed command of the 1st Battalion. Major J. Hargest, D.S.O., M.C., was appointed to command the 2nd Battalion of the Regiment, with promotion to the rank of Lieut.-Colonel. By this step he terminated a long and distinguished connection with the 1st Battalion of the Regiment. The posts of Second-in-Command were filled by Major L. M. Scott, M.C., appointed to the 1st Battalion, and Major W. Ward, to the 2nd Battalion.

On September 24th the 2nd Battalion was inspected by General Russell, G.O.C. New Zealand Division, and on the following day the 1st Battalion came in for similar attention. The tour in reserve was drawing to a close.

Units of the 2nd Infantry Brigade received orders on September 26th to move forward to the Bertincourt area. The Regiment marched out of camp in the cool of the evening, and the 1st Battalion proceeded to Barastre and the 2nd Battalion to Haplincourt Wood. On the 27th an attack was launched by the 5th and 42nd Divisions, and subsequently the enemy was reported to be retiring eastward. It was further reported that the 42nd Division had occupied Welsh

Ridge, and troops of the New Zealand Division were ordered to pass through and continue the pressure. The report of the capture of Welsh Ridge proved to be premature. The Regiment accordingly remained comparatively inactive throughout the 27th; but on the morning of the 28th, a dull and stormy day, the two Battalions advanced to a point of rendezvous in the neighbourhood of Havrincourt Wood.

The New Zealand Division received orders to take over the front held by the 42nd Division and part of that held by the 5th Division, preparatory to a resumption of the general attack on the 29th. At 5.30 p.m. the two Battalions commenced their approach march, but the congested state of traffic on all roads forward, which preceded every attack, made progress slow and difficult. When the head of the 2nd Battalion reached Beaucamp, the enemy commenced to shell the village and roads, but fortunately the straffing was of brief duration. The appointed rendezvous was reached at 11 p.m., and the guides met. The reconnoitring parties sent forward by the 2nd Battalion had been unable to gain any definite information as to the situation in front, except that Welsh Ridge was still held by the enemy, and that the 42nd Division occupied a line approximately 400 yards west of it. Major W. G. A. Bishop, who was commanding the 2nd Battalion in the temporary absence of Lieut.-Colonel Hargest, proceeded to 2nd Infantry Brigade Headquarters for information, and it was decided that in the meantime the Battalion should go back through Beaucamp to the sunken road directly west of it. This was accomplished with very great difficulty, as the roads were blocked not only with troops but with long lines of ammunition limbers temporarily held up. The sunken road was reached just after midnight, and at 1 a.m. Major Bishop returned and announced that the attack was to be carried out in the morning as originally ordered. Zero hour was 3.30 a.m., which left little time for Companies to make their dispositions and to get into positions of assembly in the darkness and over unknown country. Assembly, despite these difficulties, was accomplished by 3 a.m. In the meantime the 1st Battalion of the Regiment had moved through Beaucamp to Plough reserve and support trenches, Highland Ridge, the selected point of assembly.

The New Zealand Division's share in the attack fixed for September 29th was allotted to the 1st and 2nd Infantry Brigades. The 5th Division was to co-operate on the right of the New Zealand Division, and the 62nd Division on the left. The dispositions of the 2nd Infantry Brigade were as follows : On the left, the 2nd Battalion of Otago, with the 2nd Battalion of Canterbury in support ; on the right, the 1st Battalion of Canterbury, with the 1st Battalion of Otago in support. Briefly, the object of the attack was the capture of Welsh and Bon Avis Ridges, in the heart of the Hindenburg system, the former to the north of La Vacquerie and the latter to the east of that village.

The assault was delivered behind an effective artillery barrage at 3.30 a.m. on September 29th. Within the hour the leading waves of the 2nd Battalion of Otago, comprised of 10th and 14th Companies, had gained the top of Welsh Ridge, and considerable numbers of the enemy had been killed or captured. On the right, Canterbury troops had also gained their first objective, but experienced considerable delay in the vicinity of La Vacquerie. Progress now became much more difficult, and consequently slower, owing to the volume of machine gun fire being encountered from the front and from the right flank. Bombing parties proceeded to work down the maze of trenches, and after some heavy fighting succeeded in reaching the sunken roads on the forward side of the ridge. Here touch was gained with Wellington troops, but there was as yet no evidence of Canterbury on the right, and enfilade fire from that direction was causing heavy damage to Otago. In face of this, the two forward Companies, 10th and 14th, pushed on towards the forward slopes of Bon Avis Ridge. When within about 400 yards of the crest, the enemy's resistance became so determined as to temporarily hold up the advance. At 11 a.m. orders were received for Otago to resume the attack on Bon Avis, 8th Company from support to form a defensive flank to the right. By 1 p.m. the task had been accomplished, and 10th and 14th Companies took up positions in Royal Avenue, overlooking the Gouzeaucourt-Cambrai Road, with 8th Company on the right flank, and 4th Company in the sunken road in rear. On the right the 1st Battalion of Canterbury cleared La Vacquerie after stiff fighting, and subsequently made good the ridge to the south-east.

The advance was now approaching the formidable obstacle of the Canal de l'Escaut, parallel to which and converging at certain points, was the River Scheldt. Patrols endeavoured to work down to the Canal, but on each occasion they encountered heavy machine gun fire and were forced to come in. It was therefore decided to wait until darkness before making any further move in this direction. Up to this stage the attack had been most successfully driven home. An advance of over 3,000 yards had been accomplished, 600 prisoners, including 30 officers, had been captured, also 30 machine guns, four 77 mm. field guns, one 4.2 cm. gun, two trench mortars, and a considerable amount of material.

During the afternoon of the 29th orders were received to the effect that on the following morning the 1st Infantry Brigade would launch an attack against the line Esnes-Esnes Mill - La Targette Road, the 2nd Infantry Brigade first to push across the Canal de l'Escaut and establish posts on the high ground east of it. At nightfall patrols were again sent out by Otago, but the enemy was still holding the ground in front in some strength, and up to midnight nothing material had been accomplished. At 3 o'clock on the morning of the 30th a strong patrol under the command of Lieut. R. D. Douglass, though twice driven back by direct fire, succeeded in reaching the Canal at a point near Vaucelles, where the bridge was found to have been destroyed. Orders were issued for 4th Company to move at once and occupy the bridgehead, and a request was also made for the Divisional Engineers to be sent forward to repair or rebuild the bridge. The 4th Company reached the bridgehead at 6.30 a.m., but was unable to cross owing to the approaches being swept by machine gun fire from the opposite bank. Vaucelles was apparently also strongly held by the enemy. The Engineers, who had now arrived, endeavoured to reconstruct the damaged bridge, but were driven off, and it was then decided not to make any further effort for the time being. Troops of the 1st Battalion of Canterbury had by dawn on the 30th, with the assistance of the 5th Division's artillery barrage, definitely gained the Gouzeaucourt-Cambrai Road, and later advanced to the banks of the Canal, touch being gained with Otago at 9 a.m. During the morning two platoons of Canterbury troops effected a crossing of the Canal, and then of the River,

N.Z. Official Photograph.

Cookers of 1st Battalion, Otago Regiment.

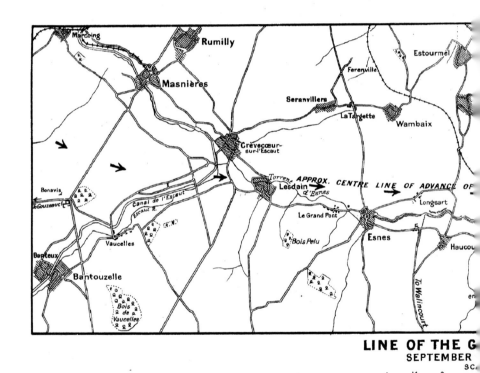

Marcoing
Rumilly
Masnières
Estourmel
Feranville
Seranvillers
La Targette
Wambaix
Crèvecœur-sur-l'Escaut
Bonavis
To Gouzeaucourt
Canal de l'Escaut
Escaut R.
Torrent d'Esnes
Lesdain
APPROX. CENTRE LINE OF ADVANCE OF
Longsart
Le Grand Pont
Esnes
Bois Pelu
Vaucelles
Banteux
Haucou
Bantouzelle
To Walincourt
Bois de Vaucelles

LINE OF THE G
SEPTEMBER
SC.
½   0

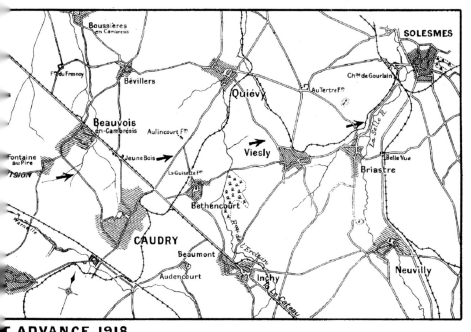

Boussières
en Cambresis

SOLESMES

F^m du Fresnoy

Bévillers

Ch^{lle} de Gourlain

Au Tertre F^m

Quiévy

Beauvois
en-Cambrésis

Aulincourt F^m

La Selle R.

Fontaine
au Pire

Jeune Bois

Viesly

Belle Vue

TSION

La Guisette F^m

Briastre

Bethencourt

Warnelle

CAUDRY

R^{au} d'Erclon

Neuvilly

Beaumont

Audencourt

Inchy

à La Cateau

T ADVANCE, 1918.
OCTOBER 12TH
MILES
2   3

by the partially demolished bridge at the Sugar Factory, north of Bantouzelle; but as there was no sign of the 5th Division on the right, and as the enemy was dribbling back, it was deemed expedient to withdraw to the western bank, and there the line was consolidated.

On the left of Otago troops of the 1st Infantry Brigade had crossed the Canal at Crevecoeur, but meeting with extremely heavy machine gun fire, finally consolidated on the Island between the eastern bank of the Canal and the River. During the night of September 30th Otago troops were relieved in their forward position by a company of the 2nd Battalion of Canterbury, and 4th Company returned to Bon Avis Ridge and took over Ripple trench, relief being completed about midnight.

Subsequent to Canterbury's capture of La Vacquerie, in consequence of the neighbouring Division not being in line, two platoons of 14th Company of the 1st Battalion of Otago were placed at Rhondda Post, and later the remaining two platoons of this Company were moved to Cornwall Cut in order to strengthen Canterbury's exposed flank. There were further slight changes in the general dispositions during the night; but when orders were received for the 1st Battalion to proceed into reserve and units were withdrawn, two Companies were established in the locality of the sunken road near La Vacquerie, and two Companies in Surrey Road further forward. A summary of the casualties sustained by the Regiment during the month of September showed that in officers alone two were killed and one died of wounds, and nine were wounded.

The dispositions of the 2nd Infantry Brigade on October 1st were that the two Battalions of Canterbury were holding the front along the western bank of the Canal de l'Escaut, with the two Battalions of Otago in support, the 1st near La Vacquerie and the 2nd on Bon Avis Ridge. During the afternoon there were indications of an enemy retirement along the Divisional front, and with a view to encouraging the opposition to fall back as speedily as possible, an artillery bombardment was put down at 5 p.m. on Vaucelles and selected trenches and suspected machine gun positions in the immediate neighbourhood. Bon Avis Ridge, on our side, was heavily shelled by the enemy for about two hours during the afternoon; but casualties were confined to four wounded. There was intermittent enemy shelling on other parts of the front, a number of gas shells being directed to the valley north-east of Villers Plough, near positions occupied by 8th Company of the 1st Battalion. At 5 p.m. an order was issued advising an alteration in the limits of the 2nd Brigade front, resulting in the 2nd Battalion of Canterbury holding the front line, with the 2nd Battalion of Otago in support, and the 1st Battalions of Otago and Canterbury in reserve.

Operations for forcing a crossing of the Canal were successfully launched by the 1st Infantry Brigade on October 1st. After very heavy fighting the whole of Crevecoeur on the eastern side of the Canal was cleared and occupied by 12 noon, over 1,000 prisoners being captured. Enemy resistance was still very strong along the line of trenches running east of the road through Bantouzelle, Vaucelles, and Crevecoeur, from which the Germans commanded the low ground west of the Canal, the forward slopes of the ridge behind it, and the Canal bank. There were no definite operations on October 2nd and 3rd. During that period officers of the two Battalions of the Regiment reconnoitred the bridgeheads and the country immediately east of the Canal.

Lieut.-Colonel Hargest now returned from Paris leave and reassumed command of the 2nd Battalion, whereupon Major Bishop proceeded to the United Kingdom on duty.

An aeroplane message received on the evening of October 3rd reported abnormal movement of enemy troops and transport in the back areas across the Divisional front, which suggested intentions of attack. Orders regarding battle stations and the necessary movements were at once issued. The morning of October 4th broke dull and misty, and the enemy's artillery was more silent than on the two preceding days. On the other hand there were indications that he was strengthening his defences east of the Canal. The day passed without any new development. On the evening of the 3rd the 1st Infantry Brigade, holding the line on the left of the 2nd Infantry Brigade, had been relieved by the 3rd (Rifle) Brigade, thereupon passing into Divisional reserve.

On the morning of October 5th the enemy commenced to shell the village of Vaucelles, the eastern bank of the Canal, and the western edge of Cheneaux Wood. Fighting patrols immediately went forward from the 2nd Brigade front, passed through the village of Vaucelles and penetrated as far as Cheneaux Wood without encountering opposition. It was now clear that the enemy had resumed his rearward movement, but the extent of it had yet to be determined. The crossing of the Canal by the pursuing troops was first effected by the aid of a primitive German raft, but later a more dependable one, constructed by a section of the New Zealand Engineers, was provided, and six men were able to cross at a time. Additional troops were thus speedily transferred across the Canal, and by 3 p.m. Cheneaux Wood and Copse had been cleared. Bel Aise Farm and the Masnieres defence line, further to the east, were found to be strongly held and protected by deep belts of wire entanglements. To the north the 3rd (Rifle) Brigade had also gained a bridgehead across the Canal, and patrols reached the western outskirts of Lesdain, but were temporarily held up by machine gun fire directed from the village. The day of the 6th passed without special event.

MASNIERES-BEAUREVOIR LINE.

Plans were now being prepared for the development of important operations against the enemy on the 8th. Simultaneously the artillery commenced a bombardment of the Masnieres trench line and wire, but the damage effected was reported to be inconsiderable. At 4.30 p.m. on October 7th the 1st Battalion of Otago commenced an approach march to relieve the right Company of the 2nd Battalion of Canterbury fronting the Masnieres-Beaurevoir defence line, and take up other forward positions. There was an absence of shell fire during the crossing of the Canal, and the relief was completed by 9 p.m. The 1st Battalion of Otago was now organised in the following order from front to rear : 14th Company in the front line ; 4th and 10th Companies in the sunken roads in rear ; and 8th Company in dug-outs to the north of Cheneaux Wood. In the same connection, the 2nd Battalion of Otago took up positions in trenches in front of Le Quennette Farm.

The operations planned for October 8th involved an attack over a wide front by the Third and Fourth Armies. The New Zealand Division, in conjunction with the 37th

Division on the right, and the 3rd Division on the left, was to attack and establish itself on the line represented by the sunken road south-west of Esnes, Le Grand Pont, Esnes Mill, and the Esnes - La Targette Road. If opportunity offered, success was to be exploited in the direction of securing Esnes and a line extending approximately 1,000 yards east of and parallel to the Esnes - La Targette Road. On the north the 3rd Division was similarly to exploit success in the direction of Wambaix village.

The New Zealand Division's share in the attack was entrusted to the 2nd Infantry Brigade on the right, and the 3rd (Rifle) Brigade on the left. The operation was to be supported by artillery barrages of considerable weight and by large numbers of tanks, and one forward section of artillery was, as hitherto, to be attached to each attacking battalion. Across the 2nd Brigade front, the 1st Battalion of Otago, on the right, was to lead the advance in conjunction with the 2nd Battalion of Canterbury. In the further subdivision of tasks, 14th Company of the 1st Battalion of Otago was assigned the capture of the first objective ; 4th Company was then to pass through and attack the second objective. Finally, 10th Company on the left, and 8th Company on the right were to advance through 4th Company ; the former to effect the capture of Esnes, and the latter to exploit success south of that village.

The night preceding the attack was wet and intensely dark, and the enemy, apparently anticipating a resumption of operations, intermittently shelled the area of assembly.

At zero hour, 4.30 a.m. on October 8th, troops of 14th Company, which constituted the leading wave of the assault, moved forward behind a splendid artillery barrage. Fairly heavy artillery and machine gun fire was encountered almost from the outset, and when the formidable Masnieres-Beaurevoir defence line was reached, the wire was found to be uncut in places and very deep. The advance in consequence became temporarily checked. The resistance of the German infantry, however, lacked determination, and by means of Lewis gun fire and bombing the enemy was finally driven from his trenches. Troops of the right Division were not yet in line, and a post on the right flank of Otago's advance caused considerable trouble until surrounded and broken up by two platoons of 14th Company under 2nd-Lieut. W. McKean, D.C.M., M.M. This post contained four machine guns and about 40 of the enemy. By 5.40 a.m. 14th Company was digging in on the high ground of the first objective, south of Lesdain.

The 4th Company now advanced through the foremost troops, and following in the wake of the artillery barrage, proceeded to the capture of the second objective. Passing to the north of Pelu Wood, comparatively slight resistance was met with, nor did the wire in front of the German trenches to the south-west of Esnes present any serious opposition. The 4th Company consolidated on the hedge line south of Le Grand Pont, and 8th and 10th Companies moved up in rear in readiness to continue the advance at 9.30 a.m., the scheduled time. During this operation Captain J. P. Hewat, whose connection with the 1st Battalion of the Regiment extended over a very long period, was killed by shell fire, and the Rev. R. S. Watson, M.C., Presbyterian Chaplain attached to the 1st Battalion, was wounded while directing and assisting casualties to the Regimental Aid Post.

At an earlier stage it had been observed that the enemy was evacuating the village of Esnes in front, but that when the advance had temporarily halted parties had commenced to filter back. At 9.30 a.m. 8th and 10th Companies passed through 4th Company and continued the advance under cover of the artillery barrage. Rifle fire was encountered from the southern edge of Esnes, also from the high ground near the Esnes-Walincourt Road, and it was found necessary in consequence of the situation on the right to refuse that flank to the enemy. The 10th Company advanced and effected the clearance of the village of Esnes and established the line on the eastern and northern sides of it. In order to secure the right flank 14th Company was escheloned south of Esnes, and machine guns posted to command the valley still further to the south, and to deal with enemy machine gun fire from that flank. On the left, heavy fire was being encountered from the factory on the road between Esnes and Haucourt, and from the high ground south-east of Longsart. The established line now encircled the village of Esnes from its eastern side, and the attack had proved entirely successful.

In the interval, the 2nd Battalion of the Regiment, in compliance with orders received at 8.15 a.m., had pushed across the Canal and taken up positions in support of the leading Battalions. During the afternoon it advanced still further, and finally settled down between the Masnieres line and that which had formed the morning's first objective.

On the left, in the course of the morning's operations, the 2nd Battalion of Canterbury encountered strong resistance at certain points in the Masnieres system, particularly from machine guns which had been over-run by the leading waves in the semi-darkness of the early morning. The first objective, a sunken road running south from the eastern edge of Lesdain, was gained at 6.30 a.m., and finally, in conjunction with the operations carried out by Otago on the right, the advance cleared Le Grand Pont and then passed to the north of Esnes, where touch was gained with the 3rd (Rifle) Brigade. This Brigade, after gaining its first objective, found that the enemy's resistance for a considerable distance beyond that point had almost completely broken down, large numbers giving themselves up without offering fight. By 9.30 a.m. the final objective along the Esnes-La Targette Road was reached. From that point patrols pushed forward until stiffening resistance was met with from the direction of Longsart.

By 1 p.m. five out of the six Artillery Brigades concerned in the attack and working under the direction of the New Zealand Division, were in action on the eastern side of the Canal de l'Escaut. The captures in material and prisoners of war during the morning had been very heavy, and included many field and machine guns. The contribution made to the total by the 1st Battalion of Otago amounted to 100 prisoners, one 77 mm. field gun, and eight machine guns ; our casualties numbered five officers and 139 other ranks. Esnes village had been heavily mined by the enemy ; while during the night abandoned dumps in the railway circuit adjoining the village were persistently shelled.

At 3.30 p.m. on the 8th about 50 of the enemy counterattacked down the gully immediately to the north-east of Esnes, but were driven off by our fire. During the same afternoon the 2nd Battalion of Canterbury relieved elements of our troops in their sector, and the line was adjusted accordingly; while later in the day touch was gained with the Somersets on the right at Hill 135, east of the Esnes-Walincourt Road.

FONTAINE AND VIESLY.

Orders were issued for a resumption of the attack by the New Zealand Division, in conjunction with the 37th Division on the right and the Guards Division on the left. The 2nd and 3rd Brigades of the New Zealand Division were still in the line ; the two Battalions of the 2nd Brigade appointed to carry out the attack on the 9th being the 2nd Battalion of Otago on the right and the 1st Battalion of Canterbury on the left. The former unit was to pass through the 1st Battalion of the Regiment and attack up the valley towards Caudry behind a creeping artillery barrage starting from the eastern side of Esnes. The final objective laid down for the 2nd Battalion was the sunken road connecting with the Cambrai - Le Cateau railway, with exploitation of success towards Fontaine - au - Pire. The Battalion moved into position of assembly over-night. The leading Companies were 4th and 8th, with 10th Company in support, and 14th Company in reserve.

At zero hour, 5.20 a.m. on October 9th, the attacking troops, now facing a direction more northerly than easterly, moved forward without opposition, either from enemy infantry or artillery. It soon became evident that the Germans had effected a deliberate withdrawal during the night. The factory on the Esnes-Haucourt Road was reached and found to be deserted, and our troops pushed on as fast as our artillery barrage would allow them. The first objective, the sunken road north-east of Haucourt, was gained and passed ; but from this stage onwards the barrage became ragged and indefinite, and the left flank was for some time held up by it. When the second objective had been passed, the barrage was stopped by orders. The Battalion now halted for a few minutes, and after reorganising and attending to the inner man, the leading Companies sent forward patrols, and deploying, followed them. The immediate objective was the high ground north of the railway and south-west of Fontaine. The patrols quickly reached this point, and on continuing their advance over the crest regained touch with the enemy, being heavily fired upon from the direction of Fontaine and Caudry. One patrol held on to its position on the forward slopes of the crest until about 4.30 p.m., when it was deemed expedient to withdraw to the reverse side, the patrol having served its purpose.

In the evening Lieut.-Colonel Hargest established his headquarters in a house alongside the railway line, and due south of Fontaine. It was at this point that 2nd-Lieut. G. Cuthbertson, M.M., and Sergt. W. Morrow, M.M., were killed by shell fire. During the night the enemy fire died down, and at midnight a patrol under 2nd-Lieut. A. E. Inkster pushed forward and entered Fontaine, and also Caudry, in both of which places there were large numbers of civilians, but no evidence of the enemy. Earlier in the day a patrol of 3rd Hussars had endeavoured to enter Fontaine, but as was the case with the infantry patrols at that stage, was forced back by machine gun fire.

On the left of the day's advance, the 1st Battalion of Canterbury had met with corresponding absence of opposition, and by the afternoon its patrols were established on the road half a mile beyond and parallel to the railway line, where machine gun fire prevented further advance for the time being. Later, patrols entered Fontaine; but further advance was checked by machine gun fire from the large factory on the western outskirts of Beauvois-en-Cambresis. Similarly, to the left again, troops of the 3rd (Rifle) Brigade were retarded in the early stages of the advance only by the pace of our artillery barrage, and did not encounter opposition until they had reached the high ground west of Fontaine.

In view of the altered situation consequent upon the enemy withdrawal, orders were issued during the morning that the 2nd Infantry Brigade, plus one battalion of the 3rd (Rifle) Brigade operating on the left, and one squadron of the 3rd Hussars, would become the advance guard of the New Zealand Division. During the same night the Rifle Brigade troops were withdrawn, the 2nd Infantry Brigade thereupon taking over the whole of the Divisional front; the 2nd Battalion of Otago and the 1st Battalion of Canterbury being called upon to extend their frontages.

Plans had now been prepared for an advance in the dark. The 10th and 14th Companies of the 2nd Battalion of Otago,

N.Z. Official Photograph.

The 2nd Battalion of the Regiment Reviewed by H.R.H. the Prince of Wales.

passing through the leading troops, moved over the crest, their first objective being the Cambrai-Le Cateau Road from north-west of Caudry on the right to north-east of Beauvois on the left. This represented a distance of approximately two miles from the starting point. Canterbury moved in unison on the left. Fontaine and Beauvois were both clear of the enemy, who had apparently effected a further retirement. Without opposition, excepting for desultory shelling of Beauvois, Otago's advance was continued in a north-easterly direction on a two-company frontage, with the leading platoons covered by patrols. The Cambrai - Le Cateau Road was reached without incident at 5.40 a.m., while it was still dark. As there was yet no appearance of the flanking troops, the Battalion remained in this position until 9.30 a.m., when Canterbury having also gained the line of the road the advance was resumed and continued through La Guisette Farm on the right and Aulicourt Farm on the left. On reaching the road between these two points, the leading troops were fired upon by machine guns and rifles from the direction of Quievy, to the north-east, and from the trench system to the south of it. Four Vickers guns were brought up to open covering fire, enabling the advance to be continued down the valley and on to the ridge north of Bethencourt. At this juncture troops of the 1st Battalion of the Regiment passed through the 2nd Battalion, and a line was formed running north from Bethencourt.

Up to this stage the 1st Battalion had been keeping pace in rear with the general movement. On the 9th it advanced as far as the sunken road south of Haucourt. On the morning of the 10th the Battalion pushed on to the north-east, skirting Fontaine-au-Pire, Beauvois-en-Cambresis, and Jeune Bois, and then over the high ground between Guisette Farm and Aulicourt Farm. By 10.30 a.m., as previously indicated, the leading Companies had passed through the line held by the 2nd Battalion of the Regiment.

The 1st Battalion was now to carry on the advance. To the north a party of the enemy, about 30 in number, could be observed carrying out a retirement. On the right, 10th Company advanced along the north-western side of Bethencourt and Clermont Wood and over the high ground towards Viesly. Enemy artillery, firing from the direction of Solesmes, was now shelling the valley north of Clermont Wood. Our patrols entered the village of Viesly and encountered opposition in the locality of the Cemetery. On the left, 10th Company experienced machine gun fire from the direction of Quievy and from Fontaine-au-Tertre Farm. The left flank now became rather dangerously exposed; and to meet this situation, Lieut.-Colonel Charters moved 4th Company into position there, strengthening the flank still further by covering it with Vickers guns and the mobile section of Field Artillery at his disposal. The 14th Company gained the high ground to the north of Viesly; the consolidated line then extending across the eastern side of that village, through the sandpit on the northern outskirts, and thence in a north-westerly direction for a distance of 500 yards. The right flank also demanded attention, and to definitely secure it from attack 8th Company was moved into position there. The general line, gained after an exceedingly rapid advance, was thus firmly established.

At 3 p.m. the 2nd Battalion of Canterbury, which had experienced some delay owing to enemy strength in Fontaine-au-Tertre Farm, and the less rapid progress of the left flank Division, reached a line more approximating to that held by Otago. At 5 p.m. advice was received that the 37th Division would endeavour to reach the high ground northeast of Neuvilly, and in order to afford protection to the left flank of this operation our line was advanced, without opposition, a distance of about 750 yards in the direction of Briastre; 8th and 4th Companies again covering the right and left flanks respectively. Among the day's casualties, increased slightly by enemy shelling of Viesly, was Captain J. N. Hines, M.C. (commanding 10th Company), who was wounded by shell fire.

A feature of the advances now being made from day to day over the open country was the effective co-operation of a mobile section of the New Zealand Field Artillery, which kept pace with the utmost limits of the advance, and time and again, firing over open sights, dealt with enemy rearguard pockets, and generally afforded the infantry splendid support.

During the night of the 10th the 2nd Infantry Brigade was relieved in the line by the 1st Infantry Brigade. The

Regiment thereupon moved back over the newly won ground to Beauvois, where, in splendid billets, acquaintance was renewed with such luxuries as sheets and feather mattresses. The Regiment remained there for several days under conditions which included good living and undisturbed rest.

On October 14th H.R.H. the Prince of Wales visited Beauvois and inspected the Regiment. A few days later General Sir A. J. Godley was in the area, and took advantage of the occasion to present medals to non-commissioned officers and men who had won distinction during the operations just concluded.

On the 17th the Officers of the 1st Battalion entertained the 2nd Battalion Officers at dinner and a convivial evening; this being the first occasion on which practically the whole of the Officers of the Regiment had been brought together under such pleasant circumstances.

During the period in reserve a large number of reinforcements arrived, and with the military and recreational training carried out daily the Regiment gained considerably in strength and efficiency.

A brief survey of events subsequent to the Regiment passing into reserve on October 10th will indicate the situation across the Divisional front when the Regiment's tour in reserve terminated. On taking over the line on October 10th, the 1st Infantry Brigade was ordered to secure the crossings of the River Selle which ran immediately east of Briastre, establish the line of the Solesmes-Le Cateau railway 600 yards still further to the east, and finally exploit success to the ridge south-east of Solesmes. Reconnoitring patrols were accordingly pushed forward, and moved on to the defined objectives practically unopposed. Briastre, in which there were 172 French civilians, all of whom effusively demonstrated their joy on relief, was occupied and the line of the Selle River reached. Small parties of the enemy were observed on the eastern bank of the river; and at an early hour two companies of infantry effected a crossing by means of a bridge thrown across by the Divisional Engineers, but came under heavy machine gun fire on endeavouring to work along the bank. There was considerable enemy shelling over the forward area during the day, to which our heavy artillery effectively replied; at the same time dealing with hostile concentrations. The situation was unchanged over the 11th. At 5 a.m. the 1st Brigade attacked in conjunction with troops of the 37th Division on the right. Strong resistance was experienced from enemy strongholds adjoining the road east of the Selle; and though all available artillery was concentrated on these points the effort proved singularly ineffective. About 3 p.m. the enemy heavily counter-attacked the 37th Division and drove it from the high ground. One result of this development was that the 1st Brigade was forced to withdraw to the line from which it had jumped off in the morning. A further attack on our part was ordered for 6 p.m. the same day. Preceded by about two hours' artillery bombardment directed on Belle Vue and the copse just north of it, the assault was successfully driven home. At 10 p.m. the line was reported as along the Solesmes-Le Cateau railway east of Briastre, where touch was gained with the 37th Division, thence north to Belle Vue and copse, north-west to the River Selle, and along the west bank to a point on the south-western outskirts of Solesmes, where the Guards Division joined up. During the same night the New Zealand Division was relieved by the 42nd Division.

VERTIGNEUL AND SALESCHES.

The Third and Fourth Armies combined were to launch an attack over a wide front on October 20th.

Over the front of the IV. Corps, which embraced the New Zealand Division, the 42nd Division, starting from Briastre at 2 a.m., advanced across a frontage of 1,500 yards, pushing forward and capturing Marou, a small village about a mile to the east of Solesmes. Subsequent to the capture of Marou, the enemy counter-attacked from the direction of Beaurain, but was repulsed by artillery fire.

On the 21st the 2nd Brigade of the New Zealand Division was notified that it was to be prepared to relieve the 126th Brigade of the 42nd Division on the following day, and to be in support to that Division. The Otago Regiment, in accordance with this development, moved from Beauvois on the afternoon of the 22nd, and headed for its concentration area. The 1st Battalion proceeded through Bethencourt, Viesly, and Briastre, and assembled in the sunken roads south of Solesmes ; the 2nd Battalion followed the route of Aulicourt Farm, Viesly and Briastre, and took up positions on the line of the railway and the Chateau. During this operation the Regiment encountered the seemingly interminable forward traffic of guns and transport preliminary to attack ; and in consequence progress was very slow. Throughout the day there had been fairly heavy rain ; but later the weather cleared and the night was fine.

The two Armies, the Third and Fourth, were simultaneously to continue the great sweep east and north-eastwards on the 23rd. Orders were that on the front of the IV. Corps, the 5th Division on the right and the 42nd Division on the left, were to attack and capture the ridge west of Beaurain ; the 3rd Division, of the VI. Corps, on the left, was to effect the capture of Romeries, north-east of Solesmes. One hour later the 5th and 42nd Divisions were to advance on the line of Beaurain village, to the south of Romeries. This having been accomplished, the New Zealand and 37th Divisions were to pass through the foremost troops of the IV. Corps, and in conjunction with the 3rd Division on the north, continue the north-eastward movement.

In this last-named undertaking, the 2nd Infantry Brigade, commanded by Brigadier-General R. Young, was to carry out the opening stages of the New Zealand Division's task. The 1st Battalion of Otago and the 2nd Battalion of Canterbury, disposed from right to left, were selected to open the Brigade's attack.

The general assault, supported by an overpowering weight of artillery, was launched at 3.20 a.m. on the 23rd. Immediate and important success was gained. The 1st Battalion of Otago moved in the wake of the attack behind an advanced guard thrown well forward as a precautionary measure. The 10th Company covered the flank of the leading Companies. A patrol sent forward to reconnoitre the high ground west of Beaurain ran into an enemy pocket which had escaped the observation of the leading troops owing to the mist. The occupants of this post were not taken prisoners on account of their treacherously wounding the officer (2nd-Lieut. F. Jenkins, D.C.M.) in charge of the patrol after throwing up their hands as a sign of surrender. The Battalion continued its forward move under the cover of a smoke barrage, passing *en route* through the valley at Marou, previously deluged by the enemy with gas. By 8 a.m. assembly in the sunken roads had been completed. A few minutes later shell fire caused several casualties in 8th Company. The time had now arrived for the Battalion to pass through the troops of the 42nd Division and take up the advance. The dispositions for the attack were as follows : 4th Company (commanded by Major G. H. Ferguson) and 8th Company (commanded by Captain J. Gillies) from right to left ; 14th Company in support, and 10th Company in reserve. A mobile section of Field Artillery and one section of Vickers guns were again attached to the Battalion for the operation.

At zero hour, 8.40 a.m., our artillery barrage opened, and the leading companies advanced through the 42nd Division. Machine gun fire was encountered from Hirson Mill on the right front and from the railway embankment skirting the southern side of Vertigneul. Under the pressure of our infantry, the enemy retired from the Mill. The railway embankment was gained and 47 prisoners and several machine guns accounted for. The enemy resistance up to this stage had not been of a very determined order, and Vertigneul was reached and passed through in the course of the advance. The River Harpies was crossed under fire, and the road north of Vertigneul quickly reached. The advance was then temporarily checked by machine gun fire from the ridge east of the village. Also, the outskirts of Vertigneul apparently still sheltered a few enemy snipers, and two sections of infantry were detailed to clear the village. The opposition encountered to the east of Vertigneul was overcome by the accurate fire of Lewis guns and rifles, but when the crest was gained, the advance attracted further machine gun fire from the vicinity of the Crucifix and the hedges near the cross-roads. 2nd-Lieut. J. Wilson, M.M., leading forward a platoon of 8th Company, delivered an attack against the flank of this stronghold with such force and skill as to effect its immediate capture. The sunken roads in the vicinity were then cleared of the enemy, and the two leading Companies consolidated on their objective. The 10th and 14th Companies, following in rear, consolidated in the orchard on the eastern side of Vertigneul. Later, our positions were subjected to intermittent artillery fire. Gas shelling of the area of the Chapelle des Six Chemins was responsible for three casualties among the officers of 4th Company.

The 2nd Battalion of the Regiment was now due to pass through the foremost troops of the 1st Battalion in continuation of the advance. Starting at 8.30 a.m., the Battalion moved along the Belle Vue-Marou Road to the cross-roads south of Vertigneul. Before reaching this point the Lewis gun limbers had unloaded in the shelter of the low ground. At 11.30 a.m. the four Companies, now extended, moved round to the south of Vertigneul, and then over the rising ground to their allotted positions of assembly. The greater part of the area was being shelled ; but the operation was completed without incurring casualties. The 4th Company was in position on the right in the sunken road, with its flank resting at the Crucifix ; 8th Company occupied the continuation of the sunken road to the north, where a junction was effected with the 1st Battalion of Canterbury ; 10th Company was in support in the low ground east of Vertigneul ; and 14th Company was disposed on the outskirts of the village.

At 12 minutes past 12 o'clock noon the artillery and machine barrages opened the attack. On account of the lengthy advance in the morning the artillery was not at full strength, and the barrage provided was weak in consequence. As the right Company, 4th (Otago), advanced over the crest of the ridge west of Salesches it came under heavy machine gun fire. The Lewis gun section, commanded by Corporal Stewart, materially contributed to breaking down this point of resistance, and the advance was resumed. The left Company, 8th (Southland), reached the vicinity of Mesnil Farm, and there similarly encountered strong opposition from enemy machine guns. The enemy was speedily overwhelmed, and a complete German battalion headquarters made prisoners. In this successful operation Sergt. J. J. Blackburn particularly distinguished himself ; it was at about the same stage that 2nd-Lieut. J. C. Fothergill, D.C.M., was killed. The 8th Company now advanced beyond the farm buildings, crossed the St. Georges River, and commenced the ascent of the slope on the eastern side. Progress was again checked by fire delivered from a series of strongly defended posts established along the slope and extending from the rear of Bernier Farm. The posts were wired, and each group contained an approximate strength of 25 of the enemy. A section of 8th Company, commanded by Sergt. F. C. Fergusson, acting as advanced guard, crept up to a hedge on the left, and at close quarters delivered destructive bursts of fire against the enemy's flank, killing several of the garrison and forcing the surrender of others with their machine guns. Across the front of 4th Company, which had effected the crossing of the St. Georges River in line with 8th Company, an attack was almost simultaneously delivered against the same series of posts by a platoon commanded by 2nd-Lieut. W. Murphy. Corresponding success was achieved; and those of the enemy who were not killed or captured gave themselves up.

It was now possible for the leading Companies to continue their advance. Further ahead, what was apparently the main enemy resistance disclosed itself. This was centred on the high ground north-east of Salesches and actually clear of Otago's front; but the situation demanded that it should be crushed. At this stage 2nd-Lieut. R. G. Charters (4th Company) was wounded. Assuming command of this officer's platoon, 2nd-Lieut. W. Murphy at once swung the two formations now at his disposal to the right, and atttacked the enemy's strongly entrenched position in enfilade. Once more our infantry were equal to the occasion. The enemy were completely overwhelmed, many of them were killed or captured, and the remainder driven from their stronghold. One platoon moved through and cleared the northern half of the village of Salesches. The operation set the Battalion had been attended by complete success. By 2.25 p.m. the whole of the high ground aimed at had been gained; heavy losses had been inflicted upon the enemy and substantial captures made in prisoners and machine guns. For their fine conduct in this operation 2nd-Lieuts. Murphy and Charters were awarded the Military Cross.

The artillery barrage, moving at the rate of 100 yards in four minutes, had proved somewhat slow, and at times retarded the pursuit of the retiring enemy. On account of the troops of the adjoining Division not being in line with

German Prisoners carrying out Wounded.

N.Z. Official Photograph.

In the Track of the Advance.

those of the Otago Regiment, adjustments were required in the direction of protecting the right flank to a depth of 1,500 yards. At 5 p.m. there were indications that the enemy was disposed to return to Salesches, a development which was accompanied by heavy shelling and machine gun fire. No definite infantry action followed. Still, the likelihood of attack presented sound reasons for stiffening the right flank.

At 7.30 p.m. Battalion Headquarters moved up to Mesnil Farm. At the same time the reserve Company, the 14th, took up new positions in the sunken road west of Salesches. At 10.30 p.m. the support Company, the 10th, advanced through the front line and established itself on the Salesches-Beaudignies Road. The reserve Company again moved, on this occasion to the road on the northern side of Salesches, with headquarters in Bernier Farm. These represented the final dispositions for the night. The day had been productive of definite and important results.

The casualties sustained during the course of these operations were as follows: Killed—one officer and seven other ranks; wounded—two officers and 54 other ranks. The Battalion's captures included 204 prisoners, 14 machine guns, and one 77 mm. field gun.

On the evening of the 24th the Battalion was relieved in the line by the 1st Battalion of the 3rd (Rifle) Brigade, and moved back to billets in Neuville.

On the left of Otago, the 1st Battalion of Canterbury reached its objective on the high ground approximately 1,000 yards to the north-east of the St. Georges River. When patrols moved out and penetrated to the southern edge of Beaudignies without encountering the enemy, it was decided to occupy the village and secure the bridges of the River Ecaillon which flowed through it. This was accomplished without opposition. It was at one of these bridgeheads that Sergt. J. H. Nicholas, V.C., M.M., was fatally shot when challenging a party of the enemy who approached his post during the night. The village was now under machine gun fire from the high ground west of Le Quesnoy; but patrols advanced along the Beaudignies-Le Quesnoy Road and drove the enemy from his outer positions.

IMPORTANT SUCCESSES.

At 9.30 p.m. on October 23rd instructions were issued verbally to the 1st Battalion of Otago and the 2nd Battalion of Canterbury to pass through the foremost troops of their respective Regiments, and continue the advance. Indications pointed to the enemy's resistance being seriously disorganised, with the possibility of an attempted withdrawal overnight. At 11.35 p.m. 10th Company (commanded by Lieut. H. R. Domigan) and 14th Company (commanded by Captain T. Sim), of the 1st Battalion of Otago, crossed the Ecaillon River and commenced a deep advance to the high ground east of Beaudignies. This was essentially a night movement. Patrols, supported by Lewis guns, preceded the Companies, which moved in artillery formation. The presence of thick hedges, interlaced with wire entanglements, accentuated the difficulties of movement by night, and demanded careful patrolling. Our scouts reported the enemy to be in strength south of the sunken road approximately half a mile east of Beaudignies. An attack under an artillery barrage was timed for 4 a.m. on the 24th, with the 37th Division disposed on the right of the 2nd Brigade of the New Zealand Division and the 3rd Division on the left. In view of that fact it was decided by the two Companies of the 1st Battalion to dig in north of the Beaudignies-Ghissignies Road, and await daylight and the arrival of the troops of the right Division. Touch was established with the 2nd Battalion of Canterbury on the left.

The advance accomplished by the New Zealand Division over the day of the 23rd had exceeded four miles.

On the morning of October 24th troops of the three Divisions, 37th, New Zealand, and 3rd, from right to left, launched their attack against the enemy as arranged. The artillery barrage under which the 3rd Division advanced on the left over-lapped the front occupied by Canterbury and necessitated a temporary withdrawal, the original line being re-established when the barrage had moved forward. At 7 a.m. English troops could be seen on the right of Otago advancing west of Ghissignies. Covering fire was directed on the practice trenches occupied by the enemy east of Beaudignies, and the two leading Companies of Otago advanced

370

and effected the capture of 75 prisoners and seven machine guns. The left Company, the 14th, pushed forward to the sunken road, and then working to the right brought flanking fire to bear on the enemy who were still holding out to the north-east. This enabled the right Company to continue; and the sunken road on the western side of the wood surrounding Farm de Beart was gained and consolidated. The enemy could now be cbserved digging in on the high ground west of Le Quesnoy. During the afternoon outposts were established on the eastern edge of the wood.

The Battalion's captures for the two days comprised 160 prisoners, 33 machine guns, four light trench mortars, and one 77 mm. field gun. Our casualties over the same period numbered six officers and 107 other ranks.

At 5 p.m. the Battalion was advised that it would be relieved by the 3rd Battalion of the Rifle Brigade; and when this was effected at 10 p.m., the Battalion marched back to Neuville.

The general situation now was that the advanced line was within a mile of the citadel town of Le Quesnoy. Minor operations during the succeeding three days established the line to the north and east of the Le Quesnoy-Valenciennes Railway. Here, as elsewhere, the succession of heavy blows delivered against the enemy's front was exhausting his strength, depleting his reserves, and creating serious demoralisation in his ranks.

Operations conducted on the Flanders front during the closing days of September had witnessed the re-capture of Messines, Ploegsteert Wood, and other places familiar to the Regiment; followed during the opening days of October by an extensive enemy withdrawal along the whole front from south of Lens to Armentieres; the resumption of the British offensive a few days later forced the evacuation of Lille and a rapid retreat over a wide front.

When the 2nd Infantry Brigade was relieved by the 3rd (Rifle) Brigade on the night of October 24th, the latter, on receipt of information of an enemy retirement in a north-easterly direction across its front, immediately sent forward fighting patrols to maintain touch with the enemy. During the day of the 25th advances were made at certain points along the general line, the foremost elements reaching the

Prechelles River, north-west of Le Quesnoy, and the level crossing over the Le Quesnoy-Valenciennes Railway.

Operations planned for the 26th included an endeavour by the 3rd Division to secure possession of Orsinval and Villers Pol to the north ; the 3rd (Rifle) Brigade of the New Zealand Division was to co-operate by advancing against the enemy defences north and north-west of Le Quesnoy. The day was marked by heavy fighting and vigorous enemy counter-attacks, preceded by increased enemy artillery, minenwerfer and machine gun fire directed against the railway and crossing north-west of Le Quesnoy. These counter-attacks were sanguinarily repulsed ; but one effect of this sudden aggressiveness was that no advance was registered by us that day. Neither did the closing days of the month witness any major operation, although several damaging raids were carried out against the enemy and his advanced positions. By reason of the greatly increased weight of artillery now being employed, and the general alertness displayed, it was clear that the enemy was bracing himself for a stand. These efforts, it will be seen, were but as the last convulsive movements of a dying beast.

CHAPTER XX.

FALL OF LE QUESNOY.

A BRITISH assault launched on the first day of November culminated in the capture of Valenciennes, to the north, and withdrawals along the Le Quesnoy-Valenciennes front.

Then followed the announcement that the First, Third, and Fourth British Armies, with an overwhelming strength in men and guns, were to deliver a combined attack over a front of 30 miles, extending from the Sambre River in the south, near Oisy, to Valenciennes in the north. The curtain was about to be rung down on the closing scenes of the great drama.

The geographical features of the country across which this great sweep was to be made presented several obstacles to a rapid advance. In the south was the Sambre River ; in the centre the deep forest of Mormal ; against the north-western flank of the forest, and standing sentinel-like over its portals, the old citadel town of Le Quesnoy.

The New Zealand Division, in conjunction with the 37th Division on the right, and the 62nd Division on the left, was to establish itself on the line Franc a Louer-Herbignies-Tous Vents ; and if opportunity offered was to exploit success through the Foret de Mormal and towards the Sambre River. The citadel town of Le Quesnoy was not to be attacked directly ; but troops moving north and south were to form a flank which would encircle the ramparts. The front over which the New Zealand Division was to operate was approximately 2,500 yards wide. Le Quesnoy occupied a considerable part of that frontage ; and moreover was only 600 yards distant from the starting point of operations. The great double moat and rampart which surrounded the town represented a serious obstacle to assaulting infantry, but afforded the enemy small protection against modern artillery ;

but the German garrison which sheltered behind its walls were comparatively secure from artillery bombardment because of the large population of French civilians also contained in the town. The decision arrived at in respect of Le Quesnoy was that the artillery barrage should search the ramparts only for a period of fifteen minutes, and then cease on the western and north-western faces while patrols pushed forward in an endeavour to ascertain if the town was still occupied, and if so, in what strength.

The opening stage of the attack of the New Zealand Division was entrusted to the 3rd (Rifle) Brigade, and the second stage to the 1st Infantry Brigade. Should the operation prove successful to the limits laid down, the 2nd Infantry Brigade was to take up the running. The general advance, immediately hitherto conducted in a north-easterly direction, was now to turn due east. At the commencement of operations the line of the IV. Corps (of the Third Army), which embraced the New Zealand Division, extended north and south, slightly west of and parallel to the Le Quesnoy-Solesmes railway line until it reached Ghissignies, where it turned to the south-east.

At 5.30 a.m. on November 4th the artillery of three Armies, massed in preponderant weight over a front of 30 miles, broke out in thunderous barrage ; behind this avalanche of destructive force advanced the thousands of indomitable infantry. The vast, complicated machinery of attack was in full motion.

The assaulting troops of the New Zealand Division met with almost instant success. Converging from right and left, they had at an early hour completed the envelopment of Le Quesnoy and its enemy garrison. Thereafter the advance swung ahead as an operation distinct from that which aimed at the capture of the town. An endeavour was made by the surrounding force of the 3rd (Rifle) Brigade to force an entrance to Le Quesnoy; but this method of attack was found to be impracticable against the heavy fire of machine guns directed from the shelter of the ramparts. In the early afternoon a German prisoner was sent into the town to inform the garrison that they were surrounded, and calling upon them to surrender. At 4 p.m. a Stokes shell bombardment was placed along the northern ramparts. It was then that the enemy fire practically ceased. Half-an-hour later parties of New Zealand troops entered Le Quesnoy by the Porte der Valenciennes, and the capture of the town and the dramatic surrender of the garrison of over 700 of the enemy, officers and men, followed.

In the meantime, troops of the 1st Infantry Brigade had passed through the 62nd Division, to the left of the New Zealand Division's front, and established themselves on a line forming a flank and facing the northern side of Le Quesnoy. Then, in conjunction with troops of the 3rd Brigade, who occupied a similar flank line on the southern side, the advance was continued to the line of Villereau-Potelle-Jolimetz, east of Le Quesnoy and fronting the Foret de Mormal. The 1st Infantry Brigade then took over the whole of the Divisional front, and at 10.30 a.m. continued the attack towards the furthest line of the detailed advance. By noon it had reached its final objective, represented by a line extending north and south through Herbignies. Strong patrols were now sent forward to maintain touch with the enemy; by midnight they had penetrated Mormal Forest to a depth of 3,000 yards.

This had proved a day of extraordinary successes for the New Zealand Division. The net results of its operations had been an advance of over six miles, the capture of Le Quesnoy, Rompaneau, Villerau, Potelle, and Herbignies (thereby liberating many French civilians), with nearly 2,000 prisoners, over 70 howitzers and field guns, many of them complete with gunners, drivers and horses, and a formidable tally of machine guns and trench mortars.

MORMAL FOREST.

The time had now arrived for exploiting to the utmost this brilliant success. The 2nd Infantry Brigade, which was in Divisional support with the commencement of operations, had moved forward at an early hour and concentrated to the south-west of Beaudignies. The Otago Regiment left Neuville at 8 a.m., and after halting in the concentration area over midday, pushed on again, past Le Quesnoy, still in the hands of the enemy, to Herbignies, where final dispositions were completed for the day. There was a certain amount of shelling over this area after arrival, and in the 1st Battalion some casualties were incurred, included among the wounded being 2nd-Lieut. A. H. King, M.C., Battalion Signals Officer, and the Rev. E. J. Tipler, C.F.

At 8.30 p.m. orders were issued to the effect that the 2nd Infantry Brigade was to pass through the 1st Infantry Brigade at dawn on November 5th, when the attack was to be renewed, supported by artillery. For this operation the 2nd Battalion of Otago Regiment was to be disposed on the right of the Brigade front, and the 1st Battalion of Canterbury Regiment on the left. On these two Battalions reaching the final objective laid down for them, the 1st Battalion of Otago and the 2nd Battalion of Canterbury were each to pass two companies through the leading formations and maintain the pressure, but were not to attempt to pierce any heavy enemy resistance.

At 1.30 a.m. on November 5th, 10th and 14th Companies of the 2nd Battalion of the Regiment advanced from Herbignies to take up positions 200 yards in rear of the foremost troops of the 1st Battalion of Wellington. At 4 a.m. 4th Company, in support to 10th Company, and 8th Company, in support to 14th Company, followed suit. Three objectives were assigned to the Battalion—first, a road running north and south 3,000 yards from the starting point; second, a road running north and south 1,700 yards further ahead; and third, a road extending across the eastern edge of Mormal Forest; involving a total advance of approximately 7,500 yards, and the whole of it through densely wooded country.

The attack was renewed at 5.30 a.m. The supporting artillery barrage descended along a line 200 yards in advance of the foremost troops, lifted 500 yards and rested there ten minutes, repeated the lift and then died out. The leading Companies advanced in the formation of patrols supported by platoons; the support Companies followed on a three-platoon frontage. No enemy resistance was encountered until Forester's House was reached. The enemy was found to be occupying this position and the high ground in rear in some strength; the machine gun and rifle fire from these points causing a temporary check. At an earlier stage the direction and speed of the advance had been seriously threatened by the dense undergrowth. Lieut.-Colonel Hargest

Forester's House, Mormal Forest—showing Graves of the Last Soldiers of the Regiment to Fall in Action.

having then with characteristic dash galloped forward and personally restored the situation, continued with the leading troops until the original impetus of the advance had been regained and the resistance at Forester's House and locality overcome. To bring about the destruction of the enemy at this point, 10th Company threatened it from the right and 14th Company from the left. A patrol from the former Company succeeded in reaching within 50 yards of the house, but there came under machine gun and rifle fire, the patrol commander, 2nd-Lieut. R. A. Savage, and one other rank being killed. An attempt was then made against the left flank, and two platoons from 14th Company worked their way to the rear. It was now observed that the enemy was preparing to evacuate the position. At 11 a.m. its capture was effected, two machine guns and about 30 prisoners being accounted for.

The Headquarters of the 2nd Battalion of the Regiment were now established at Forester's House. It was not long before the building became the target of accurate shell fire. Lieut.-Colonel Hargest was standing at the entrance as one of these shells burst, and was momentarily stunned ; almost as he withdrew a second shell demolished the front of the house.

When Companies were reorganised, the advance was resumed. The line of the secon . objective was reached without material opposition. At this point there was occasion for further reorganising, the heavy undergrowth having made it almost impossible to maintain connection and direction. It was also decided by the Commanding Officer to adopt a new formation. In accordance with this decision, the Battalion was disposed on a three-company frontage, with one Company, the 8th, and the attached Vickers guns in support. At 1.30 p.m. the Battalion advanced to the capture of the final objective. The left and centre Companies encountered very little opposition, but the right Company, the 4th, was obstructed by machine gun fire until the enemy was driven from his ground.

At 3 p.m. orders were received to the effect that the Battalion was to cease its advance for the day at 4 p.m., and that a definite line was to be formed so that the 42nd Division could effect the relief of the New Zealand Division that night. The Battalion thereupon moved forward rapidly in order to reach its final objective within the appointed time. At 3.45 p.m. the advance had penetrated to the most extreme point set by operation orders, which was beyond the great Foret de Mormal and approximately 7,500 yards from the starting point. The enemy had endeavoured to maintain his hold on the eastern edge of the Forest ; but the strong and relentless pressure of our troops, and the accurate bursts of Lewis gun and rifle fire broke down all resistance. Many of the enemy were killed, a number of prisoners and machine guns were captured, and the remainder of the garrison beat a hasty retreat across the open in the direction of the Sambre River.

The advance of the 2nd Battalion of the Regiment had been closely attended by the 1st Battalion, which had to contend against the same difficulties of maintaining connection and direction. It was originally intended that the 1st Battalion should pass through the foremost troops of the 2nd Battalion east of Mormal Forest, in order to secure the line of the Sambre south of Hautmont. This intention was not carried out ; and when the 2nd Battalion, on reaching its final objective, found that the troops to right and left were not up in line, 4th Company of the 1st Battalion formed a defensive flank to the right, while 8th Company took up a corresponding position to the left.

During the night the 42nd Division relieved the New Zealand Division in the line. The two Battalions of the Regiment thereupon commenced their long trek back through the Forest towards Le Quesnoy. The 1st Battalion completed an unbroken march to billets in the citadel town, a distance of about nine miles ; the 2nd Battalion halted at Maison Rouge, and at 9 a.m. on the 6th resumed its journey to Le Quesnoy.

The casualties sustained by the 2nd Battalion of the Regiment on the 5th included two officers and nine other ranks killed, all of them during the earlier stages of the advance. They were among the last New Zealanders to fall in action on the Western Front ; on the following day, November 6th, their bodies were reverently laid to rest alongside Forester's House, in the shade and silence of the forest.

The enemy resistance encountered during the deep advance through Mormal Forest had been more remarkable for its surprise possibilities than for its stubbornness; but the density of the undergrowth, the persistent rain, the heavy crashes of artillery fire among the tall trees, and the great distance covered, made the operation an exhausting one. But its success was decisive and complete; and as the last offensive action of the World War in which the Regiment was engaged, it represented a fitting climax to the gallant and enduring service performed by those who had travelled down the long, hard road to Victory.

CHAPTER XXI.

DEFEAT AND SURRENDER.

THE events of the next few days proclaimed in striking and dramatic form that the final stage in the mighty concentration of effort for supremacy between the great nations of the earth had at length been reached; that the German spirit had been irretrievably broken, and both its ability and its willingness for further effort hopelessly destroyed. The enemy now commenced to fall back along practically the whole front of battle. The growing demoralisation was intensified by the ceaseless and tremendous pressure exerted by the Allied Armies. On November 9th all semblance of organised resistance was abandoned, and the retreat became general over the Western Front. On November 10th the enemy was rolled still further to the east; and only at Mons was any serious attempt made to dispute the British advance; but this was quickly swept aside and the town entered early on the following morning.

There is conclusive testimony, even from German official sources, that the enemy was now moving helplessly towards the worst phases of a demoralised and beaten force. It was drifting rapidly frcm its disciplinary moorings, was suffering equally from the attacks of the pursuing army in its rear and the overwhelming fear of its own helplessness. It had reached that point in the last stages of a beaten Army where its thoughts turn exclusively on its own safety.

Under such conditions no other course remained to the German Supreme Command but to appeal to the consideration of the Allied Commander and sue for an armistice. An armistice was accordingly granted, amounting substantially, and in effect, to a complete surrender of the enemy. All that could have been gained by fighting came into the hands of the Allies more speedily, and without the loss in lives which would have followed the adoption of a more extreme course.

At 11 a.m. on November 11th—a memorable and unforgettable moment in history—hostilities on the Western Front were suspended under the terms dictated by the Allies. Peace was at last to be restored to a world prostrate and bleeding under the scourge of war.

In order to understand the full meaning of Germany's defeat, it has to be remembered that the spirit or *moral* of the German people was as completely broken as that of its Armies in the field. It was a defeat so overwhelming in its magnitude of consequences as no nation can seriously risk more than once in its life ; and in the grave of its defeat must slumber for many generations the ambitions that led Germany to the abyss, and nearly wrecked the World.

The declaration of an Armistice was received by the Regiment when at Le Quesnoy without demonstration or outward show of enthusiasm. It first became known to the general number of troops through the civil population of Le Quesnoy, who in the early hours of the morning were heard excitedly repeating the news along the streets. But, in strange contrast to the extraordinary demonstrations in other parts of the World, there was barely a shout from the billets, except perhaps as a protest against so much noise ; and the weary soldier, with a sigh of relief as after a task well done, turned over and went to sleep again.

The German occupation of Le Quesnoy, practically since the commencement of the War, had left the town in a deplorably filthy state. After all, this was typical of the German soldier's standard of cleanliness. On this occasion some satisfaction was to be derived from the fact that they were required to clean up the mess which they had made.

On November 10th M. Poincare, President of the French Republic, had visited Le Quesnoy, and was received by the civil and military population with demonstrations of extraordinary enthusiasm. The Regiment contributed to the guard of honour accorded M. Poincare.

At midday on November 11th the Regiment marched out of Le Quesnoy, and headed south-west for Beauvois. The journey was completed on the 12th, after staying the night at Quievy. The Regiment now settled down to a period of rest and training, the latter sufficiently strenuous to preserve physical fitness.

On November 13th all officers of the New Zealand Division attended an address delivered by Major-General Sir A. H. Russell, G.O.C. Division. The announcement was then made that the New Zealand Division was to form part of the Allied Army of Occupation of Germany.

On November 14th, on the outskirts of Beauvois, the Regiment participated in a Thanksgiving Service held to mark the cessation of hostilities. On this occasion practically the whole Division was assembled.

IV. CORPS ORDER.

On the conclusion of the Armistice, the following letter of farewell was addressed to the New Zealand Division by Lieut.-General Sir G. M. Harper, K.C.B., D.S.O., Commanding IV. Corps :—

" As the New Zealand Division is leaving the IV. Corps, I desire to place on record my appreciation of the valuable services it has rendered, and to thank all ranks for the magnificent fighting qualities which they have invariably displayed.

" The Division joined the IV. Corps at a critical time on the 26th March, 1918, when it completely checked the enemy's advance at Beaumont Hamel and Colincamps, and thus closed the gap between the IV. and V. Corps. By a brilliant stroke it drove the enemy from the commanding ground at La Signy Farm and gained observation over the enemy's lines, which greatly assisted in his defeat on the 5th April, 1918, when he made his last and final effort to break our front. Throughout the summer the Division held portions of the Corps front with but a short interval of rest. During this period I never had the least anxiety about the security of this portion of the front ; on the other hand, by carefully conceived and well executed raids, the enemy was given little respite, and identifications were secured whenever required—in this connection I deplore the loss of that brave man, Sergt. Travis, V.C.

" It was the ascendancy gained by this Division over the enemy that compelled him to evacuate the ground about Rossignol Wood.

" At the commencement of the great attack on 21st August, 1918, only a minor part was allotted to the Division, but subsequently the Division was ordered to attack, and swept the enemy from Grevillers, Loupart Wood, and Biefvillers, and gained the outskirts of Bapaume. Stubborn fighting was experienced around Bapaume, but eventually the enemy was overcome and pushed back to the east.

" From 24th August till 14th September the Division was constantly engaged, and drove the enemy back from Bapaume to the high ground west of Gouzeaucourt, where very heavy fighting occurred at African Trench.

" After a short period of rest the Division was put in again on 29th September to complete the capture of Welsh Ridge and to gain the crossings over the Canal de l'Escaut. A night advance over difficult country, intersected by the trenches and wire of the Hindenburg Line, was brilliantly carried out and entirely successful, and resulted in the capture of over 1,000 prisoners and over 40 guns. On the 1st October the Division captured Crevecoeur against strong opposition, and held it in spite of heavy shelling and several counter-attacks throughout the subsequent days until the great attack on 8th October, when the Division broke through the northern portion of the strongly organised Masnieres Line, and penetrated far into the enemy's line at Esnes and Haucourt.

" Going out to rest on the 12th October, the Division was again in the line on 23rd October, and drove the enemy back from the outskirts of Romeries to Le Quesnoy. Finally, on the 4th November the Division, by an attack which did much to decide the finish of the War, forced the surrender of the Fortress of Le Quesnoy and drove the enemy back through the Forest of Mormal, the total captures by the IV. Corps on that day amounting to 3,500 prisoners and some 70 guns.

" During the period the New Zealand Division has been
in the IV. Corps, it has captured from the enemy
287 officers and 8,745 other ranks, 145 guns, 1,419
machine guns and three tanks, besides much other
material.

" The continuous successes enumerated above constitute
a record of which the Division may well be proud.
It is a record which I may safely say has been unsurpassed in the final series of attacks which led to
the enemy's suing for peace.

" I send every man of the Division my heartfelt good
wishes for the future."

ADVANCE INTO GERMANY.

Preparations were now commenced for carrying out the
projected advance into Germany. A certain measure of
dissatisfaction prevailed over the fact that the journey was
to be undertaken on foot instead of by rail, but this was to
some extent dispelled when it came to be realised that the
railway system ahead had been seriously disorganised by the
blowing up of bridges and culverts and the general destruction
caused to the permanent way by the enemy during the course
of his retreat.

There was a small section which represented that the
Division should not proceed into Germany under any circumstances, their contention being that members of the N.Z.E.F.
should now be returned to their homes. Curiously enough,
some of those who exhibited this feverish desire to return to
New Zealand had left its shores only a few months previously.
It was then pointed out that the fact of an armistice prevailing did not imply that the War was at an end ; and furthermore, that an honour had been conferred upon the New
Zealand Division when it had been selected to form part of
the Army of Occupation.

On November 18th a Divisional route march of a test
nature was held, and the standard of march discipline attained
was good. The weather during this period was exceedingly
cold, though dry, and with comfortable billets, adequate
supplies of fresh vegetables, facilities for hot baths and frequent

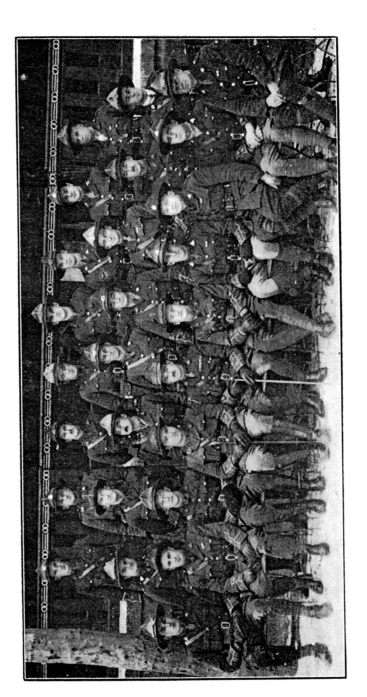

OFFICERS OF 2ND BATTALION, OTAGO REGIMENT—*Germany, February, 1919.*

changes of underclothing, and plenty of diversity in the way of football matches and cinema performances, the time passed pleasantly enough.

At this stage a Divisional Education Scheme was propounded and subsequently discussed in the course of frequent lectures and conferences.

On November 26th Lieut.-Colonel Charters assumed temporary command of the 2nd New Zealand Infantry Brigade; whereupon Major L. M. Scott took over command of the 1st Battalion of the Regiment.

On November 28th the Otago Regiment, as part of the New Zealand Division, commenced its victorious march into Germany. The selected route lay through the Valleys of the Sambre and Meuse, along which, down the ages, had passed many great Armies, but never before an Army of Conquest from so remote a part of the World.

Proceeding along the main Cambrai-Le Cateau highway, thence striking almost due north through Bethencourt, Viesly, Briastre, and Solesmes, and accorded a hearty despatch by the fife and drum bands of the 37th Division, the Regiment reached and halted for the night at St. Martin and Bermerain. Thereafter the direction of the march was always north-easterly. Rain fell almost continuously during the first day, and the heavy going under the weight of full packs provided a severe test for the opening stage of the journey. In fact a great deal of rain was experienced on subsequent days; but the assurance of comfortable billets at the termination of each day's march and the warm greetings of the civil populations *en route* lightened the discomforts of the road. Periodical spells of two and at times three days broke the monotony of distance. At many of the towns where the Regiment halted over night householders became deeply grieved if they did not receive one or more soldiers under the arrangement of billeting. The course of this great march brought the Regiment to such places as Maubeuge, Charleroi, Namur and Liege; but it was at Verviers that the most demonstrative reception of all was accorded our troops, men and horses being decorated with garlands of flowers.

On December 1st a Church Service was held at Bavais, when His Majesty the King and the Prince of Wales were present.

The roads traversed were for the most part in good order, but the typical cobbled highways of Northern France and Belgium proved severe on footwear, and the greatest difficulty was experienced in securing supplies of new boots, or even leather for repairs, at a time most urgently required. In order to lessen the burden of the march, great-coats and steel helmets were discarded on December 7th, when at Montignies-sur-Sambre, and deposited there for despatch by rail at a later date.

On December 20th, after a march of 170 miles on foot, the Regiment crossed the Belgian-German frontier. At Herbesthal, on the border line of the two countries, the Regiment entrained and completed the final 60 miles of the journey by rail through German territory. The detraining point was Ehrenfeld, on the outskirts of Cologne. From this point the Regiment marched through Cologne City, crossed the River Rhine by the Bridge-of-Boats, and thence into Mulheim. There it took up its station along with the other troops of the New Zealand Division, now established as one of the Bridgehead Garrison units of the Allied Army of Occupation.

The successive halting places on the line of march were as follows :—

		1st Battalion.		2nd Battalion.
November	28	Bermerain	...	St. Martin
November	29	Orsinval	...	Villers Pol.
November	30	Bellignies	...	Bellignies
December	3	Rousies	...	Ferrier-le-Grand
December	4	Erquelinnes	...	Erquelinnes
December	5	Thuin	...	Thuin
December	7	Montignies-sur-Sambre	...	Montignies-sur-Sambre
December	8	La Sarte	...	Auvelais
December	9	Flawinne	...	Temploux
December	11	Marchovelette	...	Vedrin
December	12	Lavoir	...	Waret-Leveque
December	13	Ampsin	...	Amay
December	17	Ougree	...	Ougree
December	18	Nessenvaux	...	Fraipont
December	19	Limbourg	...	Limbourg
December	20	Mulheim	...	Mulheim

The remarkable feature of the whole journey was the unrestrained enthusiasm and the almost embarrassing hospitality of the French and Belgian civil populations. As our victorious troops, marching to the stirring music of the Regimental Bands, advanced through a succession of towns and villages, the people excitedly crowded the road-sides, now able to realise, with feelings of emotion not easily suppressed, that the long days of enemy invasion and subjection were definitely ended.

Across the border, the attitude of the German people was first one of timidity, which might have suggested fear of retribution, and later one of attempted conciliation, or desire to make friends, supported by acts intended to convey goodwill. Of course, the presence of Allied troops in the area assured the civil population a sense of security against rioting and internal strife, such as was threatened or had occurred elsewhere. But in any case the German mentality was not to be understood on so brief an acquaintance. There was no evidence of hostility to our troops in a general sense ; in fact, the temper was that of a nation completely subdued,—a state of mind and action conveying an illustration of the expression " knocked sick."

ARMY OF OCCUPATION.

The New Zealand Division's occupation of the Cologne Bridgehead involved the additional duties of maintaining guards over German war material and factories, and the supplying of picquets and Regimental guards. The dislocation of the railway service consequent upon the blowing up of delayed action mines laid by the enemy during his retreat, and the severe strain imposed on rolling stock by the rapid advance of the Allied Armies, at times threatened to interfere seriously with the commissariat arrangements. Certainly there was grievous disappointment when the turkeys and other good things ordered for Christmas Day failed to arrive, and their consumption had to be deferred to New Year's Day, when no less gusto was exhibited because of the postponement.

During the month of January the Regiment was employed in the forenoons on educational training under the

Divisional Education Scheme; in the afternoons recreational games were played. River excursions on the Rhine always proved popular. The occupying of battle stations in defence of bridgeheads, factories, railway stations, and public buildings was practised in view of possible civil disturbances, and was certainly impressive from a military point of view.

On January 13th Lieut.-Colonel A. B. Charters, C.M.G., D.S.O., who had commanded the 1st Battalion of the Regiment through its successes and vicissitudes of fortune in France and Flanders over a period of three years, bade farewell to officers and men, and departed for the United Kingdom and New Zealand. Under the command and influence of Lieut.-Colonel Charters, the Battalion had at all times, and under the most desperate conditions of warfare, maintained its splendid reputation for discipline, fighting efficiency, and *esprit de corps*, all of which qualities were remarkably in evidence during the many difficult operations carried out in the course of the Campaign on the Western Front. Major W. G. A. Bishop, M.C., now took over command of the Battalion.

On January 16th His Royal Highness the Prince of Wales visited the New Zealand Division.

Several drafts were now being despatched to the United Kingdom preparatory to return to New Zealand. With this development commenced the termination of the Regiment's existence as such on the Western Front. On February 4th, in consequence of the rapidly decreasing strength, the 1st and 2nd Battalions of Otago Regiment were amalgamated, and the double formation designated the Otago Battalion.

On the same day Lieut.-Colonel J. Hargest, D.S.O., M.C. (F.), terminated his service with the Otago Regiment in the Field, and departed for England. In the course of his long connection with the Regiment, Lieut.-Colonel Hargest, by his thoroughness, his soldierly ability and bearing, his great sense of military honour, and his extraordinary energy and unexampled dash in action, commanded the highest admiration and confidence of all ranks; while the rapid and exceptional success which attended his military career has won for him a foremost place among the distinguished soldiers of the New Zealand Division.

The regular despatch of drafts to England continued. On February 27th the Otago Battalion amalgamated with the Canterbury Battalion, and the two formations became C and D Companies of the South Island Battalion.

By the end of March the New Zealand Division had ceased to exist as an active unit on the Western Front.

In the triumphal march of Over-Seas Troops through the streets of London on May 3rd the Regiment was fully represented, and shared in the acclamations showered upon the Colonials by an enthusiastic populace. But a brief space of time elapsed and the last members of the Regiment had left the shores of England for New Zealand—and Home.

CHAPTER XXII.

CONCLUSION.

AND so, after those long years heavily freighted with death and suffering, years of changing horizons, of alternating periods of lowering clouds and looming disaster, of clear skies and glowing hope, but always and under every change of fortune keeping its brave and unquenchable spirit aflame, the Regiment had come to the end of its great task.

The Regiment had in those years been made familiar with all the hard and merciless conditions of a war that made unceasing exaction of every ounce of effort and every extreme of sacrifice, and for which every unexplored region of Science had been laid under contribution in all its dark and frightful places in the search for new methods and new agencies of devastation and death. And the results, measured in suffering and death, were such as to make all the previous great wars of the world look mere feeble amateur experiments in the art of killing.

The losses of the Regiment had been continuous and heavy down to the last stages of the war, and its ranks had many times been sadly thinned and weakened ; but the new accessions to its diminished strength quickly absorbed the old martial spirit of the Regiment, and so its identity as a hard fighting unit was preserved, and to the last it remained the Infantry Regiment of Otago whose dash and gallantry and contempt of death will remain as one of the proudest memories of our soldiers in the Great War.

The traditions of a regiment, it may be said, live in the deeds of its most daring soldiers ; and in the collective spirit of the Otago Regiment will be found something of the individual bravery of such men as Travis, and Brown, and Cockerell, and of many others whose personal heroism was lost to observation in the turmoil and din of battle.

It is not pretended that the attempt made in this volume to follow closely the varying fortunes of the Regiment during the years of its brilliant service in the Field is equal in comprehensiveness and detail to the vastness and complexities of the subject. No writer of history of such a war, no matter how fully informed or how well equipped for his task, could hope to do more than present an incomplete, but perhaps a suggestive, picture, leaving the rest to the sympathetic imagination of his readers.

The full story of the Waterloo Campaign, the shortest and most decisive in history—it lasted less than five days—has not yet been fully told, though it occupies a space equal perhaps to the whole output of history of all other British wars. What hope is there, then, that the story of the greatest war of all the ages, numerically equal in years to the days of Waterloo, can ever see the light in full and complete historical form. And relatively and in modified form may not the same be said of the history of a fighting force so closely identified with every phase of the Great War as the Otago Regiment.

But the chief purpose of the History will have been served in keeping alive memories that in time will be woven into our national life and become great and appealing traditions, giving strength and dignity and a due sense of their own worth to our people both of to-day and of the future.

To those who suffered and died for their Country posterity must owe an everlasting debt and cherish hallowed memories ; for those who fought and suffered and lived for it, there must be no less admiration and gratitude ; for the stimulus and inspiration of their lives are not of to-day, but must live for ever.

APPENDIX.

RESERVE OR TRAINING BATTALION.

THE Reserve or Training Battalion of the Otago Regiment had its inception in Egypt at the beginning of April, 1916, with the establishment at Moascar of Infantry Training Battalions for each Brigade of the New Zealand Division. The function of the training cadres was to absorb all surplus strength and reinforcements, and ensure their efficient training before being drafted to a definite service battalion of the Division. On April 18th, 1916, the Training Battalion of the Otago Regiment moved from Moascar to Tel-el-Kebir. The arrival of the 10th and 11th Reinforcements from New Zealand called for renewed activities on the part of the training staffs; but towards the middle of May the weather became so extraordinarily hot that it was decided to carry out training operations between the hours of 2 a.m. and 8 a.m.

With the departure of the New Zealand Division from Egypt to France, it was decided by Administrative Headquarters that the reception and training camp for troops arriving from New Zealand should be established in England. In accordance with this decision the Training Battalions and their instructional staffs, under the command of Major G. Mitchell, were despatched to England. The troops concerned entrained on May 24th, and on May 30th embarked at Alexandria and sailed for England the following day, Plymouth being reached on June 9th. On arrival at Plymouth, disembarkation was effected and the troops immediately entrained for Sling Camp, on the Salisbury Plains.

Sling Camp, comfortable enough in many ways, was situated on rising ground within close distance of the permanent military camp above Bulford village, and comprised hutment accommodation which, though cool in summer time, failed to keep out the intense cold of an English winter. The sudden change in temperature and climate after the torrid days of Egypt proved exceedingly trying, and the sick parades almost immediately assumed large proportions.

393

No. 1 Camp was allotted to the training units of the 1st Infantry Brigade, No. 2 Camp to the 2nd Infantry Brigade, and No. 3 Camp to the 3rd (Rifle) Brigade. Command of the group was held by Major G. Mitchell, of Otago Regiment. A few days later this command was taken over by Col. V. S. Smyth, A.D.C., N.Z.S.C.

No reinforcements had as yet arrived, and the intervening time was profitably spent in training the non-commissioned officers selected for the instructional staff. The 12th Reinforcements had been detained in Egypt, and the first reinforcement troops to arrive in England were the 13th, who reached Sling Camp on June 26th. The 12th Reinforcements arrived on August 5th.

In the meantime several changes in the organisation of the Camp had occurred. It was first decided to institute an Otago-Canterbury Training Battalion and an Auckland-Wellington Training Battalion. This decision was given effect to, and the combined Otago-Canterbury Battalion took over No. 1 Camp, Captain Bishop, M.C., commanding the 1st Company of Otago, and Captain W. Domigan the 2nd Company. The arrangement did not, however, prove satisfactory, and independent headquarters were in consequence established for each unit. The Otago and Canterbury Training Battalions continued to occupy No. 1 Camp, commanded by Major G. Mitchell and Col. G. J. Smith respectively. A month later it was again decided to change the organisation ; and on this occasion the original formation was reverted to, i.e., 1st and 2nd Infantry Brigade Training Battalions. Col. G. J. Smith took command of the 1st Brigade Training Battalion in the No. 1 Camp, and Major Mitchell moved to No. 2 Camp and there assumed command of the 2nd Brigade Training Battalion.

Such frequent changes naturally militated against efficiency in training ; but once the organisation was considered to be established along sound lines no time was lost in meeting the demands of the Division in France for trained reinforcements. The interior administration of the Camps was also being gradually improved ; although it is recorded of the Officers' Mess at No. 1 Camp, that while it was claimed to be the best in the Group, the ambitions of the committee were such that the bailiffs called and took away the furniture and crockery, which could not be paid for owing to the non-arrival of reinforcements, and the fact that the initial expenses had to be faced by a few officers.

At this period the time available for training and putting the finishing touches on drafts for over-seas was very limited, owing to the demands of the Division in France, then deeply engaged in the Somme Offensive. The result was that operations had to be commenced at a very early hour in the morning and conducted at high pressure. The lines on which training was carried out at Sling Camp were much more advanced and more aggressive than those in operation in New Zealand. The long working hours, the exertions demanded in the "Bull Ring," and the stringent discipline insisted on in regard to both training and administration provided a rude awakening for troops who were accustomed to a comparative laxity of discipline in New Zealand, and had passed through two months of idleness on board ship. In addition to being responsible for the training of all drafts forwarded to the Regiment in France, the Reserve or Training Battalion ensured that every man was completely equipped before being sent over-seas.

On arrival in France, reinforcement drafts were received at the Divisional Base established in the great British camp at Etaples. After a further period of "Bull Ring" training, carried out alongside men from practically every Regiment in the British Army, drafts were sent straight to the Division, and there absorbed into one of the service Battalions of the Regiment. The Divisional Base was established at Etaples for a lengthened period.

Reinforcements who were in Sling Camp, on the so-called Salisbury Plains, will remember the winter of 1916 because of its extraordinary severity and duration. It was commonly regarded as the severest season experienced for over 30 years. Major J. B. McClymont was in command of the Reserve Battalion at that period, and remained there until the formation of the 4th New Zealand Infantry Brigade at the close of March, 1917, when Major J. L. Saunders, D.S.O., Otago Regiment, assumed command of the Otago-Canterbury Camp.

Towards the end of April about 150 non-commissioned officers and selected privates with active service to their credit assembled at Sling Camp and passed through a lightning course of training as officers for the New Zealand Division in France. A large number of these cadets belonged to Otago Regiment.

On April 27th, on the Bulford Fields, His Majesty the King reviewed some 8,000 men of the New Zealand Forces in England. This number included the 4th Infantry Brigade (which embraced the 3rd Battalion of the Regiment), members of the Officers' Training Corps, and large drafts on the point of proceeding over-seas.

Reinforcements were arriving regularly from New Zealand, and training was being carried on at high pressure. On September 7th, 1917, the Reserve Battalions of Otago and Canterbury Regiments separated, Canterbury remaining in No. 1 Camp, and Otago taking over No. 2 Camp, which, from an administrative point of view had long been unoccupied. Major W. G. Wray, M.C., assumed command of the Reserve Battalion of Otago Regiment, Major J. L. Saunders at this time acting as G.S.O. for the Brigade Group.

The system of training obtaining in the " Bull Ring " was altered at this period. The Group " Bull Ring " was abolished, and separate " rings " were allotted to each Battalion ; but it was doubtful if this operated as well as the former system.

The arrival of the 28th Reinforcements at Sling Camp in September, 1917, was marked by a tragic occurrence during the journey from Plymouth to Bulford, nine men being killed and two injured as a result of being run down by a fast through-train at a wayside station where the reinforcements had temporarily halted.

On October 1st Lieut.-Colonel J. L. Saunders took command of the Reserve Battalion, Major Wray proceeding to New Zealand. During the following month the despatch of drafts to the Regiment in France left the Camp practically empty. At the close of November Lieut.-Colonel Saunders left for New Zealand on transport duty, and Lieut.-Colonel G. S. Smith, C.M.G., D.S.O., up till then commanding the 2nd Battalion of the Regiment in France, arrived and took over the vacant command.

The winter months of 1917 were not as severe as those of the previous season, but yet there was a considerable amount of sickness. In fact, from time to time, epidemics of influenza, measles, and the like were experienced, demanding the adoption of special precautionary measures, by which training operations were seriously interrupted. For reasons of health, and in view of the fact that several deaths had taken place during the month of February among the latest reinforcements to the Battalion, arrangements were completed for placing the 33rd Reinforcements in a special camp at Larkhill. There the Otago Reinforcements were administered as a complete unit, and strict isolation insisted upon for a definite period. These epidemics were invariably associated with the winter months, and with the approach of fine weather there was an immediate improvement in the general health.

The internal arrangements of the Otago Camp, which provided for an excellent standard of food, every opportunity for recreational as distinct from military exercise, dry and sufficient clothing, healthy sleeping accommodation and efficient medical attention, assured a sound state of general health, and quickly combated any epidemics which arose.

The e.istence of " wet " canteens as a regular camp institution met the legitimate demands of a large percentage of the men without in any way contributing to excesses or abuse of the privileges granted.

Towards the close of July, 1918, Lieut.-Colonel G. S. Smith assumed command of the 4th New Zealand Infantry (Reserve) Brigade, and command of the Reserve Battalion, Otago Regiment, passed to Major McCrae, D.S.O., who in the following month was succeeded by Lieut.-Colonel J. B. McClymont.

The declaration of the Armistice on the Western Front on November 11th, 1918, was duly celebrated. On November 16th the last draft, comprising 93 other ranks, was despatched from the Reserve Battalion over-seas. The routine of the camp was now altered, more time being devoted to educational classes and lectures.

On December 5th a draft of 122 men, ex 43rd Reinforcements, marched into Otago Camp, this being the last reinforcement to arrive from New Zealand.

On December 26th, 1918, the Reserve Battalion, Otago Regiment, terminated its long and useful service. A new formation, the Otago Provincial Detachment, at once came into being, and under it were grouped all ranks whose destination in New Zealand was the provincial district of Otago.

It was not long before large drafts commenced to arrive from France and Germany, followed over the succeeding months by a steady despatch from Sling Camp of Homeward-bound soldiers.

HONOURS AND AWARDS.

* *Denotes killed in action, or died of wounds or sickness.*
† *Denotes Commissioned in the Field.*
(D.) *Mentioned in Despatches.*
[F.] *Foreign Decoration.*
Figure in brackets denotes the number of times mentioned in Despatches.
The rank shown is invariably that held at the time the Award was made.

Following is a list of the Honours and Awards won by members of the Otago Regiment in the Great War :—

VICTORIA CROSS.

* SERGT. DONALD FORRESTER BROWN.

For most conspicuous bravery and determination in attack (south-east of High Wood, France, on September 15, 1916), when the company to which he belonged had suffered very heavy casualties in officers and men from machine gun fire. At great personal risk this N.C.O. advanced with a comrade and succeeded in reaching a point within 30 yds. of the enemy guns. Four of the gun crew were killed and the gun captured. The advance of the company was continued until it was again held up by machine gun fire. Again Sergt. Brown and his comrade, with great gallantry, rushed the gun and killed the crew. After this second position had been won, the company came under very heavy shell fire, and the utter contempt for danger and coolness under fire of this N.C.O. did much to keep up the spirit of his men. On a subsequent occasion in attack, Sergt. Brown showed most conspicuous gallantry. He attacked, single-handed, a machine gun which was holding up the attack, killed the gun crew, and captured the gun. Later, whilst sniping the retreating enemy, this very gallant soldier was killed.—*London Gazette*, June 14, 1917.

* SERGT. RICHARD CHARLES TRAVIS, D.C.M., M.M., [F.].

For most conspicuous bravery and devotion to duty (North Hebuterne, France, on July 24, 1918). During "surprise" operations it was necessary to destroy an impassable wire block. Sergeant Travis, regardless of all personal danger, volunteered for this duty. Before zero hour, in broad daylight, and in close proximity to enemy posts, he crawled out and successfully destroyed the block with bombs, thus enabling the attacking parties to pass through. A few minutes later a bombing party on the right of the attack was held up by two enemy machine guns, and the success of the whole operation was in danger. Perceiving this, Sergeant Travis, with great gallantry and utter disregard of danger, rushed the position, killed the crew, and captured the guns. An enemy officer and three men immediately rushed at him from a bend in the trench and attempted to retake the guns. These four he killed single-handed, thus allowing the bombing party, on which much depended, to advance. The success of the operation was almost entirely due to the heroic work of this gallant N.C.O., and to the vigour with which he made and used opportunities for inflicting casualties on the enemy. He was killed 24 hours later, when, under a most intense bombardment prior to an enemy counter-attack, he was going from post to post, encouraging the men.—*London Gazette*, September 27, 1918.

COMPANION OF ST. MICHAEL AND ST. GEORGE.

LIEUT.-COL. A. B. CHARTERS, D.S.O.
LIEUT.-COL. J. A. MACKENZIE
LIEUT.-COL. G. S. SMITH, D.S.O.

DISTINGUISHED SERVICE ORDER.

LIEUT.-COL. A. B. CHARTERS, C.M.G.
† 2ND-LIEUT. A. R. COCKERELL
LIEUT.-COL. D. COLQUHOUN
† CAPTAIN A. S. FALCONER, M.C. (attached 2nd N.Z. Infantry Brigade Headquarters)
MAJOR J. HARGEST, M.C.
LIEUT.-COL. G. F. HUTTON
MAJOR F. H. LAMPEN
MAJOR J. MCCRAE
LIEUT.-COL. G. MITCHELL
MAJOR J. L. SAUNDERS
MAJOR G. S. SMITH
MAJOR W. MCG. TURNBULL

ORDER OF BRITISH EMPIRE.

CAPTAIN R. R. GOW   CAPTAIN J. MCPHERSON

BAR TO THE MILITARY CROSS.

LIEUT. C. B. McCLURE, M.C.
* LIEUT. J. C. MACLEAN, M.C. (attached N.Z. Light Railway
    Operating Company)
† LIEUT. K. SCOTT, M.C.

MILITARY CROSS.

LIEUT. E. J. ANDERSON
LIEUT. R. E. ANDREW
LIEUT. C. F. ATMORE
2ND-LIEUT. L. W. BASSETT
LIEUT. W. G. A. BISHOP
CAPTAIN D. E. BREMNER
† 2ND-LIEUT. A. E. BYRNE
CAPTAIN W. W. CHAPMAN
† 2ND-LIEUT. R. G. CHARTERS
LIEUT. H. R. DOMIGAN
† LIEUT. R. D. DOUGLASS
LIEUT. F. J. R. EARL
† 2ND-LIEUT. J. W. ELLIS
† LIEUT. A. S. FALCONER
* LIEUT. E. V. FREED
† 2ND-LIEUT. R. E. FYFE
2ND-LIEUT. R. S. HALLIWELL
CAPTAIN J. HARGEST
REV. D. C. HERRON (N.Z. Chaplains' Department)
*† LIEUT. R. J. HILL
CAPTAIN H. S. HILLS
LIEUT. J. N. HINES
† 2ND-LIEUT. A. H. KING
† SERGT.-MAJOR R. J. KNOX
*† LIEUT. J. R. R. LEYS
CAPTAIN F. W. LUMSDEN (N.Z. Medical Corps)
† LIEUT. D. McAULEY
2ND-LIEUT. C. B. McCLURE
† 2ND-LIEUT. A. MACDONALD
† 2ND-LIEUT. S. G. McDONALD
LIEUT. F. McINTOSH
† LIEUT. K. J. MACKENZIE
* LIEUT. J. C. MACLEAN (att. N.Z. Light Railway Operating Company)
REV. W. McLEAN (N.Z. Chaplains' Department)
† 2ND-LIEUT. E. S. MAYN
LIEUT. J. A. MILLER
* CAPTAIN C. H. MOLLOY
† 2ND-LIEUT. W. MURPHY
LIEUT. O. R. OLSEN
2ND-LIEUT. A. D. PAISLEY
† LIEUT. F. C. PASCOE
* SERGT.-MAJOR A. W. PORTEOUS
CAPTAIN N. H. PRIOR (N.Z. Medical Corps)
*† 2ND-LIEUT. J. RODGERS, M.M.
† 2ND-LIEUT. K. SCOTT
CAPTAIN L. M. SCOTT
† 2ND-LIEUT. G. H. SEDDON

MILITARY CROSS.

† Captain E. F. Selby
Lieut. E. H. Sharp
Lieut. T. M. Sim
Captain P. W. G. Spiers
† Lieut. G. Swan
Lieut. W. F. Tracy
Rev. R. S. Watson (N.Z. Chaplains' Department)
Captain M. McP. Watt
Captain F. N. Whitmore
Lieut. W. H. S. Widdowson
† 2nd-Lieut. J. H. Wilson, M.M.
2nd-Lieut. R. Worley (att. N.Z. Light Railway Operating Company)
Captain W. G. Wray

DISTINGUISHED CONDUCT MEDAL.

Pte. A. G. Akroyd
Pte. T. J. Beck
Sergt. L. A. Berg, M.M.
L.-Sergt. H. Bellamy
Sergt.-major P. C. Boate
Pte. H. Boreham
Sergt. R. D. Brown
† C.S.M. T. A. Bunbury
Pte. V. Cruickshank
C.S.M. W. Deuchrass
Sergt. L. R. Dickinson, M.M.
Corpl. A. Dunlop
† C.S.M. L. L. J. Du Flou
* L.-Corpl. J. P. Egan
Sergt. W. D. Evans
Sergt. F. C. Fergusson
Sergt. R. Fitzgerald
Pte. C. A. Fitzpatrick
Sergt. R. E. Fortune
*† C.S.M. J. C. Fothergill
L.-Corpl. W. Friend
† Sergt. I. D. Guy
L.-Corpl. G. Hayton, M.M.

*† Sergt. A. G. Henderson
† C.S.M. A. L. Hibbs
† Sergt. E. C. H. Jacobs
Sergt. J. P. Kennett
Sergt. J. McG. Lamb
Pte. A. Macdonald
C.S.M. A. McFadyen
Sergt. P. McGregor
Pte. R. C. McLeod
† L.-Corpl. J. MacPherson
Pte. H. Melville, M.M.
Sergt. A. C. Mills
† Sergt. F. Mitchell
† Sergt. P. T. Moir, M.M.
Corpl. W. C. S. Moorhouse
† Sergt. W. P. Morrin, M.M.
Pte. G. J. Nesbit
Sergt. W. J. Pauling
* Sergt. T. Rielly
Corpl. H. D. Skinner
Sergt. D. Sterritt
* Pte. R. C. Travis

BAR TO MILITARY MEDAL.

L.-Sergt. A. W. E. Cole, M.M.
* Pte. W. C. Espie, M.M.
Sergt. R. B. Foote, M.M.

Pte. G. Gilbert, M.M.
Sergt. A. Swainson, M.M.
† Sergt. J. H. Wilson, M.M.

MILITARY MEDAL.

Pte. R. M. V. Abbott
Pte. E. A. Anderson
† Pte. J. Angell
Pte. R. G. Angus
Sergt. A. C. Arthur-Worsop
Corpl. G. Arundel
L.-Corpl. G. Avis
Pte. A. E. Balneaves
Sergt. R. T. Barnett

Sergt. J. Beaton
Corpl. T. J. Beck, D.C.M.
Pte. C. W. Beeby
Sergt. D. J. Bennetto
Corpl. L. A. Berg
Pte. J. R. Bird
* Sergt. L. J. Bissland
* Sergt. J. J. Blackburn
Pte. P. Blackburn

PTE. C. D. BONIFACE
SERGT. A. G. BOWATER
* CORPL. J. McK. BOYLE
PTE. A. D. BRASH
SERGT. J. BROWN
PTE. J. BROWN
SERGT. C. T. BROWNE
PTE. J. K. H. BURROWS
PTE. W. J. BUTLER
PTE. T. H. BUTT
* PTE. G. CAMERON
L.-CORPL. J. CAMERON
CORPL. T. M. CAMPBELL
SERGT. F. J. CARTER
PTE. J. P. CAULFIELD
PTE. G. CHANDLER
PTE. J. CHISHOLM
† SERGT. W. S. CLANCY
† L.-CORPL. J. T. CLEARWATER
* PTE. A. D. D. CLYDESDALE
CORPL. A. W. E. COLE
PTE. R. V. CONWAY
SERGT. J. A. COOK
* L.-CORPL. W. J. COUSINS
PTE. O. CREIGHTON
† SERGT. B. W. CROKER
PTE. H. CROWTHER
* SERGT. J. T. CUNNINGHAM
PTE. A. W. CURRY
*† CORPL. G. I. CUTHBERTSON
* PTE. A. DIACK
PTE. C. T. DICKINSON
PTE. L. R. DICKINSON
PTE. N. DICKSON
PTE. W. DOLMAN
PTE. A. R. DOYLE
SERGT. C. M. DUNCAN
PTE. G. EBERT
PTE. H. A. ELLIS
* PTE. W. C. ESPIE
L.-CORPL. D. FALLS
L.-CORPL. J. M. FINDLAY
* L.-SERGT. G. E. FLETCHER
PTE. J. FOLEY
SERGT. R. B. FOOTE
PTE. M. FORD
† L.-CORPL. G. B. FOTHERINGHAM
PTE. H. S. FRASER
L.-CORPL. J. FREW
L.-CORPL. R. W. FROST
PTE. J. A. GALBRAITH
PTE. G. L. GERKEN
PTE. L. I. GIBBS
PTE. G. GILBERT
PTE. A. W. GORDON
† CORPL. L. G. GORDON
† CORPL. W. E. GORDON
L.-CORPL. A. GRANT
PTE. E. GRIEVE

CORPL. A. GUNN
PTE. A. W. GUTHRIE
L.-CORPL. A. HALL
SERGT. G. HALL
L.-CORPL. L. J. HALPIN
L.-CORPL. F. W. HAMILL
* PTE. J. HAMILTON
PTE. C. J. HAWKES
* CORPL. R. W. HAWKES
L.-CORPL. G. HAYTON
PTE. A. M. HELM
PTE. W. G. HENNESSEY
C.S.M. C. C. HENRY
CORPL. P. HENRY
CORPL. R. S. HILL
PTE. J. HILLIARD
PTE. H. C. HOLGATE
PTE. E. HOLMAN
PTE. A. HUDSON
CORPL. C. W. HUMPHRIES
CORPL. J. HUNTER
PTE. J. R. HUNTER
* PTE. W. G. HUNTER
PTE. G. T. HUTCHINS
L.-CORPL. H. INGRAM
PTE. R. F. B. IRVING
PTE. A. D. JACKSON
CORPL. C. W. JACKSON
† SERGT. J. JACKSON
PTE. J. E. JAMES
* CORPL. R. S. C. JEFFERIS
PTE. R. JEFFREY
L.-CORPL. H. JENKINS
SERGT. W. A. JOHNSTON
PTE. T. A. KEEN
PTE. W. R. KELLY
* PTE. A. M. KENNEDY
PTE. T. O. KENNEDY
SERGT. R. J. KILROY
* PTE. H. F. KIRK
PTE. J. KIRKWOOD
PTE. T. W. KNIGHT
* PTE. W. T. LACEY
PTE. T. LAINCHBURY
† PTE. H. L. LANG
PTE. D. LAURISTON
PTE. A. LAW
CORPL. J. G. LAY
PTE. R. H. LOUDEN
PTE. J. R. LYALL
CORPL. G. MACAULEY
CORPL. W. T. McCAW
PTE. H. McDONALD
CORPL. A. S. McDOUGALL
L.-SERGT. C. E. McINTYRE
PTE. D. R. McINTYRE
SERGT. H. P. McINTYRE
L.-SERGT. D. MACKAY
PTE. G. A. McKAY

MILITARY MEDAL.

PTE. R. McKAY
PTE. J. McKENDRY
PTE. D. McKENZIE
L.-SERGT A. MACLEAN
*† SERGT. I. McLEAN
PTE. J. F. McLELLAND
* SERGT. W. A. McMILLAN
L.-SERGT. R. A. MARSHALL
L.-SERGT. F. R. MARTIN
PTE. H. MELVILLE
L.-CORPL. H. C. MILLER
CORPL. J. MILLER
PTE. S. A. MILLER
PTE. E. A. MILLIS
CORPL. G. MITCHELL
† CORPL. P. T. MOIR
PTE. T. A. MOONEY
CORPL. N. R. MOORE
PTE. R. MORELAND
† SERGT. W. P. MORRIN
PTE. H. W. E. MORRIS
PTE. K. MORRISON
* SERGT. W. J. T. MORROW
CORPL. C. T. MUNRO
* PTE. P. MURPHY (attached N.Z. F.A.)
L.-CORPL. J. MURRAY
CORPL. J. W. MURRAY
L.-CORPL. N. S. MURRELL
CORPL. G. S. NAPIER
PTE. R. A. NEEDS
PTE. F. NEWRICK
PTE. S. A. NOBLE
PTE. J. O'BRIEN
PTE. J. W. O'BRIEN
CORPL. J. O'DONNELL
PTE. S. OSBORNE
CORPL. E. OXENBURY
* PTE. J. PALMER
CORPL. R. A. PALMER
† CORPL. H. R. PARKER
* PTE. L. J. K. PARKER
* CORPL. B. PAULSON
PTE. G. D. PAYNE
* PTE. B. L. PETHERICK
CORPL. R. PHILLIPS
PTE. E. L. PINCHING
PTE. E. W. PULLAR
L.-CORPL. R. QUIN
PTE. F. RATCLIFFE
PTE. E. R. RAE
PTE. H. S. RAINES
SERGT. W. J. RAMSAY
PTE. W. F. REEVE
PTE. R. A. RESTON
PTE. J. REYNARD

PTE. E. A. RICHARDSON
PTE. W. ROBERTSON
*† SERGT. J. RODGERS
PTE. S. E. RUTHERFORD
PTE. J. A. RYAN
CORPL. J. SCOTT
† CORPL. S. SCOTT
L.-CORPL. G. V. SHIRLEY
CORPL. V. W. SHIRLEY
L.-CORPL. J. W. SIM
PTE. C. SIMS
* CORPL. J. H. SIMON
PTE. F. S. SINCLAIR
* SERGT. W. G. SINCLAIR
* PTE. C. L. SMITH
PTE. K. B. SMITH
L.-SERGT. S. H. SMITH
PTE. J. SMITH
L.-CORPL. T. J. SMYTH
PTE. A. S. C. SNOWDEN
CORPL. A. T. STEWART
PTE. N. STEWART
PTE. A. STRODE
PTE. A. STUART
CORPL. J. B. STUART
CORPL. R. STUART
PTE. J. SULLIVAN
* L.-CORPL. W. SULLIVAN
PTE. J. S. SUTHERLAND
CORPL. A. SWAINSON
L.-CORPL. V. SWAN
† L.-CORPL. L. L. TALLKE
SERGT. C. W. TEPENE
PTE. N. THOMSON
L.-CORPL. H. TILSON
L.-CORPL. G. D. TOD
PTE. J. TORRANCE
* SERGT. R. C. TRAVIS, D.C.M.
L.-CORPL. J. TREMBATH
PTE. J. TRIPP
* SERGT. J. H. TURNBULL
PTE. S. R. TUTTY
† SERGT. G. A. VINCENT
† SERGT. G. R. WADDEL
† CORPL. W. H. T. WALDERS
PTE. J. WALLACE
PTE. R. J. WARD
PTE. K. G. WEBLEY
PTE. L. T. WILLIAMS
PTE. A. G. WILLIAMSON
SERGT. C. G. WILSON
† SERGT. J. H. WILSON
PTE. G. E. WINTER
PTE. R. WITTERS
L.-CORPL. N. WRIGHT
PTE. J. W. YOUNG

MERITORIOUS SERVICE MEDAL.

S.-SERGT. J. A. BROWN
SERGT.-MAJOR A. L. EMERSON
PTE. A. FLINT'
SERGT. A. FRANCIS
C.S.M. H. W. T. JONES
SERGT. C. KEENAN
L.-CORPL. W. LYNN
† SERGT. G. B. MENZIES
C.Q.M.S. G. MILLER
PTE. A. MITCHELL
S.-SERGT. H. K. NICHOLSON

S.-SERGT. E. W. T. NOLAN
SERGT. J. O'CONNOR
* PTE. J. PALMER, M.M.
PTE. T. F. PERRY
S.-SERGT. G. F. PULSFORD
S.-SERGT. C. C. ROBB
S.-SERGT. W. A. SCOTT
SERGT.-MAJOR A. W. SPRAGG
S.-SERGT. H. C. STEVENSON
SERGT. H. J. TURNER
S.-SERGT. E. C. WILLS

MENTIONED IN DESPATCHES.

CORPL. E. ALDRED (2)
* CAPTAIN F. B. ALLEY
* CAPTAIN N. H. ARDEN
* LIEUT. J. H. BARR
LIEUT. C. BARRY
* 2ND LIEUT. J. J. BISHOP
MAJOR W. G. A. BISHOP, M.C. (2)
SERGT.-MAJOR P. C. BOATE, D.C.M.
CAPTAIN H. G. BRODIE
S.-SERGT. J. A. BROWN, M.S.M.
* CAPTAIN C. BRYCE
LIEUT.-COL. A. B. CHARTERS, C.M.G., D.S.O. (4)
CAPTAIN D. S. CHISHOLM (2)
† 2ND.-LIEUT. A. R. COCKERELL, D.S.O.
* LIEUT. J. G. COWAN
* SERGT. J. T. CUNNINGHAM, M.M.
* PTE. H. J. CURLINE
LIEUT. J. E. CUTHILL
SERGT. G. R. EDWARDS (2)
CORPL. A. F. FLUGGE
† CAPTAIN A. S. FALCONER, D.S.O., M.C. (2)
SERGT. F. C. FERGUSSON, D.C.M.
2ND-LIEUT. E. M. GABITES
CAPTAIN S. C. GREER
* C.S.M. W. HADLEE
2ND-LIEUT. S. ST. C. HAMILTON
LIEUT.-COL. J. HARGEST, D.S.O., M.C. (2)
*† SERGT. A. G. HENDERSON, D.C.M.
* LIEUT. J. L. HERBERT
PTE. J. B. HEY
*† CAPTAIN R. J. HILL, M.C.
* SERGT. H. L. HOFF
*† 2ND-LIEUT. W. HOWDEN
* PTE. W. G. HUNTER, M.M.
LIEUT.-COL. G. F. HUTTON, D.S.O.
† 2ND-LIEUT. A. E. INKSTER
† SERGT. W. G. JENKINS
* CAPTAIN L. S. JENNINGS
* CAPTAIN W. D. JOLLY
*† 2ND-LIEUT. C. A. KERSE
MAJOR F. H. LAMPEN, D.S.O.
† LIEUT. A. P. McCORMACK
MAJOR J. McCRAE, D.S.O.
† CAPTAIN S. G. McDONALD, M.C.
LIEUT. A. E. McKEOWN

405

MENTIONED IN DESPATCHES.

*† 2nd-Lieut. D. McLean, M.M. (2)
† Sergt. F. Mitchell, D.C.M.
Lieut.-Col. G. Mitchell, D.S.O.
Sergt. L. D'A. Mitchell
* Lieut.-Col. A. Moore, D.S.O.
* Sergt. G. E. Morris (2)
Sergt. E. J. Naylor
* Lieut. T. J. Nisbet
* Sergt.-major A. W. Porteous, M.C.
Captain D. McF. Rae
Major S. Rice
† 2nd-Lieut. W. D. Rutherford
Major J. L. Saunders, D.S.O.
* Sergt. W. A. Schaumann
Captain L. M. Scott, M.C.
† Captain E. F. Selby, M.C.
Corpl. H. D. Skinner, D.C.M.
Lieut.-Col. G. S. Smith, C.M.G., D.S.O. (3)
* Major F. H. Statham
C.S.M. W. H. Sullivan
* Pte. R. J. Summers
Corpl. T. A. Timpany
Captain W. F. Tracy, M.C.
Major W. McG. Turnbull, D.S.O.
* Major W. W. Turner
Major D. White
*† 2nd-Lieut. C. F. Wilkie
* Captain L. G. Wilson (2)

The names of the following were brought to the notice of the Secretary of State for War for valuable services at Home towards the successful conduct of the War :—

† R.S.M. A. J. Kerse   Sergt. I. McEwen
Sergt. H. G. G. Lyttle   Lieut.-Col. J. A. MacKenzie,
† 2nd-Lieut. A. E. Martin   C.M.G. (2)
Captain J. McPherson, O.B.E.

FOREIGN DECORATIONS.

FRENCH.

LEGION OF HONOUR (CROIX de CHEVALIER).
Lieut.-Col. J. Hargest, D.S.O., M.C.

CROIX DE GUERRE.
Sergt. J. McG. Lamb, D.C.M.

MEDAILLE MILITAIRE.
SERGT.-MAJOR P. C. BOATE, D.C.M.

MEDAILLE D'HONNEUR AVEC GLAIVES EN BRONZE.
S.-SERGT. J. A. BROWN, M.S.M.

RUSSIAN.

MEDAL OF ST. GEORGE, 3RD CLASS.
* PTE. A. M. KENNEDY

ITALIAN.

ITALIAN BRONZE MEDAL.
PTE. H. BENNY

BELGIAN.

CHEVALIER DE L'ORDRE DE LEOPOLD II.
† CORPL. F. J. TEMPERO

BELGIAN CROIX DE GUERRE

* SERGT. J. J. BLACKBURN, M.M.   CORPL. O. KING
CORPL. A. R. COX   PTE.- J. ROSS
L.-CORPL. P. FLOYD   * SERGT. R. C. TRAVIS, V.C., D.C.M.,
CORPL. J. HILL   M.M.

SERBIAN

ORDER OF KARAGEORGE, 4TH CLASS (WITH SWORDS).
LIEUT.-COL. G. MITCHELL, D.S.O.

Lightning Source UK Ltd.
Milton Keynes UK
UKOW08f1618160517
301249UK00001B/30/P